100
GREAT
Film Performances
You <u>Should</u>
Remember
—BUT PROBABLY DON'T

100
GREAT
Film Performances
You **Should**
Remember
—BUT PROBABLY DON'T

John DiLeo

To
Don Johnston,
"The Nutley Flash,"
I hope you
enjoy this
book.
Best,
John DiLeo

LIMELIGHT EDITIONS
New York

First Limelight Edition   July 2002

Copyright © 2002 by John DiLeo.

All rights reserved including the right of reproduction in whole or in part in any form.
Published by Proscenium Publishers Inc., 118 East 30th Street, New York, NY 10016.

Manufactured in the United States of America.

Library of Congress Cataloging-in-Publication Data
DiLeo, John, 1961-
    100 great film performances you should remember, but probably don't / John
DiLeo.—1st ed.
      p. cm.
   Includes index.
   ISBN 0-87910-972-6
    1. Motion pictures—United States. 2. Motion picture actors and actresses—
United States—Biography. 3. Motion picture acting. I. Title: Great film perform-
ances you should remember, but probably don't. II. Title: One hundred great film
performances you should remember, but probably don't. III. Title.

PN1993.5.U6 D46 2002
791,43'75'0973—dc2l
                                                           2002069393

Designed by Mulberry Tree Press, Inc. (www.mulberrytreepress.com)

Acknowledgments

HEARTFELT thanks to Naomi Wittes Reichstein, Louise Quayle, Anne Savarese, Tom Dickson, Shira Levin, Randy Buck, Pat Clark, Craig Seligman, Silvana Nova, Maureen Caliendo, Maureen Tucker, Lazaro Delgado, Joe Gannon, Caroline Wallace, Melle Powers, Peter Cummins, and Roxanna Font.

Inestimable thanks to Mel Zerman, a most supportive and generous editor; Kathryn Koldehoff, my copy editor, for her eagle eye; Cynthia Sealy, for her boundless helpfulness and unwavering patience; Tony Razzano, who continues to teach me the meaning of friendship (and computer skills); Earl McCarroll, my life partner and sanity regulator; John and Vera, my extraordinary parents; and, finally, the late, great Pauline Kael, to whom I would like to dedicate this book.

Contents

Contents

Preface

I DON'T ALWAYS KNOW why I respond to certain actors more than to others (I haven't been able to resist Diane Keaton since I was eleven), but I feel a certain protective quality toward the ones who have taken me on journeys that I'll never forget (and like to revisit now and again). That protectiveness increases when I discover performances that have never garnered the attention they deserve or those no longer as popular as they once were. Our acknowledged list of film classics is impressive but limited, and hundreds of worthwhile movies and amazing performances have been unfairly bypassed in favor of the screen's agreed-upon treasures. In this book, I do some corrective surgery on our film history by placing the spotlight on my favorite underrated or overlooked performances and some once-heralded ones now in need of renewed attention. So, no Scarlett O'Hara, Michael Corleone, or Margo Channing here. But you will find Vivien Leigh, Al Pacino, and Bette Davis in outstanding performances that have been overshadowed by their signature roles.

Why hasn't Laurence Olivier's phenomenal work in *Carrie* (as in *Sister Carrie*, not Sissy Spacek's) joined his pantheon of legendary performances? How is it that Katharine Hepburn's greatest performance, in *Long Day's Journey Into Night*, remains one of her least seen? Can we please recognize the *dramatic* skills of Julie Andrews and Steve Martin and the *comic* élan of Eleanor Parker and Ronald Colman? And isn't it about time we pay respect to Jeanette MacDonald and Doris Day for their invaluable contributions to movie musicals? Most film lovers are crazy about Gary Cooper in 1936's *Mr. Deeds Goes to Town*, but isn't he nearly as irresistible in a little gem titled *Desire* from that same year? Why didn't Jan Sterling's unforgettable performance in *Ace in the Hole* catapult her from character actress to leading lady? What does Jeff Bridges have to do to get the recognition he deserves as the best actor of his generation? Why didn't anyone seem to notice that "glamour girls" Linda Darnell and Ann Sheridan showed genuine depth when given the opportunity? Everyone knows that *The Band Wagon* is a glorious musical, but has Fred Astaire's *acting* in it ever been properly regarded? Frank Morgan and Thelma Ritter may have often played minor roles, but could their talents have been any more major? Buster Keaton and W. C. Fields were comic geniuses, but couldn't we simply call them great comic *actors*? How long can I stand the fact that Joel McCrea and Ida Lupino are not the screen icons they deserve to be? How many people even remember who Kay Kendall was? Did Barbara Stanwyck give her peak performance in *Double Indemnity*, or was she even better in the small masterpiece *Remember the Night*? Wouldn't any sensible person prefer to watch Laura Dern and Diane Lane over their more in-demand contemporaries? The answers to these and other obsessive questions are not so much answered as wrestled with throughout this book.

Do not take this group of performances as a "hundred best" list; they're simply a collection of acting feats that have had a considerable impact on me, marking high points in my career as a movie fanatic. Focusing on performance gives me license to incorporate far-from-great movies, but rest assured, I do not include any bombs. With remarkably few exceptions, the films are very good indeed, although in most cases, the best things about them are the performances I've selected to discuss. And don't worry, I don't reveal the films' endings. My intention is to whet your appetite, not deprive you of each film's full impact. I wish I could have made room for every screen performer of the last eighty years whom I deeply admire (sorry Marlon, sorry Meryl). This book is my way of saying thank you to one hundred of them.

100 GREAT
Film Performances
You <u>Should</u>
Remember
—BUT PROBABLY DON'T

Lowell Sherman and Lillian Gish
on their "wedding night."

Lillian Gish

IN

Way Down East
(1920)

WHILE director D. W. Griffith was making trailblazing strides in film technique at the dawn of the movies, Lillian Gish, his favorite star, was doing the same for film acting. Silent-screen performing would be a short-lived art, but no one was better at it than Gish. The first time I saw her in *Way Down East*, I felt as if I were watching the moment when movie acting became legit and could never again be dismissed as dumb show. Although she had appeared in Griffith's two epic milestones, *The Birth of a Nation* (1915) and *Intolerance* (1916), her ability to reveal character before the camera's eye reached its first peak with three of the director's most popular melodramas: *Broken Blossoms* (1919), *Orphans of the Storm* (1921), and, in between, *Way Down East*, the one with the famous ice-floe climax. That thrilling, terrifying finale and the intimate pathos of Gish's performance were the chief reasons this film of Lottie Blair Parker's old chestnut of a play was not undone by its hackneyed, positively prehistoric plot, with "everything but the bloodhounds snapping at her rear end" (to quote *All About Eve*'s Thelma Ritter). Lit like a haloed angel, Gish thrives under the less-is-more scrutiny of her frequent close-ups, where she often covers her mouth to bring the focus to her blazingly expressive eyes.

Poor-relation Anna Moore (Gish) arrives on the doorstep of her snooty Boston relatives where her virginal loveliness catches the eye of Lennox Sanderson (Lowell Sherman), a lady-killing ne'er-do-well. He woos innocent Anna and, to get her into his bed, stages a mock marriage. Anna is deliriously happy (despite Lennox's insistence on keeping their union a secret), but he is soon ready for new conquests. He discloses the truth to a pregnant Anna and then abandons her. After her baby dies, Anna finds household work at the nearby Bartlett farm. There, the owner's handsome son, David (Richard Barthelmess), becomes smitten with her. Anna fearfully guards her dark past and is further shaken when she discovers that Lennox has a country estate near the Bartletts' place.

Anna is no stock ingénue because Gish gives her a playfully spirited personality, and she also finds opportunities for endearing light humor, such as when she shows off her thought-to-be-stylish gloves to her unwelcoming "wicked stepsister" cousins. Aided by a "fairy godmother" aunt, this doomed Cinderella emerges at the family's ball in all her porcelain-doll beauty and is quickly surrounded by suitors. Naïvely mistaking Lennox for a "prince" and carried away by his attentions, Gish, who only *looks* fragile, will later defend herself capably from his physical advances, until he turns the subject to matrimony. On their wedding night, Gish's blushing modesty is superseded by her erotic pleasure in feeling desirable. Her storybook world is shattered by Lennox's confession of his dirty deed. At first numbed by the revelation, Gish gives Anna wrenching flashes of touching disbelief, stifled fury, unbridled laughter, and desperate pleading, before Anna's vitality is extinguished by despair. In a grim boardinghouse, her gravely ill baby is born, and, fearing it may die before being baptized, she performs the rite herself. With heartbreaking courage, she humbly sprinkles water on the infant's head, looking searchingly to heaven to see if her action has been accepted. A scene of exquisite delicacy, it is bested only by the one that follows, where she unwillingly comes to terms with the fact that her baby is dead. She registers the truth at the touch of the newborn's cold hand, but, repeatedly blowing her hot breath on its tiny fingers, she clings to disintegrating hopes. When the doctor arrives and confirms what she already knows, Gish slowly stiffens, then lets out what appears to be a pitifully weak cry before becoming hysterical. The ice-floe sequence may be the film's showstopper, but Gish's boardinghouse scenes are its dramatic high points, acted with a striking specificity that renders them ageless.

An emotionally deadened Anna finds peace and safety working for the Bartletts, until her situation is complicated by two events: Lennox's unexpected reentry into her life and young David's growing infatuation with her. Though Gish's Anna fights back tears when she encounters Lennox at the farm, she later stands up to him and his continuing demands that she leave the area. She defiantly resents the double standard that has left her unfit to be any man's wife. So, when she falls in love with David, who's as innocent as she once was, she purposefully tries to discourage him. In an idyllic scene by the river, Anna, starting at the touch of his hand, rebuffs him regretfully. In loving him privately, she lives yet another kind of torture. Later, when he proposes, she has tears of joy but catches herself in horror, remembering that their pairing can never be. When the family learns the truth about her (in Lennox's presence) and David's father orders her to leave, Anna has nothing left to lose. Gish cuts loose angrily, in a liberating release from Anna's victimization, naming her seducer, then exiting into the blizzard. In the spectacular storm, you'll not soon forget the image of Gish with frozen eyelashes and her cape flapping in the wind or her poetic placement on the ice floe: her hair and one hand dangling in the freezing water as she heads for the falls (and movie history).

Griffith, with his visceral feel for outdoor locations and nature's elements, and with his ingenious instincts for suspense-building editing, created a sweeping entertainment. It is far from a great film: it's marred by the patience-shredding screen time given to the comic relief of the Bartletts' neighbors, a determinedly unfunny group. Ironically, when this film, which had been cut up over the years, was restored in the mid 1980s, all these unbearable scenes were back. (You might want to hit that fast-forward button or visit the fridge.) Matinee idol Barthelmess, Gish's costar from *Broken Blossoms*, has an undemanding role, but he gets quite a workout on the ice. Lowell Sherman's Lennox, lacking only a mustache to twirl, is the kind of villain who provokes hisses.

Hollywood's first great actress hit another artistic peak, at MGM, in two dramas directed by Victor Seastrom: *The Scarlet Letter* (1926), featuring the ravishing scene where, in a burst of self-proclaimed freedom, she removes the *A* from her chest and lets down her hair; and *The Wind* (1928), with its blood-chilling moment where, from her window, she sees that the man she killed and buried in the sand has been uncovered (by the title role). She starred in two undistinguished talkies, thereafter relegating her film work to occasional character parts, finding greater challenges in the theatre (notably as Ophelia to John Gielgud's Hamlet on Broadway in 1936). Though she received an honorary Oscar in 1971, her only nomination came for her supporting role in, of all things, that garish guilty pleasure of 1946, *Duel in the Sun* (where she has an extravagant death scene in which she crawls out of bed and over to hubby Lionel Barrymore before expiring). Her one classic "talking" performance was in Charles Laughton's stunner *The Night of the Hunter* (1955); no one could have fulfilled her earth-mother role as beautifully as she. Her final film, the anesthetizing *Whales of August* (1987), was far from a career capper, but it was a last chance to gaze upon a star who did as much as anyone to bring respect, even awe, to screen acting. There is no more fitting subject with which to begin this book.

Buster Keaton as Sherlock Jr.

Buster Keaton

IN

Sherlock Jr.

(1924)

WHEN the Regency Theatre, New York City's long-gone revival house, had its Buster Keaton retrospective in the spring of 1987, I made my way through his major works with an all-you-can-eat insatiability. Prior to this, the only Keaton film I'd seen was an inferior television print of *The General* (1926). I wasn't prepared for a virtual onslaught of masterpieces (seeing *The General* on the big screen made clear its reputation not only as a comedy classic but as a great Civil War epic as well). The ten independent silent features that Keaton starred in (he directed or codirected eight of them) in 1923–28 constitute the greatest burst of comic creativity in American film. (The only comparable artistic frenzy is the 1940–44 rush of Preston Sturges comedies, and he didn't *star* in his films.) Keaton's films display a timeless combination of technical wizardry, compositional poetry, beguiling storytelling, hair-raising stunts, and, of course, consistent hilarity. His tag as "The Great Stone Face" marks his deadpan approach to comedy, but it shouldn't be taken to mean that he was always the same in his films; he played a nice assortment of pampered rich boys, ambitious workingmen, and mild-mannered heroes (who all just happened to share superhuman physical grace). *Sherlock Jr.*, running a mere forty-four minutes, is my favorite Keaton film; in the time it takes to balance your checkbook, you can see one of the more magically transporting and inventive comedies ever made. And please don't miss his other must-sees: *The Navigator* (1924), *Seven Chances* (1925), and *Steamboat Bill Jr.* (1927).

Sherlock Jr. tells the simple (at first) story of a projectionist (Keaton) with ambitions of becoming a great detective. He loves a local girl (Kathryn McGuire), but his marriage plans are thwarted when a nasty rival (Ward Crane) plants a pawn ticket on him, thereby framing him for stealing the pocket watch of his would-be father-in-law (Joe Keaton, his real-life father). After a disastrously inept attempt to solve the case on his own, he returns to work, dejectedly. He falls asleep while screening

19

Hearts and Pearls, a swanky melodrama, and dreams that he walks *into* the film, taking on the role of Sherlock Jr., the world's greatest detective, in a plot that soon parallels his own story.

Can anyone catch Keaton *pushing* to get a laugh? I wouldn't advise trying. The humor comes from his total absorption in his plight of the moment. His nameless protagonist freezes with trepidation whenever he's near his ladylove. He can barely look her in the eye as he hands her a box of candy and seems to want to be elsewhere as he nervously places a ring on her finger. This potentially blissful experience is played with all the tight terror of a dreaded doctor's visit. His attempt to hold her hand has the calculating gravity of a covert operation; he finally slams his hand upon hers with a pleasureless jolt. Later, in the projection booth, he imitates the smooth moves of the leading man on the screen. With one eye on his beloved and his other on the film, he carefully mimics the debonair fellow's technique, getting slightly bolder with each successive move: turning her toward him, patting her hand, kissing her hand, placing a ring on her finger, pecking her on the mouth. Instantly aware that he's pleasing her, he's soon more eager to get back to the screen for the next "lesson" than he is in enjoying his romantic victory. Even *inside* a movie, you can learn how to make love *from* the movies.

The sequence where he enters the film within the film is, mildly put, one of the more astonishing in movie history: brilliantly conceived, technically seamless, and performed by Keaton with gasp-inducing agility and out-of-this-world timing. He gets thrown out of the movie (literally) by one of the actors, but his second entry is momentarily more secure. Suddenly, the mansion-entrance setting changes to a garden, and Keaton is off on a ride that hurls him through an unpredictable succession of scene-changing backgrounds, confronting speeding cars, a train, a rocky cliff, lions, the desert, crashing waves, and snow. If this two-minute miracle isn't the apex of silent-screen comedy, what, pray tell, is? (Chaplin must have wanted to kill himself after seeing it.) When the film returns to the plot at the mansion, he arrives as Sherlock Jr., having been called to investigate a lady's stolen pearls. Sherlock is a nattily attired sophisticate who is unshakably confident in his skills; Keaton's air of blasé superiority suggests that most of his time is spent on boring, unchallenging cases. The story climaxes in an elaborate chase through town in which Keaton spends most of his time on the handlebars of a riderless motorcycle, speeding through all manner of stunt-requiring situations (prepare to be left breathless). When he foils the villains, retrieves the pearls, and wins the girl (he gets his arm around her without *any* timidity), he makes it appear as if all the madness has been part of some carefully devised plan only he could have masterminded.

Buster Keaton in *Sherlock Jr.* (1924)

When Keaton relinquished the creative control of his independent status to sign with MGM in 1928, it was the beginning of the end. Did someone get a bonus for coming up with the lame idea of teaming him with Jimmy Durante? I have nothing against Durante, but why pair Keaton with *anyone*? When I saw *Speak Easily* (1932), one of their three (surprisingly popular) efforts, I wanted to yank an obviously miserable Keaton from the film as easily as he had jumped into *Hearts and Pearls*. MGM's decision to fire him in 1933 was brought on by his work-interfering alcoholism, relegating him to two-reelers at minor studios and low-budget films abroad. He eventually returned to MGM as a gag writer, primarily for reigning comic Red Skelton. Hardly a comeback, he made a haunting cameo (as one of Norma Desmond's bridge-playing waxworks) in *Sunset Boulevard* (1950), followed by a momentous one-time-only appearance with Chaplin in the otherwise heavy-going *Limelight* (1952). By the mid 1950s, *every* hard-luck showbiz life was fodder for the movies, and *The Buster Keaton Story* (1957) fit right into the *I'll Cry Tomorrow* genre. Keaton coached Donald O'Connor in the title role (I can't think of anyone else who could even have attempted it), but the film was a failure. There couldn't be a sadder low point than Keaton's unfortunate appearances in four beach movies of the mid 1960s. Only Joan Crawford's achingly sincere scenes opposite the gorilla in *Trog* (1970) can compete in the Did-it-have-to-come-to-this? department.

Keaton, who died in 1966, lived long enough to enjoy the revival of interest in his silent work. (He received an honorary Oscar in 1960.) By the 1970s, you couldn't find a ten-best-movies-of-all-time list without *The General* on it. (Nowadays, it's *The Searchers* [1956] that makes every list, but, moving as that western undoubtedly is, I can't understand how a movie with so many bad scenes can be rated *that* high.) With all of his major work now on video (sorry to say, *Sherlock Jr.* has an off-puttingly "modern" score attached), Buster Keaton should acquire countless new fans. If *Sherlock Jr.* hasn't aged in its first seventy-five years, is there any reason to believe it ever will?

Lon Chaney as Paul Beaumont

Lon Chaney

IN

He Who Gets Slapped
(1924)

L ON Chaney's billing as "The Man of a Thousand Faces" was not too much of an exaggeration. Chaney made more than one hundred fifty silent movies, and his legendary use of makeup made him unrecognizable from role to role. He specialized in conveying the humanity behind monsters, as in *The Hunchback of Notre Dame* (1923) and *The Phantom of the Opera* (1925). Through painstaking physical characterization and his penetrating eyes, he brought these creatures to throbbing life. As with any of the great silent-film actors, you don't long for sound and dialogue when you watch him because you're not being deprived of anything essential. Chaney also played roles with his plain, ordinary face (1926's *Tell It to the Marines* was one of his biggest hits). *He Who Gets Slapped*, based on a play by Leonid Andreyev, gave him a chance to illuminate the kind of guy no one notices. Although he spends much of the film in clown makeup, his emotions are so strong that his white face and overdrawn lips can hardly contain them.

He Who Gets Slapped tells an utterly bizarre story. Paul Beaumont (Chaney) is a brilliant scientist on the verge of proving his theories on "the origin of mankind." Baron Regnard (Marc McDermott), his trusted benefactor, steals his discoveries and presents them to the academy as his own. Beaumont witnesses this, and when he tries to claim his discoveries, Regnard slaps him. The assembly roars with laughter. The final blow is Regnard's affair with Beaumont's wife. We meet Beaumont again years later as a circus clown known as "He Who Gets Slapped — The World's Quaintest Clown." He has taken the moment of his destruction and turned it into an astonishingly creepy act. He finds renewed interest in life when he falls in love with the new bareback rider, Consuelo (Norma Shearer), whom he must protect from a grasping father and the return of Regnard. A circus lion is responsible for the violent climax.

Chaney displays youthful energy and naïveté as Beaumont's pursuit of his work leaves him oblivious to the cruel world around him. When the slap comes, he's so startled that he doesn't know how to react. The ensuing laughter is overwhelming, and Chaney vividly draws Beaumont's descent into despair. He lets the passion and fury drain from his face and the light go out of his eyes. Beaumont seems to have aged considerably by the end of the scene, when he's led away in a trance. By the time his wife walks out on him, the Paul Beaumont we've come to know is completely ruined. He must be someone else if he is to exist at all. He becomes "He," and no more specific name is required for this new incarnation.

The most shocking thing about his circus act is that it's an almost literal reenactment of the scene at the academy (with the addition of clown costumes). Every time He speaks, a clown slaps him down. Chaney's intensity transports us right back to the academy. The vulnerability returns, and there's nothing funny about watching this fragile figure humiliate himself. But the crowd goes wild! Humanity does not come off very well in this movie: laughter always seems to come at the expense of someone's misery. Beaumont knows what the world is really like, and he reminds himself of his gullibility and misguided trust every day in the center ring.

While Chaney is a nimble and raucous clown, his more intimate scenes are the ones you'll remember. His heart has to be sewn back on to his costume after each performance because of the necessarily merciless handling he receives from his fellow clowns. There's a gorgeous scene in which Consuelo sews it on for him. She holds his heart in her hand, in essence, and the look on his face shows his gentle but all-consuming love for her. Chaney doesn't take his eyes off Shearer, and it's as if Beaumont were coming back to life before our eyes. Sound and dialogue would add nothing and might even detract from such visual poetry. When he summons the courage to reveal his love for her, he kneels and buries his face in the feathers of her costume as he speaks. We haven't seen such naked emotion from him since he cried on his wife's lap after the academy debacle. In the time it takes for him to realize that Consuelo thinks he's kidding, Chaney offers a stunning transition from horror to acceptance and, finally, to the kind of too-hearty laughter that makes it seem a big joke. This broken man is invigorated by his determination to protect her from the world that destroyed him, and it is moving to watch him realize that his life may have some kind of meaning after all.

Chaney's acting is very theatrical, as befits such an operatic story. He knows how to play the big emotional scenes for maximum impact, but it's the fact that we always know what's going on in his head that makes us feel so close to his character. No one in the story gets to know him the way we do. Chaney even cuts through the obvious masochism in the story by making us believe that the depths of Beaumont's suffering could lead him to make the choices he makes (unusual, to say the least, as they are). To find another story this odd, one must go to another Chaney circus drama, *The Unknown* (1927), in which he pretends to be armless because he's wanted by the police *and* because frigid Joan Crawford can't bear to be touched by men. He later has his arms surgically removed. *The Unknown* makes *He Who Gets Slapped* look like *State Fair*.

He Who Gets Slapped will always be remembered as the first film released by the newly formed MGM. (Is that Leo himself munching on cast members at the end of the movie?) Norma Shearer and John Gilbert (as her love interest) are both on the verge of stardom here, and they fulfill their duties gracefully. Shearer would become MGM's reigning queen in the 1930s, and her vehicles got increasingly bloated. (*Marie Antoinette* [1938] is a monstrosity, and her portrayal of the doomed monarch is about as subtle as the guillotine itself.) Swedish director Victor Seastrom packs an enormously exciting and visceral experience into a mere seventy-two minutes. (In 1957, Seastrom starred as the old man in the Ingmar Bergman classic *Wild Strawberries*.) One chilling effect is the between-scenes use of a clown as something of a Greek chorus (or God himself?) who is always laughing at a spinning globe. This unsettling device adds to the story's overall pessimism and inevitability. And you certainly can't miss the world-as-circus metaphor running through the film.

Chaney resisted the talkies until 1930, when he starred in a remake of his 1925 hit *The Unholy Three*. It was a success, and Chaney got to show that his vocal versatility was nearly as impressive as his physical skills. His career in the new medium seemed secure, but he died of cancer one month after his first talking picture opened. Boris Karloff continued the Chaney tradition of finding the souls inside the monstrous, and Lon Jr., when he starred as *The Wolf Man* (1941), proved that he had observed his father well.

John Gilbert as Jim Apperson

John Gilbert

IN

The Big Parade

(1925)

JOHN Gilbert is better remembered as a casualty of Hollywood's transition to the talkies than as a superstar of the silents. Despite the legend, he did *not* have a high-pitched voice that embarrassed him off the screen. There is no clear-cut, satisfying explanation for his talking failure. Rather, there are several, each playing a part in his demise: ill-conceived vehicles, none-too-secret animosity from his boss (Louis B. Mayer), and worsening alcoholism. Had his brand of romantic ardor gone out of style? If so, why did Greta Garbo, his four-time costar, continue her grand passions without interruption? Only a few short years before, in 1925, Gilbert, who had been in films for a decade, had become a huge star in two MGM blockbusters: Erich von Stroheim's opulent *Merry Widow* and King Vidor's World War I epic *The Big Parade*. Gilbert was the Gable of the 1920s, and *Big Parade*, a phenomenally popular, no-expense-spared love story set against a raging war, was his *Gone With the Wind*. Even with a charming romance at its core, *Big Parade* is a laceratingly powerful war film. Its emotional weight is carried by Gilbert, who, without his trademark mustache, makes a finely tuned transition from a carefree innocent to a soldier ignited by love to a young man disillusioned beyond his years. It takes more than a mere matinee idol to pull off such a stirring feat, and it's *that* for which Gilbert should be remembered.

Jim Apperson (Gilbert), a pampered rich boy, is uninterested in enlisting when the United States enters the European war in 1917, but, like so many others, he's swept away by the flag-waving excitement all around him. Leaving his family and his fiancée, Justyn (Claire Adams), behind, he's sent to Champillon, a muddy French village, where he waits to be sent to the front. Jim spends his days in mischievous shenanigans with his new buddies until he falls in love with Melisande (Renée Adorée), a feisty, non-English speaking peasant girl. At last called to fight, Jim experiences the war's horrors head-on, and, when he learns that Champillon has been attacked, he's determined to find his beloved.

Gilbert, first seen getting a shave, his eyes closed as he gracefully removes excess cream from his lips, personifies idle privilege. This spoiled Jim will be obliterated by the war, and the power of that transformation is all the stronger for the indelibility of Gilbert's first impression. Once in Champillon, he begins the maturation process through the camaraderie of his unit, forging sturdy bonds with blue-collar types, and, later, when he falls for Melisande. This part of the film is a comedy, and Gilbert is keenly funny. After he impulsively kisses Melisande, she slaps him to the ground. As he plays the injured party, she kisses his cheek to soothe his pain; Gilbert's Jim, now floating, repeatedly (and delightfully) points to his "wound" to reap, and bask in, more kisses. Their endearing courtship peaks when he introduces her to chewing gum. The concept of gum mystifies her, and Gilbert's beautifully timed reactions to her confusion make it a scene of peerless charm. (Because of their language barrier, they are an ideal "silent" couple.) Add a healthy dose of physical comedy, as in his barrel-wearing scene or the one in which he tries to avoid being maimed by a sword-wielding speech maker, and you have irrefutable proof of his considerable comic talent. Then his unit is suddenly summoned. Realizing the depth of his feeling for Melisande and frantically searching for her so that he can say good-bye, Gilbert's character is never again the frolicsome doughboy. When he at last finds her, amid the departing truckloads of soldiers and hundreds of female well-wishers, the intensity of the situation (they may never see each other again) arouses extreme emotions. As his truck pulls away, Jim, desperate to maintain their connection, throws her a series of personal items (including a shoe!), an overwhelming gesture signifying his commitment to her. More alive than ever, Jim now has that much more to lose.

After valiant fighting, Jim ends up in a shell hole, where he can hear the nearby moans of a dying friend. After risking his life to save him and finding the man dead, Jim goes on a rampage, headed for the enemy. Gilbert's Jim is possessed by a seething hatred and, even though wounded, crawls after a German he has shot, determined to finish him off. Face to face with the dying fellow in another shell hole, Jim can't bring himself to murder the helpless boy. In an unbearably moving scene, Gilbert fluctuates between vindictive anger and gentle compassion; he gives the boy a cigarette, then pushes his limp face away in disgust, regretting his cruelty instantly. Through the furious clash of his contradictory impulses, he comes harrowingly close to madness. Jim returns home a ghost of his prewar self; Gilbert plays him tightly unsmiling and hopelessly resigned. While he's embracing his loving mother, his fiancée kisses his cheek; turning as if to find Melisande, Jim is momentarily stricken at the sight of Justyn instead. He tenderly comes to life when telling his mother about his lost love, and it's clear that he is not quite defeated yet. Melisande and the war have completely changed Jim, and Gilbert's nuanced performance expands the character with enriching humanity; he has been forever altered through love and pain into a far more complicated person.

The Big Parade, released only seven years after the actual war ended, is a silent masterpiece and a great war film. King Vidor directed with spectacular artistry: the awesome "big parade" of trucks, bringing countless soldiers to the front; the forty-minute combat sequence, featuring an unendurably tense march through a sniper-laden forest; the aforementioned parting of the lovers in Champillon, which ingeniously contrasts the couple, focused solely on each other, with the frenzy around them. Vidor dares to allow the comic antics in Champillon to play at a leisurely pace, lulling the viewer into a false sense of security, rendering the rest of the film that much more unexpected and shocking: you wait seventy minutes for the "action" to start. Its ending will remind you of a key Ashley-Melanie scene from *Gone With the Wind*. Round-cheeked Renée Adorée, a spunky Melisande, was reunited with Gilbert and Vidor on *La Bohème* (1926). Vidor continued to direct for thirty-five years, but Adorée died of tuberculosis in 1933 at age thirty-five, and Gilbert died of a heart attack in 1936 at forty.

Like a number of MGM's stars, Gilbert made his sound debut in the extravaganza *The Hollywood Revue of 1929*, performing a bit of the balcony scene from *Romeo and Juliet* with Norma Shearer; they're terrible, particularly Shearer, who, go figure, had immediate success in the talkies. The stilted clips I've seen of Gilbert's first talking vehicle, the ironically titled *His Glorious Night* (1929), seem to have been the inspiration for the early-talkie calamities portrayed hilariously in *Singin' in the Rain* (1952). Gilbert floundered in nearly a dozen talkies, with one classic exception, *Queen Christina* (1933); Garbo insisted on his being cast opposite her in a last-ditch effort to salvage his career. His star wattage is noticeably dimmed and his handsomeness worn, but he gives a solid performance (his voice is *fine*), still responding intimately to his former teammate. Sadly, it had no impact on his decline, however, as John Gilbert joined the big parade of silent stars into career oblivion.

Greta Garbo and a framed Dorothy Sebastian

Greta Garbo

IN

A Woman of Affairs

(1928)

WITHOUT benefit of her husky Scandinavian moan, an ostensibly essential component of her artistry, mega-goddess Greta Garbo was a major *silent* star of the final few pre-talkie years. Her accent would limit the parts she could play; she certainly could not have been cast as English Diana Merrick in *A Woman of Affairs* had it been a talkie (though her accent would be deemed all-purpose regarding roles with Continental nationalities). Her Diana is a great performance, but not in the usual terms. Garbo's work here is more elemental than "inhabiting a character" or "bringing psychological depth" to one. She's the personification of undiluted passion; she's the essence of eternal love. The plot is twaddle, the motivations perplexing, but there stands Garbo, soulfully forging a primal link to Diana, rising far above claptrap material to create something beautiful, universal, and ageless. This is the movie that contains her amazing hospital scene, one of the silent era's peaks, an enthralling display of her emotional virtuosity.

Reckless, filthy-rich Diana and high-class, not-as-rich Neville Holderness (John Gilbert) are eager to marry, but his disapproving father, Sir Morton (Hobart Bosworth), packs Neville off to Egypt, having conveniently arranged a post for him. After two years, Diana marries admirable David Furness (Johnny Mack Brown), whom she doesn't love, though he's idolized by her drunkard brother, Jeffry (Douglas Fairbanks, Jr.). Soon after, David commits suicide (turns out he's wanted by the police), but Diana, in saying her "past" caused his despair, preserves David's reputation, choosing not to shatter her brother's idealism. But she scandalizes herself. So, she sleeps with most of Europe, returning to England seven years later when Jeffry is dying. Neville finds her, and days before his marriage to sweet Constance (Dorothy Sebastian), he and Diana have sex. Their love is undying, but it doesn't look like they will ever find happiness together.

Garbo's exciting Diana is an impossibly gorgeous, teasingly humorous "flaming youth." Sporting cloche hats and turned-up collars, she's devastatingly modern, smoking freely and slouching in her seats. When things start to crumble, Diana, though pained, seems unsurprised by the way the world works; Garbo brings a knowing skepticism to the surface. She makes Diana the film's strongest character, never wallowing in regret or making apologies for her sometimes screwy actions. Garbo plays her as a realist, protecting those she loves (Jeffry and Neville) at her own expense, certain she's better equipped to cope with misery than they are. She commits to making her marriage to second-choice David work. There's a shivering moment just after he comes to her bed and she welcomes him fondly. His lips touch her forehead, and Garbo's face goes instantly dead: he isn't Neville. (You can read the thoughts of some great film stars, but Garbo makes you *feel* hers.) After David's suicide, Diana accepts her designation as a scarlet woman, though she's still defined by her hopeless love for Neville. Flash seven years ahead to their reunion, when he brings her to his home and she sees a framed photo of Constance, his fiancée. Without a shred of jealousy, she's transfixed by her rival's purity, and Garbo, in an unusually touching scene, bonds intimately with the inanimate portrait. Shortly after, the hypnotic power of Diana's gaze is aimed at Neville, willing him to kiss her: as she inches closer to his lips, you can practically hear Garbo's heartbeat.

Nine months after her brother's death and Neville's wedding, Diana, now without the will to live, is in a Paris hospital. Summoned by Dr. Trevelyan (Lewis Stone), Neville and Constance pay a visit. Diana's spirits are lifted by the roses Neville has sent, but while she's sleeping, they are removed from her room. That's the setup for the magnificent five minutes that follow. The roses personify Neville to Diana; she's distressed when they're gone and leaves her room in search of them. Garbo, moving aimlessly through the hallway, is tearfully frantic, then glowingly transformed by the becalming, far-off sight of them on a desk. Approaching purposefully, with outstretched hands, she lifts them out of the vase and embraces them as if they were Neville himself. Garbo closes her eyes and tilts her head back, caressing the flowers the way she would a lover's neck and back, even speaking to them with tears and laughter. It's the single greatest screen expression of total ecstasy I've ever seen. Turning, she sees the real Neville standing there and drops the now superfluous bouquet. She wraps her arms around him, happy beyond imagining. Then her joy evaporates at the unsettling sight of Constance. Agonizingly slammed back to reality, she removes the one arm still around Neville's shoulder, then selflessly focuses her attention on forlorn Constance, sympathetically reassuring her (despite what the young bride has just seen). Accepting the loss of

Neville once again, Diana asks a nun for her cherished roses, needing her Neville stand-in as consolation. Exiting with the flowers, she stops, bravely, to shake his hand; Garbo tenses at the unbearable desire ignited by his touch, then returns to her room. From the first panicky moment to her ultimate resignation (and every high and low flicker of feeling in between), Garbo sorcerously seems to encompass the breadth of human emotion in just a few minutes of screen time.

A Woman of Affairs is a top-of-the-line MGM product, featuring Cedric Gibbons's swanky sets, William Daniels's luxuriantly fluid camerawork, and Adrian's fashionable clothes. Clarence Brown, Garbo's most frequent director (seven times, including *Anna Christie*, her 1930 talkie debut), wisely stresses style and mood over substance, keeping your mind off the story's lapses of logic. It's based on Michael Arlen's novel *The Green Hat* (with the syphilis lost in the translation). John Gilbert, in his third of four films with Garbo, gives stable backseat support; though they are an exceedingly glamorous couple, their films together are decidedly *her* films. Lewis Stone is his drably dependable self, and poor Dorothy Sebastian, pretty in her own right, looks positively homely beside guess-who. A consistently hysterical Douglas Fairbanks, Jr., doesn't seem to know he's playing a homosexual. (If his "hero worshiper" isn't gay, then he makes no sense at all.)

Was any star equally great in silents *and* talkies? With her accent immortally in place, Garbo triumphed throughout the 1930s: she's spellbindingly larger than life (*nothing* "real" about her) as the unhappy ballerina in *Grand Hotel* (1932); both a commanding monarch and a gentle lover in *Queen Christina* (1933); a deadpan delight in the comic soufflé *Ninotchka* (1939); and, best of all, as ill-fated Marguerite in *Camille* (1937), she gives one of the movies' paragon female performances, an experience so moving that it once kept me in full sob for a twenty-block walk home from the theatre.

Edward G. Robinson and Aline MacMahon

Edward G. Robinson

IN

Five Star Final

(1931)

WHILE all those silent stars were trying to hold on to their careers with the arrival of sound, there was fresh competition to contend with: stars *created* by the new technology. Early talkies are notable for the look of terror on many of the actors' faces, so when someone like Edward G. Robinson came along, with such verve and self-assurance, it's easy to see why the public made him one of the first and most enduring "talking" stars (despite his pronounced lack of movie-star attractiveness). *Little Caesar* (1930) was the perfect fit of actor and role, and Robinson's colossal performance has lost none of its primal power. As preening mobster Rico Bandello, a cigar-chomping, possibly homosexual egomaniac, he commands the screen (though, at times, he seems to be doing a shameless impersonation of himself). In *Five Star Final*, his second film after *Caesar*, he plays another roughened character but gives a more realistic (and less prone to parody) performance. It's not a star vehicle, but Robinson, as an ace newspaperman self-aware enough to be sickened by his reprehensible behavior, dominates it. The film is woefully uneven, with long stretches of poorly acted melodrama, and yet Robinson's sterling work looks like it was photographed yesterday. That the movie still packs a punch is due to the fullness with which he embodied his character's inner struggle.

New York's *Evening Gazette* is losing circulation fast, and its managing editor, Mr. Randall (Robinson), who has tried to inject integrity into the newspaper, is to blame. The boss, Mr. Hinchecliffe (Oscar Apfel), wants a return to "human interest" (meaning smut) coverage, and Randall goes along, valuing his salary over his principles. They serialize an old scandal about Nancy Voorhees (Frances Starr) who, twenty years earlier, shot her lover dead when he refused to legitimize her pregnancy; motherhood led to her acquittal. The piece is brought up to date when the *Gazette* locates Nancy and begins wreaking havoc with the happy life she now shares with her husband (H. B. Warner) and grown daughter (Marian Marsh), who is about to marry into a prominent family and knows nothing of her mother's notoriety. The story proves a financial boon for the paper but results in a shocking tragedy, leading Randall to face his own festering accountability.

Robinson first appears in the restroom of a speakeasy. Acting on a compulsion (which is repeated throughout the film), he's washing his hands, an obvious but effective manifestation of his need for purification. But hand washing, and his desk-drawer liquor bottle, can't expunge the self-disgust Randall derives from working for a filthy rag. That insuppressible conscience, of varying degrees of strength, provides an ongoing subtext to Robinson's performance. Most of the anger and sarcasm that Randall flings at his coworkers is, of course, indirectly aimed at himself. (Robinson is funny tossing stinging insults like grenades.) And because he knows the paper needs him, he vents his aggravation without fear of reprisal. When his boss begins to lecture him about the sensational "moral values" approach they are to adopt, Robinson barely looks up from his desk, working busily, not bothering to conceal his loathing for this man and what he's saying. But because he needs his paycheck, he rationalizes his subsequent complicity: "Ideals won't put a patch on your pants." Shelving what's left of his self-respect, he resurrects and augments the Nancy Voorhees story, abetted by his top henchman, Isopod (a goofily creepy, pre-*Frankenstein* Boris Karloff), who worms his way into Nancy's home by posing as a minister. Robinson is a dynamo, machine-gunning his dialogue as he barks orders and brainstorms strategies; whatever scruples remain beneath the surface, it's plain that Randall gets an undeniable charge from his job. The clash of being invigorated *and* repulsed by his own handiwork is the driving force behind Robinson's performance.

Randall's secretary, Miss Taylor (likeably acerbic Aline MacMahon), is in love with him, but, more than that, she sees the good guy lurking inside him. It's frustrating for him to be around this "visible conscience," whose disapproval can prompt a hand-washing moment, but she's also a life preserver of decency whose nearness is a comforting reminder that he can still be saved. Robinson connects with her in a way that is unique for Randall: he respects her, values her opinions, and genuinely likes her; each seems always to know what the other is thinking. Perhaps his romantic remoteness comes from not wanting to pollute her, especially after he reignites the scandal. Despite his pangs of guilt (he's disturbed by a telephoned plea for mercy by Nancy), the ensuing tragedy (involving suicide) stuns him, making it impossible for him to think about anything else. Shaken by having engineered a senseless catastrophe, he tries to drown his grief with alcohol, but it's no use. Robinson doesn't court our pity, knowing that Randall doesn't deserve any. For having had the sense to know better, he's the worst offender in this atrocity, but he won't shirk responsibility any longer. In a climactic tirade, directed at Randall's boss, Robinson displays the galvanizing impact of the new phenomenon: the talking screen actor. His crisp, pointed phrasing of this speech, a breaking-point aria of accelerating speed and emotion, is incisively controlled; his raging bitterness is offset by the fact that Randall will be forever haunted by what has happened.

Director Mervyn LeRoy (who also helmed *Little Caesar*) does crackling good work with the newspaper scenes, but he fails miserably with the scandal victims. You can say the same for Byron Morgan's screenplay (based on the play by Louis Weitzenkorn, adaptation by Robert Lord). The scenes with Nancy (and family) reek of ancient, laughable theatrics. Frances Starr and Marian Marsh, as mother and daughter, are both abysmal. (Marsh's screeching last scene threatens single-handedly to ruin the film.) It's like watching two movies, a good one and a bad one, inexplicably stitched together. The basic subject matter, out-of-control tabloid journalism, has remained relevant, and that in itself makes it worth a look. Karloff, doing his mock clergyman, is pretty slimy and blackly comic (not too far from one of his horror creations); he overacts to his own and our delight. To see "Frankenstein's Monster" get pushed around by "Little Caesar" is an indelible sight. If that's not enough of a bizarre intertwining of iconic screen personae, in walks Ona Munson (*Gone With the Wind*'s Belle Watling) as a hot-stuff reporter. The movie was nominated for the 1931–32 Best Picture Oscar, but lost to *Grand Hotel*.

Are you sitting? Edward G. Robinson not only never won an Oscar but was never nominated for one—not for *Key Largo*, *The Sea Wolf*, *Double Indemnity*, *Dr. Ehrlich's Magic Bullet*, not even *Little Caesar*. (I'll avoid *The Ten Commandments* as part of my defense of his award-worthy career.) He died just before he was to receive an honorary Oscar in 1973. It came two months too late. Make that forty years too late.

James Cagney and cohorts

James Cagney

IN

Jimmy the Gent
(1934)

DIMINUTIVE James Cagney was arguably the toughest of movie tough guys. His streak of unpredictable violence certainly made him the scariest. He became a star in the shocking moment when he rammed that grapefruit into Mae Clarke's kisser in *The Public Enemy* (1931). Though that landmark film portrays gangster life in a most harrowing fashion (its grisly ending is a surefire nightmare inducer), Cagney's winning personality gives it an exciting allure. His inexhaustible supply of energy and his white-hot concentration secured him as one of the more riveting presences in movie history. And was anyone harder to kill than Cagney? His almost balletic death on the church steps in *The Roaring Twenties* (1939) showed just how difficult it was to put out his bright light. The surprise of his career is how he was able to use his electricity outside the realm of dramatic pictures. In the musical *Footlight Parade* (1933), he almost single-handedly puts three Busby Berkeley extravaganzas on their feet (and stars in one of them at the last minute too!). In the breathlessly paced comedy *Jimmy the Gent*, his firecracker performance is the sun around which everything else spins.

Jimmy Corrigan (Cagney) is in the "personal contacts" business, which means that when a wealthy person dies without a legal heir, Jimmy and his cohorts swoop down to locate (or invent) one. Jimmy lies, cheats, bribes, and punches his way to an eventual 50 percent cut. Speed is the name of the game in this racket, as one hot tip can put him ahead of his competitors. Despite his dirty dealings, Jimmy aspires to become a real gentleman. He loves Joan (Bette Davis), his classy rival's assistant, and she loves him, even though she disapproves of his disreputable tactics. Love finds a way, but not before several double crosses, shady deals, and physical outbursts have taken place.

Jimmy is a real mug. Don't tell him he ain't got ethics or he'll pop you one. Cagney's dese-dem-dose accent is coarser than usual and suggests just how high Jimmy has had to climb. In a movie filled with crooks, tramps, and con artists, no one is quite in his league. Cagney's Jimmy talks, moves, and thinks faster than anyone around him. And yells louder! The inconsequential plot has the kind of drive that can only be fueled by an actor who does everything full out. Even in quieter moments, his powers of persuasion overwhelm. When he smooth talks a nightclub tootsie into one of his schemes, his cocky charm ensures that he'll get what he wants from her now and be able to brush her off later.

Although he employs a get-out-of-my-way approach to living, Jimmy isn't completely invulnerable. His love for Joan is no con. Of course, he won't alter his business practices to please her, but his personal feelings are genuine and unwavering. Cagney is even more endearing in his attempts to become the "gent" of the title. Jimmy knows he's an uncouth hoodlum, but he's determined to become a class act. In the film's funniest sequence, he shows up at Joan's office as waiting clients are being served afternoon tea and thumbing through *Vanity Fair*. Jimmy is awestruck by such outlandish elegance and refinement, even though he doesn't really understand what he's looking at. He even tries hard to like tea, but it only makes his stomach growl. Cagney plays this scene like an alert kid who wants to fit in with the grown-ups. You can see him absorbing everything around him with an appealing mix of savvy and innocence.

Michael Curtiz directed this sixty-seven-minute marvel with lightning speed. It was the first of four collaborations with Cagney that include the classics *Angels with Dirty Faces* (1938) and *Yankee Doodle Dandy* (1942). Cagney got Oscar nominations for those two and won it for the latter. So, under Curtiz's guidance, he scored in a comedy, a drama, and a musical. (Their other film is the forgotten *Captains of the Clouds* [1942].) *Jimmy the Gent*'s screenplay, by Bertram Milhauser, plays like a textbook of American slang circa 1934. The snappy dialogue is volleyed by the cast with such precision as to make you want to live in a world where a wisecrack lands about every five seconds. A very blond Bette Davis is the height of working-girl chic. As the only decent character in the entire movie, she's a formidable foil for Cagney. Not many actresses could have held their own against his brand of life-or-death intensity, but she was one of them. (Davis was just one film away from recognition as a major screen actress with her shockingly raw, go-for-the-jugular performance in *Of Human Bondage*.) There's also memorable support from Allen Jenkins as Jimmy's right-hand man (and frequent punching bag) and from Mayo Methot (Humphrey Bogart's third wife) as a gold-digging dame who, in her wedding scene, gets the choicest wisecrack of them all.

James Cagney in *Jimmy the Gent* (1934)

Cagney would appear in comedies sporadically in his long career but in none as unpretentious and pleasing as *Jimmy the Gent*. These include the overproduced, often screechy film version of *A Midsummer Night's Dream* (1935), in which he gamely played Bottom. He and Bette Davis were reteamed in *The Bride Came C.O.D.* (1941), a forced, aggressively unfunny film sorely lacking the easy confidence of *Jimmy*. *Mister Roberts* (1955) is perhaps his best-remembered comedy, but have you seen it lately? Cagney is the one lively spot in this leaden movie. His last starring role was in Billy Wilder's *One, Two, Three* (1961), which cast him as a fast-talking, quick-thinking executive very close in spirit to Jimmy Corrigan. Cagney showed that he still had the charisma and vitality that had made him a star thirty years before. Unfortunately, *One, Two, Three* is nearly twice as long as *Jimmy the Gent* and only half the fun.

Frank Morgan and Fay Wray

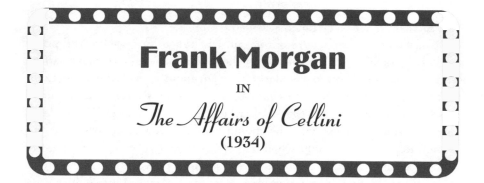

Frank Morgan

IN

The Affairs of Cellini

(1934)

Y OU may have found yourself watching an old movie and blurting out, "That's the Tin Man, with his *real* face, dancing with Shirley Temple!" or "What's the Wicked Witch doing in *My Little Chickadee*?" All of the cast members of *The Wizard of Oz* (1939) would forever be identified with their roles, and Frank Morgan was no exception. The title role in the most beloved Hollywood film of all time was just the *most* memorable of many wonderful parts for Morgan; he was one of the movies' more talented character men, equally good in comedy and drama (although he is best remembered for his ditheringly funny characters). *The Affairs of Cellini* took full advantage of his comic bag of tricks, primarily the vocal mannerisms that were his trademark. Morgan was never the kind of reliable, competent actor who would show up in a movie, do his bit, and modestly fade into the background; he was a bona fide scene stealer throughout his long career. Poor Fredric March: he starred as Benvenuto Cellini in Gregory La Cava's lavish comedy, but Morgan (re-creating his stage role) dominated the proceedings so thoroughly that it might as well have been retitled *The Affairs of Duke Alessandro*.

The *Affairs of Cellini* is no stuffy historical biography of a sixteenth-century renaissance man. Bess Meredyth's screenplay, based on a play (*The Firebrand*) by Edwin Justus Mayer, might best be described as a period screwball comedy, utilizing Cellini's adventurous exploits as a springboard for a surprisingly dizzy sex farce. The public activities of the court of Florence take a decided backseat to the bed hopping on everyone's mind. The Duke (Morgan), the only de Medici whom no one fears, is an ineffectual ruler dominated by his far craftier Duchess (Constance Bennett). Renowned for his artistic, romantic, and swashbuckling achievements, Cellini arouses the interest of the Duchess (who's used to having her way with any man she wants). Meanwhile, the Duke has his eye on Cellini's dimwitted model, Angela (Fay Wray). The Duke and Duchess try their best to cheat on each other but don't have an easy time of it. The film boasts a sword fight, a near hanging, a poisoning, and, happily, not a single moment that's to be taken seriously.

The Duke is very unsure of himself, frightened by his wife, and prone to brattiness. Since he's no match for the Duchess, he takes his frustrations out on his underlings, particularly his right-hand man, Ottaviano (Louis Calhern). Morgan's childish rantings are consistently funny as he helplessly tries to convince everyone that he's the man in charge. Sorely lacking in dignity, he runs when he should walk and has an unfortunate tendency to gesture flailingly when he gets overexcited. Most prominent of all, he becomes verbally unhinged at the slightest provocation. As he grows more flustered, he finds it impossible to get through a sentence before leaping to a new thought; sometimes he leaves phrases dangling, never to be retrieved. These scattershot monologues are delivered with such phenomenal clarity that you always know what the Duke is trying to say (even when *he* doesn't), and you're able to follow his every haphazard transition. You become accustomed to Morgan's stop-start comic style, but his rhythms are always unpredictable (unlike, say, Jack Lemmon's). Morgan raises stammering to an art, and his shtick never feels mechanical because he always seems to be making it up as he goes along.

The only time the Duke is able to focus on anything is when he's pursuing Angela. Morgan is delightfully foolish when convincing her to call him "Bumpy" in private (which will, of course, come back to haunt him). When the Duchess arrives unexpectedly, she sends the Duke to bed. (Morgan plays this exchange like a disappointed child whose mommy won't let him wait up for Santa.) With Angela hiding on the balcony and Cellini arriving in the Duchess's boudoir, a classic farcical situation is set in motion. The Duke and Duchess soon lose track of their "guests" and try to locate them without being found out. Whether crashing into a vase, pretending to be sleepwalking, or turning his calls of "Angela" into mock sneezing sounds, Morgan uses this sequence to exploit his expert physical agility and crackerjack timing. Another splendid bit is a moment in the torture chamber: while addressing the hangman, he's smacked in the face by the swinging noose *twice*, resulting in the loss of what little royal bearing he had been able to muster. He gets a rare moment of public satisfaction when he giddily demonstrates his edible jewelry at the banquet, behaving as if he's accomplished something of national importance.

Director La Cava gave this film an infectious air of tongue-in-cheek silliness. It shares an unforced appeal with his two indisputable classics, *My Man Godfrey* (1936) and *Stage Door* (1937). Fredric March, clad in tights and attractively goateed, lacks the devil-may-care flair that would have rendered Cellini as irresistible as we're told he is. Luckily, his blandness is not contagious. Constance Bennett (star first, actress second) plays the Duchess with an imperious grandeur that's more Beverly Hills than Renaissance Italy, but this only adds to the anachronistic fun. She has a naughty glow about her (and is costumed within an inch of her life!). But the biggest surprise is gorilla-enticing icon Fay Wray. One year after escaping Mr. Kong's clutches, she's flat-out marvelous as nearly brain-dead, mostly stone faced Angela. The role brought some much-needed variety to her victim-laden résumé; the most famous screamer in movie history was suddenly a confident, proficient comedienne. (Why didn't major comic roles follow?)

There were no supporting categories at the 1934 Academy Awards, but that didn't stand in Morgan's way. He joined Clark Gable *(It Happened One Night)* and William Powell *(The Thin Man)* as the three Best Actor nominees that year (Gable won). One can only wonder how non-nominees Fredric March and John Barrymore *(Twentieth Century)* felt about that. But there was simply no denying that Morgan had made the Duke hilariously his own (much the same way Peter Ustinov would do with supporting roles in his era). Although Morgan's best roles of the 1930s were comic (notably his hapless sugar daddy of *The Good Fairy*), the 1940s brought him a string of excellent dramatic parts. He gave deeply heartfelt performances in *The Shop Around the Corner* (1940), *The Mortal Storm* (1940), *Tortilla Flat* (1942), *The Human Comedy* (1943), and *The Great Sinner* (1949). Surprisingly, only *Tortilla Flat* put him back in an Oscar race (where he could now be accommodated as a supporting actor). Morgan died during the 1949 filming of *Annie Get Your Gun*, and, interestingly, it was Louis Calhern, his *Cellini* sidekick, who replaced him as Buffalo Bill.

W. C. Fields as Harold Bissonette

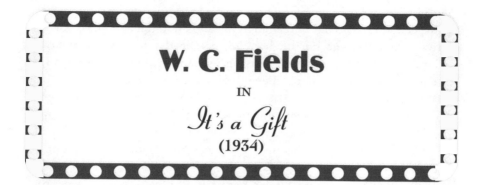

W. C. Fields

IN

It's a Gift
(1934)

IT's a Gift was the first of W. C. Fields's major works that I ever saw, and, because I laughed my way through all sixty-eight minutes of it, I was determined to see all his tailor-made starring vehicles. As it turns out, none is as good as *It's a Gift*, though each provides at least a few golden Fields moments. *My Little Chickadee* (1940) and *The Bank Dick* (1940) may be his best known and *Never Give a Sucker an Even Break* (1941) his most outrageous, but, trust me, they don't measure up to *It's a Gift*; it's the one I turn to for a Fields fix. The tide seems to be turning in its favor: it was the only Fields film on the American Film Institute's list of Hollywood's one hundred funniest comedies, ranked very respectably at number fifty-eight. Fields remains one of the great iconic images of old Hollywood: a middle-aged man, devoutly pledged to alcohol and cigars, muttering snide comments (often aimed at children) with a nasality produced by one of the more famous noses in movie history. *It's a Gift* casts him as a henpecked husband and befuddled father whom you'll root for instantly; his presence here is kinder and gentler than one usually associates with the tart-tongued legend. With a story by Charles Bogle (one of Fields's less outlandish pseudonyms), it's basically a series of comic set pieces stitched together by slight plotting, but Fields gives it unity. The comic plays his role with an actor's art, creating a three-dimensional, even touching, portrait of one man's stupefying collision with marriage, fatherhood, and business, sustained by an everlasting belief in the future.

Harold Bissonette (Fields), a grocery-store owner in New Jersey, lives with his battle-axe wife, Amelia (Kathleen Howard), and his two less-than-perfect children: Mildred (Jean Rouverol), a marriage-minded young lady, and her younger brother, Norman (Tom Bupp), a roller-skating terror. Harold's dream is to move to California and own an orange ranch. When he inherits money from a deceased uncle, he purchases some land of questionable value and sells his store. He packs up his skeptical family in a broken-down jalopy and heads west.

Fields is achingly sympathetic when trying to get respect, or even no-tice, in his own home. In his first scene, his bathroom shave is interrupted by his daughter, who has barged in to fix her hair and makeup. As she gets between him and the mirror, bobbing her head this way and that, he valiantly struggles to continue shaving without slitting his throat. In an extended, essentially silent sequence, Fields goes to increasingly drastic lengths to get on with his shave. He hangs a small mirror in the center of the room, but he can't prevent it from rotating. After striving to stay with it as it slowly turns, he decides to wait for it to spin around to him, mak-ing mad razor scrapes to his neck as he catches fleeting glimpses of his face whenever the mirror glides by. Fields's execution of this painstak-ingly detailed business puts him on par with the great silent clowns, prov-ing just how underappreciated his physical dexterity has been, in favor of his inimitable skill with an acidic line. The film's most ambitious (and probably funniest) scene is another intricately staged incident, an eleven-minute episode in which Harold tries to get some early-morning sleep on his back-porch swing, a futile attempt to escape his wife's nagging. On the middle level of an impressive three-story set, he must withstand a steady barrage of noises: a milkman's jangling glass bottles, a coconut's pro-longed descent down the back stairs, a brash traveling salesman, a bom-bardment of grapes (and an ice pick!) from a wicked child, a tedious mother-daughter conversation, a squeaky clothesline, and a fruits-and-vegetables vendor. The sight of Fields desperately seeking rest and exas-peratedly responding to, and trying to rid himself of, each distraction is one of the high points of movie comedy. By the time he resorts to arming himself with a shotgun, he has already stopped the show.

No one registers frightened surprise like Fields, be it caused by a per-son or an object: his shoulders nearly hit his ears while his arms, hands, and fingers go momentarily haywire. This never ceases to be funny (no matter how often he does it) because it always happens without warning; you never know what will set him off, and so you fall for it every time. In this movie, no one scares him the way the shrewish Amelia can. Always correcting him, badgering him, suspecting infidelity, and disapproving of everything he says, she's a horror (she even pretentiously insists he pro-nounce their name "Bis-on-*ay*"). As he attempts to comfort his weeping daughter, he tells her that *he's* the master of the house, though he is care-ful to whisper his words so Amelia cannot hear him. As worn down as he is by her constant criticisms and frustrating misperceptions, he never bears her any real malice. Domineering and unpleasant as she is, he wants to make her happy, and more surprising, he doesn't want to run away from her. Masochistic as that may sound, it makes Fields's performance endearing; he's committed to his wife and children despite their total lack of faith in him. Determined to follow through with his orange-grove fantasy, he takes everything in stride. When it looks as though his dream is a washout, his private moment of disappointment, quietly absorbing the blow of another failure, is unexpectedly affecting; it hurts him deeply to see his family walk out on him. But don't worry, folks, it's not too late for Harold to find his place in the sun.

It's a Gift, directed by Norman McLeod (who had just helmed two Marx Brothers pictures and would later direct Danny Kaye and Bob Hope), plays like a best-of reel for Fields; its comic situations build bit by bit to delirious heights. Other highlights include Harold's inadvertently sending a blind man into a stream of fire-engine traffic; his farewell to New Jersey in a sputtering, overpacked heap; the family's estate-trashing picnic on private property, complete with a pillow's feathers blanketing the grounds. Kathleen Howard, one of the movies' first-rate harridans, is so far beyond over the top that she makes Marie Dressler and Margaret Dumont look like Method actresses. And you don't want her to pull back one inch! (You won't be shocked to learn that she spent the early part of her career at the Metropolitan Opera.)

I'll leave you with one memorable breakfast exchange: after little Norman has snitched on Harold, the child asks, "What's the matter, Pop? Don't you love me anymore?" As he physically threatens to punch the kid, Harold shoots back, "Certainly I love you." Amelia shouts, "Don't you strike that child," to which Harold replies, "Well, he's not going to tell me I don't love him." And no one's going to tell me I don't love W. C. Fields.

Bit player Cesar Romero and Margaret Sullavan

Margaret Sullavan

IN

The Good Fairy

(1935)

S TAGE actress Margaret Sullavan made her screen debut playing an unwed mother in *Only Yesterday* (1933). Its plot may have been indistinguishable from dozens of girl-makes-mistake melodramas of the period, but there was nothing regular about Sullavan's acting. Though fairly ordinary looking by Hollywood standards, she had a face that made hearts melt when she smiled and ache when she cried. She also had a toughness of spirit in her that was an effective contrast to the physical fragility of her characters, who were often ill. But even when cast as robustly healthy, she still seemed easily breakable. More than anything else, it was Sullavan's delicately husky voice that audiences responded to and could never forget; it seemed to scrape its way yearningly out of her throat. Some actresses used their raspiness for grand theatricality (Tallulah Bankhead) or come-hither sexuality (Lauren Bacall), but Sullavan used hers to modulate a fluid range of emotional colors. With only sixteen films to her credit, she belonged more to the theatre than to the movies; *The Voice of the Turtle* (1943) was one of Broadway's more popular plays of the 1940s and a career-topping triumph for her. *The Good Fairy*, a most beguiling romantic comedy, is also notable for its behind-the-scenes drama. Sullavan and her director, William Wyler, clashed furiously during its making, wed before it was completed, and divorced soon after. Whatever it took to get it made, the result is a lollipop treat in which none of the background chaos got onto the screen.

Preston Sturges's screenplay, based on a play by Ferenc Molnár, begins in an all-girl orphanage in Budapest. Luisa Ginglebusher (Sullavan), a grown-up orphan who has been taught to do a good deed every day, is selected to become a movie-palace usherette, thereby allowing her to enter the outside world. Luisa is soon pursued by a millionaire, Mr. Konrad (Frank Morgan), but she tells him she's married to discourage his sugar-daddy impulses. Undeterred, he offers to make her

51

husband rich; unable to resist being someone's good fairy, she picks a name out of the phone book to claim as her spouse. Thus it is that struggling lawyer Max Sporum (Herbert Marshall) suddenly becomes a high-earning legal representative of Konrad's meat-packing company. Luisa goes to Max's office, intending to explain what has happened to him, but she decides to let him hold on to his illusion that his steadfast integrity has finally paid off. They fall in love, but Luisa is now juggling more well-intentioned lies than she may be able to handle.

Sullavan wisely plays the comedy straight: she assumes her usherette role with the utmost seriousness. In a glitzy toy-soldier uniform, she directs patrons with her electric wand, smiling on cue, too conscientious to relax. Outside the confines of the theatre, life is far more confusing. Detlaff (Reginald Owen), a waiter who becomes her first friend, wangles her an invitation to a posh hotel party, and she arrives with a mix of wonder and dread, delightfully fumbling to find her invitation. Sullavan's Luisa is even more enchantingly clueless when asked by the maître d' for her cloak, trying her best to make sense of the etiquette, ultimately tipping him with her coat-check chip. Even worse, Luisa completely misses the onslaught of sexual innuendo that comes her way. Earlier, she had explained to Detlaff that the orphans once gave a garden party at the penitentiary, but they weren't asked back because "it worried the prisoners or something." Here and throughout, Luisa's obliviousness about sex is a major source of amusement. In a private dining room, Mr. Konrad instigates a naughty game in which he's a mountain lion chasing her, a little lamb; she plays along as if it were make-believe time at the orphanage. Sullavan's teamwork with the hyperactively hilarious Frank Morgan provides the film's biggest laughs. Their cross-purposed conversations (they rarely know what the other is really talking about) are sheer bliss as her blithe embodiment of blank-slate innocence causes mounting frustrations for the would-be lecher. (Note that Morgan, when trying to tempt her with lavish gifts, refers to himself as a "wizard" four years before he immortalized himself as the most famous wizard of them all.)

Soon after Luisa has closed her eyes and excitedly stabbed the phone book to find her "husband," she looks out on the lights of Budapest and is enlivened by her anticipation of the joy she's going to bring. She declares herself Max's good fairy, and Sullavan's glowing enthusiasm creates the kind of spell that only a real star can cast. Despite the fact that Luisa becomes smitten with Max, her most touching relationship is with an inanimate object. It's love at first sight when she spots a department store display of "genuine foxine" fur pieces. She tries one on, which leads to the irresistible scene in which she admires herself between two mirrors, tickled by the funhouse effect of an endless chorus line of foxine-wearing Luisas. She then steps out of the ranks for her aptly overdramatized, suffering-like-Garbo imitation of the refined, fur-swathed actress she had seen on the movie screen. Max buys her the foxine, the first present she's ever received, and it becomes her security blanket. Thereafter, Sullavan is never seen without it (until the last scene), tenderly attached to that cheap, sorry-looking thing no matter how ragged it gets. While still in the store, Luisa naïvely tells Max that she can't see him later because she has to meet a man (Konrad) in his hotel room; she's hurt and bewildered when this makes Max angry and he walks out on her. When she calls him from a phone booth to say farewell, Sullavan utilizes her special gift, an incandescent vulnerability, as Luisa asks him to "think of me . . . kindly . . . almost . . . almost as if . . . I loved you." (She just about whispers those last three words.)

It's a shame that Wyler rarely directed comedies because this one and his next one, *Roman Holiday* (1953), demonstrate his adeptness in the genre; the laughs come without unnatural exertion. Written five years before his emergence as a star writer-director, Sturges's clever script is a polished jewel. Herbert Marshall likeably thaws Max from a pompous stiff to a humbled and grateful man. (Marshall would reteam with Wyler as *two* much-abused Bette Davis husbands in *The Letter* [1940] and *The Little Foxes* [1941].) *The Good Fairy* would be remade as *I'll Be Yours* (1947), a flat, semimusical Deanna Durbin vehicle.

Sullavan had her biggest critical success in the movies as the dying heroine of *Three Comrades* (1938), receiving the New York Film Critics' Best Actress Award and her sole Oscar nomination for her luminous performance (she easily outacted the titular trio). But her best film is Ernst Lubitsch's sublime romantic classic *The Shop Around the Corner* (1940), the third of her four films opposite a boyish James Stewart. (Frank Morgan is also in it and in the fourth one, the 1940 anti-Nazi drama *The Mortal Storm*.) In 1960, at age forty-eight, Sullavan died from an overdose of barbiturates that was ruled a suicide. The undimmed radiance of her Luisa Ginglebusher is a fitting legacy; Sullavan was a good fairy to anyone who loves the movies.

Mary Boland and Charles Laughton (in his drunk scene)

Charles Laughton
IN
Ruggles of Red Gap
(1935)

PORTLY Englishman Charles Laughton is my choice for the screen's greatest ham. Did anyone appear to enjoy acting as insatiably as he? He was often outrageous (Nero in *The Sign of the Cross* [1932]) and sometimes unrecognizable (buried under extensive gross-out makeup as Quasimodo in *The Hunchback of Notre Dame* [1939]—a performance almost entirely dependent on his exposed left eye). Laughton is best remembered for two towering turns: his definitive, Oscar-winning portrait of the title role in *The Private Life of Henry VIII* (1933) and his sadistic Captain Bligh in the impressively mounted *Mutiny on the Bounty* (1935), performances achieved with bold strokes and a wicked flair for theatricality. (His Bligh lives in my memory the way the best of Disney's animated villains do.) How lucky for us that he found time for the change-of-pace title role in *Ruggles of Red Gap*, a comedy of emancipation and one of the decade's sunniest treasures. As an English manservant who comes out of his shell in the American West, Laughton gives a tickling performance.

In 1908 Paris, Marmaduke Ruggles, valet to the Earl of Burnstead (Roland Young), learns that the Earl has bet (and lost) him in a poker game. His new employers are the wealthy Flouds of Red Gap, Washington: fun-loving Egbert (Charlie Ruggles, no relation) and grander-than-grand Effie (Mary Boland). Aching for social prominence, Effie hopes that Ruggles can turn her unwilling, good-ol'-boy husband into a gentleman. Ruggles inadvertently becomes Red Gap's most sought-after citizen when a newspaper identifies him as "Colonel" Ruggles ("late of the British army"), misinterpreting Egbert's nickname for him. Transformed by this unforeseen freedom, and smitten with a local widow, Prunella Judson (ZaSu Pitts), Ruggles is suddenly thrown by the news that the Earl is coming to Red Gap and intends to take his longtime valet back home with him.

Despite his doughy, double-chinned presence, Laughton, through the flawless execution of a servant's duties, makes Ruggles all but invisible.

Taking enormous pride in his work and anticipating his master's every need, Ruggles is devoted to his role as the man *behind* the man. When his world is turned upside down, Laughton's Ruggles retains his formal control, but his eyes, swimming in their sockets, always betray him. These optic spasms, signaling the thoughts and feelings his staid, timid body wouldn't dare register, humanize him. Swallowing his horror at being sold, he accepts his fate without complaint. The first time he says "Red Gap," Laughton pauses slightly between the words as if the name cannot be real. He's particularly discomfited by Egbert, who, uninterested in master-servant protocol, treats him as an equal. Ruggles musters time-honored resistance to familiarity between classes, disturbed by this heedless break with tradition and aghast at being called "Bill" and "Colonel." Laughton's drunk scene, begun at a Paris café, is the first step in Ruggles's conversion. After many highballs (with Egbert and one of his cronies), he becomes deadly silent, staring straight ahead until he cuts loose with a sudden "Yahoo!" (soon followed by a string of "Yippees!"), jolting even himself. An honest-to-goodness grin is, at last, coming through. (His smile grows in confidence the more practice it gets.) Still drunk when he faces a displeased Effie, he leans on her, slides down her buxom body, and happily sprawls out on the floor. Laughton's accompanying staccato laugh is uproarious, unrestrained, and triumphant; it appears to be the laugh Ruggles has been stifling, out of tastefulness, his whole life.

In Red Gap, it's a while before Laughton relaxes Ruggles's expression of disbelief at finding himself in such a rowdy place. But once he's accidentally freed by the news item declaring him "an honored houseguest" of the Flouds, he gets a taste of what it's like to be a somebody; feted at dinner parties, the man who's never drawn attention is now the center of it. He blooms with each successive, convention-busting experience, even finding a lady friend in Prunella. This welcome ugly-duckling romance is steered from cuteness by his know-it-all criticisms and her resulting snippiness. (Great bit: sparked by her invitation to tea, he attempts to leap over her white picket fence, overestimating his agility and doing little more than a hitch-kick, recovering as if it never happened.) In a saloon (with Prunella, Egbert, et al.), he officially declares his independence from lifelong servitude, determined to explore his revelatory individuality. Egbert mentions Lincoln's Gettysburg Address, and, after no one in the bar can recall a single line of it, Ruggles softly begins to speak it. Laughton's eloquent recitation, gaining in power, is infused with Ruggles's reverence for his new nation. A hush falls, and the patrons draw near to him. It is a tribute to Laughton that the director keeps the camera primarily on the listeners' awed faces, trusting the actor's voice to carry the scene. Ruggles, set to open a restaurant, will now use his considerable talents to serve himself. Laughton, tingling with possibility, reveals that freedom is not only a thrilling notion for the ex-valet but a deeply moving one. "When people think you are someone, you begin to think you are," Ruggles later tells the Earl. It helps that he's played by one of the most colossal someones the movies have ever known.

Leo McCarey's assured direction allows the best sequences to play at leisurely, but never slack, tempos; he maximizes the material's charm and the players' distinctiveness. For example, witness the fresh, unforced, and heavenly scene in which the Earl is taught the drum accompaniment to "Pretty Baby" by beautiful Nell Kenner (Leila Hyams) as she plays the piano part, as well as sings the vocal. The compact screenplay by Walter DeLeon and Harlan Thompson (adapted by Humphrey Pearson and based on Harry Leon Wilson's 1915 novel) is first-rate comedy writing, both in situation and in character. And for all of Laughton's authority in his role, it is far from a one-man show, containing three of the funniest, most expert supporting performances of the era: a frisky Charlie Ruggles, a bone-dry Roland Young, and an extravagant Mary Boland (who gives what may be the most hilarious portrayal of nouveau-riche affectation ever filmed) are each brilliant. (Unfortunately, Oscars for supporting roles did not begin until the *following* year.) ZaSu Pitts, a spunky ragamuffin, is yet another of this movie's indispensable ingredients. *Ruggles of Red Gap* received one Oscar nomination, for Best Picture, one of twelve films cited. Laughton was nominated too but for Captain Bligh rather than for Ruggles. (The New York Film Critics Circle named him the year's Best Actor for both.) *Ruggles* had already had two silent-screen versions and was later reworked for Bob Hope as *Fancy Pants* (1950).

Two of Laughton's late-career highs merit mention: *The Night of the Hunter* (1955), the only film Laughton directed (and a flat-out masterwork), and the credulity-straining but vastly entertaining *Witness for the Prosecution* (1957), in which he's sensational as the decrepit barrister, netting his third and final Best Actor Oscar nomination.

Jeanette MacDonald and Nelson Eddy

Jeanette MacDonald

IN

Naughty Marietta

(1935)

RELAX: I'm not going to make a case for Jeanette MacDonald as a great actress. But I would like to counteract her negative reputation as a humorless, eye-fluttering diva who starred in ludicrous, stiff musicals that can only be enjoyed as camp. That she appeared in her share of stinkers (beware of *Broadway Serenade*) was no reason for the *That's Entertainment!* films to treat her and her perennial partner, Nelson Eddy, so mockingly. You can imagine my surprise when I saw *Naughty Marietta* (their first of eight MGM pictures together) for the first time. I thought, "Hey, wait: this is funny, and Jeanette and Nelson *know* it's funny, and *they* are funny." I had been led to believe that their pictures would be numbing to sit through, and it's simply not true. *Naughty Marietta* and *Maytime* (1937) rank with the best musicals of the 1930s.

Jeanette MacDonald was the first major female star of movie musicals. Ernst Lubitsch teamed her with Maurice Chevalier in *The Love Parade* (1929), and it was a sensation. She made three more sexy and sophisticated musicals with Chevalier. (Yes, there was a time when Chevalier was actually sexy.) Two of them, Rouben Mamoulian's *Love Me Tonight* (1932) and Lubitsch's *Merry Widow* (1934), are among the best movie musicals of all time (their other one is 1932's *One Hour with You*). The wholesomeness of the Eddy pictures was a departure from the risqué nature of the Chevalier pictures. (Speaking of wholesomeness, the plot of her 1936 crowd pleaser *San Francisco* spends an awful lot of time on her valiantly protecting her virginity from the clutches of scoundrel Clark Gable.) *Naughty Marietta* was already an old-fashioned operetta by 1935, but MacDonald's attractive personality and her instantaneous chemistry with Eddy made it a huge hit. She and Chevalier had been excellent together, but now, with a classically trained singer as her costar, she began the most successful chapter of her screen career.

Set in the eighteenth century, *Naughty Marietta* tells the silly but enchanting story of Princess Marie (MacDonald) of France who, to avoid an arranged marriage, takes a ship to New Orleans disguised as her servant, Marietta. She's rescued from pirates by mercenary scout Richard Warrington (Eddy) and brought safely to New Orleans. Her uncle (Douglas Dumbrille) tracks her down, but Warrington helps her escape. She is caught, but not before she has fallen in love with Warrington. Her uncle insists she return to France and the impending marriage. Can she give up the man of her dreams in the name of duty? What do you think?

Has anyone played as many princesses as Jeanette MacDonald did? She had the requisite poise and grace and a certain royal distance from the masses. Her Princess Marie loves her people but is clearly not one of them. She is nobody's pushover either, and MacDonald shows Marie's real strength in dealing with her uncle as he tries to plot her future. Her resourcefulness comes into play aboard ship as she tries her best not to be recognized. MacDonald is delightful wearing glasses, stuffing her mouth with food, and trying to look as homely as possible. It's fun to watch this beauty let go of all vanity and give herself completely to her new adventure.

Naughty Marietta is that rare musical in which the characters always *know* they're singing. Whenever MacDonald or Eddy finishes a song, the other comments on the loveliness of the singing. The characters sing to impress each other, to compete with each other, and, finally, to give utterance to their deepest personal expression. When Warrington discovers that Marie can sing ("The Italian Street Song"), he knows he's found the mate of his dreams. Singing is the most intimate way for them to communicate. It is also a joyous celebration of being alive, as in MacDonald's first number ("Chansonette"), in which a houseful of people join her for a nonsensical but thrilling outburst of communal spirit. MacDonald grabs the movie by the collar here and dominates it with ease and self-assurance. The princess's people love her, and so now do we.

The most affecting thing about MacDonald's work is the way she lets us feel the princess's private yearnings for love. She hears the melody of "Ah, Sweet Mystery of Life" in the first scene, but there is no one for her to sing it to. When Marie meets Warrington, their relationship is all sparring and flirting, and she doesn't take him seriously. Then he sings "I'm Falling in Love with Someone" to her in a rowboat, and we see her realize *he's* the one she's been waiting for. He has given her a love song and awaits one in return. The emotional thrust of the movie becomes finding the moment when she can sing "Ah, Sweet Mystery of Life" to him. In the party scene, she believes she'll never see him again; as he's about to leave, she begins the song. Her full-throated rendition builds beautifully as she reveals who she is and what she wants. The heart beneath all the comic shenanigans has risen to the surface, and that heart belongs to MacDonald. When Eddy joins her at the staircase to make it a duet, they create one of the peak moments of singing in movie history. Because it's so simply staged, nothing can interfere with its sincerity. MacDonald and Eddy concentrate so completely on each other that the crowded room seems to disappear. (Try to forget Madeline Kahn's sidesplitting send-up of the song in 1974's *Young Frankenstein*, if you can.)

Naughty Marietta is swiftly directed by W. S. Van Dyke, and MacDonald is lavishly costumed by Adrian (the man who gave Joan Crawford her first pair of shoulder pads). There's very amusing support from Frank Morgan as the ever-bumbling governor and Elsa Lanchester as his sour wife. (She played you-know-who's "bride" that same year.) Eddy doesn't appear in the first half hour, but when he shows up singing "Tramp, Tramp, Tramp," his glorious voice could not be more welcome. This film, Oscar nominated for Best Picture, created the formula that would carry its two leads through seven more outings, but none of them would seem as fresh and spontaneous as this one. In fact, their *New Moon* (1940) plays like a virtual remake of *Marietta*, with Sigmund Romberg's music taking the place of Victor Herbert's. World War II changed the tastes of movie audiences, and the operetta phase had played itself out. Judy Garland became MGM's top singing sweetheart, and MacDonald left the studio in 1942. She returned six years later for two pictures *(Three Daring Daughters* and *The Sun Comes Up)* that failed to reignite her stardom. It would be two decades before another soprano (Julie Andrews) would gain the public's affection the way Jeanette MacDonald had.

Katherine DeMille and Boris Karloff (as Gregor)

Boris Karloff

IN

The Black Room
(1935)

SEVENTY years after it was filmed, Boris Karloff's numbingly creepy entrance as the Monster in *Frankenstein* (1931) remains as shocking as ever, and his performance still astounds. Why? Well, more than his hulking gruesomeness or indestructible strength, it's the Monster's private miseries, primarily his tortured inability to understand why he's so despised, that resonate so unforgettably. Who can forget his instinct for kindness, his childlike wonder, or his questioningly expressive hands? All are signs of the humanity coming through his stitched-together mass. It's as painful a portrait of loneliness as the screen has ever seen. In the nearly as great (but not as scary) sequel, *Bride of Frankenstein* (1935), Karloff, essentially a supporting player in the original, was now billed above the title, alone, as simply "Karloff," a literally towering superstar. (In *Bride*, the Monster, no longer sporting bangs, discovers speech, music, wine, cigars, and romance, becoming a much more regular guy.) Right after *Bride*, Karloff had one—make that two—of his best roles, playing good and evil twins in the non-supernatural but nonetheless horrifying film *The Black Room*, the best Karloff movie you've never heard of.

In central Europe, near the end of the eighteenth century, the Baron de Berghman (Henry Kolker) is shaken when his wife gives birth to twin boys, fearing the fulfillment of a centuries-old prophecy that the family will end when the younger of twins kills the firstborn in the castle's black room. As a precaution, the onyx-walled room is sealed up. Forty years later, Gregor, the elder twin, rules tyrannically and lecherously, swooping down on the local, never-seen-again females (a love 'em and kill 'em policy). At Gregor's request, his gentle brother, Anton, whose right arm has been paralyzed since birth, returns home after ten years in Budapest. With his people's hatred for him growing violent, Gregor relinquishes his power to the well-liked Anton, intending to murder his unsuspecting sibling so that he can assume his identity. He accomplishes this swiftly.

Gregor is irredeemably diabolical, and Karloff, with a mask of sado-masochistic glee and the gruffest of manners, is able to insinuate even darker depravities than the screenplay dares to name. Greedily addicted to his predatory pursuits, he's an all-too-*human* monster whose slovenly appearance well reflects the ugliness inside him. When sitting slouched in his tilted-back chair, his leg dangling over its arm, Karloff cuts a defiantly arrogant figure, believing himself invincible and savoring the fear he instills in others. With his oily version of charm, he sets his sights on virginal Thea (Marian Marsh), barely containing his brewing lust. Gregor has no plans to curb the excesses of his lifestyle.

Gregor is prime Karloff, but you'll be surprised at how immediately convincing he is as Anton, a man of fur-trimmed elegance, almost a fop. Anton genuinely likes people, and Karloff plays him with an open smile for everyone he encounters. For all his worldliness, Anton is an innocent; Karloff utilizes a softspoken approach to the character, with a light, higher-placed voice than the coarse depths of Gregor's (although both characters share the actor's distinctive lisp). With his paralyzed arm bent at the elbow and his hand at his chest like a boutonniere pinned to his lapel, Anton carries his deformity with grace. He refuses to believe that his brother is a demon until Gregor casually lures him, via a secret passage, into the dreaded room of the title (with its deep, enemy-eliminating pit) to kill him, even though the prophecy names Anton the murderer. In Anton, Karloff creates a deeply humane, highly respectable contrast to the sickening darkness of Gregor.

With Anton disposed of, Gregor, still inside the black room, practices his "Anton" before his onyx reflection, fixing his hair and placing his newly paralyzed arm, mere technical adjustments. But then his posture rises and his head leans back distinguishedly, and suddenly Anton is present, as are the cultured tones of his speech. It's believable that he's able to fool everyone because Karloff, playing it very cool, doesn't keep reminding us that he's really Gregor; he only occasionally lets his ulterior, patiently lurking thoughts pierce through. Thea's uncle, Colonel Hassel (Thurston Hall), requests Anton's signature on a formal agreement after he gives his consent for Thea and Anton to marry. With the right-handed Gregor's right hand now unusable, he's in a tight spot. He stalls until he can connive a sly solution, but when he's found out, he daringly unleashes Gregor: he unfolds the fingers of his lifeless hand, leans back in his chair, and luxuriates in his true, dastardly self. Later, in front of a mirror, he bids farewell to his healthy right arm (intending not to use it again, even in private), placing it, in ritualistic fashion, securely into its inactive position. Resolved to stay in power and marry Thea, Karloff plays this scene like a sinisterly twisted pep talk. An interesting note: the real Anton's paralyzed hand is somewhat limp, but when Gregor pretends to be Anton, *his* paralyzed hand is a fist. No one notices the marked difference. Is Karloff showing us that Gregor missed a detail in his impersonation? Or did he decide that Gregor's natural force would unconsciously clench the hand? Mighty subtle, Boris.

With a screenplay by Arthur Strawn and Henry Myers (story credit to Strawn), *The Black Room* is set at a page-turning pace, running only sixty-eight minutes, but it is filled with enough inspired grisliness for a film twice as long. Director Roy William Neill, who would helm eleven Sherlock Holmes pictures in the 1940s, gives it a stylish luridness, embellishing the theme of duality with mirrors of all sizes, seemingly everywhere. He also makes prominent and striking use of religious statues, all sympathetically, if quietly, observing the proceedings. With sets that suggest a macabre operetta, the film appears to take place in the same village as *Frankenstein*. And, oh boy, that blaring background score has got to go!

The horror craze would subside; in the late 1930s and early 1940s, Karloff's vehicles were mostly B- and C-grade. He was so typecast as a figure of fright that everyone seemed to have forgotten he was an accomplished actor capable of surviving the genre's decline. He played the Monster one last time in *Son of Frankenstein* (1939) and made a final appearance in the series in the pitifully awful *House of Frankenstein* (1944), which affords the matchless sight of him, as a mad scientist, acting with *someone else* (Glenn Strange) as the Monster; they even share a quicksand death together. Karloff had a brief artistic resurgence when he starred in three of producer Val Lewton's very fine (more suggestive than explicit), low-budget horror films: *The Body Snatcher* (1945), *Isle of the Dead* (1945), and *Bedlam* (1946), with the middle one, a psychological stunner, the standout. Though he made his name in a genre that tends to keep you off Oscar ballots, Karloff, like Lon Chaney before him, repeatedly proved that horror films and superlative acting are not mutually exclusive.

Carole Lombard and Fred MacMurray

Carole Lombard

IN

Hands Across the Table

(1935)

MORE than anyone else, Carole Lombard personified the key ingredients of screwball comedy: fearless unconventionality, innate daffiness, and devastating glamour. After paying her dues in silent Mack Sennett shorts in the late 1920s and racy, run-of-the-mill melodramas in the early 1930s, she was rescued from possible career oblivion when Howard Hawks cast her opposite the outrageous John Barrymore in the slaphappy farce *Twentieth Century* (1934). As stage and screen star Lily Garland (formerly Mildred Plotka), Lombard showed more enthusiasm and raw talent than skill, but she had, at last, found her niche; screwball comedy brought out her sparkling personality and screen magnetism and quickly endeared her to the mass audience. In between the Hawks picture and her two greatest vehicles of the 1930s, *My Man Godfrey* (1936) and *Nothing Sacred* (1937), Lombard starred in the modest, not-quite-screwball *Hands Across the Table*. It's not in the same league with those three classics or with her final film, Ernst Lubitsch's brilliant *To Be or Not to Be* (1942); let's call it her fifth best comedy (amid such competition, that's nothing to sneer at). The confidence she'd gained working with Hawks and the irrepressible Barrymore is apparent here: Lombard's thoroughly natural performance combines bruised strength and cloaked innocence, stubborn cynicism and childlike zaniness, to create a character who's easy to care about and hard to resist.

New York manicurist Regi Allen (Lombard) has one thing on her mind: snagging a rich husband. At the swanky hotel where she works, she forms a friendship with wheelchair-bound Allen Macklyn (Ralph Bellamy), a wealthy hotel resident who falls for her instantly but whom she regards as a sympathetic confidant. She sets her sights on Theodore Drew III (Fred MacMurray, in the screwball role), a handsome, lighthearted fellow from a distinguished family who schedules a manicure to pursue her. After a fun-filled date, Regi may have found love *and* money in one package. Well, it turns out that not only is Ted engaged to the daughter of "The Pineapple

King," but he hasn't got a dime to his name (the crash of '29 took care of that) and is only marrying for the money. When he misses his boat to Bermuda (an engagement present from his future father-in-law so that he won't be around for the wedding preparations), Ted asks Regi if he may spend his "vacation" as her roommate. After all, they're both just a couple of gold diggers. (I can't imagine that the manicurists who saw this movie had apartments as roomy as Regi's or were clad in Travis Banton wardrobes, but isn't that part of the fun?)

Regi's likeably wry attitude toward life makes her appear more hard-boiled than she really is. Warm conversations with Allen in his spacious suite are a therapeutic respite for both of them: from her drudgery and his loneliness. Lombard lets Regi come radiantly alive in these scenes, leaving her ready-for-battle sarcasm outside and letting the sweet, uninhibited Regi emerge. But even Allen's influence cannot sway her from her financially driven approach to matrimony. Regi's relationship with Ted achieves a similar openness once they admit to each other that they're both money-minded heels, but she pulls back when her feelings for him deepen, and the sexual tension of their arrangement becomes noticeably thick. Lombard plays their last night together with a sexy brew of tangible desire and agonizing determination to stay away from him. She turns chilly to discourage his increasing inability to resist her; Regi's afraid he'll later resent her if she takes him away from his heiress's bankroll. The pain of loving Ted (and driving him away) drains all the joy from her, and she's in an irritable daze the next day when she meets her rival, Vivian Snowden (the easy-to-dislike Astrid Allwyn). Regi's unimpressed by this bitch's clever ploy to arrange a manicure in order to meet her, but she perks up when Vivian implies that Regi's a whore with some money due her. Lombard enhances Regi's steely composure with a rising anger, but she waits until the following scene to fall apart, tearfully disclosing to Allen all the pent-up emotions and frustrations of her tattered love life.

Despite its dramatic flourishes, *Hands Across the Table* still affords Lombard plenty of opportunities to get laughs and charm us to distraction. Whether trying to impress Ted with her bogus thoughts on polo (as she nervously manicures his fingers to bloody stumps) or wreaking havoc with Allen's tea service, Lombard is delicious. When Ted moves in, it becomes obvious that they're made for each other because of all the fun they're having. His casual bursts of lunacy awaken Regi's antic side, which gives Lombard her cue to unleash her plucky gift for comic mayhem. (She really enjoys their phony brawl to scare off one of her suitors.) Their most inspired moment of mischief comes when they decide to fool Vivian into thinking that Ted is phoning from Bermuda. Pinching her nose to get the right nasal effect, Lombard goes all out as a long-distance operator, infuriating Vivian with frequent nonsensical interruptions.

Director Mitchell Leisen was particularly good at blending a film's comic and dramatic material in a most effortless way (a gift best demonstrated in 1940's *Remember the Night*). Cinematographer Ted Tetzlaff photographed Lombard as if her bone structure were lit from within (you can see why he was her favorite cameraman). Ralph Bellamy's gentle performance effectively navigates the self-pitying pitfalls of his potentially maudlin role. It's easy to forget that Fred MacMurray was once a brightly energetic comic actor; he was hardly what you'd call lively on the television series *My Three Sons*. (Notice that he and his sitcom costar William Demarest share a scene in this movie.) This was the first, and unquestionably best, of MacMurray's four pictures with Lombard (the others: *The Princess Comes Across* [1936], *Swing High, Swing Low* [1937], and *True Confession* [1937]). They surely made an attractive and easygoing team.

After *Fools for Scandal* (1938), an embarrassingly strained romp that deservedly flopped, it was time for Lombard to take a break from comedy. She gave lovely, restrained performances in four consecutive dramas: *Made for Each Other* (1939), *In Name Only* (1939), *Vigil in the Night* (1940), and *They Knew What They Wanted* (1940). But it was back to comedy for her two final films: the witless *Mr. and Mrs. Smith* (1941), whose only distinction is that it was directed (cluelessly) by Alfred Hitchcock, and *To Be or Not to Be*, which contains her wittiest performance. Lombard, at age thirty-three, was killed in a 1942 plane crash. Today, she is primarily remembered as Clark Gable's wife, but that is an insufficient way to acknowledge one of the great female stars of Hollywood's Golden Age.

Marlene Dietrich and Gary Cooper

Gary Cooper

IN

Desire

(1936)

IT'S no surprise that Gary Cooper, man of few words, became a star in the silent era (at the tail end). An immediate success in talkies, notably *The Virginian* (1929), *Morocco* (1930), and the well-made *Farewell to Arms* (1932), his career leapt into superstardom with the title role in Frank Capra's *Mr. Deeds Goes to Town* (1936). One of the director's best, it showcased Cooper's laid-back comedic flair, loosening him up to audiences (sort of like what *Twentieth Century* did for Lombard). As Deeds, the tuba-playing "Cinderella Man" who inherits a fortune and wants to give it to the poor, he's simply terrific and effortlessly funny. Cooper received an Oscar nomination and, thereafter, took on occasional Deeds-like characters (such as Bertram Potts in *Ball of Fire* [1941], his best post-*Deeds* comedy). *Desire*, the movie he made just before *Deeds*, looks like his warm-up for his role in the Capra film. In both, he plays innocents (smarter and tougher than they look) who not only come up against sinister forces but fall in love with women who aren't what they seem to be. High-gloss *Desire* isn't as good as *Mr. Deeds*, but it's still a marvelous hybrid of light comedy, romantic melodrama, and exotic intrigue, reteaming Cooper with his *Farewell to Arms* director, Frank Borzage, and his *Morocco* costar, glamour-drenched Marlene Dietrich. Cooper, six-foot-three and unreasonably handsome, is totally engaging as a midwestern fish out of water dropped into a European pond, amplifying his subdued screen personality with game-for-anything high spirits and an ear-to-ear grin and generously sprinkling his work with casually humorous grace notes.

American-in-Paris Tom Bradley (Cooper), a motor engineer for a Detroit car company, completes his business trip and sets off for an adventure-seeking Spanish vacation. At the border, stunning Madeleine de Beaupre (Dietrich), a jewel thief posing as a countess, slips a stolen pearl necklace into Tom's suit-jacket pocket to get it safely through customs, but she's unable to swipe it back. She hitches a ride with him, even resorts to stealing his car, but still no necklace. He tracks her down in San Sebastian (still un-aware that he has the necklace), and although furious about his car (she wrecked it), he can't resist her: *she* is the adventure he's been seeking. He joins her and her "Uncle" Carlos (John Halliday), her partner in crime, at a mountain villa, where, after the necklace has been retrieved, Tom and Madeleine fall in love. He still doesn't know she's a criminal, and besides, Carlos isn't going to let her go without a fight.

Tom, a valued up-and-comer in the company, is first seen alone, prac-ticing a forceful, vacation-demanding speech he intends for his boss. As he rehearses himself into a steam, Cooper makes Tom's guilelessness in-gratiatingly transparent. When his boss (*I Love Lucy*'s William Frawley) offers him a vacation before he even asks, Tom is at first thrown but re-laxes into aw-shucks modesty as the boss praises him. Now, with a com-pany car, nothing can stand in the way of his realizing his boyhood dreams of bullfights and senoritas. When elation spontaneously over-takes him, as it does on the road, he sings "Cielito Lindo," making up his own simple lyrics (in this case, "I'm driving, I'm driving"). When he gets to "Ai, ai, ai-ai," he's crooning at the top of his lungs, but you sense that he hopes for a better companion than the sound of his own voice. An-other of Cooper's prize moments comes when Tom pulls over to photo-graph himself on holiday, striving for a look of rakish abandon (leaning against the car, a guitar in his arms, and a self-consciously dashing ex-pression on his face), only to have Madeleine's car race by and splash him with mud. When they actually meet, he tries his homegrown brand of seductive smoothness on her, but it flops. Perhaps the most pleasura-ble aspect of Cooper's work is that, no matter how many indignities he suffers at her hands, he just can't stifle his giddiness at being in her pres-ence. He cannot stay mad at someone he's so happy to be around. (Sure, he wants his car back, but mostly he wants to see her again.) When she explains with a lie that she stole the car (and left him stranded) because she was afraid of his virile advances, he's so flattered that he blushes.

Up at the villa, Madeleine and Carlos manage to get the necklace back, but he sees fit to warn her against becoming emotionally entangled with Tom. So, when she and Tom are alone, she feigns sleep just as he's revving up to woo her (emboldened by a shot of alcohol). He confesses his love to the sleeping beauty with the smoldering conviction that only a movie star extraordinaire such as Cooper can summon. He's hurt by her yawn, but later, under the Spanish moon, she reciprocates his feelings; Cooper's wistful demeanor is lifted. They *finally* kiss, but it's worth the wait (for them and for us). Cooper's erotic heat also expertly layers his line read-ings. The pauses he brings to "All I know about you is . . . you stole my car . . . and I'm insane about you" make it one of those magical funny *and* sexy moments; he breathes the line on her cheek. But beneath his lusty urges and fancy-free energy is rock-hard dependability, a tenacity to protect their future together, especially as Carlos takes steps to block them. And so, American know-how battles European sophistication. Cooper, now a gleaming white knight, dominates the climactic dinner scene, jockeying to outfox his opponent, without sacrificing his lightly funny manner. You may, on occasion, catch Cooper milking the boyish charm, but I find that forgivable in light of moments such as this: while packing his suitcase for America, he sings about the voyage home, improvising his latest rendition of "Cielito Lindo" ("We are sailing, we are sailing"), but interrupts himself to check his departure date on a telegram, then confidently resings the verse with the now-correct information.

Creamily directed by Borzage, and graced with the sly, entrancing "touch" of its producer, Ernst Lubitsch, *Desire* is an intoxicant. The script, by Edwin Justus Mayer, Waldemar Young, and Samuel Hoffenstein and based on a German film, provides a gloriously escapist scenario, its cleverness matched by its amorous zeal. Dietrich, luxuriously furred and feathered (thank you, Travis Banton, you mad boy!), gives a soft, insinuating performance, an ideal contrast to Cooper's sprightly appeal. Her one song, the swoony "Awake in a Dream," is effective foreplay for the sparks-flying couple. Suave John Halliday (Kate Hepburn's *Philadelphia Story* father) is a villain worthy of Claude Rains.

Cooper won two Best Actor Oscars, for *Sergeant York* (1941) and *High Noon* (1952), the second more justified than the first. Let me mention my soft spot for two much-derided films of his: *The Fountainhead* (1949), deliriously over the top and perhaps the greatest bad film of the 1940s (certainly the most phallic); and *They Came to Cordura* (1959), a Mexican-set treatise on courage and cowardice. In the former, his acting is, unfortunately, as stiff as the power drill he brandishes, but in the latter, he gives a thoughtful, often moving performance in a one-man-stands-alone plotline (shades of *High Noon*). And then there's the gritty *Man of the West* (1958), a good western worth catching for the incredible scene in which, after pummeling Jack Lord, Cooper strips him of nearly all his clothes, repeating and expanding the humiliation Lord inflicted on Julie London. And, to think, he can sing a mean "Cielito Lindo" too.

Spencer Tracy, William Powell, and Jean Harlow

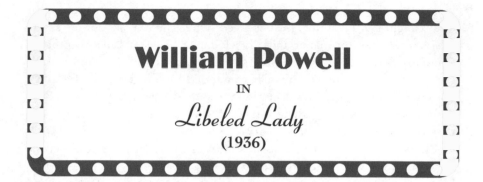

William Powell

IN

Libeled Lady
(1936)

DAPPER, good-humored William Powell had quite a year in 1936. Oh, he'd been a familiar screen face through the silent 1920s and found early talking success as mystery-solving Philo Vance and also as the six-time costar of clotheshorse Kay Francis (don't miss their exquisite romance *One Way Passage* [1932]). Superstardom was his when, blissfully cast opposite divine Myrna Loy, he played spiffy, cocktail-swilling detective Nick Charles in *The Thin Man* (1934), a true 1930s classic (though it's little more than a B picture whenever he and Loy aren't onscreen). The bantering duo's depiction of marriage made domesticity seem sexier than any backstreet affair. Nick brought Powell an Oscar nomination, and his ascending career peaked with five 1936 films. Not only did he star in *After the Thin Man*, a popular not-as-good sequel, and *The Ex-Mrs. Bradford*, a *Thin Man*-styled comic caper with Jean Arthur, but he also played the title role in the musical blockbuster *The Great Ziegfeld* (which only *feels* like the longest movie ever made). Best of all, he headlined two grand screwball comedies, *My Man Godfrey* and *Libeled Lady*. *Godfrey*, the quintessence of Depression-era make believe, paired him with ex-wife Carole Lombard; her breathless ditsiness complements his elegant understatement. *Libeled Lady* isn't as cherished as *Godfrey*, but it's still a dilly of a comedy, not only starring Powell and Loy (after *The Thin Man*, it's their next best of *fourteen* films together) but also Jean Harlow (top billed) and Spencer Tracy. And yet it's Powell's show; a tip-top light comedian gives a note-perfect performance.

Newspaper editor Warren Haggerty (Tracy) postpones his wedding to tough-talking Gladys Benton (Harlow), yet again, when heiress Connie Allenbury (Loy) sues his paper (for five million dollars) for printing a libelous story about her ("Peer's Wife Routs Rich Playgirl"). A frantic Warren rehires ex-employee (and libel specialist) Bill Chandler (Powell) to use his lady-killing skills to put Connie into a compromising situation, whereupon she'll be compelled to drop her lawsuit. The plan: Bill will marry Gladys (suckered into the scheme by Warren); then, after he's "caught" with Connie, his bereaved "wife" can expose Connie as the husband stealer the paper initially claimed she was. Bill's wooing of Connie gets off to an unpromising start, but as she falls for him, he falls for her. Now seeking to shield his intended victim, he stalls for time, hoping he can *talk* her into dropping the suit. Warren, suspecting a double cross, and Gladys, now in love with Bill, do their damnedest to see that Bill carries out the plan as arranged.

Bill is a real smoothie. He spends most of the story lying to everyone but, no matter how daftly the situation escalates, you'll not lose faith in his ability to surmount any complication with ease, good cheer, and shrewd ingenuity. The beauty of Powell's performance is the way he juggles all the other characters, supplying the called-for persona that will get him what he wants. When Warren first tracks him down, he matches the cagey editor's street smarts with his cultured brand of wise-guy snappiness, all the while concealing beneath a carefree demeanor that he's in debt and needs a job. And he surely enjoys his work. Powell's Bill has an exuberant flair for mischief, whether committing full out to his public, playacting ardor for Gladys (his "Fuzzy Wuzzy" bride) or cramming, while shaving, to memorize all he can about angling in order to impress Connie's trout-enthusiast father (Walter Connolly). His nonchalance is so reassuring that, whenever Bill hits a real snag, Powell has prime opportunities for laughs. Following the Allenburys aboard an ocean liner, he's stunned by their imperviousness to his charms and the thuds that greet his jokes. Wondering if he's lost his touch, he realizes that he'll have to work harder than anticipated. His most precarious moment comes later on, after he's won over Mr. Allenbury and been invited to his mountain lodge for a dreaded fishing weekend. (Now he must prove he's the ace fisherman he's touted himself as being.) A last-minute lesson in his hotel room reveals his inexplicable perfection at executing an underhand cast, which he will later grandiosely display to the Allenburys before wandering upstream with his hidden how-to book. It's a classic city-boy-in-nature scene, and Powell gets a slapstick, waterlogged workout, accidentally wowing father and daughter in the process. It is a joy to watch a sophisticated funnyman like Powell brave a low-comic obstacle course.

Before long, Bill has both Connie and Gladys in love with him. He needs Gladys as an ally in delaying Warren from humiliating Connie, and it is easy for him to attain her fancy. He melts this brassy dame with gentlemanly attentiveness, something she craves. By lending a sympathetic ear to her complaints about Warren's treatment of her, and by tossing compliments her way, Bill soon has her hanging on his every word. But Connie is no Gladys. She's smart and suspicious but not nearly as aloof as she seems (Loy thaws her winningly), and Bill and Connie start to bond. The magic of the Powell-Loy team is that they radiate a teasing affection for one another, tickled by their pleasure in having found a wit-sharing soulmate. After a moonlit swim, she confesses how wrong her first impressions of him were, and Powell's face registers guilt, shame, and regret. It's a rare moment of self-reflection for Bill, a life-changing acknowledgment of what a heel he's been. Determined to protect her from the already-in-motion frame-up, he tries his best to convince her to abandon the libel suit (she still doesn't know he's employed by the paper). Though he hardly ever utters a truthful word to Connie, Warren, or Gladys, he actually has all of their best interests in mind: marriage for him and Connie and for Warren and Gladys and a suit-free newspaper. Before the merrily mixed-up finale in which all four stars converge, there's a winsome scene in which Connie proposes to Bill, rendering the exceedingly verbal Powell just about speechless.

Directed by Jack Conway at a *Front Page*-ish clip, *Libeled Lady* is frivolous fun. From a story by Wallace Sullivan, the screenplay, by Maurine Watkins, Howard Emmett Rogers, and George Oppenheimer, has a humdinger of a plot, zingy dialogue, and four terrific roles. An iridescent Loy and a feisty Tracy are flawless; though Harlow isn't in her costars' league, she is splendidly cast and supremely likeable (even though her star-making, explicit sexuality had been tamed by the newly enforced Production Code). When she died of uremic poisoning in 1937, at age twenty-six, she was engaged to marry Powell. The movie was remade as *Easy to Wed* (1946), an Esther Williams vehicle, with Van Johnson in Powell's role, but Lucille Ball, in the Harlow role, is the film's sole virtue.

Libeled Lady was nominated for a Best Picture Oscar (ten films made the final ballot) but received not a single other nomination. Powell was nominated that year for Best Actor but for *My Man Godfrey*, which got five other nominations, including those for Best Director (Gregory La Cava) and Best Actress (Lombard) but *not* for Best Picture. Go figure. And what *was* Oscar's Best Picture that year? None other than *The Great Ziegfeld*. Yep, 1936 was the heyday of William Powell.

Thurston Hall looks on as Irene Dunne "goes wild"

Irene Dunne

IN

Theodora Goes Wild

(1936)

IRENE Dunne arrived in Hollywood at the outset of the talkies and systematically won popularity and acclaim genre by genre. She first made her name in drama, in the lumbering epic *Cimarron* (1931), one of those baffling winners of the Best Picture Oscar. Then, more specifically, she was a soap star, engendering audience sniffles via the original versions of *Back Street* (1932) and *Magnificent Obsession* (1935). She clicked in musicals next, and her lilting soprano, which had brought her stage success in the 1920s, distinguished the Jerome Kern-scored hits *Roberta* (1935) and *Show Boat* (1936), the latter one of the top Broadway-to-Hollywood adaptations ever done. Finally, and most enduringly, Dunne became a screwball comedy star, one of the roughly half dozen funny females who dominated that miraculous comic era. Unlike, say, Claudette Colbert, Dunne didn't make a slew of comedies; her considerable reputation in the genre is built on her three good ones: two fondly remembered, marital mix-up romps, *The Awful Truth* (1937) and *My Favorite Wife* (1940), both costarring a peak-form Cary Grant, and *Theodora Goes Wild*, the sleeper that established her as a deluxe comedienne. No longer as widely known as the two with Grant, *Theodora* is the showiest showcase of Dunne's comic art. (It helps that her title role has a dazzlingly broad arc.) For all her other talents, it was in comedy that she revealed just how smart an actress she was, not to mention one with a glimmering screen presence, the kind that keeps you an essential star sixty-odd years after the fact.

Caroline Adams, author of *The Sinner,* a sexy best-seller, is the pseudonym of Theodora Lynn, a Sunday school-teaching, church organ-playing virgin who lives with her two maiden aunts in Lynnfield, an upstanding (and gossipy) Connecticut town. She keeps her writing a secret and, therefore, can't take pleasure in her success. At the office of her New York publisher (Thurston Hall), she meets Michael Grant (Melvyn Douglas), the artist who designed her book cover; he can't believe that fresh-faced

Theodora is *the* Caroline Adams. Michael follows her home on a goodwill mission to *force* her to come clean with Lynnfield and embrace her true self and blackmails her into hiring him as the gardener. Well, they fall in love, whereupon Michael runs scared. Theodora, having finally taken his advice and gone "wild," follows him to the city, where, relishing her overdue celebrity, she's ready to return the favor: despite his resistance, she'll help Michael free himself from his bullied-by-daddy existence, hoping that, at last, they can both just be themselves.

Dunne gives a sympathetic portrait of life "in the closet": carefully monitoring her every move, suppressing her impulses, living a safe but inauthentic life. Theodora lives in constant fear of exposure. Although the stress of keeping up the charade is exhausting, the alternative seems much worse. The antithesis of her alter ego, she's headed for the spinsterdom in which she was raised. While reluctantly out to dinner with her publisher, his wife, and a party-crashing Michael, she's embarrassed by her own purity and becomes daring (via many cocktails), winding up in Michael's apartment and determined to play it cool (the way Caroline Adams would). He asks if she'd like a "scotch"; when she repeats the word in assent, Dunne says it in a too-precise way, implying that Theodora has never said the word aloud before. When she spots his bed, Dunne, in a beautifully orchestrated bit, physically reacts as if she's just come upon the edge of a cliff, then spins around, recovering by gracefully waltzing herself away from it. When he reaches to kiss her, she snaps. Her woman-of-the-world pose (never very convincing) is shattered in her frantically funny exit; she schoolgirlishly turns into everything she wanted to prove she wasn't, running and screaming out the door. When Michael shows up in Lynnfield, she must go along with his gardener routine (or he'll blab the truth), and though she wants him to leave, it's the most exciting thing ever to happen to her. Theodora soon springs to life, laughing full out in his company, as if she were making up for a lifetime devoid of spontaneity and silliness. (Dunne finds plum moments for her wickedly amusing, deliberately phony laugh, cunningly used to convey victory.) But she still can't bring herself to make the big leap; Dunne believably clings to Theodora's security blanket of fear, guilt, and shame. But when gossip about her and Michael intensifies, she makes an unplanned declaration of independence to the biddies of her "literary circle." In a defiant, angry, yet firmly-in-control speech, Dunne frees Theodora from decades of moldy convention; her Yankee spirit, spurred on by love, has risen at last. When she proudly reenacts the scene (for Michael), Dunne is positively aglow. There's no turning back.

When Theodora "comes out," look out! She arrives at Michael's apartment, only to learn that, though he cares for her, he is trapped in a love-less marriage, having promised not to disgrace his father's political career with a divorce. Now it's Theodora's turn to play fairy godmother (Dunne's single-mindedness has a gleeful invincibility), and Michael is just as mortified as she once was. She moves into his apartment (he immediately moves out) and becomes the Caroline Adams the world's been waiting for. Arriving at the publisher's office smothered in black feathers and with the obligatory dog on a leash, Dunne makes quite the grand entrance, luxuriating fully in her diva persona. (She appears, at times, to be giving a zesty, decades-early audition for *Auntie Mame*.) In a fabulous turnaround, she *demands* publicity. Thereafter, a press corps is never far off, and a vivified Dunne flamboyantly toys with the reporters as if they were her own band of stage-door Johnnies. Freed by the headlines about her true identity, Theodora is committed to making Michael just as happy (and single) as she is. She loves him, but that doesn't mean she can't have fun upturning his life; a teasing Dunne enjoys the merciless revenge of doing to him what he did to her, and she does it with a lot more splash. (Bernard Newman's whimsical costumes swathe her in enough fur and glitz for a pair of movie queens.) It is a rare pleasure to watch Dunne bask in Theodora's seemingly scandalous, gal-about-town lifestyle, which climaxes at the hoity-toity reception for the governor. Dunne's resourceful performance is an *A*-to-*Z* comic turn, stylishly and cheerfully hitting most of the letters in between.

Jauntily directed by Richard Boleslawski (a veteran of the Moscow Art Theatre), *Theodora Goes Wild* holds up very well; it is a hypocrisy-slamming lark that affectionately pokes fun at all concerned. Sidney Buchman's screenplay, from Mary McCarthy's original story, has a zippy momentum, building steadily on its adorable premise. One subpar scene: the nighttime battle of the noises, Michael's whistling versus Theodora's piano playing and singing; it's as annoying to us as it is to them. Melvyn Douglas may not have had Cary Grant's good looks, but he was a polished light comedian (*Ninotchka*, anyone?), and he adroitly partnered Dunne. She received an Oscar nomination, her second of five, for this film but you can put her on the woefully long list of Oscar's nonwinning casualties.

Humphrey Bogart as Frank Taylor

Humphrey Bogart

IN

Black Legion

(1937)

I N 1936, Humphrey Bogart became a "name" when he re-created his 1935 Broadway role of gangster Duke Mantee in Warner Brothers' film version of *The Petrified Forest*. In 1941, he became a full-fledged Warners star as Roy Earle, another gangster, in *High Sierra*. Well, in between, he languished at the studio, appearing in twenty-eight films during this five-year limbo. Playing second fiddle to Edward G. Robinson, Pat O'Brien, George Raft, and providing occasional target practice for James Cagney, Bogart was clearly not regarded as star material. Witness some of the oddball assignments he was subjected to: the title role in *The Return of Dr. X* (1939), a schlocky horror movie in which he sports a Bride-of-Frankenstein streak in his hair; Bette Davis's startlingly Irish-brogued stable groom in *Dark Victory* (1939), in which he seems to be wondering how he got there (he isn't the only one); and his—heaven help us—Mexican bandito in the Errol Flynn epic *Virginia City* (1940). Only twice during this dues-paying period did he get roles worthy of the talent he bared as Duke Mantee. William Wyler's *Dead End* (1937) is a superb stage-to-screen adaptation, and Bogart, on loan to producer Samuel Goldwyn, is unforgettable in the supporting role of Baby Face Martin, yet another gangster. *Dead End* remains a classic, but Bogart's other prime showcase of the era is virtually unknown. *Black Legion*, directed by *Petrified Forest*'s Archie Mayo, is one of the final films in the cycle of socially conscious dramas that were a mainstay of Warners in the 1930s. Intended to scare the pants off its audience, it's a compact, tough little B picture, a tale of one man's descent into the inescapable clutches of a KKK-like organization. The variety in Bogart's performance makes the melodrama hold up in a way that wouldn't have been possible with a less intuitive actor in the leading role. He connects the rapid-paced plot developments with a moment-to-moment psychological truth that makes dramatic sense of his character's downward spiral.

Frank Taylor (Bogart) is a happy-go-lucky drill-press worker, devoted to his wife, Ruth (Erin O'Brien-Moore), and their young son. When a better-qualified guy (with a foreign-sounding last name) gets the promotion Frank was counting on, he is stunned and furious. A buddy tells him about the Black Legion, a strong-arm group dedicated to keeping America for "Americans" via vandalism, beatings, arson, and so forth. Frank joins the secret gang, wears its uniform of black hood and sheet, and, at first, feels empowered by their ruthless, result-getting tactics. His "lodge" activities soon dominate his lie-infested life, alienating his family and his best friend, Ed (Dick Foran). By the time he wants out, it is, of course, too late; he must live up to the legion's oath of allegiance . . . or else.

Despite Bogart's ordinary looks, who thinks of him as a portrayer of ordinary guys? But here, before he became devastatingly cool, he is utterly believable as a regular Joe. Frank is popular at the factory, a good worker, the kind of guy who is whistling when he arrives home from work and enjoys listening to radio adventure programs with his boy. Though Frank will soon change drastically, we retain the image of the gleaming guy he was and could have continued to be. The impending promotion sparks dreams of material gains, puffing him up into feeling like a big man. But when he's passed over for the job, the humiliating rejection depletes his surface cockiness, leaving him susceptible to the Black Legion's call to arms. Bogart's about-face transformation into a sulking, resentful man (for whom blaming others is the only balm) proves just how precarious Frank's semblance of stability really was, and the actor maintains an undertow of uncertainty behind the character's subsequent actions. At the initiation ceremony in the woods, kneeling before a fire (with a gun to his head), he has a regretful ache in his voice by the time he reaches the end of the blood-curdling oath. Without the confidence we associate with a Bogart character, Frank finds a spineless and misguided outlet for his anger, unleashing a shocking capacity for cruelty, thereby setting his fall into motion.

Bogart has a great scene alone in his living room, admiring his oversized, gun-brandishing shadow on the wall, then moving to a full-length mirror to continue his big-shot posing. It's a peerless sight to see the tough-guy legend look woefully, and convincingly, uncomfortable with a gun, playing with it like a kid handling something he knows he shouldn't. The approaching nights of mayhem, followed by lots of drinking, invigorate him temporarily, but violent action doesn't make him feel more in control. Bogart's use of increasingly foul temper conveys the depths of Frank's festering self-loathing. Ruth walks out on him and he is suddenly helpless. Though he wants to break free of the legion, he knows that it's impossible. When Ed confronts him, a very drunk Frank inadvertently reveals certain details about the legion, prompting Ed to speak of going to the cops. In a shuddering instant, Frank sobers at the terrifying realization that he's broken his oath, snivelingly begging his friend to say nothing. Frank is disintegrating. After the police arrest him for a murder, Ruth visits him in prison. The look on Bogart's face at the sight of her is one of profound anguish; he walks slowly to her and then, in a burst of sorrow, drops to his knees, puts his arms around her, and sobs. If Bogart didn't make us believe that Frank deeply loved and needed Ruth, the character's senseless destruction would not be as powerful to behold as it is. It's a tribute to the humanity in the performance that Frank's plight can move us, despite all the awful things he has done, as he tries to find a way back to decency and take responsibility for his reprehensible choices. The climax puts Frank on the witness stand, and Bogart has one of those emotional courtroom speeches that only happen in the movies. However, he nails it with such conviction that he handily overrides the clichés in the material.

Written by Abem Finkel and William Wister Haines, *Black Legion* has a blistering, rough-hewn energy, though it sometimes races too swiftly through a story that would have benefited from a bit more breathing room. Unfortunately, it does slow down for a nice long lecture from the judge in the final scene, just in case we're morons and missed the film's cautionary message. As nurturing Ruth, Erin O'Brien-Moore is just right (she would turn up twenty years later as Russ Tamblyn's crone of a mother in *Peyton Place*). Dick Foran is easily likeable as Ed, the strong, dependable contrast to Frank, and lovely and tart Ann Sheridan (as Ed's girl) is clearly, at any second, about to emerge as a star.

Once *High Sierra* (soon followed by *The Maltese Falcon*) catapulted Bogart to the top, he would be a superstar for the remaining fifteen years of his career, leaving a legacy of outstanding films equaled by few screen actors. In *Black Legion*, you'll catch him early in the icon-making process, exploring the insecurities and doubts beneath a seemingly sturdy façade, a gift that would later enhance, among other films, *Casablanca* (1942) and *The Treasure of the Sierra Madre* (1948).

Spencer Tracy and Clark Gable share a bed

Spencer Tracy

IN

Test Pilot

(1938)

SPENCER Tracy as a gay man in love with his straight best friend? That's not the official plot synopsis of *Test Pilot*, but it's all right there on the screen. You have to go to the more explicit days of Peter Finch's performance in *Sunday, Bloody Sunday* (1971) to find as moving a portrait of one man in love with another. We'll never know what Tracy was thinking while playing *Test Pilot*'s Gunner Morris, but it's clear that Gunner's love for Jim Lane (Clark Gable) informs every moment of his performance. Tracy and Gable had first been teamed in the blockbuster *San Francisco* (1936), which tells a fairly routine story until its phenomenal earthquake sequence. They played so easily together, and the picture was such a smash, that a reunion was inevitable. Add Myrna Loy to the mix and the three-way star power of *Test Pilot* is nearly blinding.

Test pilot Jim Lane crash-lands on the Kansas farm of Ann Barton (Loy). They marry after a whirlwind romance, and Ann discovers the constant fear and stress that come with marriage to a man in such a dangerous profession. Gunner, Jim's buddy and mechanic, helps her cope as Jim goes off on one life-threatening assignment after another. Ann hopes that Jim will eventually take a job on the ground, but it seems that his heart will always be in the sky. A mission to test the altitude limit of a bomber becomes the decisive event in their three lives.

Gunner's whole world is Jim. There's no one else in his life. Getting Jim to bed after he's had too much to drink, waking him up on flying days, and keeping tootsies away from him are all part of Gunner's routine. He gripes and makes wisecracks, but we never doubt his fulfillment in being the one who takes care of Jim Lane. Watch Tracy's face anytime Gable is in the air. He stares at the sky so intensely that it's clear nothing else exists for Gunner. There's no life on earth while Jim is airborne. On the ground, Gunner conceals his tender feelings behind a tough-guy façade. Tracy's gruff, gum-chewing exterior is the protective armor that allows Gunner to move comfortably in his macho world. Since there's not the remotest possibility that Jim could ever love him as more than a chum, Gunner is embarrassed whenever Jim is playfully affectionate. When Gable grabs his head in a clinch, Tracy flinches. As long as Gunner maintains a safe distance, Jim need never know how he really feels. In their final scene, Tracy expresses Gunner's feelings more openly, and his last line confirms that his love goes deeper than what one feels for a buddy.

Instead of her arrival causing a rivalry between Ann and Gunner, they become soulmates who call each other "pal." Gunner is initially unfriendly to her because he sees her as just another one of Jim's girls, but things change when she officially replaces him as Jim's caregiver on their wedding night. After taking his leave, Tracy's Gunner is the very picture of loneliness as he walks off into the night. He becomes close to Ann when he realizes that she truly loves Jim as much as he does. Tracy's best scene is the one in which he lets down his guard with Ann for the first time. Jim's plane has caught fire during a race, but Gunner tells Ann not to worry because Jim is made of asbestos. When she snaps at him for this careless remark, he loses his temper and speaks of having been on this emotional roller coaster with Jim for ten years. As tears begin to well up, he stops himself from saying too much and steps away. Instead of barking back, Ann moves to comfort him, having just figured out how much Gunner loves Jim. She is the first person to see the real Gunner and is touched by what she sees (as are we). No one can understand Gunner and Ann as they understand each other. They connect through their mutual love of Jim, and they seem more intimate with each other than with Jim. Gunner becomes Ann's emotional anchor whenever distress and panic overwhelm her. She externalizes the feelings that he's been internalizing all these years. Gunner knows what she's going through, and Tracy's gentleness with Loy creates a bond between the characters that is the loveliest element of the movie.

Test Pilot was a big hit for MGM and an Oscar nominee for Best Picture. It's a case of top-notch commercial filmmaking that blends drama, comedy, action, and romance. Its surprising and unmistakable gay subtext makes it cry out for rediscovery. Victor Fleming's crackerjack direction brings suspense to the flying sequences and heartfelt attention to the human drama. Tracy made five films with Fleming, including *Captains Courageous,* which won him the 1937 Best Actor Oscar. (Tracy seems mighty ill at ease as a Portuguese-accented fisherman, and this wonderful film's effectiveness really derives from little Freddie Bartholomew.) Gable and Loy's *Test Pilot* performances rank with the best of their respective careers. They are charming and funny during their breezy courtship and affecting when they have less to laugh about. Lionel Barrymore, as Gable's boss, gives the identical performance he gave in countless MGM productions (which means that he's a mass of irritating mannerisms). Fresh from her overtly lesbian vampire in *Dracula's Daughter* (1936), Gloria Holden plays Mrs. Benson, another pilot's wife, in a manner that proves she was less comfortable when playing human beings.

In *Test Pilot*, it's easy to see why Spencer Tracy was widely regarded as the best movie actor of his generation. With the possible exception of Cary Grant, did anyone make acting seem so effortless? Good as Gable and Loy are in this film, you can't take your eyes off Tracy. He may seem to be doing the least amount of acting, but you can always read his thoughts on his face. His consummate underplaying draws you into whatever he's doing, and if you look away you might miss some telling moment. Tracy won the 1938 Best Actor Oscar for the bathetic *Boys Town*, but his work in *Test Pilot* was more deserving: Gunner is a richer creation than dear old Father Flanagan (a role he could have played in his sleep). Tracy and Gable were reteamed one final time for the awful (but popular) *Boom Town* (1940). In that endless oil-drilling epic, the boys alternate between being rich and poor so many times that you end up wishing the San Francisco earthquake would just move east and put an end to it. In a career that brought nine Oscar nominations and nine teamings with Katharine Hepburn, there are still several Tracy films that have been unjustly overlooked. After you catch *Test Pilot*, move on to the smart-aleck comedy of *Me and My Gal* (1932), the pre-*Citizen Kane* political saga *The Power and the Glory* (1933), and the vastly underrated World War II drama *The Seventh Cross* (1944). Give *Father of the Bride* (1950) a rest and expand your experience of Spencer Tracy's greatness.

Francis Lederer, Mary Astor, Don Ameche,
Claudette Colbert, and John Barrymore

Claudette Colbert

IN

Midnight
(1939)

T HOUGH solidly effective in drama (despite a tendency to suffer nobly), Claudette Colbert thrived in romantic comedy and made the genre the bread and butter of her career. Three films stand out as the great triumvirate of Colbert comedies. Frank Capra's transporting *It Happened One Night* (1934), in which she plays a spoiled heiress to Clark Gable's slick reporter, is one of the rare early Best Picture Oscar winners that defies time: it's not only one of the freshest and most naturally funny comedies ever made but also an unpretentious, vivid contemporary portrait of the Depression. Colbert and Gable were dynamite together, and both deservedly walked off with Oscars for their effortless efforts. Her two other knockout comedies cast her as gold diggers frustratingly in love with low earners. Preston Sturges's *Palm Beach Story* (1942), the dizziest (and one of the more uproarious) of screwball comedies, has her gracefully juggling many outlandish plot turns, all the while clicking with costar Joel McCrea as winningly as she had with Gable. Mitchell Leisen's heavenly *Midnight*, a Cinderella update written by Charles Brackett and Billy Wilder, mixes a zany situation with an air of Lubitsch-like sophistication. Colbert sails through this one like the balmiest of breezes; the lightness of her touch is the keystone of her technique. No other Cinderella ever manipulated her own fate as cunningly or as dazzlingly as Colbert's ever-resourceful Eve Peabody.

Eve is a down-on-her-luck American chorus girl stranded in a rainy Paris train station (with nothing but the evening gown she's wearing) when she meets Tibor Czerny (serviceable Don Ameche), a Hungarian taxi driver. Romantic sparks fly unmistakably between them but, due to her determination to marry a bankroll, Eve flees his cab. She crashes a society party where she encounters wealthy Georges Flammarion (John Barrymore, in the fairy godfather role), his unpleasant wife, Helene (Mary Astor), and Helene's lover, Jacques Picot (glossy, if a bit Draculaish, Francis Lederer). Georges figures out that Eve's an impostor, and he hires her to lure Jacques away from Helene. Now calling herself Baroness Czerny, Eve is stunned when Tibor tracks her down at a ball at the Flammarions' Versailles estate, casting himself in the role of her husband, the baron.

Colbert plays Eve with a likeably straight-shooting demeanor; her coolheaded directness in her dealings with Tibor (and later with Georges) can be attributed to Eve's hard-knocks New York background. Despite her pesky habit of being attracted to guys without money, Eve doesn't lead Tibor on, yet Colbert exudes enough stifled ardor to let him know she'll succumb if she doesn't get away from him (and his forty-francs-a-day income) fast. After sneaking her way into that posh party (a pawn ticket poses as her official invitation), she tries to find a seat as unobtrusively as possible, while everyone's attention is on a wailing opera diva. In an inspired bit of comic business, Colbert sits on a tiny unseen dog, yelps impulsively and loudly, and springs back into a standing position. Thoroughly enchanted by Eve by evening's end (and setting his plot in motion without telling her), Georges arranges rooms for her at the Ritz after she's lied to everyone that she's staying there. She can't make sense of the chain of events that lands her in a luxurious suite stocked with the latest fashions; considering madness, Eve tests her sanity with her very own oral quiz. When Georges arrives, revealing himself as the man pulling the strings, Eve assumes that he's looking for a mistress, and she's not interested. (She is still hoping to combine money with *marriage*.) He is, in fact, looking for a partner in crime tempting enough to lure Jacques out of Helene's arms. One of the more engaging elements of this film is the harmonious, father-daughter bond that develops between Barrymore and Colbert. Despite the characters' opposite origins, they become like-minded chums (and liars of complementary abilities).

With to-the-manor-born confidence, Eve begins her all-expense-paid mission to snare Jacques when she catches up with him and Helene at a fancy hat shop. Colbert and Mary Astor have a grand time with the bitchy dialogue; Colbert casually smiles her way through her most pointed verbal jabs. It comes as no surprise when she exits with Jacques on her arm; he's been putty in her hands since he first saw her. Once the action shifts to Georges's eighteenth-century chateau, the stakes become higher; Helene suspects that Eve is no baroness. Then, of course, there's the unexpected arrival of Tibor, who wants Eve to return to Paris with him. So, she must play along as the dutiful wife of the "baron." The film peaks with the chateau's breakfast scene in which Tibor fakes a telegram (designed to force Eve into leaving) about their sick child, but he's no match for Eve's ingenuity. Colbert convinces you that Eve has the smarts to improvise her way out of anything. She triumphs with an emotional, maternal telephone performance (to "Budapest"), which assures everyone that her little girl is just fine after all. Eve eventually resorts to persuading Jacques, Helene, and Helene's gossipy friend Marcel (Rex O'Malley in a rare, for that censorship-laden era, portrayal of a gay best friend) that Tibor is *insane*. Colbert "bravely" delivers Eve's painful confession of the burden that Tibor's dementia has placed on her; Eve is so pathologically good at spinning fantastic yarns about her past that even Georges is amazed. When Tibor reenters the scene, she treats him like an escaped mental patient, meekly agreeing with whatever he says and feigning fear of his supposed violent streak. Colbert is priceless as she intersperses knowing glances to the others while Tibor rages on implausibly, yet telling the absolute truth.

Mitchell Leisen was an underrated director, and *Midnight* is among his top films. Because he began as a costume and set designer, he always made sure that his films looked fabulous (check out *Kitty* [1945]), and this one certainly shimmers with black-and-white opulence. (In 1945, Leisen directed *Masquerade in Mexico*, a semimusical remake of *Midnight*, with Dorothy Lamour in the Colbert role.) The Brackett-Wilder script is an intricately constructed farce that lags only in the below-par scenes in which Tibor and his fellow cabbies try to locate Eve. Barrymore and Astor, silent-screen costars and former lovers, are both seen to advantage here: he with his gift for merry lunacy, she with her ice-queen formidability. Astor also appears with Colbert in *The Palm Beach Story*, but they get along swimmingly in that one.

Colbert's final romantic comedy was *Let's Make It Legal* (1951); her last popular one had been the huge hit *The Egg and I* (1947). But be it the intermittently sublime film *The Gilded Lily* (1935) or the strained *It's a Wonderful World* (1939), Claudette Colbert could be counted on to inject any comedy with a champagne fizz that never flattens.

Frank Albertson and Ginger Rogers at work

Ginger Rogers

IN

Bachelor Mother

(1939)

I N her first decade in the movies, Ginger Rogers's talent seemed limitless: she introduced several song standards (notably "We're in the
Money" from *Gold Diggers of 1933*); she became half of the greatest dance
team in movie history via Mr. Astaire; she won acclaim as one of the
screen's top comediennes; and, finally, she achieved Oscar-winning approval as a dramatic actress with *Kitty Foyle* (1940). (Only Irene Dunne
was equally at home in comedies, dramas, and musicals, but Rogers's
singing *and* dancing skills one-upped the singing-only Dunne.) The magic
of "Fred and Ginger" brought her deserved immortality, but I feel that her
greatest gift was as a funny lady. More than any of the Golden Age's comediennes, Rogers epitomized the plight of the working girl, leaving the
wacky heiresses to Hepburn and Lombard. She had been used to getting
laughs early on; her "Anytime Annie" of *42nd Street* (1933) is one of that
legendary film's enduring treats. And, of course, the Astaire musicals were
festive, foolish romps. But it was in *Stage Door* (1937) that her comedic talent took center stage. As the *most* hardboiled of a group of quick-witted
boardinghouse actresses, Rogers's casually sharp delivery of the film's
choicest one-liners had her stealing the film from Katharine Hepburn and
a female supporting cast that would only be rivaled by *The Women* (1939).
Her comedy career peaked with Billy Wilder's film *The Major and the Minor*
(1942): the role of a grown woman posing as a twelve-year-old to get a
half-fare train ticket could have spelled disaster (she keeps up the masquerade for most of the film), but Ginger's joyously fearless work made it
a smash. In between these high points was another big hit that's less talked
about today. *Bachelor Mother* is a little miracle that's a worthy, if modest, addition to the lineup of Hollywood's 1939 classics. The role of Polly Parrish
plays to Rogers's strength: locating the tenderness in weary cynics,
thereby bringing real feeling to the most lightweight vehicles.

Polly, a clerk in the toy department of John B. Merlin (Charles

Coburn) and Son, receives notice that she's to be discharged. While walking during her final lunch hour, she spots an elderly woman placing a baby on the doorstep of a foundling home. After the woman runs off, Polly goes to the baby's aid. The door opens. Despite Polly's protests, the home's employees assume the baby is hers; after inadvertently revealing that she works at Merlin's, she hurriedly leaves the baby in their care. They reveal her situation to the junior Merlin, David (David Niven), who sympathetically reinstates her. She's not happy when the home "returns" the baby to her. Since no one will believe the truth, she eventually gives in and admits to being little John's mother. David's active interest in the twosome's well-being leads to suspicions that he's the baby's father.

In her first scene, between offhand jokes, you feel the quietly devastating impact of losing a job in hard times with no one to lean on. It's satisfying to watch her relationship with the baby turn her life around; at first a colossal inconvenience, he becomes her support system. Baby John is also responsible for bringing David into her life on an increasingly steady basis. Polly's too smart to fall for a rakish rich boy; she moves cautiously through their unlikely friendship. To keep her job, she lets him believe that the baby is hers, creating an elaborate lie about the baby's brutal father. (Polly seems genuinely surprised, even invigorated, by her easy flair for fabrication.) When it's obvious that David has romantic interest in Polly, she confesses to the baby, "I think he likes me." In that moment, Rogers coalesces Polly's burgeoning love for David and her closeness to the baby, giving us a wholly happy Polly. Now it is too late to protect herself from the risk of being hurt. When the notion of marriage (his father's idea) panics David, Polly refuses to let him see her get emotional about it; she brushes off the subject and then brushes him off.

Polly first meets David when he inexplicably rehires her, providing Rogers with a rare speechless moment; her baffled expressions, as she tries to figure out what's going on, prove that the actress didn't have to rely on sarcastic quips to get laughs. Other (more typical) highlights: her sleep-deprived description (beautifully paced in a mechanical daze) of the tedious and difficult process of putting the baby to sleep; her I-told-you-so glee during David's unsuccessful attempt to disprove her claim that it's impossible to make exchanges at Merlin's. But the film's centerpiece is the New Year's Eve party where Polly's a last-minute fill-in for a dateless David. As they enter the ritzy festivities, she looks swell (gown and mink coat courtesy of Merlin's), but she's painfully aware that she is out of her element. To ease her fear of having nothing to say to his tony friends, David impulsively introduces her as a Swedish manufacturer's daughter, who cannot speak a word of English. Instead of showing the slightest tinge of terror, she gracefully picks up his challenge and is enlivened by the thrill of pulling off such a charade. And so they begin their priceless mock Swedish exchanges, with Rogers trading in her dry wit for something more playful. Her departing "Opp-ee Noo Cheer" is a crowning triumph for the now-popular Swede. (Rogers's arduous overarticulation is the magic ingredient.) The scene is capped by her home-run zinger (aimed at a society bitch) that *must* be included in any reel containing Rogers's greatest moments.

Soon-to-be-famous playwright Garson Kanin (*Born Yesterday* opened in 1946) had a briefly successful movie-directing career, and this is his best film. (His other one with Rogers, 1941's *Tom, Dick, and Harry*, was also well received, but it lacks *Bachelor Mother*'s unforced charm and proved that Rogers was not at her best playing dimwits.) Norman Krasna's bright screenplay (from a story by Felix Jackson) is a peak in a long career of writing romantic comedies for stage and screen. (Its flat musical remake, 1956's *Bundle of Joy*, starred Debbie Reynolds and Eddie Fisher.) Niven, behaving Cary Grant-like in a perfect Grant role, is quite winning; his sophistication and Rogers's down-to-earth appeal create a chemistry similar to the one she shared with Astaire. They made two less-felicitous films together: *Magnificent Doll* (1946) and *Oh, Men! Oh, Women!* (1957). Irascible Charles Coburn is a softhearted delight, single-mindedly staking his claim as the baby's grandfather. And as Fred, Polly's coworker, Frank Albertson partners her in a swinging dance contest sequence. (Will Ginger dance *only* with guys named Fred?)

The Oscar she won for *Kitty Foyle* was an excessively generous gesture (beating Katharine Hepburn in *The Philadelphia Story* and Joan Fontaine in *Rebecca*), particularly since she was better in that same year's *Primrose Path*. Her popularity began to slip after the war, but she worked steadily in movies until the late 1950s. I suggest you seek out some of these forgotten films; despite their sometimes considerable flaws, they feature some of Rogers's best acting: *Storm Warning* (1950), *Forever Female* (1953), *Tight Spot* (1955), and *Teenage Rebel* (1956).

Marlene Burnett, Miriam Hopkins, and Bette Davis

Bette Davis

IN

The Old Maid
(1939)

No other movie actress had a five-year career high like the one the inestimable Bette Davis, Queen of Warner Brothers, had from 1938 to 1942. Beginning with *Jezebel* (for which she won her second Best Actress Oscar, little brother to the one she got for *Dangerous* in 1935), her run of classic performances continued with *Dark Victory* (1939), *The Private Lives of Elizabeth and Essex* (1939), *The Letter* (1940), *The Little Foxes* ([1941] on loan to Sam Goldwyn), and *Now, Voyager* (1942). (It's a list that could make the 1980s Meryl Streep feel like an underachiever.) Davis, who alternated staccato-rhythmed bitch roles with long-suffering martyrs, appeared in eight other films during this phenomenal half decade; from among these nonclassics, her standout performance is in *The Old Maid*, a heavy-duty "woman's picture." It's the actress's undercurrent of anger that fortifies her through the masochistic self-sacrifice of Charlotte, the title role. (*Now, Voyager* and *Hush . . . Hush, Sweet Charlotte* also cast her as much-abused Charlottes.) Made after *Dark Victory*, with the same director (Edmund Goulding) and screenwriter (Casey Robinson), *Old Maid* isn't quite in the former's league of divine weepers, but Davis's performance is nonetheless a doozy.

In 1861 Philadelphia, Charlotte Lovell has a brief affair with Clem Spender (George Brent), the former flame of her newlywed cousin Delia (Miriam Hopkins). Clem is killed in the Civil War, never to know that Charlotte, who supposedly went out West for her health, gave birth to his daughter. After the war, Charlotte opens a nursery for war orphans so she can raise her little Tina without scandal. She becomes engaged to Delia's brother-in-law, Joe Ralston (Jerome Cowan), but her future is secretly sabotaged by her cousin, who's filled with jealousy once Charlotte confesses that she slept with Clem. After Delia is widowed, she invites Charlotte and Tina to live with her and her two children in splendor. Fifteen years pass. Tina (Jane Bryan), raised to think she was a foundling, believes that Charlotte is the family's old-maid aunt. To ensure that Tina will never suspect the truth, Charlotte is deliberately harsh with her, avoiding the slightest favoritism, watching as her beloved daughter looks upon Delia as her "Mummy."

Davis, lovely in sausage curls, first appears in a burst of youthful energy; Charlotte is caught up in the excitement of Delia's wedding. She may be vivacious, but Charlotte is neither immature nor foolish. When she admits her feelings to Clem, Davis cuts through Charlotte's girlish impulsiveness to convey the gravity of her once-in-a-lifetime love. When his train is about to depart, she asks him to "come back" from the war and tries not to become too emotional, but she is powerless to mask her dread at losing him. Five years later, Charlotte's spiritedness has been muted by grief (for Clem) and fear (for Tina), and she opts to marry wealthy, kindly Joe. Moments before her wedding, Charlotte makes the mistake of seeking Delia's counsel, confiding the truth about Tina (and Clem). As Delia's jealousy rises, the scene becomes the first of several juicy showdowns between the cousins; a bracing Davis often looks ready to bite her cowed costar's head off (their famous offscreen antipathy enhances their onscreen rivalry). The wedding is off. Six months later, Charlotte, summoned to Delia's side (her husband is dying), runs into a now-married Joe and discovers that it was Delia's lies about Charlotte's health that caused their split. Watching her compute this information is a vintage Davis moment: eyes ablaze, arm and fingers twitching, emotions roiling inside her. Confronting her nemesis moments later, Davis is electrifying, spewing her rage in a feverish whisper, hate seething from every pore. (Charlotte may be victimized at every turn, but she always puts up a good fight.) Later reconciled, Charlotte moves in with Delia, offering Tina normalcy and security; and though Davis loosens neither Charlotte's pride nor her determination to stay in control, she wills her to accept a place on the sidelines of Tina's life.

There is no way to prepare for Davis's fifteen-years-later entrance as the old maid. Charlotte can't be any more than forty, but she seems much older in her gray-haired primness (though she still has the tiniest waist in showbiz). Businesslike and humorless, she's the taken-for-granted mechanism that makes the household function efficiently. (She reminds me of *Rebecca*'s Mrs. Danvers, another crone stalking through an enormous house.) Nothing remains of the buoyant Charlotte we first met. Dramatizing Charlotte's need to keep her mind occupied, Davis is always doing *something*, distracting herself with domestic tasks, compulsively tidying. The grown Tina all but despises her critical aunt (the disciplinary contrast to the spoiling, adored Delia), but that's Charlotte's own doing; Tina will thereby never figure out that Charlotte is her mother. Commitment to this objective is the driving force of Davis's performance. Her severity makes better sense once Charlotte tells Delia of the self-consciousness of her "Aunt Charlotte" persona; Davis wears her like a Halloween costume. In an emotionally gruesome Jekyll-and-Hyde scene, Davis sits alone in a darkened room, affording us a glimpse into Charlotte's twisted world. She speaks aloud to Tina (who has just gone off to a ball) with all the maternal warmth she suppresses in the girl's presence, and then, straightening her back and raising her chin, she *becomes* "Aunt Charlotte," essentially saying the same things, but assuming the cold, imperious manner that shields her true feelings; it's a dress rehearsal for their next meeting, and Davis's total absorption eclipses the scene's innate nuttiness. The clash between these cross-purposed identities pulsates through a never-wispy Davis for the rest of the film. Particularly in her articulately expressed, undissipated bitterness for Delia, Davis refuses to play Charlotte as a helpless drudge, making what might easily be nauseating into something unexpectedly moving.

With tasteful direction from Goulding, *The Old Maid* manages to surmount its flagrant manipulations and frustrating nobility. If you go for this sort of handsomely produced, Kleenex-demanding fare, you're in for a satisfying, eye-reddening experience (though its first half is superior to its second). Still, it's surprising that it is based on a 1924 Edith Wharton novella that became a 1935 Pulitzer Prize-winning Zoe Akins play. Miriam Hopkins is hopeless as the young beauty of the early scenes, but she gets better, though Davis still acts rings around her (they would reteam in 1943's *Old Acquaintance*). George Brent, in one of his *eleven* films with Davis, makes do with his nothing role (male leads in Davis's biggies rarely do much), but Jane Bryan is a colorful, feisty Tina. And could it *be* a Bette Davis movie without costume designer Orry-Kelly and composer Max Steiner?

Davis's dominance at Warners began to fade in the mid 1940s (ironically, just as MGM has-been Joan Crawford was becoming Warners' hottest female star via *Mildred Pierce*), hitting rock bottom with *Beyond the Forest* (1949). Bouncing back, Davis gave her greatest performance (and among the *screen's* greatest) in Fox's *All About Eve* (1950), but it was a fleeting comeback. Thereafter, it was mostly "camp" over quality (*The Star* [1952] is a terrible movie that I highly recommend), self-parody over artistry. But she never did enough damage to alter her stature as one of Hollywood's supreme talents, whose gallery of characters remains one of the most awe inspiring the movies have ever given us.

Myrna Loy and George Brent

Myrna Loy

IN

The Rains Came

(1939)

MYRNA Loy was a major screen presence for one simple reason: she was at home up there, living and breathing on celluloid as if it were the most natural place on earth. I don't think Loy ever misjudged the playing of any scene in her entire fifty-five-year movie career; you'll certainly never hear anyone refer to one of her films and comment, "Oh, she's so bad in that!" Even so, she had a tricky rise to fame, starting at the bottom (including a bit part in *The Jazz Singer* [1927]) and working her way through the ranks (notably as a series of "exotics" in films like *The Mask of Fu Manchu* [1932]) until she played Nora, the heiress wife of detective Nick Charles (William Powell), in the eternally captivating film *The Thin Man* (1934), where she found her merrily witty, sophisticated but approachable persona. (Nick aptly describes his wife as a "lanky brunette with a wicked jaw," neglecting her celebrated upturned nose.) She was tagged the screen's "perfect wife," and when a 1937 national poll hailed Clark Gable King of Hollywood, it was Loy, not Garbo, Lombard, or Colbert, who was voted Queen. At the peak of her popularity, her studio, MGM, loaned her to Fox to star in *The Rains Came*, a romantic blockbuster, a real *movie-movie*, distinguished by the intelligence of its performances, primarily that of Loy who, blessedly never one to pull out all the stops, draws us into her Edwina, a decidedly imperfect wife, with discerning understatement.

Set in Ranchipur, India, in 1938, *The Rains Came* follows two British visitors: artist Tom Ransome (George Brent), the alcohol-prone son of an earl, who had arrived seven years earlier to paint a royal portrait and never left; and bored Lady Edwina Esketh, a woman with a shady past, traveling with her insufferable, much-older husband, Lord Albert (Nigel Bruce). Tom and Edwina, former lovers, are coincidentally reunited at a palace dinner. Major Rama Safti (Tyrone Power), a high-caste Indian surgeon, catches Edwina's roving eye, and she systematically pursues him, despite his lack of interest. Meanwhile, Fern (Brenda Joyce), the virginal daughter of American missionaries, falls in love with the dissipating Tom. Well, the seasonal rains come, followed by an earthquake, floods, and plague. Edwina's attraction to Rama becomes the real thing, and, with her husband conveniently killed in the quake, she sees her chance for lasting happiness.

The lady may be a tramp, but, since she's encased in breeding, you'd never guess it to look at her; Edwina is as serenely confident as the actress playing her. (Loy doesn't do a British accent, probably because Hollywood speech of the 1930s was close enough.) With ex-lover Tom, she can be her jaded self, as in the scene where he gives her a tour of the palace. Loy takes vain pleasure in her jewels and assortment of white gowns, camouflage for the deadness inside Edwina; she's sleepwalking through her loveless, jackpot marriage, finding temporary distraction in playgirl escapades. When she tells Tom that her life is exciting "now and then," Loy's reading of the line neatly implies extracurricular sex; in her desirous first glance of Rama, it's clear that Edwina approaches romance as a thrill-seeking sport. All of Loy's effects are softly achieved; she puts the moves on Rama with graceful persistence, and though you wouldn't call her technique invisible, she's never blatant enough to scare him away. Tom warns her not to toy with the esteemed Indian, but Edwina, stunned that Rama is unreceptive to her allure, has no intention of ceasing her delicate assault. Here and in all of the likeable, direct Edwina-Tom scenes, Loy and George Brent connect with a two-of-a-kind, talk-the-same-language rapport. (You believe that they go way back.) Loy's playing is levelheaded, honest, and wry, never letting us forget that Edwina is used to getting what she wants with little effort. What a difference an earthquake makes.

The impact of her authentic feelings for Rama, whom she no longer thinks of as an exotic conquest, is a revelation to her, whether or not Rama ever returns those feelings. Edwina's conversion may be a sentimental notion, but the humbling humanity in Loy's performance sneaks up on you (as it does on Edwina), and it's what gives the film a soul. She volunteers as a nurse at the hospital, tirelessly and uncomplainingly caring for plague victims and occasionally seeing Rama in his official capacity as physician. Being near him makes her happy, but she also finds enrichment in her unselfish usefulness. Oblivious to the extent of her love, he asks her why she has endured the arduous nursing duties, and Loy, wearing a hospital mask that exposes only her eyes, transmits the profundity of Edwina's love without a word. But the Maharani (a cigarette-smoking Maria Ouspenskaya) wants Edwina out of India, fearing the undoing of her plans for Rama to rule Ranchipur one day; she sends Tom to the hospital to convince Edwina to go. Free of lingering cynicism and secure in the rightness of her path,

Edwina's refusal is calm but emphatic, strengthened by her newfound lightness of spirit, a stark contrast to the grim setting. (I can't help feeling that Edwina and Tom would be happier with each other than with their saintly love interests.) When Rama reveals his love for her and his willingness to give up everything to be with her, she is sincerely overcome. Tragedy strikes, and Loy's portrayal of sacrificial love is wisely tearless, devoid of off-putting masochism. Nourished by their love (which, incidentally, remains kiss-free), she's able to face what comes.

Director Clarence Brown balances lavish spectacle with low-key performance values, resulting in a solid, old-fashioned entertainment. Based on Louis Bromfield's novel, the screenplay, by Philip Dunne and Julien Josephson, is well crafted, juggling a host of characters and plotlines with impressive precision. Wearily insouciant George Brent is exceptionally good, but poor Tyrone Power, saddled with a role of wooden goodness, is not able to do much more than avoid embarrassment, though he looks mighty fetching in his dark makeup and array of turbans. Following *San Francisco* (1936), *The Hurricane* (1937), and *In Old Chicago* (1937), in what was a heyday for disaster movies (not to be rivaled until the 1970s), *The Rains Came*'s biggest claim to fame is that, for its colossal destruction of Ranchipur, it won the Oscar for special effects over *The Wizard of Oz*! It was listlessly remade as *The Rains of Ranchipur* (1955), with a different ending, and the Edwina of Lana Turner, lacking nuance, was no more than a soap queen in second-rate mush.

Loy received an unforgivably late honorary Oscar in 1991 (two years before her death), but, in what may be the cruelest shutout in Academy history, she not only never *won* an Oscar, she was never even *nominated*. Not for this film, for *Test Pilot*, for *The Thin Man*! And not for her role (one of her perfect wives) in *The Best Years of Our Lives* (1946); her sublime reunion scene with Fredric March is the most memorable sequence of her career (if this great film has a flaw, it is Loy's relegation, despite top billing, to supporting-player status following this unforgettable early scene). But even when her characters, such as Edwina, were far from perfect, the actress playing them surely was.

Fred MacMurray and Barbara Stanwyck

Barbara Stanwyck

IN

Remember the Night
(1940)

M Y favorite Barbara Stanwyck performance is in a black-and-white 1940s film in which she plays a shifty dame opposite Fred Mac-Murray. No, not *Double Indemnity* (1944), but a small masterwork titled *Remember the Night,* a bittersweet love story with romantic-comedy flourishes. Brooklyn-born Stanwyck, the most "regular" of the Golden Age's great divas, gives a beautiful performance that is something of an amalgam of the best-remembered roles of her career: she incorporates the unsentimental approach to sentiment that she brought to *Stella Dallas* (1937); the glamorous, naughty wit with which she would grace two dandy 1941 comedies, *The Lady Eve* and *Ball of Fire;* and the calculating cool of *Double Indemnity*'s femme fatale. Though it sounds like a greatest-hits medley, Stanwyck melds these seemingly disparate traits into one carefully modulated characterization. In a story that may seem cloying in the telling, she overrides potential mawkishness with her believable transformation from a longtime cynic and schemer into someone forever altered by a new force in her sorry life: the kindness of others. Stanwyck, aided by her striking features and her gifts for economy and restraint, has a way of getting under your skin.

Mink-wrapped Lee Leander (Stanwyck), formerly Anna Rose Malone, is arrested in New York for swiping an expensive bracelet, standing trial just before Christmas. The prosecutor, Jack Sargent (MacMurray), fearing a holiday-induced acquittal, finagles a continuance but, feeling guilty about her being locked up over Christmas, he arranges for Lee's bail without her knowing. The bondsman, who has a dirty mind, takes her to Jack's apartment; as she has nowhere to go, Jack takes her to dinner. He discovers that she shares his Indiana roots and offers to drive her home for the holidays on his way to his family's place and pick her up on the way back. Lee, seeing a chance to make peace with her estranged mother, likes the idea, but her reunion is a disaster, and so Jack brings her home with him. Lee is bowled over by the Sargent family's whole-hearted hospitality. Despite the likelihood of her postholiday conviction, Lee and Jack fall in love.

At the trial (Lee's third offense), Stanwyck projects a mad-at-the-world hardness, suggesting she's done whatever she's had to do to make it on her own (and acquire nice things). When deposited at Jack's apartment, she assumes that he expects her to sleep with him; Stanwyck's far-from-shocked, even amused, reaction speaks volumes about Lee's tawdry past. But the more she realizes what a good guy he is (a novelty for her), the less eager she is to leave (besides, she has no place to go). Out to dinner, they talk more freely, and Stanwyck makes it clear that beneath her confident, lacquered veneer lies the real Lee: tender, regretful, and lonely. On the dance floor, they discover they're both "Hoosiers," from nearby towns, but their pasts couldn't be less alike. Without saying much, Stanwyck registers the pain of Lee's early years, mingling it with her poignant desire to see her mother and resolve their differences. Grateful for this chance, her anticipation turns apprehensive as the moment arrives. In a sequence filmed with the foreboding darkness of a murder mystery, Lee is met by the stern, unforgiving righteousness of her mother (Georgia Caine) and is soon futilely defending herself from long-ago accusations. Outside with Jack, after the crushing finality of the meeting, her emotions are uncontainable; Stanwyck, with a distraught fragility, exposes a Lee with all her defenses down.

At Jack's family farm, run by his widowed mother (Beulah Bondi) and maiden aunt (Elizabeth Patterson, who would be immortalized as *I Love Lucy*'s Mrs. Trumbull), Lee is met with open arms. Enveloped by their thoughtful embrace, she sees a kind of life she never believed existed, the starkest possible contrast to her own experience. Jack hasn't told them the truth, and she soon wishes she were the girl they think she is; yet, in essence, she *is* that girl. A family this idyllic could be revolting company if they weren't drawn with such care: teasing or bickering affectionately, they feel like people with a shared history. Stanwyck has several remarkable moments where, in amazement, Lee takes in her surroundings. As they all sit in the parlor listening to Jack singing "Swanee River" (accompanying himself on the piano), watch her absorb her good fortune with every pore, moved and nourished by their warmth. Tears well up when she's alone in her lovely guestroom; her pleasure clashes with the reminder that it's all temporary. Never losing her capacity to be genuinely overwhelmed by their fondness and generosity (Christmas gifts, baking lessons, a vintage gown for the barn dance), Stanwyck's simply expressed, humbling gratitude doesn't get old; Lee allows the healing power of love to work its magic on her. But as she falls for Jack, she's hurt when it appears to be one-sided. (There's a brief, funny scene in which she, furious, flings a popover at him when he laughs at the notion of their coupling.) Jack's mother (who now knows the truth about her) tactfully admits her concern for her son's future if he, in fact, loves Lee. Stanwyck, after allowing a split-second flash of anger to cross her face, sympathetically sees the mother's point, though it's tearing her up inside. But, neither a martyr nor a masochist, Lee is a realist ready to pay the piper. No longer the harsh, grasping woman we first met, her self-actualization is unmelodramatically achieved, thanks to Stanwyck's from-the-gut commitment to humanizing Lee honestly and with newfound dignity.

Gorgeously crafted by director Mitchell Leisen, *Remember the Night* is one of the top romantic films of its era, though it's marred by unevenness until Lee and Jack arrive in Indiana. (The low point is a cow-milking scene.) Preston Sturges's delicately woven screenplay (his last before he started directing his own material) tells a memorable story with characters you'll care about, though the laughs at Jack's black servant's expense are unfortunate. (Stanwyck's next project would be Sturges's *Lady Eve*.) But there's no faulting Ted Tetzlaff's lustrous cinematography nor old-timers Bondi and Patterson, both marvelous in refreshing, three-dimensional maternal roles. MacMurray, in his first of four films with Stanwyck, is a smart, amiable leading man, and he and Babs are a sexy, playful, fervent team. They have a markedly different, equally effective dynamic—rottenness—in *Double Indemnity*, in which (despite her ridiculous blond wig) Stanwyck is the poster slut for ruthless heartlessness. She was top billed on *Remember the Night*, whereas MacMurray snagged that honor on *Double Indemnity*. Their other two films are *The Moonlighter* (1953), a western, and *There's Always Tomorrow* (1956), a glossy soap.

Stanwyck made dozens of negligible movies, far below the caliber of her stardom, but let me recommend a few other lesser-known, worthwhile films: *The Miracle Woman* (1931), an evangelist drama and the best of her five Frank Capra films; *Baby Face* (1933), an entertaining, smutty pre-Code affair; three handsome, juicy soaps, *My Reputation* (1946), *East Side, West Side* (1949), and *All I Desire* (1953); and one terrific, incestuous western, *The Furies* (1950), the one where she throws a pair of scissors into Judith Anderson's face. But it's still *Remember the Night*, despite its disposable title (*which* night?) that I turn to for a revivifying dose of Barbara Stanwyck.

Vivien Leigh as Myra Lester

Vivien Leigh

IN

Waterloo Bridge

(1940)

OKAY, you've just played the most famous female role in movie history. What do you do for an encore? Following her dazzling and indestructible Scarlett O'Hara, Vivien Leigh screen-tested for the role of the second Mrs. de Winter (potentially appearing opposite soon-to-be husband Laurence Olivier) in David O. Selznick's production of *Rebecca*. Having just produced *Gone With the Wind*, Selznick had to know that audiences would never accept the stunning Leigh playing anyone's mousy paid companion. Joan Fontaine rightly got the part, and Leigh (who was actually the ideal image for *Rebecca*'s never-seen title character) went over to MGM for a new version of the 1931 weeper *Waterloo Bridge*. It reteamed her with Robert Taylor, her leading man from *A Yank at Oxford* (1938), in an impeccably mounted production directed by Mervyn LeRoy. *Waterloo Bridge* was pretty dicey stuff, as it dealt with a young woman's descent into prostitution. It's a wonder it got made at all. The original had the advantage of being filmed in the racy days before the strict Production Code went into effect. Even with many alterations to the story, *Waterloo Bridge* was still fairly explicit for the Hollywood of 1940, and for the family-oriented MGM, no less!

We know we're in for something tear-jerking when the film begins with sad-eyed and aging Colonel Roy Cronin (Taylor) flashing back from the Second World War to the First. The story begins simply enough. Roy, a highborn soldier, meets Myra Lester (Leigh), a beautiful ballet dancer, during a London air raid. They fall in love and try to get married before he goes back to the front. Bad luck and worse timing prevent this from happening, and Roy is suddenly called back to service. Myra is fired from the ballet and trying to make ends meet when she reads that Roy has been killed in action. Jobless and miserable, she becomes a streetwalker on the bridge of the title. Months later, she discovers that Roy is alive when she runs into him at the train station. Will she tell him the truth? Will he ac-

111

cept her after all that's happened? Like *The Old Maid*, it's pure soap opera; so if you don't have the stomach for that, perhaps you should skip it. However, what could have been sappy and laughable is restrained and dignified in Vivien Leigh's accomplished performance.

We meet Myra as a practical working girl touring with a second-rate ballet company (headed by the daunting yet unintelligible Maria Ouspenskaya). Myra wants to believe in love and happiness but can't deny her pessimistic tendencies. Roy calls her "defeatist," and there's certainly a melancholy quality about her from the beginning. Myra blossoms when she allows herself to believe in a future for her relationship with Roy. Leigh's transformation from skeptical pragmatist to someone deliriously in love is touching to behold. She and Robert Taylor have a romantic chemistry that's quite engaging in their playful courtship scenes. You can't help being entranced by Leigh's beauty and charm, but her performance deepens once things take a turn for the worse. Myra has her first meeting with Roy's mother (the formidable Lucile Watson) moments after learning that he is dead. She's too overcome to reveal the tragic news, and her unintentional rudeness breaks your heart. This botched meeting is excruciating to watch as Leigh balances Myra's attempts to conceal her devastation with her obvious failure to do so convincingly.

Leigh is believable as a prostitute. (Did anyone really believe that Helen Hayes was turning tricks in *The Sin of Madelon Claudet* [1931]?) The dazed look in Leigh's eyes and the hopelessness behind her forced gaiety identify her as someone who is already dead but keeps on breathing. Perhaps Leigh's best moment comes when she accidentally meets the suddenly back-to-life Roy. It's a joyful but shattering reunion, and for the rest of the film we share Myra's dilemma over how to handle it. Her confession to Roy's mother is another standout scene. Her delicacy and emotional fragility contrast with her resolve to do what she feels she must. Leigh refuses to let Myra's story be ludicrous. It may be hackneyed in its plotting, but she gives it a grace and intelligence that turn the character's melodramatic path into an affecting experience.

If you know Leigh only as Scarlett O'Hara and Blanche DuBois, I suggest her Myra Lester as the next performance with which to familiarize yourself. *Waterloo Bridge* is the only film that captures her still in the glow of her recent emergence as a true Hollywood star. The following year she made *That Hamilton Woman*, which, although filmed in Hollywood, was distinctly British (and costarred Olivier). In the next decade, she starred in British film versions of *Caesar and Cleopatra* ([1946] in which she's a kittenish delight) and *Anna Karenina* (1948) and also did a great deal of stage work. When she returned to Hollywood to play

Blanche in *A Streetcar Named Desire* (1951), it was as a celebrated actress rather than as a movie star. It's interesting to note that Myra bears resemblance not to the win-at-all-costs Scarlett but to Blanche, as both characters try to shake off their pasts in an unforgiving world.

Robert Taylor must have loved working with Leigh because he never seemed so relaxed and spontaneous in front of a camera. (He'd improved remarkably in the three years since his not-quite-ready-for-Garbo performance in the otherwise great *Camille*.) Leigh also has a lovely rapport with Virginia Field as her best friend (and fellow hooker). Everyone connected with this movie treated it as something more than trash, and this commitment resulted in a memorable picture. (Check out the sanitized 1956 version, *Gaby*, whose only distinction is that it cast a genuine ballerina, Leslie Caron, in Leigh's role.) The black-and-white photography of Joseph Ruttenberg is not only as lushly romantic as you'd expect (particularly in a candle-lit dance), but it affords Leigh the kind of close-ups that linger in the memory. Leigh's legend is deservedly based on her Oscar-winning turns in *Gone With the Wind* and *A Streetcar Named Desire*, and while *Waterloo Bridge* is hardly in their league, it's another opportunity to witness her particular brand of brilliant acting and incomparable beauty.

Lucy Goes Hawaiian

Lucille Ball

IN

Dance, Girl, Dance
(1940)

I T seemed that Lucille Ball had been around forever when she finally conquered show business with her legendary television series *I Love Lucy* in 1951. She'd been in the movies for nearly twenty years, working her way up from the bottom. You can spot her as a platinum blond in a few of the Astaire-Rogers musicals and in two with Eddie Cantor. Her first good role in a major film was as one of the wisecrackers in *Stage Door* (1937), where she held her own alongside Ginger Rogers and Eve Arden. RKO kept her busy in B pictures, such as *Five Came Back* (1939), and then finally gave her a big chance opposite Henry Fonda in the drama *The Big Street* (1942). It was a courageous attempt at a hard and unsympathetic (even when she's in a wheelchair) character, but her daring "ugly" performance was ultimately undone by the film's off-putting mix of relentless masochism and sloppy sentiment. Her monotonous unpleasantness grows wearisome as the film plods on. (Maybe Barbara Stanwyck could have made *The Big Street* work, but even she would have had a tough time of it.) Then MGM took their turn, giving Lucy the henna rinse and building her up as a Technicolor musical star (1943's *DuBarry Was a Lady* and *Best Foot Forward*) despite the fact that she really didn't sing or dance. The panther-taming number from *Ziegfeld Follies* (1946), complete with cracking whip and writhing showgirls, is perhaps the oddest use of Lucy's talent in her entire career. It seemed she had missed her chance at stardom, and she spent the rest of the 1940s in mysteries *(The Dark Corner; Lured)* and mild comedies *(Sorrowful Jones; Miss Grant Takes Richmond)*. Then came the television series to rescue her and give full flower to her gargantuan comic gifts.

How is it that nobody could figure out what to do with a talent as big as Lucy's? She just never got the right role in a hit picture that would have made all the difference. You would think that, after her sensational performance as the gold-digging Bubbles in *Dance, Girl, Dance*, directors would have clamored to hire her. Well, *Dance, Girl, Dance* was no smash,

115

and it's really a case of a great performance in a not-so-hot movie. The film has something of a reputation as an early feminist piece, and it is interesting on that level. Dorothy Arzner directed it, and she was the only female director working in Hollywood at the time. It's definitely a cult film and certainly worth seeing, but more for Lucille Ball's performance than for anything else.

Dance, Girl, Dance follows the careers of two beautiful dancers with different ambitions. Judy (Maureen O'Hara) wants to be a great ballerina, and Bubbles basically wants to snag a millionaire. When Bubbles becomes a highly paid burlesque queen, she hires Judy to be her stooge. Jimmy (Louis Hayward) is an unhappy rich boy interested in Judy but still in love with his soon-to-be ex-wife (Virginia Field). Judy is more interested in her career than in her love life anyway, but Bubbles finds Jimmy highly appealing (and in the right tax bracket). The relationship between Judy and Bubbles becomes increasingly strained, and it takes a courtroom scene to iron out the ending.

The first time we see Bubbles, she's performing with an all-girl dance troupe in an Akron dive. She spots Jimmy in the audience and starts making eyes at him during the routine. Lucy sets up Bubbles's personality in that first moment: this girl is going places, and she knows how to get there. Bubbles is one tough cookie, and Lucy tosses off her sharp one-liners like the pro she is. When the troupe reconvenes in New York, Bubbles gets a job doing a hula dance, which leads to her break on the burlesque circuit. Lucy is startlingly sexual in her hula audition. It's the kind of number that she would have spoofed on her series, but she plays it here with all the rawness and abandon that the censors would allow in 1940. Bubbles exhibits so much confidence in her ability to arouse men that you can see why they would pay good money to see her dance.

When Bubbles makes it big, she's renamed Tiger Lily White. She visits Judy's modest apartment and plays the oh-so-grand star to the hilt, although she can't quite conceal her innate trashiness. Luckily, we get to see two of Lily's burlesque numbers ("Mother, What Do I Do Now?" and "Jitterbug Bite") in their entirety. Lucy, singing in her own perfectly acceptable voice, cuts loose and is a tremendous performer. When told to "Give 'em all ya got," she replies, "They couldn't take it." And you believe it. Her performance brims with an irresistible playfulness, remarkably free of inhibition. Liberal use of a wind machine raises her skirt, which adds a nice smarminess to the milieu. Not that Lucy needs any help in making you believe this is burlesque. Her brassy, one-of-the-boys rapport with her male audience is perfectly pitched. Lucy convinces you that she could have left the movies and given Gypsy Rose Lee some real competition.

Lucille Ball in *Dance, Girl, Dance* (1940)

Maria Ouspenskaya appears yet again as a ballet instructor. (She's much nicer to the girls here than she was in *Waterloo Bridge*.) It's worth the price of admission to hear her wrap her impenetrable accent around the word *oomph*. The worst scene in the movie features Maria's unconvincing demise under the wheels of a car. (Had the driver been forced to watch her earlier scenes?) Louis Hayward and Virginia Field must carry the most irritating part of the plot, and you won't care if they get together at the end or not. In a strange bit of casting, Ralph Bellamy is the head of a dance company. (We sure do see enough of their work!) His attempts to connect with Maureen O'Hara's character are tiresome. Despite these flaws and a highly implausible climax at the burlesque house, *Dance, Girl, Dance* is still a must-see for any fan of Lucille Ball.

Lucy is billed after O'Hara and Hayward, and her role is a supporting one in terms of actual screen time, but it's her picture all the way and should have done more for her movie career than it did. If you only know her as television's Lucy Ricardo, Lucy Carmichael, and Lucy Carter, then her gutsy, hard-edged Bubbles should prove a revelation. She's so good that you might even forgive her performance in *Mame* (1974).

Charles Boyer and Olivia de Havilland

Charles Boyer

IN

Hold Back the Dawn
(1941)

WITH the glaring (and I do mean *glaring*) exception of Joan Crawford, Frenchman Charles Boyer, Hollywood's greatest Continental lover since Rudolph Valentino, romanced his way into the onscreen hearts of nearly every major female star of the 1930s and 1940s. With Parisian sophistication, brooding intensity, and sad-eyed but glamorous fatalism, he was irresistible to Greta Garbo and Marlene Dietrich, Bette Davis and Katharine Hepburn, sisters Olivia de Havilland and Joan Fontaine, plus Barbara Stanwyck, Ingrid Bergman, Claudette Colbert, Irene Dunne, Hedy Lamarr, Rita Hayworth, Loretta Young, Jennifer Jones, Margaret Sullavan, and Jean Arthur. In *Algiers* (1938), which is little more than a collection of movie clichés pleasurably strung together, Boyer played Pepe le Moko, a sleek thief hiding out in the Casbah (until he risks everything for love), firmly establishing his suavely jaded, yet passionate persona. It earned him a second Best Actor Oscar nomination; his first was for his impressive Napoleon in *Conquest* (1937), one of MGM's duller costume epics. Better than both of those performances is his unnominated work in the uncommonly fine drama *Hold Back the Dawn*, where he penetratingly charts the redemption of a velvety rascal (as in *Algiers*, love is the catalyst), an unintended victim of his own devious plotting. With his deep, heavy-accented growl, Boyer also narrates, suffusing his words with biting world-weariness.

Romanian Georges Iscovescu (Boyer), a gigolo and sometime ballroom dancer, comes to a Mexican border town; his hope is to enter the United States because all the rich women fled Europe for America at the start of World War II. But due to the quota system, his wait could be from five to eight years. A despondent Georges runs into his old dancing partner (and fellow hustler), Anita Dixon (Paulette Goddard), who tells him that the fastest way to enter the States is to marry one of its citizens, just like she did (though she's now divorced). Georges sets his sights on visiting California schoolteacher Emmy Brown (Olivia de Havilland) and sweeps her off her feet and into an impulsive marriage. With four weeks to wait before he's allowed to cross the border, he must sidestep the inquisitive immigration inspector, Mr. Hammock (Walter Abel), and whisks Emmy off on an impromptu honeymoon through the outlying areas. Soon dreading his cruel plan to dump her once he's an American, Georges begins to fall in love with Emmy; it wasn't supposed to happen this way.

After Georges is stunned by the news of his interminable wait, he makes his way to the seedy, purgatorial Hotel Esperanza. Like a deposed prince, Boyer suppresses Georges's devastation behind elegant grandeur, aided by a dapper walking stick. Jump ahead five months, and Georges is as shabby as his surroundings: bitter, out of hope (and money), and uncharacteristically in need of a shave. He springs back to life when Anita suggests he snag an American tourist. Like a panther on the prowl, Boyer's Georges slinks through town with insinuating charm, especially when bright-eyed Emmy becomes his target. Concealing his desperation with warmhearted attentiveness, he slyly makes himself indispensably helpful to her and her field-trip carload of overexcited schoolboys as their station wagon is being repaired. Portraying himself as lonely and romantically scarred, Georges is a coldly confident, professional love maker, overwhelming the starved-for-romance Emmy with European courtliness and his gently persuasive, intoxicating ardor. When she and her brats are ensconced overnight in his hotel's lobby, Georges comes downstairs for a middle-of-the-night wooing session; Boyer oozes with the cynicism of just how easy this sort of thing is for Georges.

As soon as they are wed, Georges is eager for Emmy to return to California. But before she goes, she asks him to say the vows he didn't get to say in their rushed civil ceremony, and although he complies, Boyer allows Georges's face to show the first hint of conscience; he is clearly uncomfortable with her genuine feeling for him. When she unexpectedly returns a few days later, Georges takes her on an improvised honeymoon to evade the snoopy inspector. They come upon a village celebrating the patron saint of brides and grooms and join the candle-holding procession of couples. When they kneel before the priest for their blessing, watch Boyer fail to complete the sign of the cross: Georges stops himself from polluting the moment any further with his falseness; the simple beauty of the ritual and his happy bride remind him what a scoundrel he is. But just as Emmy was susceptible to his polished technique, Georges begins to fall under the spell of her untarnished goodness and sincerity. They spend the night in the woods of the innless town in her station wagon, but Georges cannot bring himself to deflower the trusting Emmy. After feigning a shoulder injury, he remains in the driver's seat while she sprawls out in the back. Boyer brims with desire when Georges looks at his ripely sensual wife in the rearview mirror, stifling himself from being even more of a heel than he already is. He abruptly turns the mirror, removing the temptation, but he's still visibly ruffled by his jumbled motives. As love and unselfishness overtake him, he becomes resolved to make things right with Emmy—if it's not too late. When a melodramatic crisis strikes, Boyer drives the remainder of the film, avoiding potentially hokey pitfalls with the singularity of purpose of a well-aimed bullet.

This is the fourth Mitchell Leisen-directed film I have included in this book. Isn't it about time he got wider recognition for his beautifully acted, richly detailed movies? From a story by Ketti Frings, the script, by Billy Wilder and Charles Brackett, boasts well-developed main characters, an unusually atmospheric setting, and an engrossing love story. It suffers from too many peripheral characters (at the hotel) and an ending that comes too easily and too quickly. Not much is gained from its framing story either; Leisen himself appears as a fictional director, filming Veronica Lake in *I Wanted Wings* (his previous film), when Georges shows up to tell (and sell) his story. Olivia de Havilland's Emmy, like her Melanie Hamilton, is a lovely performance enhanced by surprisingly sturdy reserves of strength. Oh-so-American Paulette Goddard is no one's idea of an Australian-Polish gold digger, but she's awfully smart, sexy, and sassy, as Anita does all she can to keep Georges for herself. The two actresses share one of those juicy good girl-bad girl confrontation scenes. The picture garnered six Oscar nominations, including those for Best Picture and Best Actress (de Havilland).

Boyer later took Georges's manipulative skills to the brink as Gregory Anton in George Cukor's *Gaslight* (1944), the highly enjoyable, handsome period thriller in which he tries to drive wife Ingrid Bergman mad (to get her dead aunt's jewels). His performance, which won him a third Oscar nod (his fourth, and final one, came for 1961's *Fanny*), is not the subtlest portrait of villainy you'll ever see; Anton lacks dimension, but, alas, he's far better remembered than Georges Iscovescu, a man caught between two countries, two women, and two codes of behavior, played by one great actor.

Joan Fontaine and Cary Grant

Cary Grant

IN

Suspicion
(1941)

CARY Grant had been in pictures five years when, in the screwball comedy *The Awful Truth* (1937), he became *the* Cary Grant, establishing his ever-after persona (call it comic sophistication fueled by Cockney assertiveness), one that was consistently popular for the next *thirty* years. On infrequent occasions, Grant challenged fans' fixed ideas about him (notably in *None But the Lonely Heart*, a turgid, enervating 1944 failure, for which he got an Oscar nomination, presumably for his valiant earnestness). In *Suspicion*, his first of four Hitchcock films, he subverts the Grant that audiences couldn't get enough of in *His Girl Friday* (1940) and *The Philadelphia Story* (1940), the latter featuring him as C. K. Dexter Haven, the quintessential Grant role. He begins as his usual charming self in *Suspicion*, then cagily exposes an alarming darkness beneath his gleaming façade. The film was a hit, but it's often talked about as a movie ruined by its ending; the wrap-up *is* a problem, but Grant still gives one of his superior performances. In fact, he *makes* the film, despite the fact that his costar, comely Joan Fontaine, netted the year's Best Actress Oscar. It's his persuasiveness in a tricky role, rather than her tedious series of "suspicious" expressions, that makes the film succeed (even though the story is told from *her* point of view).

In an English province, well-off Lina McLaidlaw (Fontaine), a beauty beneath her bookishness, seems headed for spinsterdom when she meets Johnnie Aysgarth (Grant), a handsome rake of the society set who lacks nothing but funds. Opposites attract, and they hastily marry. Lina soon learns that her husband *borrows* money rather than earns it, and, worse, he's an inexhaustible liar. Things take an ominous turn when Beaky (Nigel Bruce), Johnnie's pal (and partner in an ambitious real-estate venture), dies, possibly the victim of foul play. Lina suspects Johnnie's involvement in Beaky's demise, and as the couple draws further apart (and his debts mount), she's convinced he's going to poison her to collect on an insurance policy.

One thing about Grant's outgoing, cocky Johnnie: rules don't apply to him. Whether trying to talk his way into a first-class train seat with a third-class ticket or crashing a high-toned ball as if he'd been invited, Johnnie always attempts to schmooze his way to whatever he wants. And, in their second chance encounter, he decides he wants Lina. He looks at her, lovely on horseback, and his attraction to her is striking in its certainty. (Johnnie is ready for someone different from the bubbly women encircling his every move.) He wears down Lina's good-girl primness with his self-amused teasing and relentless brashness; Grant also silkily implies the promise of sexual gratification. His charisma makes it easy to believe whatever Johnnie is saying, and yet you can't be sure that you're not simply being taken in, seduced the way Lina is. Even so, I don't think there's any doubt: Johnnie genuinely falls in love with her. His discomfort, that of a rogue floored by never-before *feelings*, is the first puncture of his flashy surface. But that doesn't mean that Johnnie has suddenly matured or has any intention of changing his no-account ways; he is still sure that he can get away with plenty. Grant employs his irresistibility as Johnnie's barricade to reality; he's a polished, smiling liar, fast thinking and unruffled. He's not stupid though, and you can see tiny rumblings of panic on Grant's face whenever Johnnie is in a bind. But since Grant has few onscreen moments without Fontaine, he has limited time to reveal Johnnie's unguarded thoughts. Within the frustrating constraints of playing a role in which he must keep us guessing, Grant is undaunted, artfully delineating the steady crushing of Johnnie's confidence as his luck runs out and as Lina pulls away.

As he lavishes Lina with gifts he can't afford, Grant transmits the basic insecurity in Johnnie: he's afraid of not being able to hold on to her. They have an unusually honest car-ride discussion after her father's death, where Grant, simply and wholly, makes it evident that Johnnie's love for her is the only constant in his haphazard life. (Just moments later, he's smoothly deflecting her inquiry about his dismissal from his short-lived job.) A wall slams down if she gets *too* nosy. Fearing that Johnnie is taking advantage of his friend's cash, she questions Beaky about his understanding of Johnnie's real-estate plan. Having overheard this, Grant flares a glacial anger we haven't yet seen in Johnnie, controlling (barely) his fury, humiliated by her meddling and lack of faith in him. Thereafter, there's a remoteness in Grant's Johnnie. (Hitchcock often has him slip into the frame as coolly and quietly as Dracula.) Without letting his performance go vague or flat, Grant draws Johnnie into himself, preoccupied with financial woes, deflating the spontaneous alacrity that was his trademark, widening the chasm between him and Lina. Johnnie can still rouse his "killer" charm, as at a mystery writer's dinner party, but that only emphasizes what a mask it really is. Lina, making excuses (and by now terrified), banishes him from their bedroom, and Johnnie takes offense. Grant instantly turns Johnnie to stone, incensed by this blatant rejection but calmly veiling the extent of his displeasure. The trouble with the ending isn't that the facts don't gel or make sense; it's the abruptness and patness of the last scene, in which explanations, coming at us left and right, feel tacked on and a bit desperate. But a lucid, livid, pushed-to-the-limit Grant, baring Johnnie's sunken manhood and whipped vulnerability, somehow pulls it off.

Grant was in the 1941 Best Actor Oscar race, but for *Penny Serenade*, a baby-driven piece of slop (though *he's* good), rather than for *Suspicion*. Fontaine's constipated, uninteresting Lina copped her a compensatory Oscar; she had lost the 1940 prize for her marvelous work in a similar (but better) role, another timid woman who marries an inscrutable man who may be a murderer, in Hitchcock's ravishing *Rebecca* (his only Best Picture Oscar winner). *Suspicion* was also up for Best Picture, but it isn't one of the director's best. It does, however, contain some classic moments, like the ill-boding appearance of the word *murder* in a game of anagrams and Grant's impassive stair climb with a glass of glow-in-the-dark (poisoned?) milk. Based on Francis Iles's long-winded novel *Before the Fact*, the script (which changed the book's ending), credited to Samson Raphaelson, Joan Harrison, and Alma Reville (Hitch's wife), is an entertaining fusion of romance, humor, and peril, but it's Grant who gives the film its kick. His provocative passage from carefree hedonism to moody disenchantment brings verve to a character conceived as little more than a device.

Grant and Fontaine had already appeared together in the adventure classic *Gunga Din* (1939), one year before *Rebecca* made her a star. Grant went on to appear in two of Hitchcock's greatest films, *Notorious* (1946) and *North by Northwest* (1959), and, in between, *To Catch a Thief* (1955), a picturesque trifle. Only James Stewart, who also starred in four of Hitch's movies, had a comparable association with the master of suspense.

Joel McCrea and Veronica Lake

Joel McCrea

IN

Sullivan's Travels
(1941)

JOEL McCrea was probably the most underrated actor of Hollywood's Golden Age. He never quite made it to superstardom (Gary Cooper was always in his way), but he had a long career and starred in an unusually high number of first-rate pictures. *These Three* (1936) and *Dead End* (1937), both directed by William Wyler, showed that he was a dramatic actor of real substance, and they put him on the A list of leading men. He underplayed in the name of economy and simplicity, and his work hasn't aged a day. He fell into the "he makes it look so easy that everyone takes him for granted" category. I'm sure that his leading ladies appreciated him, as he tends to bring out the best in them. He really listens to them, and the results include some of the more memorably intimate pairings of the period (with Ginger Rogers in *Primrose Path*, with Claudette Colbert in *The Palm Beach Story*, with Jean Arthur in *The More the Merrier*). And he was versatile. Although people may remember him as a cowboy star of the 1950s, he happened to be one of the better light comedians of the 1940s. His boyishness makes him particularly funny when he's pursued by a man-hungry woman, such as Mary Astor in *The Palm Beach Story*. In that same film, his love scenes with Claudette Colbert have an erotic charge that's rare in a comedy. Of course, it didn't hurt that he was great looking. McCrea had it all, and as you've already surmised, it's difficult for me to contain my enthusiasm for his underappreciated contribution to American movies.

It's somewhat odd to me that, although *Sullivan's Travels* has become one of Hollywood's best-loved films, McCrea's performance has never received its due. I don't wish to take away an ounce of praise from Preston Sturges for his wonderful script and inspired direction, but I do wonder whether it would be as good a film with another actor playing John L. Sullivan. Yes, Gary Cooper or Henry Fonda or even Fred MacMurray could have played it, but certainly not better than McCrea. I don't think any of them could have combined the role's intelligence, warmth, irritability, and wisecracking humor in such a winning way. McCrea's skill with Sturges's dialogue is the perfect union of actor and writer. He seems instinctively to know when to speed through the words and when to take his time. There's certainly sentimentality in the story but none in Mc-Crea's acting. He is the movie's sturdy and dependable backbone.

Sullivan's Travels tells the story of a wildly successful comedy director (McCrea) who wants to address the suffering in the world by making a message picture titled *O Brother, Where Art Thou?* When he's told by the studio people that he knows nothing about suffering, he decides to learn about it firsthand. Dressed as a hobo and with only a dime in his pocket, he goes out to discover what real trouble is. Despite many failed (and hilarious) attempts, he finds the trouble he's seeking and is a changed man. Along the way, he also finds the luscious Veronica Lake as a discouraged Hollywood hopeful eager for an introduction to Ernst Lubitsch.

When we first meet Sullivan, he seems naïve and idealistic. His intentions to do good are utterly genuine, but how can his quest possibly succeed? It takes him about five attempts to find the trouble he seeks. The first try ends with a slapstick car chase, but Sturges wisely makes each succeeding attempt less funny than the last. Sullivan gets closer and closer each time, and Sturges subtly prepares us for the shift in tone. Much of the humor in McCrea's performance comes from his increasing surliness toward those who stand in the way of his mission (mostly the studio employees who are forever on his trail). An affable presence, he can nevertheless handle a wisecrack with as much aplomb as Thelma Ritter. Yet he never seems rude because, although misguided, he's always admirable for his resolve. There's a charming scene where he's burning with fever in the studio's trailer and being terribly cranky. He stops in the middle of his tirade to tell Lake's character how pretty she looks, and it's funny and touching at the same time.

When Sullivan faces true brutality, McCrea conveys the terror of a man who has lost his safety net for the first time in his life. Sullivan learns more than he ever wanted. The film ends with his famous speech about this "cockeyed caravan," and I'd say it's a perfect moment. The words come out of McCrea in a simple but deeply felt way. There isn't a trace of actorly self-consciousness in his line readings, and the result is the finest moment of his entire career in the movies. That's high praise indeed. And the movie gets to have it both ways: it's a feel-good comedy *and* the humane message picture that Sullivan wanted to make.

Veronica Lake is another of those actresses who shines in McCrea's presence. They make a great screen couple, as their romance comes out of the fact that the two characters like each other so much. Their first scene is a tender meeting of two persons down on their luck (though he's pretending), and she buys him breakfast. Their dialogue is peppered with smart-aleck remarks, but we can feel their real connection. Sullivan is married to a loathsome creature (for tax-friendly financial reasons), but we ache to see him get together with his new love (who remains as nameless as Joan Fontaine in *Rebecca*). Lake is luminous in this film: smart, funny, and terribly in love. And, of course, we have the great Preston Sturges stock company on hand. (Unlike the members of John Ford's stock company, Sturges's actors could actually *act*.) Each one, from Eric Blore to William Demarest, makes a unique and vital contribution to a genuine classic.

McCrea became a Preston Sturges favorite. In 1942, they made the lightning-speed screwball farce *The Palm Beach Story*, and then came a critical and box-office disaster titled *The Great Moment*, filmed in 1942 but released in 1944, which was an oddly comic medical drama. The one-two punch of *Sullivan's Travels* and *The Palm Beach Story* marked McCrea's apex. If he had never put on those cowboy boots and gotten on a horse, his status as a screen legend would still be firmly secure for this movie lover.

Robert Cummings and Ann Sheridan

Ann Sheridan
IN
Kings Row
(1942)

WHEN you're tagged the "Oomph Girl," it's clear you're not being groomed to be the next Bette Davis. Perhaps the most beautiful actress at Warner Brothers, Ann Sheridan found her wise-gal niche when her gift for street-smart sass clicked with James Cagney's in *Angels with Dirty Faces* (1938), resulting in reteamings on *Torrid Zone* (1940) and *City for Conquest* (1940). For a lesson in how to hold the screen, watch her in her first scene as the truck-stop waitress in *They Drive by Night* (1940), slinging more deadpan wisecracks than hash and making quite an impression on George Raft and Humphrey Bogart. With her caressingly low voice, melting eyes, and (black-and-white) red hair, she was *all* movie star, but could she really act? *Kings Row*, an irresistibly absorbing melodrama, answered with a resounding *yes*, but it's still primarily remembered as Ronald Reagan's best film. Oh, it is that; but in a picture that plays like a period *Peyton Place*, it's Sheridan who provides its heart and soul. Among the (still) shocking, sometimes gruesome plot turns (murder, family secrets, suicide, sadism, madness, and illicit sex), Sheridan's Randy Monaghan stands out, grounding the picture with low-key strength amid the considerable hysteria around her. Although top billed, she does not appear in the film's first *hour*. Once she enters, though, it's as if she's always been there.

Beginning in 1890 and crossing into the new century, *Kings Row*, based on Henry Bellamann's novel, uncovers the ugliness behind the closed doors of the titular town, a seemingly perfect Everytown, U.S.A. It follows two rich boyhood friends: Parris Mitchell (overearnest Robert Cummings), who dreams of becoming a doctor, and Drake McHugh (Reagan), a fun-loving guy without a serious thought in his head. Parris comes under the tutelage of moody Dr. Tower (Claude Rains) and soon renews his interest in Tower's shut-in daughter, Cassie (Betty Field), his childhood sweetheart. They begin an intense affair that ends tragically, whereupon Parris goes to Vienna to study a new field: psychiatry. After a breakup with

131

wealthy Louise Gordon (an effective Nancy Coleman), Drake falls in love with literally wrong-side-of-the-tracks Randy. When he loses his trust fund in a bank scandal, Drake becomes a railroad employee. An accident on the job results in the loss of both legs, which destroys his will to live. Randy cares for him and marries him, and Parris, now a psychiatrist, returns home to help treat his broken friend.

Sheridan has a great entrance, poking her head around a corner at the train station as Parris has his sendoff for Vienna. Her radiant healthiness is a breath of fresh air, especially after a full hour spent with Cassie's crumbling psyche. Randy's love for Drake is unmistakable; from the way Sheridan looks at Reagan, you know it's the real thing. The levelheaded poor girl and the hedonistic rich boy are a perfect match; her straight-talking common sense is just what careless-living Drake needs. In the scene where he tells her of his unresolved feelings for Louise, she deals with it admirably: head-on, rationally, and without undue drama. Later, when he's working at the railroad, she visits him for a rail-side coffee break and tells him that she's happier than anyone has a right to be; and despite tough times and their class difference, you believe her, and you go on believing her after calamity strikes. If Randy sounds too good to be true, you don't think that while you're watching her. Since Sheridan's style is so unvarnished (and she says her lines fairly rapidly), Randy never seems insufferably noble. She stays focused on Drake rather than on her self-sacrifice; everything she does is motivated purely by her love and concern for him. As gorgeous as Sheridan is, Randy's beauty comes from within.

After Drake's accident, Randy refuses to let him wallow in self-pity. She bristles at his mention of a "home" where he can go (and hide) and launches into a quiet but firm speech about her determination to marry him, despite his protests. Sheridan's calm steadfastness and thoughtful restraint make it an unusually moving scene, abetted by the way bedridden Reagan covers his face and turns away from her as she speaks, ultimately reaching out a hand to her. (Please pass me a *box* of tissues.) Randy tries to build up Drake's confidence, to convince him that she needs him, to encourage him without pressuring him; and when he finally wonders aloud about a possible real-estate venture for himself, she lights up like a Christmas tree. Her train-station reunion with Parris is another overwhelming emotional release for her; to be with someone who, in his way, loves Drake as much as she does is a great comfort. When the two men have their bedside reunion, Randy leaves them alone, closes the door behind her, and whispers, "Mary, Blessed Mother of God," three times to herself. It is a deeply private moment, and Sheridan makes it a joyously tear-filled expression of Randy's answered prayers. Randy finds a true confidant in Parris, someone with whom she can freely discuss her hopes and fears. Sheridan develops an intimate bond with costar Cummings, a bond as warming and simply honest in its way as the one she shares with Reagan.

Sam Wood's direction is most compelling in the Randy-Drake scenes and in the disturbing episodes involving the creepy, fascinating Tower and Gordon families. The film disintegrates into unbearable sludge when Parris is given an insipid new love (Kaaren Verne). And, sadly, the plot ties up too neatly in the rushed final minutes, with Parris ludicrously spouting poetry at a most inopportune moment. James Wong Howe's black-and-white cinematography may be voluptuously beautiful, but it also has the lurking grimness of a horror film. (You get both qualities in a lightning-lit love tryst between Parris and Cassie.) William Cameron Menzies's ambitious and impeccably crafted production design is nothing less than you'd expect from the man who designed *Gone With the Wind*. Erich Wolfgang Korngold's magnificent score might have been intrusive but, instead, enhances the film's emotional content. Reagan is ideally cast and appealing; his "Where's the rest of me?" is a justifiably classic moment. Cummings has some well-played scenes, but his Parris is too Andy Hardy for me; it's a pretty drippy performance. Betty Field's Cassie goes well over the top, but there's coldly incisive work from Claude Rains, Charles Coburn (cast against type as evil Dr. Gordon), and Judith Anderson (Mrs. Gordon). The film got Oscar nominations for picture, direction, and cinematography. (How did it miss for music and art direction?)

Sheridan, who died of cancer at age fifty-one in 1967, never topped her work here; she had few roles remotely as good, but two manage to stand out: *The Unfaithful* (1947), an interesting reworking of *The Letter* in postwar America, which gave her a bona fide Davis role to sink her teeth into (alas, once again, Eve Arden steals a movie); and *Come Next Spring* (1956), a lovingly told tale of an ex-drunk (beautifully played by Steve Cochran) who returns to the wife (Sheridan), children, and farm he ran out on nine years before. And you don't have to wait an hour for her to show up in either of them.

Ronald Colman, Clyde Fillmore (as a senator), and Jean Arthur

Ronald Colman

IN

The Talk of the Town
(1942)

ENGLISHMAN Ronald Colman was one of the American silent screen's
more dashing stars, popular for his romantic teamwork with Vilma
Banky and also for the title role in *Beau Geste* (1926). And fans hadn't even
been acquainted with the most distinctive of his gifts: a cultured voice of
resonant beauty, warmly enveloping rather than snooty. Adapting to the
talkies was a nonissue for Colman, who snagged *two* Best Actor nominations, for *Condemned* and *Bulldog Drummond*, at the 1929–30 Academy
Awards. His career peaked in the mid 1930s as the thinking man's Errol
Flynn with a series of stirring adventures: *A Tale of Two Cities* (1936), with
his gorgeous rendering of Sydney Carton's "far, far better" last words;
Frank Capra's sometimes exciting, more often wrongheaded *Lost Horizon*
(1937); and, best of all, *The Prisoner of Zenda* (1937), the definitive version
of the durable dual-role vehicle. By decade's end, Colman, pushing fifty,
was looking a bit old for such exploits, and his decline seemed imminent.
But in 1942, he was back on top in two Best Picture Oscar nominees, *Ran-
dom Harvest* and *The Talk of the Town*. The former, *the* amnesiac love story,
has a see-it-to-believe-it plot so ludicrous that there's nothing to do but succumb to its high-gloss excesses. For falling in, out of, and back into love
with Greer Garson, Colman got an Oscar nomination, but he should have
gotten it for *Talk of the Town*'s Michael Lightcap (who's a lot more fun to be
around). Why am I writing about third-billed Colman when the movie also
stars Cary Grant and Jean Arthur? Well, the success of George Stevens's
highly enjoyable Capraesque comedy is due primarily to Colman's exhilarating transition from an overregimented academic, shielded by the
"fortress" of a beard, to a vigorously involved member of the human race.

Up in New England, factory employee Leopold Dilg (Grant), framed
for arson and murder by the boss, escapes from jail in the midst of his trial.
He stumbles upon the doorstep of friend Nora Shelley (Arthur), who's fixing up the house she's about to rent to Professor Lightcap, a distinguished

135

law-school dean seeking summer solitude. When Lightcap arrives early, Dilg, unable to leave because of an injured ankle, hides in the attic. Nora arranges to stay on as Lightcap's cook-secretary so she can watch over Dilg. To hide his true identity from the professor, Dilg plays the role of Joseph, the gardener. The two men become unlikely friends, engaging in lively philosophical discussions about the law. When Dilg is caught and Lightcap realizes he's been harboring a wanted man, risking his impending appointment to the Supreme Court, the professor overcomes his feelings of betrayal and sets out to prove his friend's innocence. But he must bend his principles to do so before it's too late.

Though Lightcap arrives in a downpour, Colman couldn't be drier; with an all-business demeanor, he's in no mood for Nora's scatterbrained antics. But when Joseph enters the plot, Lightcap, initially put off by the inappropriateness of the gardener's familiarity, soon finds invigorating pleasure in the situation. Here Colman relaxes Lightcap's formality, bonding with the ever-surprising Joseph; the more Colman defrosts, the more irresistible his character becomes. Though the film is a love triangle, with Nora as the prize, the core of the story is the relationship between the men. Today, the delight that confirmed-bachelor Lightcap displays in Joseph's presence might raise eyebrows. Despite growing affection for Nora, Lightcap gets much more of a charge from his contact with Joseph, which proves to be life altering. If, after my essay on Spencer Tracy in *Test Pilot*, you suspect that I see homoeroticism in every old movie about two men and one woman (there's *none* in *The Philadelphia Story*), let me say that both *Talk of the Town* and *Test Pilot* are especially alive for the sexual-orientation complexities brought to them by Colman and Tracy. After Dilg is captured, Lightcap, consoling a teary Nora, says, "I know now you couldn't help feeling the way you do about him." Colman, a master of gentlemanly restraint, makes it transparent that neither can Lightcap.

Lightcap's feelings for Joseph and Nora run too deep to be undone by the revelation that Joseph is, in fact, Dilg. And although Colman has already made Lightcap a far more appealing fellow than the stiff who showed up that rainy night, the fun has only begun. Lightcap takes action, reckless action, to see that justice is done, thereby imperiling the low profile he's supposed to be keeping before his senate approval for the Supreme Court. In a symbolic act signifying the new him, he shaves his beard (but not his pencil-thin mustache, a Colman trademark); he begins with a swordlike flourish of his scissors, à la *Prisoner of Zenda*. Suspecting that beauty-salon owner Regina Bush (Glenda Farrell) has information regarding Dilg's frame-up, the now smooth chinned but woefully inexperienced Lightcap puts himself in her manicuring hands. Like an awkward teenager, he checks to see who's looking, then swallows before actually asking for a date. Colman makes a charming babe in the woods: Lightcap races out of the beauty parlor when, after Regina's acceptance, another young lady winks at him; at a nightclub, he tries to finesse Regina with his rather stilted compliments and, when given permission to kiss her, opts for a fatherly forehead peck. As he lies, uses his fists, wields a gun, and challenges everything he's held to be true, Lightcap has never had a better time or felt more purposeful. Cary Grant and Jean Arthur take their positions on the sidelines as Colman carries the film, all the while nourishing the inner life of Lightcap, who, via companionship, learns to follow his heart and give his overworked head a rest.

Despite seven Oscar nominations, the black-and-white *Talk of the Town* is not widely remembered; it is overshadowed by the two George Stevens comedies that sandwiched it: *Woman of the Year* (1942) and *The More the Merrier* (1943). (While both have great moments, *Talk of the Town* is still my favorite of the three.) The screenplay, by Sidney Buchman and Irwin Shaw, wisely allows the relationships and the humor to take precedence over the message: a warning that our democracy could collapse if each of us doesn't keep an eye on it. (You won't be surprised to learn that Buchman wrote 1939's *Mr. Smith Goes to Washington.*) The writers manage to keep the love-triangle resolution dangling until the last moment. There are flaws: the dumb scene in which bloodhounds chase Colman outside the house; and the cringe-inducing misuse of black actor Rex Ingram as Lightcap's overly devoted manservant. Cary Grant is oddly cast as a rebel, but he and the ever-adorable Jean Arthur shine (though their roles don't have the variety that Colman's has).

Colman won the 1947 Best Actor Oscar for *A Double Life,* playing an actor who takes the role of Othello off the stage with him. His work in it is admirable, but the script, written by Garson Kanin and Ruth Gordon, two theatre pros who should have known better, is utterly unconvincing. His final movie was, oops, *The Story of Mankind* (1957), the kind of film that doesn't have a problem with casting Hedy Lamarr as Joan of Arc. I'm surely not able to make Colman's Michael Lightcap the talk of the town, but I can certainly champion the performance as a model of light-comic perfection, on par with the best of Cary Grant, even, in this instance, outclassing Grant himself.

Joseph Cotten as Charlie Oakley

Joseph Cotten

IN

Shadow of a Doubt
(1943)

I T is just about impossible to make a list of the all-time great films without including several featuring Joseph Cotten. Owing to an association with Orson Welles that solidified at New York's Mercury Theatre in the late 1930s, Cotten was a member of the powerhouse ensembles of three of Welles's movie milestones: *Citizen Kane* (1941), *The Magnificent Ambersons* (1942), and *Touch of Evil* (1958). Even in Carol Reed's stunning film *The Third Man* (1949), in which Cotten memorably starred as pulp writer Holly Martins, Welles was on hand to steal the spotlight as satiny criminal Harry Lime. *Kane* marked Cotten's Hollywood debut, following his 1939 Broadway stint opposite Katharine Hepburn in *The Philadelphia Story* (playing the soon-to-be Cary Grant role). He quickly became one of the key leading men of 1940s films, costarring with many of the top female stars of the day. Handsome without being beautiful, gifted without being showy, and intelligent without being dull, he was Spencer Tracy without the acclaim. Cotten was never an Oscar nominee, not even for his Charlie Oakley, a serial killer with elegant manners, in Alfred Hitchcock's gripping family-ties thriller *Shadow of a Doubt*. His calmly terrifying performance ranks with Hitchcock's other two classic sociopaths: Robert Walker's Bruno in *Strangers on a Train* (1951) and Anthony Perkins's Norman in *Psycho* (1960). *Shadow of a Doubt* is essentially the story of a young woman's loss of innocence, but without a performance as icily controlled as Cotten's at its dark center, the movie would not be the rare frightener it is.

Easterner Charles Oakley, wanted by the police, visits his doting sister, Emma Newton (Patricia Collinge), and her family in idyllic Santa Rosa, California. His eighteenish niece and namesake, Charlie (Teresa Wright), worships her worldly uncle, convinced they share a twinlike bond. Detective Jack Graham (Macdonald Carey) shows up on the pretext of conducting a survey, and young Charlie soon figures out that he's trailing her uncle. On her own, she puts together enough clues to conclude that her beloved relative is the Merry Widow Murderer, strangler of wealthy matrons. She promises her uncle that she'll keep quiet if he'll leave town, but once the police believe they have nabbed the real killer back east, there's just one thing left for Uncle Charlie to do: silence the only person who knows the truth, even if she is his niece.

In Cotten's first appearance, lying on a bed in a dingy apartment and smoking a cigar with his eyes closed, he suggests a vampire at rest. Though you'll later become accustomed to Charlie's charming public persona, you'll never shake that first glimpse of the private man: worn out and rock hard. He keeps out of sight on the train to Santa Rosa by feigning illness and arrives hunched over, requiring a cane to walk. When the coast is clear and he sees his niece, Cotten springs into the role of the glamorous Uncle Charlie, gliding toward her, his cane now a classy walking stick. With his soft-spoken gentility and unhurried movements, Cotten masks Charlie's seething hatred of our "foul sty" of a world with hollow but ingratiating goodness. His reunion with his sister overwhelms her, but watch him: he says all the right things and beams in the right way, but Charlie's dead eyes have no capacity for love. Cotten, with cunning reserve, never lets Charlie show any real familial feeling; his manner is like that of an alien who can replicate the behavior of an earthling but can never actually be one.

The psychology behind Charlie's sickness is hinted at, yet nothing said is particularly illuminating; he was a spoiled child who fractured his skull in a bicycle accident and has needed to "blow off steam" ever after. I don't really want an explanation anyway; it's more fun to be startled by the inexplicable presence of pure evil in a typical American home. Cotten pays meticulous attention to those moments when Charlie's true nature can't be suppressed. He brutally grabs his niece when she innocently confronts him with the incriminating page he's removed from the evening paper, but he's able to smooth things over with a dose of warm-smiling tenderness. The next morning, when his sister mentions Jack Graham's interest in interviewing *all* of the family for his survey, Charlie tears a piece of toast in half as if he were ripping Jack in two. Cotten's creepiest moment is his measured delivery of a diatribe against useless money-wasting widows. Photographing the right side of Cotten's face as he spews his venom, Hitchcock moves in slowly, as close as you can get, while Cotten continues, unblinking. When Charlie responds to his niece's interruption, he turns his head, looking directly into the camera (at *us*), and his blank stare is bone chilling. In a booth at a bar, he absentmindedly strangles a cocktail napkin while talking to his now-disillusioned niece; he drops his hands below the table when he sees the look on her face. Later, after learning that he's no longer under suspicion, he enters the house and uncharacteristically bounds up the stairs, but he stops before reaching the top, turning slowly with the realization that his niece *still knows*. Looking at her framed in the entranceway, Cotten reveals a surprising pang of humanity in Charlie; he regrets (momentarily) that he must kill his underestimated "twin" in what will amount to a battle between the good and bad halves of the one whole—uncle and niece together—Charlie.

Hitchcock and cameraman Joseph Valentine provide many unforgettably eerie black-and-white images, coolly aided by Cotten's alarming stillness as an object of menace. And notice how Hitchcock emphasizes the connection between the two Charlies by introducing each in exactly (camera angle and all) the same way: resting, face up, on a bed. (You can spot the director playing cards on the train.) The superb script was written by Thornton Wilder, Sally Benson, and Alma Reville. For Wilder, it was like turning his *Our Town* on its ear by placing a maniac in the middle of Grover's Corners. The film is a black-comic joke on our inability and unwillingness to see the evil under our noses. Henry Travers (as Mr. Newton) and Hume Cronyn (as a neighbor) are a delight as they concoct "perfect murder" scenarios, oblivious to the horror beside them. Patricia Collinge (so great as Birdie in *The Little Foxes*) is quite moving as Emma, while fresh and pretty Teresa Wright is ideal as strong-willed young Charlie.

After *Shadow of a Doubt* and *The Third Man*, my next favorite Cotten performance is his struggling artist in the neglected, highly imaginative time-bender *Portrait of Jennie* (1948), his last of four films with Jennifer Jones. (If *Gone With the Wind* had been made in the mid 1940s, I bet Cotten would have played Ashley to Jones's Scarlett because both were by then under contract to its producer, David O. Selznick.) Cotten reunited with Hitchcock for *Under Capricorn* (1949), a period dud that I've seen but about which I can't recall a single frame. He got Uncle Charlie's hands back into shape to choke Marilyn Monroe in *Niagara* (1953), but he never again got his clutches on a role as heart stopping as Charlie himself.

Joel McCrea, Jean Arthur, and Grady Sutton

Jean Arthur

IN

The More the Merrier
(1943)

JEAN Arthur's gurgling voice, an aural highlight of Hollywood's Golden Age, sounds like a prepubescent boy's on the cusp of changing. The *Annie Hall* of her day, Arthur was a lovably befuddled, highly inventive comedienne. Two of my favorite Arthur moments: in *The Talk of the Town* (1942), she prevents Ronald Colman from seeing Cary Grant's "wanted" newspaper photo by throwing an off-the-wall fit, lunging to cover Grant's face with Colman's fried-egg breakfast; in the majorly minor movie *A Lady Takes a Chance* (1943), she downs a lethal "cactus milk" cocktail, going from dazed to screamingly berserk, running around the bar like a wild animal. A film actress since the silent days, Arthur became a big star (under Frank Capra's heavenly direction) in *Mr. Deeds Goes to Town* (1936). As a hard-boiled newspaperwoman who develops a conscience when she falls in love with her "victim" (Gary Cooper), her transitions are richly felt, and the overall effect is magical. If you can resist her in this, you're a pretty hard soul; it remains her top performance. The joyous film *The More the Merrier* also ideally cast her, and Arthur, one of the funniest of screen criers, gives her tear ducts a real workout. She also makes another enchanting conversion, from an uptight, mechanized woman to one born anew by head-over-heels love (and the awakening of lust).

There's a wartime housing shortage in Washington, D.C., and working girl Connie Milligan (Arthur) patriotically decides to rent half her apartment. However, it's with reluctance that she agrees to take in elderly Benjamin Dingle (Charles Coburn), who's in D.C. to discuss the housing plan. Dingle senses that Connie could be happier, and he decides to play matchmaker. He secretly rents half of his half to Sgt. Joe Carter (Joel McCrea), "a high-type, clean-cut, nice young fellow" who's awaiting his mission to Africa. Dingle plots to rid Connie of her stuffed-shirt fiancé, Charles Pendergast (unfunny Richard Gaines), and replace him with Joe. Though Connie is infuriated by the unapproved appearance of a second roomer, she is soon smitten (as is Joe). Will her prolonged engagement and his impending orders keep them apart? Not if Mr. Dingle, their fairy godfather, has anything to say about it.

For all Connie's semblance of being in charge, an endearing Arthur makes it clear that her efficiency and orderliness are substitutes for spontaneity, romance, and contentment. Arthur's lambent softness and girlish vulnerability permeate the film, enriching Connie's situation beyond mere light-comedy convention; her life doesn't reflect who she really is. Arthur's spunk is adorable rather than cloying as she stands up to Dingle's steamrolling invasion of her status quo. Her task is to bring Connie's miles-apart head and heart together. There's a touching resignation in Arthur; diary-writing Connie knows that her private romantic yearnings have little chance of being realized, so she opts, instead, for a life of routine. With her trusty floor plan, she rapidly explains to Dingle the minute-by-minute morning schedule she's devised for them. Arthur is marvelous here, straight-facedly behaving as if it were perfectly normal to live in such a regimented way. (Why do they have to wake up at the same time?) Dingle is the catalyst for nudging her out of this; Joe is the prize. Connie meets Joe when they pass each other in her hall, and her cold-creamed face can't conceal her immediate attraction to the handsome, bathrobed stranger. In an astute bit, she's so focused on him that she doesn't even notice Dingle when he walks between her and Joe. She says she wants them out of her apartment (I love Arthur's scrunched-up anger), but she's not fooling anyone.

Arthur beautifully plays the push-pull of being both aroused by Joe *and* scared to death of succumbing to her urges, all the while melting under his incessant, amorous gaze. The sexual tension is palpable, but it's also consistently amusing. In some inspired foreplay, Arthur and McCrea, seated across from each other in a restaurant, rumba with only their shoulders, oblivious to all else. He escorts her home; as they amble down their street amid a stream of smooching couples, he can't keep his hands off her. She repeatedly spins out of his clutches, but she never *really* tries to stop him. (Connie's no-no-no and yes-yes-yes impulses are at war.) She chatters on with questions about his love life. The bliss of watching this sequence comes in the moments when Arthur shows signs of losing the battle, meaning the times when she involuntarily shuts up. He collapses them onto her front steps. As she talks about her fiancé and her engagement ring, she's pleasurably silenced when he kisses her hand. His lips reach her neck, leading to her closed-eyed ecstasy and a breathy pause. (Arthur gets back to reality by blinking several times.) He kisses her mouth while she's talking, and she woozily finishes her sentence when released. Finally, she grabs his face with both hands and kisses him back; wholesomeness has never been hotter. (There's a split-screen bed scene with them side by side, separated by a thin wall, predating the similarly titillating Doris-and-Rock tub scene from 1959's *Pillow Talk*.) The plot gets a bit silly, but Arthur has a pip of a crying jag, a kind of tremulous chanting, at an airport lunch counter. There's a surprise ending, and her reaction is a sustained squeal, a whimpering whine. Mostly, it's a unique mating call.

The movie nabbed six Oscar nominations: for Best Picture, Best Actress (Arthur's *only* Oscar recognition), Best Director (George Stevens), Best Original Story (Robert Russell and Frank Ross, Arthur's husband), Best Screenplay (for Russell and Ross, as well as for Richard Flournoy and Lewis R. Foster), and Best Supporting Actor (Charles Coburn). The wonderful Coburn, who confidently pulls the story's strings, was the only winner. Joel McCrea, the all-American Cary Grant, is also perfection: sexy, funny, and tender (his plain style is swell alongside Arthur's effervescence). Stevens's direction is often spot-on in its staging and timing (as in the front-steps scene), and he knows how to simmer the romantic longing, but some of his work (primarily the slapstick) feels overengineered. These labored antics, notably Dingle's disastrous attempt to keep up with Connie's schedule, deflate the film's buoyancy (so does the final chunk of the plot, involving a "Japanese" sighting and a feared sex scandal). I prefer the first Arthur-Stevens comedy, *The Talk of the Town*, also noted for the crack teamwork of its three leads, in which Arthur plays another "landlady."

Arthur worked with Stevens a third time, on *Shane* (1953), her last film and one of the great westerns. She again plays a woman restraining her romantic feelings (this time for the title character), wringing a dense emotional subtext from what is, basically, a supporting role. The Arthur-Stevens trio of films are as enduring as the trio of performances that make *The More the Merrier* so very merry.

William Eythe and Tallulah Bankhead

Tallulah Bankhead

IN

A Royal Scandal

(1945)

AFTER Tallulah Bankhead's phenomenal success as chic journalist Constance Porter in Alfred Hitchcock's sublime one-set thriller *Lifeboat* (1944), she should have immediately been cast in a custom-tailored vehicle designed to showcase the stinging wit, been there-done that malaise, and daring sexuality that audiences loved in *Lifeboat*. Guess what, folks: she got that ideal follow-up role and no one cared. As man-eating Catherine the Great in the frivolous black-and-white romp *A Royal Scandal*, the Ernst Lubitsch-produced remake of his silent *Forbidden Paradise* (1924), Bankhead is a high-comic virtuosa. It wasn't her fault that the film died an unjustly quick death at the box office, providing a *second* finish to her movie career. She'd been among dozens of stage stars who'd entered studio soundstages in the early 1930s, answering the call for "talking" actors. After making little impression in a handful of disappointing films, she returned to Broadway where she had her two greatest triumphs: *The Little Foxes* in 1939 and *The Skin of Our Teeth* in 1942. These plays made her so hot that Hollywood beckoned once more, and the Hitchcock picture proved that she could score in the movies. It won her the New York Film Critics' Best Actress Award, but she was denied an Oscar nomination (an outrage). Most people think of *Lifeboat* as the only film that effectively used Bankhead, but I'm happy to report that *A Royal Scandal* preserves her comic brilliance at its peak. Rarely seen, it's the Holy Grail of her movie career.

A Royal Scandal is a sex comedy very much like *The Affairs of Cellini* (1934), with eighteenth-century Russia standing in for sixteenth-century Italy. It will come as no surprise that *Scandal*'s screenplay (which supplies Tallulah with remarkably few of her signature "dahlings") was written by Edwin Justus Mayer, the man whose play *(The Firebrand)* was the source material for *Cellini*. Not a moment of either film is meant to be taken seriously, and that's why both are enchantingly light, libido-engined treats. Treason lurks behind every palace door, but Empress Catherine doesn't let that interfere with her appetite for the fellas. When Alexei (William Eythe), a sweet-faced young soldier, arrives to warn her of a dangerous plot, Catherine realizes she's just found her newest plaything. Alexei doesn't realize that his startling rise to Commander of the Palace Guard has more to do with his eye-filling torso than with his laborious edicts for the betterment of Russia. Countess Anna (Anne Baxter), one of Catherine's ladies-in-waiting, is Alexei's fiancée, and she isn't going to give him up without a fight.

It's hard to resist a movie in which the jewel-laden czarina's first utterance is a "Shut up!" to her crooked chancellor (Charles Coburn). Catherine may be known as Mother Russia, but don't dare call her that to her face or you'll get a look that'll freeze your blood (she apparently has good aim with vases too). Whipping a busy handkerchief around to stress certain points, Bankhead takes a delicate prop and makes it a witty acting partner. With her insinuatingly low growl of a voice, a husky instrument capable of surprising nuance and flawless diction, she can get anyone to do anything she wants: any *man* anyway. She opts for sisterly warmth as a tactic to get her twenty-two-year-old rival, Anna, out of her way. Bankhead's a hoot offering Anna a chance to visit her *"dear* little mother." She wrings so much comic juice out of the word *dear* that it's suddenly a two-syllable word. But Anna is immune to Catherine's calculating friendliness. When the empress points out that she's an older-but-wiser thirty-three years old, Anna corrects her with, "Thirty-*seven.*" Aghast at the girl's temerity, Catherine fires back with unbridled cries of, "Siberia!"

When Alexei literally bursts into her life, Catherine's initial displeasure quickly turns to lust. Upon learning that he possesses the stamina to ride three days and three nights to see her (he's *still* not tired) and that he's just twenty-four years old, Catherine slips into predator mode. Bankhead brought a carnal hunger to her roles that was rare in 1940s Hollywood. (Remember the blatantly open-mouthed kiss she planted on John Hodiak in *Lifeboat*?) William Eythe's Jimmy Stewart-like innocence is the perfect contrast to her world-weary grandeur, and they make a delectably funny mismatch (reminiscent of aggressor Mae West putting the moves on a boyish Cary Grant). In the seduction scene, Bankhead flaunts herself in an off-the-shoulder, white-feathered gown, just the right mix of sin and purity (designer René Hubert clearly having a wonderful time). Her Catherine poutingly speaks of her loneliness and, after maneuvering their first kiss, tosses her head back with a dramatic, "I wish you hadn't." But to keep her white-uniformed hunk happy, she must pretend to be interested in his ideas for progress, which leads to an exquisite exchange about the peasants that raises the film to loopy heights. Supremely uninterested in the peasants, she rattles off her comments as if fascinated by the topic. ("There's nothing like a good peasant.")

Producer Lubitsch, in failing health, didn't take on double duty, leaving the directing chores to Otto Preminger. Unfortunately, Preminger's halfhearted work offers little visual imagination, resulting in a film that too often feels talky and stagy. But the jaunty script and game cast come to the rescue. Anne Baxter, who years later would inexplicably do a Tallulah imitation when she infamously groaned, "Moses, Moses," in *The Ten Commandments* (1956), makes Anna a saucy, fresh ingénue. Eythe is a most appealing comic foil whom you may remember from dramatic parts in *The Ox-Bow Incident* (1943) and *The Song of Bernadette* (1943). The supporting cast is a melting pot: Charles Coburn, Sig Ruman, Mischa Auer, and a drawling Grady Sutton, each delightful in his own idiosyncratic way. Then there's Vincent Price as the French ambassador; is he kidding with that untraceable accent? This oddball assortment is on hand to remind you that this glittery diversion will make no attempt to bring you anything resembling history, Russia, or even Catherine herself. Sadly, 1945 audiences were not in the mood.

No one but Bankhead could have given the role as much haughty glamour (or could have so commandingly carried such a perilously high hairdo); okay, Marlene Dietrich could have, but she lacked Tallulah's take-no-prisoners comic precision. (Dietrich played Catherine in Josef von Sternberg's 1934 drama *The Scarlet Empress*, a candidate for most insane, over-the-top movie *ever*.) I'm sorry to say, Bankhead would star in only one other film; I'm even sorrier that it was *Die! Die! My Darling!* (1965). Oh, it's compulsory camp: she tries to outdo Bette Davis in the "Baby Jane" sweepstakes, easily getting me to root *for* her deranged Mrs. Trefoile and *against* glossy victim Stefanie Powers. But it's still a depressing waste of her talent. You can cure that depression with *A Royal Scandal*.

Jerry Austin, Flora Robson, and Ingrid Bergman

Ingrid Bergman

IN

Saratoga Trunk

(1945)

A FTER director Sam Wood and his stars, Gary Cooper and Ingrid
Bergman, made Paramount's *For Whom the Bell Tolls* (1943), they
were reassembled, this time at Warner Brothers, for another grand-scale
literary adaptation, Edna Ferber's *Saratoga Trunk*. The first film, from
Ernest Hemingway's novel, is an epic-length, memorable picture, successful as both poignant love story and nail-biting action-adventure.
Cooper's stoicism and Bergman's soulfulness created bona fide chemistry
in their depiction of an earth-shaking love, their shared blue-eyed beauty
enhanced by Technicolor. As the war-ravaged Maria, Bergman, fresh
from playing *Casablanca*'s own war-torn heroine, is radiance personified.
In a showy change of pace, she went from blond Maria's simplicity and
faithfulness to *Saratoga Trunk*'s Clio Dulaine, a dark-haired, man-dangling
fortune hunter. Clio was a rare comic role for her, a chance to indulge a
more explicitly sexy and gutsy Ingrid Bergman. Unfortunately, the surrounding film, a late-nineteenth-century spectacle in high-sheen black-
and-white, is lumbering and disjointed, but Bergman doesn't let that get
her down and tears into this opportunity to overthrow audience perceptions of her as angelic, victimized, and serious. Clio is a Cajun-spiced
Scarlett O'Hara: both characters are gorgeous; both make us laugh; and,
most fascinating, both know how to make things *happen*.

Paris-raised Clio returns to New Orleans, her birthplace, and reno-
vates her late mother's dilapidated house. She is eager to take revenge on
her father's aristocratic Creole family, whom she blames for ruining her
unwed mother's life. (They had exiled her to Paris after she accidentally
shot her lover, Clio's father, dead.) Clio seeks to marry a millionaire and
grab respectability so she'll never be unprotected the way her weak, all-
for-love mother was. She meets a virile Texas gambler, Clint Maroon
(Cooper); though he's not rich, they begin a tempestuous affair. After set-
tling her score with her mortified relatives, she follows Clint to Saratoga,

151

millionaire land, setting her sights on Bartholomew Van Steed (John Warburton) and soon has him eating out of her gloved hands. Yet Clio, who can't forget Clint, is frustrated by being unsure of what she really wants. (There's a pointless subplot about railroad corruption, giving Cooper more to do, but it's a snore.)

Rules don't apply to Clio; a self-assured Bergman glides through this movie like a goddess utterly aware of, and tickled by, her beautiful attributes. Extravagantly gowned and coiffed, she accepts her looks as a happy given and has a ball wielding them to her advantage. Clio has her father's elegance and her mother's passion, a personality as striking as her defiantly pronounced eyebrows. There's nothing half-way about her, be it her bratty tantrums or her voracious appetites: her laugh is unbridled; her smile is wicked; her bursts of singing are seductively enrapturing. I particularly enjoy Bergman's eating scenes, such as her first taste of jambalaya, which makes me want to pull up a spoon and join her. She gets all worked up over the sounds of a peach vendor (like a child at the ice-cream man's bells), soon reveling in her favored libation: champagne with a fresh peach floating in it. In a performance that can truly be described as sensual, Bergman embraces *all* her senses. There's no mistaking what she's thinking the first few times she gets an eyeful of Cooper. He's a tall drink of water, and she's mighty thirsty. Clio and "Cleent," as she calls him, have a sparring, two-of-a-kind, Scarlett-and-Rhett dynamic—she'll not be tamed, and he won't be a chump. She maddens him with her selfish willfulness, but, damn, she's the most exciting creature he's ever met. And she knows it. (When she tells him there is no one like her, it won't even occur to you to doubt her.) Clio treats him like a boy toy, delighting in their lovemaking and cat-and-mouse games, but she does not want him to interfere with her plans. She'll not be dissuaded from brazenly taunting the Dulaines, flaunting her glittering presence all over town. Bergman relishes the playacting aspect of Clio without losing the real rage beneath the artifice. Clio's birthright setbacks are coal in her furnace, and even when playful, Bergman doesn't let us forget that.

Passing herself off as a widowed countess, and treating all in her path with a gracious superiority, her arrival in Saratoga is a triumph. Clio's barrage of magnetism, glamour, and enthusiasm is intoxicating; her wheels are always turning, but Bergman's engine is so smooth that she makes it all seem a lark. Clio's theatrical sense is impeccable, as is Bergman's. (There's a scene where she bolts out of bed, a breathtaking force of nature, joyfully ready to devour the world.) Always at her side are her two loyal servants, Angelique (a heavy-on-the-makeup Flora Robson) and Cupidon (little person Jerry Austin), both bearing the brunt of Clio's quicksilver moods.

Ingrid Bergman in *Saratoga Trunk* (1945)

Bergman, under her breath, is casually, caustically funny when she tosses off, "Keep quiet, Angelique, or I'll send you away somewhere to starve." She meets a near match in Sophie Bellop (Florence Bates), an influential old bat willing, for a purse, to help Clio nab Van Steed. Sophie calls Clio "bold and dramatic and believable," and it's certainly true of Bergman. But the closer Clio gets to her goal, the more rankled she is by a nagging, amatory feeling for Clint. It's a realization that disrupts her surefire agenda, and Bergman flares with petulance. The film ends with a so-called comic scene, undermining Clio in a chauvinistic way. Better to remember Bergman up until then: fearless, scintillating, and crafty.

Long and lumpy, *Saratoga Trunk* is entertaining junk, elevated whenever Bergman takes it by the reins. The railroad subplot, including a train wreck and a cast-of-hundreds brawl, is so poorly done and is such a desperate ploy to give the film action that all I'm thinking is, "Where's Ingrid?" Casey Robinson's screenplay gives her savory material, but its obvious *Gone With the Wind* pretensions are futile (despite the resplendent period decor). It's fun to spot the blatant *GWTW* nods, such as Clio's I'll-think-about-that-tomorrow close-up when Clint leaves New Orleans, or the scene in which she hovers while he packs a bag (and then leaves her), reminiscent of Scarlett and Rhett's last scene. Cooper breezes through the film in a Rhett-ish, peripheral way. His light Texas twang and laid-back composure complement Bergman's fanciful allure. The movie, completed in 1943, didn't open until 1945 and wasn't widely distributed until 1946, so Flora Robson waited a long time for her supporting Oscar nomination, a tribute for surviving bizarre casting. (A better idea would have been to nominate lethal Florence Bates, a shark who merely looks like a granny.) Speaking of looks, Bergman's dark hair heightens her resemblance to her daughter, Isabella Rossellini, but it's Sophia Loren, with her flair for naughty amusement and grand "attitude" (in the best of her 1960s Italian comedies), that Bergman may bring to mind.

Dorothy McGuire on the title role

Dorothy McGuire

IN

The Spiral Staircase

(1946)

A N incandescent Dorothy McGuire revived the art of silent-screen acting when she played Helen, the mute servant in Robert Siodmak's *Spiral Staircase*, a scary movie for grown-ups. It was her fourth film, and she'd been a fast-rising young film actress since her debut as the childlike wife *Claudia* (1943), a role she had played to acclaim on Broadway. Her second film was Elia Kazan's adaptation of *A Tree Grows in Brooklyn* (1945) in which she's highly impressive as the rigid mother, a realist plainly bruised by her disenchanted life. She then scored as the homely girl physically transformed by love in the memorable fantasy *The Enchanted Cottage* (1945), costarring Robert Young (who was also her leading man in *Claudia* and its 1946 sequel, *Claudia and David*). McGuire possessed a girl-next-door prettiness and an unforced screen presence, but it was her genuine talent that separated her from scores of equally attractive contract players. I can't imagine that many of them could have sustained a hold on an audience as gripping as McGuire's when she played Helen. Without words, without screams (Fay Wray need not apply), she focused on Helen's every thought and action and never fell into the obvious trap of overdoing her gestures and eye movements.

Mel Dinelli's tightly crafted screenplay, based on Ethel Lina White's novel *Some Must Watch*, is set at the dawn of the twentieth century. A serial killer is on the loose in a small New England town; his victims are defenseless women, each with some kind of disability. The film takes place over the course of a single action-packed day and primarily unfolds at the sumptuous mansion of bedridden dowager Mrs. Warren (Ethel Barrymore). Her son Steven (Gordon Oliver) and stepson Albert (George Brent) are great disappointments to her, but she has a maternal fondness for Helen and fears for the young woman's safety. Helen is in love with Mrs. Warren's physician, Dr. Parry (Kent Smith), but he's been unable to convince her to seek help in facing the trauma that has rendered her speechless since childhood (and has now made her a prime target). It's not too long before Helen discovers a dead body in the basement, realizes there's no one in the house who can save her and, while a storm rages, comes face to face with the killer.

The first time we see Helen she's being thoroughly entranced by a silent movie. This is a cleverly fitting start to a film that reminds us of the unique spell a dialogue-free performance can exert. Helen is a pleasant young woman, comfortable with her coworkers and employers, and shares a particularly warm and caring relationship with Mrs. Warren. There's an amusing playfulness between them that is our first clue that there's more to Helen than wide-eyed innocence and domestic efficiency. Just don't bring up the subject of her past. When Dr. Parry mentions a visitor from Helen's hometown, she knows that he's learned her family history and that he intends to dredge it up. McGuire tenses Helen like a frightened animal with no means of escape. As Parry recounts the story he's heard, everything he says is magnified in her face; she soundlessly relives a personal tragedy that's as immediate for her as the day it happened (and still impossible to confront). Under the penetrating scrutiny of an extended close-up, Helen's rising agony peaks in McGuire's heartbreakingly choked squeal. The happy-in-her-work servant dissolves into an emotionally crippled child.

The surprise of McGuire's performance is its core of strength and calculating ingenuity. Even though Helen would appear to be a classic victim, she's no cowering waif tied to the railroad tracks. Despite a failed attempt to phone for help, painfully struggling for words that will not come, she's remarkably coolheaded. When she uncovers a corpse in the basement, there's a chilling moment when the breeze from an open door tells her she's not alone. McGuire turns her head very slowly, almost calmly, but we know Helen is terrified. (Who wouldn't be?) Now, I've always believed that any candle-clutching heroine who ventures into a pitch-black basement while a madman is lurking *deserves* to be murdered. But McGuire's intense awareness of her surroundings inspires confidence; she transmits each of Helen's suspicions and flickers of discovery as she *thinks* them. Notable, too, is the pulse-quickening physical agility of her work. She races through that house at the speed of terror, hurling herself from one potentially life-saving situation to the next. Her final scene provides a much-needed cathartic release that is delicately played and deeply touching.

The Spiral Staircase is the ultimate stormy-night, spooky-house, psycho-killer thriller. Although its mystery isn't difficult to figure out, the film delivers consistently tingling entertainment. Siodmak's unsettling and imaginative handling of the murders (including the murderer's point-of-view shots) is worthy of Hitchcock at his best. Nicholas Musuraca's moody black-and-white photography prowls the gloriously designed house with the menace of a nightmare (the titular staircase is forebodingly showcased). Roy Webb composed the lush *Rebecca*-like score, enhancing the romantic nature of the material and its classy period setting. Ethel Barrymore, who does her grand-dame bit perhaps more nurturingly than usual, got an Oscar nomination. George Brent's complicated Albert was a nice break from the cardboard "love interest" roles that were his mainstay. (He must have been tired of wooing Davis and Stanwyck over and over again.) And the always-welcome Elsa Lanchester, as the brandy-nipping cook, is the quirky treat you'd expect her to be.

McGuire's next big one was Elia Kazan's *Gentleman's Agreement* (1947), a Best Picture Oscar winner that made good use of her gift for playing unlikeable ordinary people (a harder task than playing larger-than-life schemers), resulting in her sole Oscar nomination. Her roles in the 1950s were less challenging, but like Jane Wyman (who won an Oscar for *her* mute role in 1948's *Johnny Belinda*), McGuire kept moviegoers happy with superficial soaps. The most popular were the unbearably dated *Three Coins in the Fountain* (1954), in which she masochistically pines for Clifton Webb when she could be outside enjoying Rome (thus completely losing my sympathy), and the slick theme-song-driven film *A Summer Place* (1959). She had worthier roles as the mothers in the overpraised *Friendly Persuasion* (1956) and the underpraised *Dark at the Top of the Stairs* (1960), the latter stolen by Angela Lansbury *and* Eve Arden (too close to call). Her last good gig was her association with Disney, which brought us *Old Yeller* (1957), *Swiss Family Robinson* (1960), and *Summer Magic* (1963). Nothing ever topped her string of successes in the mid 1940s, with *The Spiral Staircase* the primary beneficiary of her radiant simplicity.

Henry Hull and Ida Lupino

Ida Lupino

IN

Deep Valley
(1947)

WHEN you're watching Ida Lupino in a quintessential role, like straight-shooting nightclub singer Petey Brown in *The Man I Love* (1946), it's hard to accept the fact that she came to Hollywood from England. Has any British performer been as consistently convincing as one of us? (Her family's theatrical roots go back to Renaissance Italy, where the Lupinos were strolling players; they emigrated to England in the seventeenth century.) She spent the mid to late 1930s wasted in ingénue roles, unrecognizable as the Ida Lupino she would soon become. Her Bessie in *The Light That Failed* (1939), the flashiest Cockney since Bette Davis in *Of Human Bondage* (1934), catapulted her in much the same way that *Bondage* elevated Davis; the two actresses shared a hyperreal style in which they seemed to set themselves on fire when angered. Signed by Warners (Davis's studio), Lupino was cast in *They Drive by Night* (1940), a remake of Davis's *Bordertown* (1935), topping her predecessor's version of the climactic witness-stand mad scene. In Americanizing the bracing bravura she brought to Bessie, she fit herself into the Warners mold of urban toughness, and it defined her persona thereafter. Ostensibly in Davis's shadow, Lupino still emerged as one of the 1940s' finer and more versatile actresses. (Consider her haunting Emily Brontë in *Devotion* [1946].) With eyes like high-beam headlights, you cannot look away from her. Though never an Oscar nominee, she won the New York Film Critics' Award for *The Hard Way* (1943), a spicy, if uneven, tale of big, bad showbiz. In the kind of grasping and manipulative role in which audiences liked her best (and one that anticipates Mama Rose in *Gypsy*), she gives a tensely controlled performance, though her ice-veined scheming starts to feel one-note after a while. I much prefer her in *Deep Valley*, her final Warners film and one that has never received its due. In one of my all-time favorite examples of casting against type, Lupino, the epitome of brittle glamour, delves into the role of a stuttering farm girl without a single cigarette or cocktail and with no defensive wisecracks as weaponry.

159

Libby Saul (Lupino) lives on an isolated and dilapidated farm near the rocky cliffs of the California coast, a virtual servant to her estranged parents (Fay Bainter and Henry Hull). Avoiding each other since a confrontation seven years earlier, her mother and father occupy different floors of the house. Libby's only solace is her walks in the woods with her dog, Joe. She sometimes watches the laboring convicts, including Barry Burnette (Dane Clark), build the new coastal highway. After a row with her father, Libby runs away to a cabin in the woods where she finds an escaped Barry. Free from the confines of their miserable lives, they fall in love, intent on having a new beginning elsewhere. Libby hides Barry in the Sauls' barn loft, sneaking up to see him whenever she can. But they cannot make their move until the posse gives up its relentless search for him.

How is Lupino believable as a psychologically battered twenty-two-year-old? Without the slightest condescension for her child-woman role, she listens and reacts with thought to everything around her. Channeling her patented electricity within, she burrows her way into Libby's withdrawn sadness. Lupino also softens the scotch-soaked gravel in her voice to make Libby's sheltered innocence and debilitating stammer ring true. Barefoot and in jeans, she's a 1940s Cinderella, with endless chores and an absence of love in her life. In her jaunts through the woods (to the hysterically happy strains of Max Steiner's score), Lupino, no longer the family drudge, releases pure pleasure in Libby's nature-girl existence. Unlike a typical Lupino role, Libby operates on emotion rather than smarts, instinct rather than calculation, and her heart is big enough to ache for all other mistreated creatures. The first time she comes face to face with Barry (when the road workers stop by the farm for drinking water), it's like looking in a mirror; his loneliness and victimization mark him a kindred spirit, and she openly weeps when he's taken away in handcuffs for striking a guard. Lupino is even more poignantly fragile in her stormy-night showdown with her father. As he cruelly belittles her, she reverts to a trapped, frightened child, a transformation that enables her to confront him with a painful memory; it's a catharsis that gives her the resolve to find her own way.

After she finds Barry in her secret cabin, it doesn't take long for the pair to fall in love. He has a definite violent streak, but Libby intuitively knows the real him. When the moment comes for their first kiss, in an idyllic woods setting, Lupino's Libby looks as if she knows it is going to change her profoundly, and it's almost more than she can bear. When their lips part, she closes her eyes, nestles her head against his chest, and is overcome with the feeling of home, a discovery of where she belongs. Transforming love is the core strength of Lupino's performance; it empowers Libby with confidence and purpose, and, of course, cures her stutter. Despite the odds against their

Ida Lupino in *Deep Valley* (1947)

bypassing the law, Libby remains unceasingly optimistic; her newfound happiness outweighs the strain of her efforts to safeguard their future. Back on the farm (with Barry hiding in the barn), the once-unkempt Libby is now a fresh, vibrant girl, showing herself off to Barry in an off-the-shoulder dress (and a flower in her hair), thrilled to be feeling attractive; the amount of genuine girlishness Lupino is able to effect is astonishing. There's a lovely scene where she tells Barry that, after they're married, she'd like to pick out his suits; Lupino's commitment to Libby's domestic fantasy is touching in its blind faith. It's a revelatory achievement that this formidable actress could pull off a character of such heartrending simplicity *after* audiences had identified her as a been-around-the-block dame.

Director Jean Negulesco is able to meld on-the-run suspense, household psychodrama, and passionate romance into one unusually compelling package. Ted McCord's evocative black-and-white photography enhances the ruggedness of the location landscapes and the scary-movie grimness of the farmhouse. The richly textured screenplay by Salka Viertel and Stephen Morehouse Avery, based on a novel by Dan Totheroh, plays like a dark fairy tale: a girl and her dog leave a "haunted" house and find adventure, love, and danger in the woods. (In the book, Libby doesn't stutter, but she does get pregnant.) The script doesn't spell out everything for us in its depiction of Libby's parents' strange relationship, which is acted superbly by Bainter and Hull. Dane Clark, the second-string John Garfield and well cast as Barry, effectively mixes tenderness and fury. Negulesco, McCord, and Max Steiner would share a major success with *Johnny Belinda* (1948), another highly atmospheric film centered on an unfortunate young woman.

Lupino reunited with Negulesco on *Road House* (1948), my other favorite of her films, which put her in a comfortably trashy milieu as chain-smoking Lily Stevens, croaking out tunes in a bowling-alley lounge. A year later, she began a career as a director, producer, and writer on a series of low-budget films, the best being *The Hitch-Hiker* (1953), for The Filmakers, a company she formed with then-husband Collier Young. As an actress of unstinting courage and considerable range, *and* as the only female director working in 1950s Hollywood, Lupino was a singular artist, a pioneer, and an obvious candidate for an honorary Oscar, which, unconscionably, never came: she died in 1995. Instead of being in Bette Davis's shadow or in anyone else's, Ida Lupino cast a pretty wide shadow herself, leaving a legacy that defies comparison with that of any other.

Wendell Corey, John Hodiak, Lizabeth Scott, and Mary Astor

Mary Astor

IN

Desert Fury

(1947)

ROM her days as an angel-faced ingénue of the silent era to her memorable swan song as Jewel Mayhew in *Hush . . . Hush, Sweet Charlotte* (1964), Mary Astor showed inexhaustible versatility without ever becoming a star of the first rank. She is best remembered as scheming Brigid O'Shaughnessy, one of her rare leading roles, in John Huston's greed-driven masterpiece *The Maltese Falcon* (1941). This femme fatale character set the standard for all the bad girls of the upcoming film noir period, which lasted from the mid 1940s to the mid 1950s. That same year, she won the Best Supporting Actress Oscar for going head to head with Bette Davis in the juicy "woman's picture" *The Great Lie*. Astor's role as a bitchy concert pianist was a showstopper, and she played it to the histrionic hilt. (Even Davis seems knocked out by her.) Her dizzy, sex-crazed Princess Centimillia of *The Palm Beach Story* (1942) proved that she was also an accomplished screwball comedienne. Can it really be just two years later that she played matronly Mrs. Smith in *Meet Me in St. Louis*? She hadn't aged all that much in the interim, and yet the warmth and wisdom she brought to the role makes her seem considerably older than the madcap Princess. After *Meet Me in St. Louis*, she was saddled with thankless mother roles (her mopey Mexican madre of twins Esther Williams and Ricardo Montalban in *Fiesta* [1947] has to be her lowest point), but every once in a while a choice part came her way. *Desert Fury*'s Fritzie Haller was a mother role and a supporting role, but that didn't stop Astor from walking off with the movie.

Fritzie, the most powerful woman in Chuckawalla, owns and operates the Purple Sage casino. Her nineteen-year-old daughter, Paula (Lizabeth Scott), has just dropped out of yet another school, and Fritzie wants to marry her off to respectable cop Tom Hanson (Burt Lancaster). But Paula is excited by gambler Eddie Bendix (John Hodiak), Fritzie's old flame, who has just arrived in town with his ever-present partner,

Johnny Ryan (Wendell Corey). Johnny resents Paula's attempts to take Eddie away from him, and thus begins a tug-of-war for Eddie's attention. (I'm not making this up!) Will Johnny quietly step aside? Can Fritzie convince Paula that Eddie is a heel? Paula must follow her heart and make her own choices regarding her future.

When Fritzie talks of her humble beginnings, Astor makes you believe that this is a woman for whom life has been a constant battle, yet she has not a shred of self-pity. She rules her kingdom with the confidence of someone who has always taken care of herself. The way she wields her cigarette holder (her favorite prop) suggests that she has had enough worldly experience to intimidate anyone she chooses. Astor plants her feet firmly on the ground, delivers her lines with bite and brains, and creates a character who lives her life without apology or explanation. She is Mildred Pierce without the sentiment, the masochism, or the piecrusts (you won't find Fritzie near a kitchen). Fritzie doesn't expect anything from people except what she's willing to buy from them. Although still very attractive (and sporting a swanky Edith Head wardrobe), she seems to have ruled out romance as an option. Men have only meant trouble in the past, and she'll never make herself that vulnerable again. If loneliness is the price, then so be it.

Paula is the only person who can disrupt Fritzie's controlled world. If Fritzie's life has any purpose, it is in what she can do for her beloved daughter; the rest is just business dealings with people she doesn't like. Fritzie wants Paula to have the respectability she never had, and she's willing to use her money to buy it for her in the form of Tom. But Paula can be as hardheaded as Fritzie. The pleasure Astor's Fritzie displays in having her daughter's companionship soon dissipates into frustration once Paula becomes infatuated with Eddie. (Shades of *Mildred Pierce* again as mother and daughter have relations with the same guy.) Fritzie's intentions are for Paula's good, but Astor plays her with an obstinacy that doesn't allow her to try to understand her daughter. Fritzie is right, and that's all there is to it. It's hard for her to sit back and watch Paula make the same mistake she made. She hasn't built up an empire so that her daughter can run off with a faithless gambler. Fritzie eventually speaks honestly with Paula about her past with Eddie, but nothing she says is as revealing as Astor's expressions every time his name is mentioned. In Astor's eyes, we see all of the regret, humiliation, and pain still there after ten years.

Desert Fury is no classic, but director Lewis Allen keeps the melodrama chugging along at a good pace, aided by the ravishing color cinematography of Charles Lang and Edward Cronjager. It's rare to see a film noir story given the Technicolor treatment (you half expect Carmen Miranda to show up in Chuckawalla). *Leave Her to Heaven* (1945) and *Slightly Scarlet* (1956) are two other noirish tales whose use of vibrant color makes you sit up and take notice. The intensity of *Desert Fury*'s colors may also remind you of the Douglas Sirk pictures, such as *Written on the Wind* (1956), of the following decade. Lizabeth Scott's wooden acting makes it easy for you to become transfixed by her crimson lips and luxurious blond hair. John Hodiak is hardly an exciting enough presence here to warrant all the lustful attention coming his way, while hunky Burt Lancaster is wasted in the dull, nice-guy role. But Wendell Corey, in his film debut, certainly makes an impression as Johnny. His hell-hath-no-fury performance is the most unambiguously homosexual characterization of Hollywood's Golden Age. Nevertheless, *Desert Fury*'s acting honors belong to Mary Astor, who dominates the film by locating the humanity beneath this tawdry tale. Her lean, unfussy approach to Fritzie cuts through the plot's extravagance, creating the only three-dimensional character in the piece. You relax whenever she appears on the screen because you know you're in good hands.

Astor made a habit of giving substance to trashy movies (she's the only reason to *Return to Peyton Place* [1961]) and making potentially bland roles luminous (Walter Huston's new love in 1936's *Dodsworth*). Another of my favorites is her role in *Red Dust* (1932) where, as Gene Raymond's prim wife, she develops an adulterous passion for Clark Gable. If all this weren't enough, she wrote two exceptional autobiographies, *My Story* (1959) and *A Life on Film* (1971), which possess the same strength and intelligence she brought to Fritzie.

Tyrone Power and James Flavin (as the carnival owner)

Tyrone Power

IN

Nightmare Alley
(1947)

No one really feels sorry for beautiful movie stars who complain about not being taken seriously as actors. And yet, when confronted with irrefutable proof of talent, I want to do my share in righting any wrongs committed by the industry and moviegoers alike. Take Tyrone Power: in the right role, he could be wonderful. He'd been a major star at Twentieth Century-Fox for a decade when *Nightmare Alley* came along. He shot to fame in spectacles like *Lloyd's of London* (1936), *In Old Chicago* (1937), and *Suez* (1938). (His appeal was strong enough to survive two frostbitten Sonja Henie musicals.) The studio toughened his image with great success in *Jesse James* (1939), *The Mark of Zorro* (1940), and *Blood and Sand* (1941). Power was always enjoyable to watch, even though his roles were usually one-dimensional. His career was interrupted by military service in World War II, and when he returned, he seemed determined to make a name for himself as an actor. *The Razor's Edge* was a big hit in 1946 (and a surprising Best Picture Oscar nominee), but it hardly proved his worth. The role of Larry Darrell is too cerebral, and his journey toward self-fulfillment is fuzzy and rather a bore. It was the trashy elements in the story that made the picture so popular. *Nightmare Alley* is a far superior film, but it flopped at the box office, and Power went back to making variations of his prewar hits, such as *Prince of Foxes* (1949) and *The Black Rose* (1950). John Ford's *Long Gray Line* (1955) and Billy Wilder's *Witness for the Prosecution* (1957) gave him good roles at the end of his career, but they were exceptions. Stan Carlisle in *Nightmare Alley* was the best role he ever got and resulted in the performance of his career.

Stan is a ruthless opportunist working in a seedy carnival with big dreams of rising to the top. He works with Zeena (Joan Blondell) and her broken-down husband, Pete (Ian Keith), in a mind-reading act, but that won't satisfy him for long. Stan wants Zeena to teach him the mind-reading code she hasn't used since her days in the big time. After accidentally causing Pete's death, Stan becomes Zeena's partner and soon finds himself learning the tightly guarded code. Having no more use for Zeena, he leaves the carnival with his new carny bride, Molly (Coleen Gray), finding success on the nightclub circuit as The Great Stanton. Stan then hooks up with crooked psychologist Lilith Ritter (Helen Walker in one of the iciest roles of all time) so that he can enter the "spook" racket. Using his charisma and her patient files, they use spiritualism to hoodwink wealthy suckers into thinking he can converse with their dead loved ones. They're making lots of money when the whole thing comes crashing down on him.

In a role in which you might expect to see Burt Lancaster, Tyrone Power is everything you could ask for. He doesn't try to pretend that he doesn't look like Tyrone Power. He uses his beauty and sexuality as a key element in his characterization. He's the smoothest of smooth operators, and neither Zeena nor Molly can resist him. Instead of being sexually rough with his women, he's intimate and gentle, and it works like a charm. Power also conveys the unstoppability of Stan's ambitions by appearing always to be planning his next move. (You can catch him several times not listening to his wife's words because he's consumed with his next plot.) But Stan doesn't seem particularly villainous; he doesn't wish to harm anyone. He has no enemies, no vendettas. He does have a general contempt for people, but it's nothing personal. Conning is just the thing that's been working for him his whole life. He thinks of everyone as the chumps in the audience. Occasional feelings of guilt, superstition, and fear don't last long.

Though utterly selfish, Stan doesn't pity himself; he just keeps on going despite any setbacks. He's not entirely free of gullibility himself, and that's one reason you never really dislike him. His treatment of Molly seems rather careless until we come to see that he has genuine feeling for her (which surprises him as well). But Stan is most alive when in control—and never more so than when performing his act or in personal contact with one of his victims. His satisfaction comes in his skill at manipulating people. He seduces his way into their psyches, and it's a powerful drug. Power projects the thrill and danger inherent in any live performance. Stan is a true actor and absorbs everything around him that may be of use to him. Watch him in the scene where he finesses the cop who has threatened to shut down the carnival. Using every trick he's learned so far, Stan persuasively passes himself off to the poor fool as a decent, sensitive human being. The cop goes off meekly, and it's Power's mesmerizing performance that has made the con so believable. At moments like these, Stan appears invincible. Of course, he's not, and Power brings his path to destruction to chilling life.

Tyrone Power in *Nightmare Alley* (1947)

Edmund Goulding, having directed this film and *The Razor's Edge*, was Power's director of the moment. In a career that included *Grand Hotel* and *Dark Victory*, Goulding's best work remains *Nightmare Alley*. It's one of those films in which everyone seems to be in peak form. Lee Garmes's extraordinary black-and-white cinematography vividly depicts several distinct locations, such as the grim and shabby carnival, the shiny, glamorous nightclub, and a hazy, lush palatial garden. Jules Furthman's screenplay (based on William Lindsay Gresham's novel) is hard-hitting, thoroughly gripping, and adult. It's also unusually cynical for the period. That cynicism (aimed at showbiz, spiritualism, and psychology) makes the film seem modern, as does the character of Stan himself.

Joan Blondell had one of her better parts in Zeena. She's particularly good at bringing out the conflict in Zeena's maternal and sexual sides. Ian Keith's Pete and Taylor Holmes's Mr. Grindle (one of Stan's wealthy followers) make indelible impressions with little screen time. Power's scene in Grindle's garden is the best scene in the movie, as all the elements come together in one unforgettable "nightmare." And what about Helen Walker as Lilith? She is one scary dame who will probably make you want to cancel your next therapy session.

The film's financial failure robbed Tyrone Power of the Oscar nomination he deserved to get. And he watched all the best roles at Fox go to Gregory Peck. Not to take anything away from Peck, but it's interesting to imagine what Power might have done with *Gentleman's Agreement* (1947) or *Twelve O'Clock High* (1949). I sure am glad we don't have to imagine him in *Nightmare Alley*.

Gladys Cooper and Judy Garland arrive in Port Sebastion

Judy Garland

IN

The Pirate
(1948)

PICK up any of the many books about the incomparable Judy Garland and read about the ghastly experience of making *The Pirate*. With her marriage to its director, Vincente Minnelli, deteriorating, and with her dependency on pills worsening, Garland's fragile health and resulting absences caused the filming to be endless, and the budget skyrocketed. When it was finally released, the unheard of occurred: a Judy Garland musical was a box-office loser. With its tongue-in-cheek sophistication and Latin fairyland setting, *The Pirate* was an oddity in an era of musicals that concentrated on composer biographies, backstage tales, and period Americana. If 1948 audiences didn't know what to make of its winking theatricality, time has surely been its ally. Second only to *Meet Me in St. Louis* (1944), the first Minnelli-Garland picture, *The Pirate* stands as MGM's next best musical of the 1940s, holding up better than, say, *Easter Parade* (1948) or *On the Town* (1949). Call it celluloid magic, but Garland's offscreen problems don't show in her performance. For all the flamboyant flair provided by Minnelli and a mustachioed Gene Kelly, it comes as no surprise that it is she who provides the heart and makes the story emotionally enchanting; without her soulful glow, it might look merely like a lot of showing off. An instinctual and fearless comedienne, she was also never funnier than she is here. In short, Judy is flat-out wonderful, and *The Pirate*, a bursting piñata of a musical, is a semiburied treasure that has been waiting more than fifty years for the acclaim it deserves.

On a Caribbean island in the early nineteenth century, Manuela Alva (Garland) escapes the doldrums of her provincial village in her dreams of Macoco, a real-life cutthroat. Aunt Inez (Gladys Cooper, in a high-comic break from her meanie roles) arranges Manuela's marriage to the middle-aged, portly mayor, Don Pedro (Walter Slezak). On a trip to Port Sebastion to meet her trousseau, she is pursued shamelessly by Serafin (Kelly), a strolling player. He learns of her infatuation with Macoco

171

when he hypnotizes her during a performance, and (still in a trance) she wows the crowd with a song. Serafin now wants her for the troupe, as well as for himself. He arrives in her village on her wedding day, discovers the real Macoco in their midst but, determined to win her, proclaims *himself* the pitiless, dashing pirate of her dreams.

Garland's Manuela is a Dorothy-like orphan, yearning for a world beyond her own, and she speaks of Macoco to her girlfriends with the impassioned relish of a loyal groupie. (Sorely missing from this first section of the movie is the opportunity for Garland to express her longings in song.) When her fiancé reveals his disinterest in travel, Manuela makes a touching private plea to her aunt for a once-in-a-lifetime visit to the port, promising that its memory will last her forever. Garland manifests a rebellious streak stewing beneath Manuela's good-girl demeanor, a convention-defying hunger for life; her youthful wonder masks grown-up appetites and fantasies about the thrills and mysteries of carnal love. When hypnotized by Serafin, Garland unleashes Manuela's obsession with bad-boy Macoco in "Mack the Black," her first and best solo. With surging, id-releasing abandon and a manic glint in her eyes, Garland taps into Manuela's aching-to-be-free sensuality (not to mention her natural gift for the stage). After Serafin's kiss snaps her out of it, she is horrified by her behavior and frightened by her loss of control. Racing back to her aunt, she begs to go home (in the movie's most blatant Dorothy reminder), retreating from her collision with the outside world. As Manuela's situation grows more complicated, Garland deftly balances the character's four-alarm feistiness with halting fearfulness. Coming of age in fits and starts, Garland's frazzled vulnerability precisely captures the push-pull tendencies of Manuela's dilemma: to find out what it is that she really wants and what will make her truly happy.

Garland, having established Manuela's interior life in all its confounding desires, is free to have a field day embroidering her performance with gustily-executed physical comedy and irritably deadpan line readings. She is a spunky delight, fending off Serafin's lecherous attentions when he accosts her as she's serenely gazing at the sea. Her firm exterior temporarily dissolves when he flusters her with talk of daydreams. After some delicious, dignity-reducing business with her floppy hat, which blows off and, when reapplied, hangs damp and drooping over her frustrated face, the capper is her utter revulsion at the discovery that he is, of all lowly things, an actor. Back at home, she caresses that soggy hat to her cheek, a cherished souvenir of her one adventure, and when he arrives seconds later, it's as if she has conjured him. She frantically tries everything to stop him (arm-flailing warnings, scissor-wielding threats, mood-shifting appeals), but he tightropes his way into her room. Deep down, she knows that if he gets too close, she might impetuously bolt from a ready-made life to a chaotic, but exciting, one. She lets the town think that she's a martyr when she sacrifices herself (eagerly) to Serafin, whom she now believes to be Macoco; from behind her bedroom door, she dramatically wails her lines to her worried townfolk while madly primping herself for her captor's pleasure. When she somberly leaves her house to go to him, a friend rushes over, offering to take her place; Garland leans in with a stinging "He asked for *me*." Manuela soon learns that Serafin isn't Macoco but decides to play along. Channeling Manuela's humiliating fury, Garland is merciless fun, overdoing her adoration of his swashbuckling exploits, mocking his acting ability, and teasingly deflecting his defensive interruptions.

The screenplay, by Albert Hackett and Frances Goodrich, based on S. N. Behrman's play, is a spirited springboard for its stars' antics. Cole Porter's songs, however, are a disappointment; Garland's two ballads, "You Can Do No Wrong" and "Love of My Life," aren't first-rate and insufficiently enhance the story or her character, though she sings the hell out of them. It's a shame that she and Kelly don't have a duet until "Be a Clown," the merrily uninhibited finale. Kelly's lavish numbers, including the muscular, literally explosive "Pirate Ballet" (in which he evokes a dancing Douglas Fairbanks), showcase his awesome, stunt-loving physical prowess. Funny as Kelly is, sending up ham actors (a trial run for *Singin' in the Rain* [1952]), Garland's comic timing offers more spontaneous surprises. This was the second and by far the best of their three teamings, following *For Me and My Gal* (1942) and preceding *Summer Stock* (1950), which contains her second funniest performance (plus her legendary "Get Happy"). Though designed within an inch of its life, *The Pirate* isn't bogged down by overdecoration; to the color-saturated whirls of Harry Stradling's camera, ringmaster Minnelli keeps it all in dazzling motion.

A Star Is Born (1954) brought Garland an Oscar nomination for what may be the most stupendous display of sheer talent in movie history. After bypassing her that year in favor of Grace Kelly *(The Country Girl)*, the Academy had a chance to make amends when she got a second nomination, a supporting one, for her brief, but tremulously effective, nonsinging work in *Judgment at Nuremburg* (1961), but voters were overtaken by *West Side Story* fever, and Rita Moreno beat her. Her final film was the British-made *I Could Go on Singing* (1963), a soapy portrait of a concert singer's messy life, to which she brought unmistakable, raw-nerved truth, making a mediocre movie seem far better than it is. You'd expect nothing less from the movies' greatest singing actress.

Ann Sothern, Linda Darnell, and Jeanne Crain

Linda Darnell

IN

A Letter to Three Wives
(1949)

ALONGSIDE Ann Sheridan and Tyrone Power, you can add raven-haired Linda Darnell to the lineup of gorgeous movie stars whose beauty posed a hindrance to their being taken seriously as talented actors. With porcelain skin, liquid eyes, and one of the lovelier speaking voices of her era, Darnell became a star at Twentieth Century-Fox while still in her teens, notably for her angel-faced virgins in *The Mark of Zorro* (1940) and *Blood and Sand* (1941), both opposite Power. (And with Rita Hayworth also in the latter, that movie plays more like a beauty contest than anything else.) After the ultimate virgin role, the Virgin Mary in *The Song of Bernadette* (1943), Darnell showed a knack for playing mean-spirited sluts in films like *Hangover Square* (1945) and *Fallen Angel* (1945). Fox used her all over the place genre-wise: the musical *Centennial Summer* (1946), the exotic drama *Anna and the King of Siam* (1946), the John Ford western *My Darling Clementine* (1946), and the Preston Sturges farce *Unfaithfully Yours* (1948). She got a Scarlett O'Hara-style opportunity, replacing newcomer Peggy Cummins, in *Forever Amber* (1947), based on the racy best-seller about Charles II's England. Audiences flocked to see her (looking surprisingly good as a blond), but it turned out to be no *Gone With the Wind*. Joseph L. Mankiewicz's highly entertaining comedy *A Letter to Three Wives* was a critical and box-office smash, but it did more for Mankiewicz (Oscars for writing and direction) than for its stars. Darnell, in particular, never received sufficient praise for her work as Lora Mae; the film would not be what it is without her smartly controlled and caustically funny contribution.

Three suburban friends, Deborah (Jeanne Crain), Rita (Ann Sothern), and Lora Mae, are about to board a ferry for their women's club picnic for underprivileged children when a telegram arrives from a fourth friend, Addie Ross (wittily voiced by a never-seen Celeste Holm), whom they are expecting to join them. Addie's "letter" informs them that she has just run off with one of their husbands, but she does not tell them *which* one. Each woman examines her marriage in flashback, revealing why she might be the jilted wife. Deborah, married to wealthy Brad Bishop (Jeffrey Lynn), remembers her calamitous introduction to his social circle at a country-club dance. Rita, a radio writer, recalls a disastrous dinner party in which her schoolteacher husband, George Phipps (Kirk Douglas), clashed with her radiocentric boss (Florence Bates). Lora Mae, once a department store employee, recounts how she calculatingly snagged her divorced boss, middle-aged Porter Hollingsway (Paul Douglas), rendering her unsure about his true feelings for her, even after three years of marriage.

Lora Mae remains cool after the telegram arrives; she's not going to let the other two see her squirm. The only wife to appear in all three flashbacks, Lora Mae is on hand in the first two to provide laughs with her sarcastic cracks, mostly aimed at her husband; she and Porter have made a habit of belittling each other in front of their friends. If she's his trophy wife, why isn't he beaming? If she married him for his money, why isn't she giddy with material gain? Darnell, who is deadpan perfection delivering some of Mankiewicz's choicest lines, has a bitter edge, conveying that her zingers aren't merely comic relief but a by-product of Lora Mae's resentment-filled marriage. When her own flashback begins, we see that Lora Mae Finney was a girl with a plan: to escape her *very* humble beginnings. She didn't grow up on the wrong side of the tracks; she grew up *on* them, or, at best, a few yards from them. Every time a train goes by, the Finney shack shakes as if it might blow down (Lora Mae and her family take the rumbling for granted as a perfectly normal interruption of everyday life). Lora Mae may not have real class, but she's mastered a damn good imitation, from which she intends to profit. She's made up her mind to go after what she wants, and Darnell's steeliness, masked by her arsenal of feminine wiles, makes Lora Mae's story not just believable but inevitable.

Lora Mae set her trap for her boss, Porter (owner of seven department stores), when he asked her out on the pretext of discussing a promotion. He's in lust and she's seeing dollar signs. She does her silky smooth, refined-young-lady bit, all coy manners and wide-eyed sweetness. He knows right away that it's an act, she knows he knows, and they both know it's *working*. Darnell's Lora Mae gleams with confidence when she tells him that she's holding out for a man who wants to marry her. She manipulates him with devastating skill: at the end of their first date, she remains seated in his car, casually glancing at her car door to let him know that she's waiting for him to get out and open it for her (she may live in a dump, but she expects to be treated like royalty); she deliberately rips her nylons, flashing a dazzling view of her gams; her full-lipped kisses and dramatic good-byes are tinged with you-may-never-see-me-again, hinting at the sexual wonders that can be his (if he's smart). At his mansion, she sees a silver-framed photograph of Addie, and it sparks a discomforting jealousy; she realizes that she wants to be wanted and adored like that. When his proposal finally comes (on New Year's Eve), it amounts to, "Okay, you win; I'll marry you." Darnell's vulnerability seeps out just enough so that only we can see how much it hurts Lora Mae to hear him call their union "a good deal." Her game of cat and mouse has paid off, but in a way she has outsmarted herself. Their unacknowledged love match will play out as a marriage of convenience because neither of them has the courage to admit deeper feelings; each instead hides behind "shut ups" and tough-talking stubbornness. Goddess Darnell and regular-Joe Paul Douglas (in his screen debut) make an unlikely but sensational team. He's a superbly concentrated actor, and Darnell, in her best role, meets his challenge; the rhythm of their give and take is masterful, and the emotional undertones in their performances sneak up on you.

Based on a *Cosmopolitan* magazine novel by John Klempner, *A Letter to Three Wives* isn't quite the scintillating adult comedy it was heralded as being, but it still shines. With lots of sharp dialogue, it feels like a warm-up for Mankiewicz's next picture, the far superior *All About Eve* (1950). *Letter*'s Jeanne Crain episode is pretty thin; she gives a phony and humorless performance, and Jeffrey Lynn is a blank. (He disappears even while he's talking.) Ann Sothern's episode is very good; she's marvelous, as always, and it's refreshing to see a pre-*Champion* Kirk Douglas as a brainy fellow. But it's the Darnell episode that makes the movie a minor classic. Mankiewicz rewarded her with a good dramatic part in his racially charged drama *No Way Out* (1950), but, like other talented 1940s glamour girls, such as Veronica Lake, Darnell had trouble finding a place for herself in the Hollywood of the 1950s. Her career was essentially over before she turned thirty; tragically, she died at age forty-one, from injuries incurred in a 1965 fire.

Betty Hutton as Annie Oakley

Betty Hutton

IN

Annie Get Your Gun

(1950)

WHEN someone is meant to play a certain role, nothing can stand in the way. Judy Garland was starring as Annie Oakley in *Annie Get Your Gun*, MGM's adaptation of Irving Berlin's 1946 Broadway musical, but she was fired because of the cost-consuming delays brought on by her unreliable health. Fate had intervened; blond dynamo Betty Hutton stepped in, gave the performance of a lifetime, and the film was a smash. Although Ethel Merman originated the role on stage and sang it through the roof, Annie Oakley found her definitive interpreter in Hutton. Hutton's big break had come as a featured player in *Panama Hattie* (Merman's 1940 Broadway hit), and it wasn't long before she became one of the top musical stars at Paramount. Playing a series of loudmouthed, boy-crazy gals, she always found time to belt out a few comic specialty numbers; she attacked songs with almost maniacal gusto. Call her an upbeat pit bull with an indestructible brass band of a voice or, at her worst, a shameless ham. (You rarely see anyone like her nowadays because "musical comedy" is practically extinct.) Her only significant role of the decade had been as Trudy Kockenlocker, mother-to-be of sextuplets, in the Preston Sturges screwball classic *The Miracle of Morgan's Creek* (1944). But by 1949, her career was fizzling, and *Annie* provided a well-timed jumpstart.

Buffalo Bill Cody (Louis Calhern) brings his Wild West show to Ohio, where he discovers Annie Oakley, a scruffy illiterate from the backwoods who's phenomenal with a gun. She beats the show's "swollen-headed stiff" star, Frank Butler (Howard Keel), in a shooting match, and Cody hires her as Frank's assistant. She doesn't mind her secondary role because she's hopelessly smitten with Frank. She cleans up real purdy, and Frank soon returns her love. But when she inadvertently becomes Cody's main attraction, Frank quits and joins a rival show. Annie goes on to international fame but is miserable until a possible merger between the two shows gives her hope for a reunion with Frank.

Entering the film by shooting the bird off a woman's hat, Hutton looks as if she's been living inside a tree for months. Her robust personality quickly emerges from behind the grime; "Doin' What Comes Natur'lly" is as good a character-introducing show tune as there is (Berlin's score is his greatest). Hutton's nothing less than a rag doll come to enchanted life, mangling her words with an appealing hillbilly twang. After her first encounter with Frank, she sings "You Can't Get a Man with a Gun" (which director George Sidney wisely lets her deliver directly to the camera). Again, Hutton cuts loose with her life-sustaining joy in performing; there's no such thing as "too big" when your heart's really in it. Her best number, "I've Got the Sun in the Morning," is sung at a New York party following Annie's European tour. Some actresses might be overwhelmed by a fire-engine-red ball gown and a glittering, medal-strewn chest, but not our Betty. She's a rocket going off; the number is one of the most irresistible outbursts of pure happiness in all of movie musicals and the quintessential Betty Hutton moment.

The character could be monotonous if she were played with nonstop razzmatazz; Hutton balances her larger-than-life charisma with an unexpectedly poignant love for Frank. You won't care about them as a couple because he's unworthy of her, but you'll want them to get together because it means so much to *her*. The first time she lays eyes on him, Hutton reacts with an eye-popping, jaw-to-her-knees "take" that must be the most extreme expression of love at first sight in movie history. It'd be an appallingly overdone moment if it weren't so endearing (it's a long time before she can look at him without repeating that reaction). Annie, never having seen anyone so handsome, is positively thrilled when he tells her that he's seen worse than her. Frank launches into "The Girl That I Marry," a tribute to doll-like femininity, and Hutton listens with deeply felt yearning, made bittersweet by Annie's awareness that she'll never be what he's describing. When she gently nestles her head against his chest as he, oblivious, plows through the song, it's the most touching moment in the film. It may be his song, but it's her scene: you never take your eyes off her. Annie's transformed by her undeniable need for him. (Their romantic duet, "They Say It's Wonderful," proves that Hutton's voice was not made for ballads.) Much later, Annie has a shipboard monologue in which she acts out both parts of an imaginary reconciliation with Frank. Beginning in a blustery comic vein, Hutton gradually (and tenderly) unleashes the enveloping warmth inside Annie.

Annie Get Your Gun isn't one of the top-tier MGM musicals, but it's still lively, candy-colored fun. It's hampered by patches of stage-bound stiffness, but at least there's nothing highfalutin about it. Mercifully, it was made before adaptations of Broadway musicals were treated with awestruck reverence (and then usually botched). In his pre-trash novelist days, Sidney Sheldon wrote the screenplay, adapting the show's book by Herbert and Dorothy Fields. Howard Keel, in his Hollywood debut, uses his natural charm, staggering good looks, and impressive baritone to survive playing a self-centered creep. (Frank's a nice guy as long as Annie remains second best.) Keel's rowdy duet with Hutton, the unforgettable "Anything You Can Do," is a genuine showstopper.

The film was out of circulation for a quarter of a century because of disputes between the rights holders, but it finally made its debut on video in 2000, making it plain, once again, that no one could touch Hutton as Annie. As a bonus, the video includes Garland's two completed numbers and one dialogue scene (each in its entirety); Judy isn't bad, just uncomfortably cast. As for the other Annies: I can't imagine that the formidable Merman emanated the childlike wonder that is key to the role; Mary Martin's 1957 television performance is sickeningly coy; Bernadette Peters, in the recent Broadway revival, made a valiant try, but she's no one's idea of a tomboy (though Reba McEntire, one of Peters's replacements, was reportedly a knockout in the part). Then there were the Annie imitations: neither Doris Day as *Calamity Jane* (1953) nor Debbie Reynolds as *The Unsinkable Molly Brown* (1964) could fill the broadness of her role without enormous, not-fun-to-watch strain. (Day even had Keel as her leading man. Was she hoping Hutton would rub off on her?)

Hutton had just one more success: Cecil B. DeMille's cornball circus epic *The Greatest Show on Earth* (1952), widely considered the worst film ever to win the Best Picture Oscar (I'd like to cast my vote for James Cameron's dimwitted *Titanic* [1997]). With DeMille's sledgehammer touch to guide them, Hutton, Charlton Heston, and Cornel Wilde strenuously vie to give the film's worst performance (Wilde's Pepé Le Pew accent gives him the edge). Hutton's "greatest show" was her triumphant Annie Oakley, and it's easy to believe "There's No Business Like Show Business" in her presence.

Gregory Peck and Millard Mitchell (as a marshal)

Gregory Peck

IN

The Gunfighter
(1950)

GREGORY Peck's film debut in the war movie *Days of Glory* (1944) was not much of an event. What a difference a year makes. He became a star in 1945 with the one-two-three punch of *The Keys of the Kingdom* (an intermittently effective but overlong religious drama), *The Valley of Decision* (the last of Greer Garson's box-office blockbusters), and *Spellbound* (Hitchcock's romantic excursion into the subconscious). Peck became the biggest new male star of the late 1940s, and he garnered three consecutive Best Actor Oscar nominations for *The Keys of the Kingdom*, *The Yearling*, and *Gentleman's Agreement.* He proved to be an earnest actor, with a rich, soothing speaking voice and devastating good looks, but he was hardly a threat to Spencer Tracy. When Peck played roles requiring more than basic sincerity, he was laughably terrible: sexing it up as bad-boy cowboy Lewt in the out-of-its-mind horse opera *Duel in the Sun* (1946) and going emotionally screwy as the amnesiac in *Spellbound* (both movies made fortunes). His most notable misstep was Hitchcock's unbearable flop *The Paradine Case* (1947), which had him ludicrously cast as an English barrister. Peck found his footing as an actor when he starred in Henry King's very fine 1949 WWII drama *Twelve O'Clock High* (he got a fourth Oscar nomination and the New York Film Critics' Award). As an exacting bomber-group commander who suffers a mental collapse, Peck's sturdy performance got exceptional support from a compelling script and King's incisive direction. Peck and King tried to make lightning strike twice the following year with the elegiac western *The Gunfighter.* Lightning *did* in fact strike a second time, but 1950 audiences didn't take notice—a shame because it marked Peck's finest hour until his indelible, Oscar-winning Atticus Finch in *To Kill a Mockingbird* (1962).

"He don't look so tough to me" is how it always starts. Jimmy Ringo (Peck) is a "top gun" of the 1880s Southwest, and he can't go anywhere without some young hotshot challenging his quick-on-the-draw prowess.

At age thirty-five, Jimmy is no longer the wild gunslinger he once was, and he's grown weary of not being able to move anonymously in his world (his full mustache aptly keeps him in a perpetual frown). In the opening scene, he is forced into a barroom shoot-out, killing yet another cocky punk, whose three revenge-seeking brothers are soon on his trail. Jimmy shows up in Cayenne to see the wife and son he left behind eight years earlier. His arrival is the most exciting thing that's ever happened in this muddy town, and every local lad wants to catch a glimpse of the great and feared Jimmy Ringo. (It's roughly the male equivalent of the female hysteria caused by another "Ringo" eighty-odd years later.) His wife, Peggy (Helen Westcott), has changed her last name and become the town's schoolteacher; her son doesn't know that he's the offspring of an infamous father. Dreaming of taking his family far away with him to start a new life, Jimmy must first rid himself of those three relentless brothers and Cayenne's own troublemaker, Hunt Bromley (Skip Homeier), each of whom wants to be "the man who killed Jimmy Ringo."

Peck carries Jimmy's whole sorry past in his worn-out physicality and exhausted eyes, emitting more telling bits of the character's history than a half hour of flashbacks could. His mix of boredom and seething misery conveys his cursed existence; every day is part of the never-ending payback for a life of myth-making transgressions. Keep your eye on Peck's riveting transitions in the two major sequences where loudmouthed youths bait him: note his eyebrow rise at the moment he becomes aware that trouble has found him again; his decision to ignore the situation; the realization that he must react; the attempt to do so peaceably; and, finally, the self-protective hardness that must rise to the surface. In the scene in which a bartender (Karl Malden) recognizes him, Jimmy wearily responds with, "Well, where was it with you?" The look of dread returns, and his here-we-go-again ability to handle things is somehow mustered once more. Later, an elderly man takes a shot at Jimmy to avenge his son's murder, but Jimmy has never even heard of his son. When the geezer asks him if he's *sure* he's innocent, Peck's stony expression is disturbed by a surprising flash of self-doubt. Jimmy can't account for all of his actions, despite the fact that he likes to think he can. Every frame of Peck's pensive performance convinces you that daily doses of unwanted confrontations have taken their toll on Jimmy; he's not really living, he's just staying alive.

Jimmy's determination to create a normal life for himself is all that sustains him. He loves Peggy and yearns to be a model husband and father (his "professional" life has brought him nothing but notoriety). When old pal Molly (Jean Parker, very good in the "Claire Trevor" role) refers to his son as being eight years old, Jimmy automatically corrects her: "Eight and a half." It's a fleeting moment, but Peck uses it to make us aware of how prevalent the boy has been in Jimmy's thoughts; you feel that he's been counting every day of his son's life. After some resistance, Peggy eventually agrees to meet with Jimmy. Peck plays this crucial scene with the sweet gentleness and long-dormant joy of a man reunited with the thing he wants most, temporarily breaking free from the nagging strain of his unbearable renown and regretful past. Jimmy is revived by her presence; his fantasy future suddenly seems closer to attainability. He tries to convince her that he's different now. (We know he means it, but is he in any position to make promises?) Peck's acting has the stirring urgency and gravity of someone fighting impossible odds.

Henry King's lean, mature film is one of Hollywood's great westerns, and it's my favorite film in the genre. It's not only a haunting, authentic-feeling portrait of the West but a potent exploration of the double-edged sword of celebrity (long before that was a trendy concept). The script by William Bowers and William Sellers, based on a story by Bowers and director André de Toth, is realistic and mournful (two things that don't exactly spell boffo box office). Cinematographer Arthur Miller (no, not *that* Arthur Miller) gave this black-and-white film the look and feel of nineteenth-century photographs; it doesn't have the spruced-up prettiness of most back-lot westerns. Peck and King made four more films together, none of them coming anywhere near the quality of the first two. They are *David and Bathsheba* (1951), the dullest Bible epic of them all (it's not even *campy* fun), followed by *The Snows of Kilimanjaro* (1952), *The Bravados* (1958), and that awful mistake *Beloved Infidel* (1959).

Juano Hernandez (as the first mate)
and John Garfield in the foreground

John Garfield

IN

The Breaking Point

(1950)

JOHN Garfield is the transitional link between the cocky tough guys of the 1930s (James Cagney, Edward G. Robinson) and the brooding rebels of the 1950s (Marlon Brando, James Dean). Garfield's quintessential role, boxer Charlie Davis in *Body and Soul* (1947), combines the brashness of an ambitious tenement dweller of the Depression era with the angst and introspection of the Method-inspired, conflicted heroes of the Eisenhower years. The vulnerability he brought to the cynical, defeatist Mickey Borden in *Four Daughters* (1938) made him a star. That capacity to portray complicated, tortured men makes his acting seem a match for the smoldering realism of Elia Kazan's best films, and Garfield is the only star of the 1930s I can imagine playing Brando's role in *On the Waterfront* (1954). Garfield was popular throughout the war years, and 1946 brought two big hits: *The Postman Always Rings Twice* is still nasty libido-driven fun, but please feel free to remind me that I never have to sit through the soggy and pretentious *Humoresque* again. It wasn't until the late 1940s and early 1950s that he really hit his acting stride, with a series of powerful, emotionally complex parts. *Force of Evil* (1948) and *The Breaking Point* weren't the moneymakers that *Body and Soul* and *Gentleman's Agreement* (1947) were, but they gave Garfield rich opportunities to explore accountability and conscience within the action-oriented crime genre. His untimely death from a heart attack at age thirty-nine in 1952 came not too long after Brando's emergence as the screen's hottest actor.

The Breaking Point, more faithfully based on Ernest Hemingway's *To Have and Have Not* than the 1944 film of that name, is set on the coast of southern California. Since the end of World War II, Harry Morgan (Garfield) has been trying to make a success of his fishing boat. His wife, Lucy (Phyllis Thaxter), wants him to go into her father's profitable lettuce business, but he can't picture himself as a farmer. Harry's financial woes lead him to become involved in a botched smuggling scheme, which results in his shooting and killing a man in self-defense. His money situation worsens, and he accepts an offer to let his boat be used as a high-speed getaway for a gang of racetrack robbers. He soon regrets his decision and tries to redeem himself for his mistakes and for the pain he has caused those who love him.

Coloring everything Garfield's Harry does is an overwhelming sense of postwar disillusionment. No longer a war hero, Harry feels his glory days have passed and his luck gone with them. Each day is a struggle to provide for his family and make a success of his business. He doesn't get lured into breaking the law because he's impulsive or seduced by avaricious dreams or impressed by natty-looking gangsters; rather, he's a smart guy whose fiscal desperation causes him to do things he wouldn't otherwise consider. His abilities with guns and his fists allow him to believe that he can control any tight situation. Physically, he's in great shape; it's the mental wear and tear that's destroying him. Harry considers the severity of his actions and comes to careful, if risky, decisions. He takes no pleasure in exercising brute force and only resorts to it when pushed to the limit. When he kills the man who tries to swindle him, he suppresses the pain of the experience until much later. Loose lipped with alcohol, he confesses the killing to his wife, and Garfield lets us see how deep Harry's sense of personal responsibility runs. His slide into criminal behavior comes from the hurt at seeing his wife make sacrifices to make ends meet. Garfield could have played him as a guy whose bruised male ego causes him to try the easy way out, but he lets Harry's struggle come from a genuine desire to provide for his wife and two daughters, unconcerned with how the outside world views him. The star-making sensitivity that Garfield brought to malcontent Mickey Borden in 1938 matures in Harry Morgan's devotion to his family.

The most unusual aspects of Garfield's performance (and the film itself) are Harry's relationships with the two lead female characters. Harry and Lucy have a surprisingly physical marriage for a film couple of 1950; you won't catch *them* in twin beds. They have to remind each other that their daughters may walk in on them as they get lost in groping each other. Lucy is no glamour-puss, but we never doubt how much she means to Harry. Garfield plays him as a man who is proud of his happy marriage, and it becomes clear that he derives his strength from its intimacy. There's no one else for him and that's that. The "other woman" is a high-class whore named Leona (a very blond Patricia Neal) whom Harry meets when her "date" rents his boat. Leona finds Harry intensely desirable, even more so when she learns how much he loves his wife. When he speaks of Lucy to her, Garfield gives Harry a sense of peace and surety that you don't otherwise see in him. Though tempted by Leona's availability, he soon recognizes that she's no substitute for what he has with Lucy, despite its seeming ordinariness. At the touch of Leona's lips, a longing for Lucy registers on his face and the foolishness of the situation becomes obvious to him. Harry may gamble with his fortunes, even his life, but he knows when to stop where his marriage is concerned. This is the rare film where the scenes with the humdrum wife are more erotically charged than the ones with the temptress. It's refreshing to see a macho character with such a deep-rooted need for his wife, and Garfield makes Harry Morgan a far gentler character than the film's background of guns and gangsters would lead you to expect.

The Breaking Point was the fourth and best collaboration between Garfield and director Michael Curtiz. Curtiz guided Garfield to stardom (and an Oscar nomination) with *Four Daughters*, followed by *Daughters Courageous* (1939), and *The Sea Wolf* (1941). Its mix of full-bodied characters and exciting action marks *The Breaking Point* as one of Curtiz's better post-*Casablanca* films. Unfortunately, lousy musical biographies, such as *The Helen Morgan Story* (1957), and popular stinkers, such as *The Egyptian* (1954), are more characteristic of Curtiz's work in the 1950s. Patricia Neal was familiar with the "bad" Curtiz; she had been ghastly as a loony Southern belle in his extravagantly dull epic *Bright Leaf* (earlier in 1950). Ted McCord photographed *The Breaking Point* with vivid, black-and-white images and a tangible feeling for the exterior locales. The final shot is a triumph for both McCord and Curtiz. Phyllis Thaxter does the best work of her career as Lucy, and Patricia Neal is slinky, bad-girl fun as Leona. Both actresses seem to know how lucky they are to be working with an actor who gave body and soul to his craft.

Jan Sterling as Lorraine

Jan Sterling

IN

Ace in the Hole

(1951)

No one, not even Gloria Grahame, is as convincing playing tramps as Jan Sterling. Attractive, but not "movie star" alluring, she does "cheap" without glamorizing it. With platinum-blond mental acuity, unrefined speech, and mean-streets education, Sterling's characters feel like the real thing, belying the fact that she was a Broadway actress and not someone discovered in a seedy bar. (She was Judy Holliday's replacement in *Born Yesterday*.) If you were sent to a female penitentiary in the 1950s, chances are your cellmate was Sterling. She played Smoochie, a likeably vacant "c.p." (common prostitute), in the campy *Caged* (1950) and returned to the clink as Brenda, a smart-tongued but goodhearted forger, in *Women's Prison* (1955), which makes *Caged* seem like a documentary. A good portion of Sterling's career was spent in stock B pictures, but she always elevated them with her no-nonsense talent for the truth. In the Hedy Lamarr-Jane Powell mother-daughter fiasco *The Female Animal* (1958), Sterling's scenes (as a has-been film star) make you forget you're watching one of the worst movies ever made. A-picture opportunities occasionally came her way, and she never squandered them, proving that she could even bring three dimensions to standard roles, such as Humphrey Bogart's supportive wife in *The Harder They Fall* (1956), his final film. She got a Best Supporting Actress Oscar nomination and a Golden Globe for the airplane nail-biter *The High and the Mighty* (1954); among a rather colorless cross section of humanity, she gives the film's best performance. With a sympathetic lack of self-pity, she pulls off the ludicrous, much-talked-about scene in which she takes off all her makeup, deciding no longer to pretend she's younger than she is (that is, if the plane doesn't go down). Nowhere near as popular but infinitely better is Billy Wilder's gripping and nasty *Ace in the Hole*. Calmly ruthless and unapologetically self-centered, Sterling's Lorraine is one of the screen's great bad-girl performances.

New Yorker Chuck Tatum (Kirk Douglas), once a big-shot reporter

191

whose career is now on the skids, arrives broke in Albuquerque. He gets a job on the local paper, confident that he can put himself back on top if he can just land one story worth national attention. After an uneventful year, he gets his wish. In nearby Escudero, a nowhere town, Leo Minosa (Richard Benedict), owner of the local trading post, is trapped in a mountain cave-in; he'd been exploring for old Indian treasures. Chuck makes his way in to speak to Leo, gains his trust, and realizes that he's found a human interest story to rival that of Floyd Collins. If he can just keep Leo down there for a week (rather than the sixteen hours proposed to free him), Chuck can create a media frenzy. He is aided by two others eager to profit by Leo's misery: Leo's greedy wife, Lorraine, and Gus (Ray Teal), the crooked sheriff. The thousands of visitors to the site are proof of Chuck's success, but as the end of the week nears, there's doubt about whether Leo will survive.

You're certainly not expecting bleach-blond Lorraine to turn up in Escudero, working behind the counter of her husband's store. Five years earlier, Lorraine, an ex-dance hall gal from Baltimore, fell for Leo's war uniform and his misleading tales about his New Mexico business and acreage. She hasn't forgiven herself for being a sucker, and it's no help that Leo remains crazy about her, even after she's run out on him several times (he always brings her back). Her bluntly sarcastic comments are her only distinctive means of self-expression; Sterling's fed-up delivery (she has all of the film's quote-worthy lines) is informed by a boredom that has beaten the life out of Lorraine. She packs her bags soon after the cave-in, but Chuck talks her into staying when he turns the subject to money. Lorraine may appear to be a floozie of limited brain power, but she's shrewd in matters of self-interest; her wheels are always turning. When the hordes descend on Escudero, Lorraine takes in more dough than she ever imagined: first charging admission to the site, then turning it into a bustling amusement park. Sterling's Lorraine never shows a shred of remorse; she has paid her dues (five years in limbo) and will now be able to afford the finer things she's been waiting for. Her marriage is finally, if inadvertently, paying off. From the moment of Leo's entrapment, she has found freedom and relegates him to her past, heartlessly cutting herself off from his agonizing struggle. Sterling suggests a tawdry Sleeping Beauty who, waking from her coma, is ready to make up for lost time and grab her ticket out.

Chuck is the only one who can get a rise out of Lorraine. Cut from the same rotten cloth, they have the makings of a match made in hell. His responsibility for her financial boon ignites a potent sexual urge in money-mad Lorraine. Sterling evokes Lorraine's dime-a-dance days when she puts the moves on Chuck, smiling naughtily (it's a shock to see that Sterling can actually smile) and raring to please him. But it's better for his news story if the "grief-stricken wife" stays faithful, and so he stuns her with two face-reddening slaps. At first humiliated and angry, Sterling will later make it masochistically clear that Lorraine much prefers Chuck's take-charge roughness to Leo's dripping goodness. Aroused by Chuck's swift rise, she'll make another play for him, hoping he'll want to reconnect with her once he returns to New York in glory. As Leo's health worsens, Chuck starts feeling pangs of guilt, but Lorraine is made of sterner stuff. One of filmdom's cooler customers, Sterling acts rings around a teeth-flaring Kirk Douglas. He may have a fireball's intensity, but she can slice right through his scene-slamming, overdeliberate technique with a single hard stare. (William Holden, a favorite of Billy Wilder, would have made a more incisive, less histrionic Chuck.) Because Lorraine is untainted by late-arriving, implausible spasms of recrimination, it's Sterling who provides the film with its sharpest sting. Even so, it's hard to feel antipathy toward a character who explains that she doesn't go to church because "kneeling bags my nylons."

Ace in the Hole, made just after his monumental *Sunset Boulevard*, was a rare box-office flop for Wilder (and rereleasing it as *The Big Carnival* did nothing to alter its financial woes). It's easy to see why audiences were turned off: it portrays the masses as insensitive idiots. Wilder's script, cowritten by Lesser Samuels and Walter Newman, still packs a firm punch, anticipating out-of-control tabloid journalism. The stark outdoor cinematography of Charles B. Lang, Jr., makes *Ace in the Hole* one of the "whitest" black-and-white movies; unforgettable are several all-encompassing shots of the sun-baked "big carnival" as it grows to awesome proportions. (The film also features one of the grimmest, "blackest" of final images.) Sterling didn't get an Oscar nomination (not enough people saw her in it), but, surprisingly, she was named Best Actress by the National Board of Review, over Vivien Leigh in *A Streetcar Named Desire*. As flawless as Sterling's work is, that win seems excessive praise for what is, essentially, a supporting role. But half a century later, Sterling merits excessive praise; she's one of the 1950s' least sung talents, many a movie's ace in the hole.

Jeanne Crain and Thelma Ritter

Thelma Ritter

IN

The Model and the Marriage Broker
(1951)

DID you ever hear anyone say, "I don't like Thelma Ritter"? Surely you haven't, and I don't expect you ever will. Brooklyn-born and middle-aged, the beer-and-pretzels Ritter was Hollywood's premier character actress of the 1950s; her New York accent (and attitude) brought a blue-collar sensibility and goodhearted toughness to a host of roles. Her first film, *Miracle on 34th Street* (1947), set the working-class tone for the parts that followed: as a worn-out Macy's shopper stunned by the store's new Santa-inspired, customers-ahead-of-profits policy, she parlayed a three-minute role into a major career at Twentieth Century-Fox. After stealing several scenes as a hilariously no-class domestic in *A Letter to Three Wives* (1949), she was rewarded by the film's writer-director, Joseph L. Mankiewicz, with an even better role in an even better picture, a little something called *All About Eve* (1950). As Birdie, Margo Channing's dresser-maid-pal, Ritter's tell-it-like-it-is performance gives as good as she gets from a matchless Bette Davis; they snipe at each other like marksmen, all the while conveying the secure, underlying affection between them. (If the film has a flaw, it's Ritter's mysterious disappearance from it after the party scene.) Ritter was put on earth to bring plain-talking, salty reality to supporting roles, but she did get one vehicle built around *her*. George Cukor's picture *The Model and the Marriage Broker* may be a modest situation comedy, but it's your only chance to watch Ritter carry a film; it's a virtual one-woman show in which she's sensational. Unfairly billed below the romantic leads, Jeanne Crain and Scott Brady, she's in nearly every scene, dominating the movie with streetwise charm, crackerjack comic know-how, and beautifully delineated heartache. It's not really all that different from the typical Ritter performance; there's just, happily, a lot more of it.

Marriage broker Mae Swasey (Ritter), whose office is in New York's Flatiron Building, finds mates for the shy, the lonely, and the unattractive. Her husband left her for another woman twenty years ago, and no one has come along to take his place. Mae is completely immersed in her not-quite-thriving "contacts and contracts" business. She meets Kitty Bennett (Crain), a fashion model who's involved with a married man, when the two women accidentally switch handbags. Mae decides that Kitty is perfect for clean-cut X-ray technician Matt Hornbeck (Brady), who's uninterested in being tied down. Unbeknownst to either of them, Mae sets her matchmaking plot in motion.

Ritter marches through this movie with enough easygoing pushiness to believably rearrange the lives of everyone around her. Most of Mae's clients need to be nudged and wheedled; she spends much of her time coaching their behavior, trying to accentuate the positive or just *find* a positive. She's damn good at what she does, earning every penny of her commissions, juggling an assortment of characters with a finesse that belies the exhausting effort. Hard work it is, but Mae really cares about what she does, and Ritter's attention to her fellow actors never lets you forget it. Once she gets it into her head that Kitty and Matt are an ideal match, she fools Kitty into thinking that she may have swallowed one of Mae's earrings (in an omelette) and insists that she get an X ray (at Matt's lab, of course). Kitty still doesn't know what Mae does for a living, but Matt does, and he's certain that this is one of her put-up jobs and tells her so. Feigning shocked outrage at his mistrust of her, Mae begins manipulating him into thinking that he and his measly salary aren't good enough for Kitty. Unstoppably determined and unbeatably fast thinking, Ritter is Dolly Levi with a thriftier wardrobe. And what about Mae's distinctive way with words? When she wants Kitty to go fix her makeup, she tells her to "jack up" her face. After being told that only God could make a tree, she replies, "Who else'd take the time?" Good lines on their own, but Ritter nails them with her no-frills directness.

Mae has shut herself off from a personal life ever since her husband walked out. Ritter buries Mae's loneliness in bustling activity, but you can still see it if you really look at her. Childless, she develops a maternal, protective feeling for Kitty, gently employing her hard-won wisdom to urge the inexperienced beauty to give up her married boyfriend. At first angered by Mae's meddling, Kitty soon seeks her counsel. Smoking a cigarette and sprawled across her bed, Mae tells Kitty what happened twenty years earlier; the pain of her husband's rejection is still much in evidence, and Ritter brings Mae's usually concealed sadness to the surface with unsentimental simplicity. Mae's personal investment in Kitty's happiness, her chance to feel like a mother, fills her with rejuvenating gratification (until it backfires when Kitty is appalled by Mae's "professional" interference in her life). Now, while all this is going on, there's another significant relationship in Mae's life, one that she takes for granted. Doberman (Michael O'Shea) is a low-key Damon Runyon type who frequently comes to her office, presumably for the business of renewing her newspaper ads but more for the pleasure of playing pinochle with her. Oblivious to his feelings for her, Mae treats him like a buddy; he waits patiently for her to wise up. The second-nature companionship of Ritter and O'Shea's characters, in which lots of talk is unnecessary, is infinitely appealing. (The final scene anticipates the romantic card-playing ending of *The Apartment*.)

George Cukor, often touted as the supreme director of actresses, sits back, smiles, and lets Ritter have a field day. He doesn't seem much interested in the young lovers though; Jeanne Crain's poised artificiality apparently bores him. The script, by Charles Brackett, Walter Reisch, and Richard Breen, delivers the feel-good goods and provides Ritter with a made-to-order showcase. Like other black-and-white Cukor comedies of its era (*Adam's Rib* [1949], *It Should Happen to You* [1954]), *The Model and the Marriage Broker* makes enough use of New York locations to give the film a shot of Big Apple adrenaline.

Ritter never won an Oscar, despite *six* Best Supporting Actress nominations for *All About Eve*, *The Mating Season* (1951), *With a Song in My Heart* (1952), *Pickup on South Street* (1953), *Pillow Talk* (1959), and *Birdman of Alcatraz* (1962). No one has received as many nods in this category. She was particularly deserving for her Moe, a broken-down pickpocket and stoolie, in *Pickup on South Street*, a performance of moving dignity amid squalor. She should have been cast in two roles that Bette Davis got: the Bronx mother in *The Catered Affair* (1956), which Ritter had played on television, and Apple Annie in *Pocketful of Miracles* (1961). Davis strenuously *acts* these roles; Ritter could have done them in her sleep. Besides, on the strength of her Mae Swasey, she had earned the right to play leading roles. However, it's unlikely that she would ever have been lucky enough to be supported by a "supporting" actress as sharply skilled as Thelma Ritter.

James Mason as Diello/Cicero

James Mason

IN

5 Fingers
(1952)

AFTER the attention accorded *The Seventh Veil* (1945) and *Odd Man Out* (1947) when they reached our shores, it was only a matter of time before Hollywood secured the services of English star James Mason. By the mid 1950s, he was one of our movies' top actors, endowed with not only film-star looks and charisma but a talent of discerning judgment and clarity. He also possessed an instantly identifiable voice, whose resonance purred along vowel sounds, tapping the consonants lightly, but crisply, with his immaculate diction. *5 Fingers,* one of the great spy films, gave Mason his first outstanding role in America, that of Diello, a truly international character: an Albanian-born, English-transplanted valet working in Turkey, spying for the Germans, and planning to pose as an Argentinean when he escapes to Rio. In glorious black-and-white, the film tells a true story that is not only a fascinating chapter in WWII espionage but a spellbinding study of a discontented nobody, a man whose fermenting resentments find their venue for retribution (it's one man's class warfare set against an actual war). Mason's performance has cunning dimension, actualizing both the robotic valet, who suppresses his personality, and the calculating, spitefully ambitious opportunist. Yet Diello is never a villain because Mason interprets him with a visceral humanity, fighting to bring his thwarted dreams to fruition.

In 1944 Ankara, capital of neutral Turkey and hotbed of wartime intrigue, Diello, valet to the British ambassador (Walter Hampden), offers himself to the Nazis as a spy, one with access to the embassy's top-secret files. Soon flush with cash, he enlists the help of Anna Staviska (Danielle Darrieux), a penniless, French-born Polish countess whom he knew when, for three years in England, he was valet to her now-deceased husband. Diello provides her with the money for an extravagant home so he'll have a place to hide his stash and conduct his undisclosed "business" transactions. He also happens to carry a torch for Anna, but his feelings are mixed with the vindictive satisfaction of seeing their roles reversed. He wants her to run off with him to Rio, but time is of the essence once the British suspect an informer in their midst.

With his dark hair slicked down and severely parted (off center), Mason has insidiously commanding poise. Stepping out of the shadows, he approaches an attaché, Moyzisch (Oscar Karlweis), at the German embassy and proceeds, with arrogant confidence, to talk the wary Nazi into his proposition. Mason's Diello has intellect and dry humor at his disposal, and his casual sophistication and effete manners heighten our sense of his certainty in his scheme (his ticket out of servitude). Ever the outsider (a man without a country), he has no interest in the war, no loyalties to anything but himself. Mason cuts an implacable, cool figure and performs a valet's duties with mechanical precision (the same skill that makes Diello a great thief), keeping up his end of a routine conversation with the ambassador, though his face registers the private thoughts belied by his pat responses. Mason embodies the toll of a lifetime's concealed dissatisfaction and contempt. With "Cicero" as his code name, he savors his new persona; Mason transmits the devilish, cynical amusement Diello takes in his ease at earning his fortune, using the Nazis and outwitting the British. (Mason is sexy as Cicero, neutered when merely Diello.) In a long, unbroken take, we see him in action: opening the ambassador's safe, removing the classified documents, photographing and returning them. Mason uses speed without panic and a surgical attention to detail. Protected by his dispassionate professionalism, Diello appears invincible, and in his dealings with the Nazis, he is the gentleman he has always dreamed of being.

Then there's Anna. He visits her, a bankrupt countess in a dingy flat, with news of his financial windfall (though he stints on the specifics). Mason, emanating how much Diello coveted her (and still does) and how much he hated her for her unattainability when he worked for her husband, plays the scene with a shrewdly wielded upper hand. With money to entice her, he has illusions of, at last, possessing her, vindicated and aroused by her economic dependency on him. Their relationship is one big power play. In subtle strokes of psychosexual longing, Mason intertwines Diello's desires to love her, own her, punish and debase her, even allowing him to believe she's attracted to him. Usually detached, he can't mask the feelings she engenders. Her mixed signals may keep him unsteady, but he opens up around her. Though both are essentially no good, she's the realist and he's the dreamer. He tells her of his Rio fantasy, which began when he was a cabin boy on a tramp steamer and saw a man in a white dinner jacket on the balcony of a villa. Mason delivers this speech with a haunted yearning, carrying the gravity of someone who's made, and been propelled by, a not-to-be-forgotten pact with himself. ("I swore then that someday I'd *be* that man.") When she finally kisses him, instead of telling her he loves her, he tells her to get him a drink, testing and relishing his control. Later, careful not to incriminate himself, he absorbs some shocking news delivered by an English counterintelligence agent (Michael Rennie). When alone, Mason lets this crushing blow burn through Diello's pores. He stoically confronts pain and humiliation, but with no time for self-pity or rage, he's on to his next move. If you've seen *5 Fingers*, no doubt you recall its twist ending, in which Mason, at first strangely impassive and emotionally incomplete, suggests a beautiful mannequin. He reacts to alarming news with a look that could slice steel, followed by a startling but entirely appropriate response, in which he unrestrainedly digests the irony of all that has transpired.

Joseph L. Mankiewicz's Oscar-nominated direction maximizes the suspense, but he also concentrates on the story's urbane humor, its one-sided romantic anguish, and the intricacies of its war games, making atmospheric use of the real-life locations (though it's obvious that Mason never set foot in Turkey). Befitting a Mankiewicz movie, Michael Wilson's Oscar-nominated screenplay is talky in the good sense; you won't want to miss a word. Danielle Darrieux is silky and alluring as Anna, money being the match that lights her flame. The title, unlike that of, say, *The 39 Steps*, has no special meaning; five fingers are all you need to *take* things.

Mason and Mankiewicz reteamed on *Julius Caesar* (1953), a respectable, unimaginative (and cheap-looking) prestige production, in which Mason is an intelligent Brutus. Two magnificent performances lay ahead: as Norman Maine in *A Star Is Born* (1954), he matches Judy Garland every step of the way in terms of poignancy and presence (they are among the more convincingly "in love" of all screen couplings); as Humbert in *Lolita* (1962), he's suavely, deviously funny in the first half, alongside a never-better Shelley Winters, then descends into passionate, pitiable desperation (for the title character). Diello, Norman, and Humbert are a troubled trio, but they share in the triumph of being played by the same ingenious actor.

Stewart Granger (behind the mask),
Henry Wilcoxon, and Eleanor Parker

Eleanor Parker

IN

Scaramouche

(1952)

A FTER more than twenty years in Hollywood, Eleanor Parker, of the flaming red hair and catch-in-the-throat breathiness, got the part for which she is best known: the worldly (and very blond) baroness in *The Sound of Music* (1965), where—costumed like a Christmas package— she's the jaded alternative to Maria's winsome purity (and the story can't abide her stylish, nonsinging presence for long). As a Warner Brothers ingénue, Parker had made her start in hits like *Pride of the Marines* (1945), but she was a bit too cool and refined for sweet-young-thing roles. By the decade's end, she needed a hit that would knock her off her remote pedestal. As Marie Allen in *Caged* (1950), the ultimate women's prison movie, she begins as her ladylike self and is transformed, little by little, into a hard-bitten career criminal. John Cromwell, who directed it like a cross between *The Snake Pit* and *Stage Door*, turned her career around, much as he had Bette Davis's in *Of Human Bondage*. For her showy (if hardly great) work, which included getting her head shaved by matron-from-hell Hope Emerson, Parker was Oscar nominated alongside Bette Davis and Anne Baxter in *All About Eve*, Gloria Swanson in *Sunset Boule-vard*, and, the eventual winner, Judy Holliday in *Born Yesterday*. Against such colossal competition, did anyone, including herself, vote for fifth-wheel Parker? With a 1951 nomination for her wife-with-a-secret in the overly hysterical police-station drama *Detective Story*, one of William Wyler's weaker play adaptations, she secured her position as one of the new decade's top actresses. After all that heavy emoting, she played Lenore, a seductive, funny, violent-tempered actress, in *Scaramouche*, the best of MGM's Stewart Granger vehicles, and gave a performance of shimmering wit and teasing sexuality, the loosest and most liberating of her career. When Lenore is called an indifferent actress, Parker shoots back, "I'm superb!" It's a wonderful relief that she happens to be right.

Set on the eve of the French Revolution, *Scaramouche,* based on Rafael

Sabatini's 1921 novel, is the story of Andre Moreau (Granger), the illegitimate son of an aristocrat whose identity is unknown to Andre. When he witnesses the death of his best friend, freedom rebel Philippe (Richard Anderson), in a duel with the villainous Marquis de Maynes (a nonchalantly effective Mel Ferrer), Andre vows revenge against the master swordsman. Two women love Andre: fiery Lenore, an actress with whom he shares a tumultuous past, and virginal Aline (petite yet bosomy Janet Leigh), who may turn out to be his sister, in addition to being the Marquis's ward. Hunted by the Marquis's men, Andre joins Lenore's troupe of strolling players, safely concealed behind the always-masked role of Scaramouche. Furiously improving his fencing skills by day and wowing audiences by night, Andre moves toward his inevitable showdown with the Marquis.

Parker's role is secondary to the main plot, but she gives the standout performance. And what an entrance! Descending stairs in a wedding gown replete with multicolored ribbons, her red hair cascading enticingly, she is a Technicolor goddess. Her tongue-in-cheek awareness that she's a stunning creature, wielding her feminine power as artfully offstage as on, infuses the film with a sophisticated comic sheen that elevates it far above the era's rash of costume pictures. About to marry "the sausage king" (Howard Freeman), from whom she's hiding her dubious past, Parker luxuriates in Lenore's gold-digging scheme, coyly wheedling her middle-aged fiancé. When he asks what he's done to deserve her, she replies, "Well, so far, remarkably little, but I'm living in hopes." In that, her first line of dialogue, Parker insinuates herself into Lenore's toying ways. When she's deserted by her wealthy groom at scene's end, she gazes triumphantly at the diamond bracelet that is still hers. Oozing innuendo throughout the film, Parker's patented throatiness becomes the sexiest of growls. When the troupe becomes a success and her dressing room is filled with suitors, she dangles men like trinkets, but Andre is the only one she wants. She deeply and unalterably loves him, but she's tired of waiting for him to marry her and is unable to trust a word he says. Whenever he takes her in his arms, though, Lenore cannot, and will never be able to, resist him. Parker's robust love scenes with Stewart Granger indicate the potency of the characters' erotic activities.

Parker's ease at exhibiting Lenore's lusty urges is a revelation, but then so is her go-for-broke physical abandon. Though you can't take your eyes off the lustrous glamour of her onstage presence (and her supply of matching eye shadow for every costume), it's her antic enthusiasm in the slapstick routines that is the delightful surprise. (All the theatre scenes are wildly colorful and, though not really funny, they elicit an innocent wonder with their magician effects.) Parker is even more physical offstage, a wildcat with a temper as blazing as her tresses; Lenore's relationship with Andre has a *Taming of the Shrew* gusto. Not content merely to hurl torrents of verbal abuse at him, she also bites and slaps, even clobbers him with a frying pan; Parker seems never to have had (or provided) more uninhibited fun. (She would have made a marvelous Amanda in *Private Lives*, utilizing both the crisp line readings and the knockabout brio she brought to Lenore.) Despite all the comic brawls and fierce attacks of jealousy (as in *The Sound of Music*, her rival is *so* virtuous), Parker permits Lenore's resilient core to shine through. More than merely the sum of her glittering effects, Parker, amid all the infectious pleasure, humanizes Lenore and her life upon the wicked stage.

Director George Sidney, best known for MGM musicals like *Anchors Aweigh* (1945) and *Show Boat* (1951), gave *Scaramouche* the swirling energy and ice-cream palette of his song-and-dance films, aided by the lushly beautiful contributions of Charles Rosher's cinematography and Gile Steele's costumes. Sidney had had a big hit with *The Three Musketeers* in 1948. Though *Scaramouche* wasn't as popular, it's ten times better (only its romantic resolution is unsatisfying). Stewart Granger comes closer than he ever did to filling Errol Flynn's tights, and his climactic swordfight with Mel Ferrer, an intricately choreographed and nimbly performed feat that wends its way throughout an elaborate and enormous theatre set, is one of the greatest in movie history. Sidney made *Kiss Me Kate* the following year; its star, Kathryn Grayson, as another temperamental actress in a volatile relationship, was given a long red wig, duplicating Parker's Lenore look. Was Sidney hoping, in vain, that this would inspire her to Parker's elusive heights?

Parker got a third Oscar nod for *Interrupted Melody* (1955), a standard showbiz biopic of polio-stricken opera star Marjorie Lawrence, in which she does an expert job of enacting whole scenes from the diva's repertoire, while lip-synching to Eileen Farrell's recordings. (The irony is that Parker's speaking voice is so hoarse that she can barely talk, let alone sing soprano.) *Scaramouche* may not have put her in an Oscar race or been intended as anything more than a rousing trifle, but I still think it's a truer celebration of Parker's talent than any of her act-up-a-storm vehicles.

Laurence Olivier and Jennifer Jones

Laurence Olivier

IN

Carrie

(1952)

WHEN director William Wyler joined forces with Laurence Olivier (then relatively unknown in the United States) on *Wuthering Heights* (1939), they created a beloved Hollywood romance, and Olivier's sublime casting as brooding, handsome Heathcliff made him an American film star (and an Oscar nominee). Sadly, the film, lacking the density of Wyler's best movies, hasn't aged all that well. It feels underdone, racing through the plot with insufficient character development (Geraldine Fitzgerald's Isabella is the most fully realized performance). Even Olivier's stirring and poetic work only hints at his potential, a potential that would be fulfilled when he and Wyler reunited on another ambitious literary adaptation. *Carrie*, based on Theodore Dreiser's novel *Sister Carrie*, vanished quickly, but it contains one of Olivier's greatest performances, and Wyler's direction is more intricately probing than his work on *Wuthering Heights*. Though the grimness of *Carrie* could never have the widespread appeal of *Wuthering Heights*'s florid romanticism, this downer looks better with each passing year. Without flashy theatrics, Olivier immerses himself in the private anguish of a man whose midlife crisis sets him on an irreversible rise-and-fall path. (And his American accent is so good you forget he's British.)

At the turn of the twentieth century, Missourian Carrie Meeber (Jennifer Jones), a virginal beauty, leaves her family to live with her married sister in Chicago. Afraid she'll be sent back home after losing her job at a shoe factory, she moves in with a traveling salesman, Charlie Drouet (Eddie Albert), who promises marriage. They are befriended by George Hurstwood (Olivier), the elegant, middle-aged manager of a first-class restaurant. While Charlie is out of town, George falls in love with Carrie, concealing the fact that he's unhappily married and the loving father of two grown children. Carrie learns the truth, but George, vowing to get a prompt divorce, woos her away with him to New York. Unbeknownst to her, he's got ten thousand dollars from his boss's safe. They live grandly until he's forced to return the bulk of the money, thereby avoiding prison but being blacklisted from the restaurant business. Things continue to worsen for George, and Carrie leaves him, finding success on the stage (it's an olden-days variation on *A Star Is Born*).

Olivier's distinguished-gray, impeccably groomed George is so smoothly integrated into the restaurant's plush surroundings that you'd never guess the pain and sense of futility lurking beneath his flawless efficiency. Carrie's innocence and beauty become the antidotes to the coldheartedness of his greedy wife, Julia (Miriam Hopkins, whose relentless severity ensures that she gets none of our sympathy). Olivier increasingly lets George's conduct be ruled by an uncontrollable need to be near Carrie, impulsively risking everything for his second chance. Since he had given up on having any real love in his life, his feelings for Carrie have a depth beyond her comprehension — she can never know what it means to him to have found her. Whenever she's about to depart, he can't bear to let her go; Olivier, holding on to her as long as she'll let him, conveys that each moment away from her is torment. She is now his sustenance, his way out of the darkness. Olivier is primarily soft-spoken; his most profoundly felt lines are delivered in hushed tones, suffused with a passion that needs no bravura to highlight it. But when she tells him she returns his love, his happiness is beyond words, beyond even a smile. Unable to contemplate losing her, he tells lie after lie, saying anything he has to to keep her with him. It's the rare performance where you accept that someone cannot *live* without someone else; Olivier looks at Jennifer Jones as if he can't believe she's real. The stakes are raised when Carrie learns about Julia, and a fumingly indignant Olivier confronts his conniving spouse. Desperate to be rid of her "loathing" and "contempt," he makes a movingly unstrung bid for his survival. However unwisely George behaves, Olivier keeps us attuned to his every passing thought and feeling. He seems reckless, but his need is so deep that he has no choice. Though still legally bound to Julia, he becomes free in mind and spirit. Whatever the cost, it feels wonderful.

As their New York life slides into poverty, George not only feels threatened that he'll lose Carrie but suffers considerable wounds to his pride. He's still in love and continues to hold her as his life preserver, but tenement life and the constant scrounging for work take their toll. George has replaced a loveless, well-ordered world with an ardent but demeaning one, exchanging one kind of misery for another. Ill-equipped for the indignities of deprivation, he's thoroughly shaken (snapping at Carrie, dissolving in tears), whereas Carrie, having been poor, takes things more in stride. Clinging to hopes he no longer has faith in,

George is a broken, frightened man. (Watch Olivier try to suppress George's unmistakable relief after Carrie's miscarriage.) He reads in the newspaper that his newlywed son is on a ship headed for New York and goes to the pier to meet him, genuinely missing their closeness (and intending to ask for help). A nervously expectant Olivier watches the happy couple arrive, but can't bring himself to sully their joy with his disgrace and heartbreakingly shields his face with his hand as they pass him. For all his despair, Olivier never lets you feel that George regrets his actions. Carrie has made him feel more alive than ever before, and however bleak the film gets, it's not a masochistic tale. George finally loves Carrie unselfishly enough to let her have her own second chance. As he sinks lower into an in-the-shadows existence, Olivier, persuasively near death, is devoid of Hollywood softening: so hungry he barely has the energy to speak, so dirty you can almost smell him. But in Olivier's tired yet subtly expressive eyes, he's still the George we have come to know so completely.

In their expertly pruned adaptation of Dreiser's dense book, Ruth and Augustus Goetz (the team responsible for *The Heiress*, which Wyler filmed in 1949) make smart additions (Carrie's pregnancy, Julia's New York visit, the pier scene, and others). Victor Milner's textured black-and-white cinematography is complemented by splendidly detailed, Oscar-nominated sets and costumes. David Raksin's fine score bears more than a passing resemblance to his subsequent great one for *The Bad and the Beautiful*. Though it's easy to lose interest in Carrie once George becomes the focus, Jennifer Jones's vapidness doesn't help (in much the same way that Merle Oberon detracts from *Wuthering Heights*). Nothing seems to puncture her comely surface, resulting in a merely adequate performance. But Eddie Albert is excellent, bringing surprising humanity to slick Charlie; Wyler deservedly rewarded Albert with an Oscar-nominated role in *Roman Holiday* (1953).

Two other Hollywood peaks for Olivier are his enduring (and *very* British) 1940 classics *Rebecca* and *Pride and Prejudice*, playing, respectively, Maxim de Winter and Mr. Darcy. (In *Carrie*, he looks much as he did in *Rebecca*, but he no longer requires age makeup to appear about forty-five.) As indelible as his Maxim, Darcy, and Heathcliff are, none has the magnificent breadth or searching complexity of his George Hurstwood.

Janet Leigh and James Stewart

James Stewart

IN

The Naked Spur

(1953)

HE most important legacy of Frank Capra's cherished *It's a Wonderful Life* (1946) is that it introduced the dark side of James Stewart, revealing his uncompromising ability to portray complex, not always attractive human impulses. Of course, we remember the film's blanketing warmth, its lovable, wingless angel, and its life-affirming finale, but Stewart, in his first postwar role, made it hard to dismiss George Bailey's restless unfulfillment, his festering anger and resentment, and his near-suicidal breakdown. These elements give the film its lasting emotional resonance and prevent it from being excessively sentimental. They're also what two great directors latched on to in shaping Stewart's career in the 1950s, his most impressive and surprising decade in films. Under Alfred Hitchcock's guidance, particularly in *Rear Window* (1954) and *Vertigo* (1958), Stewart applied nervous energy and disturbing insecurities to create characters who are startlingly modern in their dysfunction. But no one put Stewart through more consistent anguish (mental *and* physical) than Anthony Mann; their collaboration on five psychological westerns rattled forever the uncomplicated goodness of Stewart's "Mr. Smith" persona. *Winchester '73* (1950), *Bend of the River* (1952), *The Naked Spur* (1953), *The Far Country* (1955), and *The Man from Laramie* (1955) constitute one of the more satisfying actor-director series in movie history. Stars of Stewart's ilk rarely took on characters as unsure of themselves as Stewart's in Mann's westerns, especially in the unrelenting *Naked Spur*, in which a drama of claustrophobic intensity unfolds against the vastness of the gorgeous yet menacing Colorado Rockies. It's my favorite of the five (followed by *The Far Country*) and unusual in its having only five speaking roles and not a town or saloon in sight.

In 1868, Kansas rancher Howard Kemp (Stewart) is on the trail of the five-thousand-dollar reward for the capture of marshal-killer Ben Vandergroat (Robert Ryan). Passing himself off as a no-nonsense sheriff (and making no mention of the reward), Howard gets help along the way from broken-down prospector Jesse Tate (Millard Mitchell) and Lieutenant Roy Anderson (Ralph Meeker), dishonorably discharged from the army. When they meet up with Ben, the "wanted" man tells how he knew the "sheriff" back in Abilene; Howard is a Civil War veteran who returned home to find that his fiancée had sold his ranch and run off with another man. His pursuit of the reward money is his desperate attempt to buy back his land and rebuild his shattered life, but now he'll have to split the cash with Jesse and Roy. Ben uses his companion, Lina Patch (Janet Leigh), a pretty and feisty blond, to help him create dissension (mainly greed driven) among the three captors as they make their treacherous way back to Abilene.

At first, Stewart comes on tough, self-consciously so, and it all makes sense when it's revealed that Howard's a fake. Aggressiveness doesn't come naturally to him, and so his hardness and quick temper have the overemphasis of someone who's afraid his weaknesses may still be showing. He's a mass of contradictory urges and guilty pangs, uncomfortable with the morality of his role as bounty hunter. Stewart's in a bad mood for most of the film because Howard can never relax, never trust that he's firmly in control of an explosive situation. He *feels* every bit of this perilous journey: after a pointlessly bloody encounter with Indians, Stewart's face and body carry the unshakable weight of accountability. He also registers every agonizing blow of his mounting physical punishments. After Howard is shot in the leg by the Indians, he strains to keep up with the others; he limps, but Stewart infuses him with more determination than ever to finish what he's begun. His dusty brawl with Roy has a believable messiness, without the obvious fight choreography or dubbed-in punch sounds we're used to; Stewart flails his way through this nasty wrestling match, looking as if he's not sure he can survive it (let alone win it). Howard *does* possess the grit to lead this band of outcasts, but he takes no pleasure in it. This experience is a means to an end, but not necessarily the end he had in mind.

Howard is tormented by the betrayal that ruined his life, and he may never again be able to trust a woman. In Stewart's harrowingly raw "mad" scene, Howard lurches out of his sleep with bloodcurdling shouts, reliving the devastating moment of his homecoming. This outburst is just the kind of unguarded moment he spends his waking hours trying to avoid. Still in a dream state, he verbally reenacts his off-to-war love scene with faithless Mary, as Lina does her best to comfort him. Even though Howard can't remember what he said, Stewart plays the morning-after scene with the awkwardness of knowing he's been exposed. Grudgingly grateful for

Lina's compassion, Howard connects with her for the first time, realizing that she doesn't belong in these volatile circumstances any more than he does. When he later covers a sleeping Lina with a blanket, it's a small but meaningful gesture; Stewart's flash of a smile signifies that Howard is beginning to care for someone again. In a nighttime chat, he learns that Lina shares his yearnings for a stable home life, and so he tells her about his ranch. Whenever he speaks of his prewar days, Stewart has a restorative calm that allows the once truly-at-peace Howard to shine through; like Dorothy, he *needs* what he had in Kansas. During this conversation, he gets carried away, and before long, he's even implying marriage; he lunges for a kiss in a clumsy, desperate grab at happiness, aching for all that life's denied him. At the film's climax, Howard faces a decision that will have an impact on the rest of his life, and Stewart brings wrenching depth and a rush of uncontainable tears to this redemptive struggle. (Did any actor of the Golden Age cry as unabashedly as Stewart?)

Most westerns feature straight-arrow good guys as their protagonists, but Anthony Mann's "heroes" occupy grayer areas; he mined his characters' tortured subtexts and made films of unsettling power. Mann's staging of *The Naked Spur*'s brutal action scenes (the Indian confrontation, the climax at the rapids) has heart-stopping excitement, but he never loses sight of the loss of life incurred by such violence. He also made exceptional non-Stewart westerns: *The Furies* (1950) with Barbara Stanwyck, *Devil's Doorway* (1950) with Robert Taylor, *The Tin Star* (1957) with Henry Fonda, and *Man of the West* (1958) with Gary Cooper. Because of its remote setting and paranoiac greed, *The Naked Spur*'s taut, character-driven screenplay, by Sam Rolfe and Harold Jack Bloom, plays like a north-of-the-border *Treasure of the Sierra Madre* (1948). Robert Ryan plays Ben with a perpetual smirk that you'll want to slap off his face (I mean that as a compliment); I also love the way he demeans Howard by calling him "Howie." Ralph Meeker's smooth, reckless Roy is pure id, and Millard Mitchell's Jesse, a gullible old codger, is quite a stretch from his movie mogul in *Singin' in the Rain* (1952). Janet Leigh's strong-willed Lina temporarily rescued her from the blandness of two-dimensional ingénue roles.

Stewart and Mann also made three nonwesterns together, but there's nothing distinguished about any of them: *Thunder Bay* (1953), which cast Stewart as a guy named Steve Martin; *The Glenn Miller Story* (1954), a popular movie, but I can recommend only its soundtrack; and *Strategic Air Command* (1955), a deadly dull film. (The last two were severely undermined by two words: June Allyson.) But whenever Stewart and Mann saddled up and hit the open spaces, it was, as they say, movie magic.

Fred Astaire and Cyd Charisse dance the "Girl Hunt" ballet

Fred Astaire

IN

The Band Wagon
(1953)

No one needs help from me in discovering *The Band Wagon;* Hollywood's greatest backstage musical is one of the acknowledged jewels in the MGM musical crown. Not since *Top Hat* (1935), the best of his ten dance fests with Ginger Rogers, had the incomparable Fred Astaire appeared in such a satisfying vehicle. With all the praise heaped on *The Band Wagon,* I still don't think Astaire has ever been given the credit he deserves for his unguarded, sharply funny *acting* as has-been movie star Tony Hunter, a man with more than a few things in common with . . . well, Fred Astaire. Writers Betty Comden and Adolph Green used an affectionately satirical tone in building the character from pieces of the man himself. Astaire was still popular, but there was no denying that he was a middle-aged, not-very-tall leading man, who had recently been partnering women young enough to be his daughters. He embraced this close-to-the-bone role, allowing himself to be seen as a man with insecurities, fears (mostly about veering too far from the formula that had made him a star), and a need to prove he's still "got it." With the same artistry and attention to detail that made him the greatest dancing star in movie history, he sensitively handled the best-written role he ever got. In its own way, it's as true a portrait of a fading star as Bette Davis's Margo Channing in *All About Eve.* With the much-younger Cyd Charisse as his partner, the extravagantly inventive Vincente Minnelli directing (he and Astaire had made the madly ornate 1945 flop *Yolanda and the Thief*), and hot choreographer Michael Kidd (fresh from Broadway's *Guys and Dolls*) creating the dances, Astaire found himself in a situation as potentially catastrophic as the one facing Tony Hunter.

With his Hollywood career on the skids, Tony Hunter returns to Broadway to star in a musical written by his married buddies Lily (Nanette Fabray) and Lester Marton (Oscar Levant, who's not nearly as funny as he thinks he is). When the Martons bring reigning genius Jeffrey Cordova (the fabulous Jack Buchanan) aboard to direct, Tony senses that it's not going to be the kind of light musical comedy in which he's comfortable. Cordova envisions the piece as a lavish, modern reworking of *Faust* and promptly lures classically trained Paul Byrd (James Mitchell) to do the choreography. Byrd's protégée, prima ballerina Gabrielle Gerard (Charisse), becomes Tony's improbable dance partner. Rehearsals are disastrous, and the show bombs out of town, but Tony thinks it can be saved if it's retooled back into the pure entertainment it was originally intended to be.

Tony Hunter's humiliations do pile up. At his first meeting with Charisse, Astaire is a sympathetic delight casually trying to gauge how tall she is while still keeping up his end of the conversation. His advancing age is the subject he's touchiest about, and Gaby's backhanded compliments about his *long* career (she loved his films at a recent museum revival) prove too much for this gentleman's composure. Here, and in a later hotel scene, Tony shoots back with some well-aimed wisecracks. (Astaire hits these often self-mocking jibes with sardonic glee.) The rehearsal process brings a more public kind of embarrassment. Encouraged by his director to go over the top in a problematic scene, Tony attempts a Cagney-like approach to acting. To watch Astaire, the man who makes everything look easy, perform his desperately revved-up rendition is a one-of-a-kind hoot. It's tinged with sadness, though, because Tony is floundering, yet he's too much the trouper to be anything but a good sport. As the ego bruises mount (he can't lift his leading lady; his part is trimmed a little each day), Tony eventually reaches a boiling point and explodes. It's obviously out of character for him to pull a "star trip," but he's now beyond civility, declaring himself neither Nijinsky nor Brando. In the finest nondancing moment of his career, Astaire delivers Tony's "good riddance" monologue as a last stand for self-preservation. Speaking with the no-holds-barred conviction of someone with nothing left to lose, his pointed anger and stinging wit mark this as a triumphant moment for Tony. Although invigorated by the sense of relief that quitting the show brings him, Astaire never lets us forget that Tony's "victory" is also an admission of bitter defeat. He finishes his speech, bows, exits, and I want to burst into applause. Whether the movie can or cannot deliver a new Tony Hunter, it has already given us a new Fred Astaire.

If Tony is the most vulnerable character in the movie, he's also the most self-aware. "By Myself," the great ballad by Howard Dietz and Arthur Schwartz (whose estimable songbook provides the film's score), establishes Tony as a survivor. As Astaire walks (as beautifully as he dances) along a train platform, he sings the words with just the right mixture of wistfulness and optimism. (Astaire was one of the greats at acting the feelings beneath the lyrics of a song.) Tony may feel discarded by the public and the movie industry, but he's not beaten yet. When the show lays an egg in New Haven, he's the only one who attends the opening-night party; he knows that flops are part of the business and you just keep going. It's Tony who raises the spirits of the disheartened company and convinces them that the show can still become a success.

Although his professional confidence is boosted by the show's back-on-track momentum, the never-married Tony is remarkably unsure of himself when he realizes that he's in love with Gaby. With young and handsome competition from Paul Byrd, how can he possibly win her? When Lester (who has figured things out) raises the issue, Tony launches into a defense of his bachelorhood, even praises his rival, but he isn't fooling anyone. Astaire's Tony is boyishly charming as he tries to cover his true feelings, rambling on about marriage and career. Finally, even he can't listen to himself anymore; Astaire shifts keys by suddenly stopping his babbling and quietly confessing his love for Gaby. The screenplay has again pushed Astaire to new depths, and he comes through with a touching, keenly perceptive performance.

If the role's requirements expanded Astaire's acting range, then Michael Kidd's challenging choreography did the same for his dancing range. In the thrilling "Girl Hunt" ballet, a twelve-minute spoof of pulp-fiction detective stories, Astaire makes a dryly hilarious Mike Hammer stand-in. The epitome of dinner-clothes elegance transforms himself into a sexy, brawling, knee-working, shoulder-rolling Michael Kidd dancer, and his versatility is astounding. The sizzling Charisse emerges as one of his greatest partners, both in "Girl Hunt" (in which, in a dual role, she is a double-whammy of scorching sensuality) and in the sublime "Dancing in the Dark" (which can stand with the best of Fred and Ginger). Nearly every number in the picture is a classic, but not quite: I could live without the bland Fabray's second-rate "Louisiana Hayride," which belongs in another movie, a crummy one.

Comden and Green obviously poured their Broadway-bound experiences into the script, which captures the nothing-else-exists mentality of putting on a show. Minnelli's breathtaking use of color and his witty staging of all the show's tribulations (the outrageous backers' audition, the out-of-control scenic elements, the zombified New Haven audience) help make it the second-best musical the director ever made (only 1944's *Meet Me in St. Louis* ranks higher). Astaire never topped his work in *The Band Wagon:* how do you improve on perfection?

Spencer Tracy and Jean Simmons

Jean Simmons

IN

The Actress

(1953)

HEN a still-in-her-teens Jean Simmons appeared as Estella in David Lean's *Great Expectations* (1946), it seemed as if Vivien Leigh had a baby sister, with all the striking self-possession that implies. Thus it is fitting that it was Leigh's husband, Laurence Olivier, who gave Simmons her big break, Ophelia in his *Hamlet* (1948), which won her a supporting Oscar nomination. Hollywood beckoned, and 1953 was the year she became a full-fledged American movie star, by virtue of her leading-lady status in *The Robe*, the kitschy CinemaScope Bible epic that everyone went to see. The National Board of Review named her the year's Best Actress, citing her for it and two other films, *Young Bess*, in which she makes a strong Elizabeth I (even if the historical drama around her is a major yawn), and *The Actress*, the pearl of the three, featuring a central performance of angelic radiance, enchanting humor, and blooming maturity. Ruth Gordon's screenplay for *The Actress*, based on her autobiographical play, *Years Ago*, is a fond look at her youthful obsession with the theatre. Now, Jean Simmons, with her arresting beauty, is just about the last actress you'd imagine playing the woman who'd later star in *Harold and Maude* (1971), but Gordon is depicted so early in her life that it's easy to suspend your disbelief.

Although she's the daughter of Clinton (Spencer Tracy), an ex-sailor now employed at a food company, and Annie (Teresa Wright), a home-maker, seventeen-year-old Ruth Gordon Jones feels destined to escape the ordinariness of her life in Wollaston, Massachusetts (circa 1912). With every fiber of her being, she craves a life on the stage, but her father wants her to become a gym teacher. Despite the financial strains on the family and the attentions of a handsome Harvard student, Fred Whitmarsh (Anthony Perkins), Ruth will not be distracted from her quest to take New York by storm.

Ruth is first seen leaning over the balcony at a performance of *The Pink Lady*, a lavish musical starring her idol, Hazel Dawn (Kay Williams), who's surrounded by tuxedoed chorus boys. Simmons, in ravishing close-up, captures the rapture of anyone who's been transported by the magic of the theatre at a tender age. In her unblinking, sparkling-eyed gaze, Ruth sees on that stage everything she could ever want; nothing else exists. In scenes like the one in which she takes a vow (on a photo of Miss Dawn) that she's going to be "somebody wonderful," Simmons is a bewitching mixture of innocent wonder, insatiable enthusiasm, and the one-track determination to make it come true. Every good thing that happens to Ruth, such as her invitation backstage to meet Miss Dawn, only confirms what she believes deep down: she is special, and her success is inevitable. She treats Miss Dawn's letter like a holy document and reads it aloud to her girlfriends with the pride and intoxication of someone whose dreams are within reach. When Fred, her beau, leaves her house later that night (following a charming scene filled with Simmons's subtly registered, mortified reactions to Ruth's parents' unrefined behavior), he gives Ruth her first kiss. This milestone causes her to float, but her joy is displaced seconds later by thoughts of Miss Dawn's invitation, which produces a far more euphoric response from her when she removes the letter from inside her blouse. Love is nice, but no one can compete with, or dissuade her from, her plans for herself.

When she finally, and meekly, confesses to her father that she wants to go on the stage, he's not unsympathetic, but he is skeptical. She bravely volunteers to audition for him, resulting in a scene of mounting humiliation; Ruth's skills clearly haven't caught up to her drive and desire. In a speech from *Twelfth Night* and a bit of a novelty song, Simmons bombs endearingly. Oh, she's loud all right, and she's got energy and spunk, but she's raw as can be, with fidgety hands and an overriding sense of desperation. Simmons delightfully displays Ruth's limited technique without making her appear untalented; she has the fearless makings of a real actress; she just needs training and experience. Defying her father's wish that she finish high school, Ruth keeps an appointment with a Boston director. Right before she goes through the stage door, Fred surprises her and proposes marriage, which she absorbs as a well-timed ego booster before her meeting. Though she's able to acknowledge her selfish tenacity, and admits to being touched by his offer, her focus is on that magical stage door, and how, upon passing through it, her life will be forever changed. With her arm outstretched, she makes a theatrical farewell, then kisses him and vanishes. (Simmons's spasms of overdramatization are an ongoing source of witty pleasure.) But as setbacks come her way, her relationship with her father deepens. He becomes committed to seeing that she gets her chance, and she comes to recognize how much alike they are: it is from him that she gets her rebellious will and adventurous spirit. As the story proceeds, watch her expand her view of him, discovering he's so much more than a grumbling ex-seaman, and realizing, in the process, just how lucky she is. As played by Simmons and Spencer Tracy, the coming together of daughter and father is lovely to behold.

A heartfelt valentine to the theatre (and a box-office bust), *The Actress* is a gently keyed, character-driven domestic comedy directed by George Cukor with meticulous care, easy confidence, and no staginess. For his funny and poignant performance as a put-upon, loving curmudgeon, Spencer Tracy, in his fifth of five films with Cukor, won a Best Actor Golden Globe. (Fredric March won a Tony when he played the role on Broadway.) Tracy has a showstopping scene in which he performs in a physical fitness exhibition (it seems Dad's a ham too), repeatedly unable to keep his pants from falling down. Teresa Wright, who seemingly moments before had been playing ingénues, is suddenly cast as a mother. (Wright also played Simmons's mother in 1969's shallow, full-of-itself drama *The Happy Ending*, sadly the only film to put Simmons in a Best Actress Oscar race.) In his screen debut, Anthony Perkins is appealing in his hopeless pursuit of Ruth and has none of the troubled rumblings he brought to later roles. Gordon's story works on several levels: as a rich, black-and-white period piece; as a distillation of individual, yet universal, yearning; as a tribute to extraordinary parents. Simmons has the ethereal shine to make it soar, pulling off the kind of role that would have gone to Katharine Hepburn two decades earlier. And, as the movie ends, there is the comfort of knowing how well it's going to work out for Ruth.

Simmons won a Golden Globe for her musical comedy versatility in *Guys and Dolls* (1955), but she would give her finest performance, as evangelist Sister Sharon, in the juicy adult drama *Elmer Gantry* (1960), a film best remembered for Burt Lancaster's Oscar-winning, spectacularly entertaining pyrotechnics in the title role. He is matched, maybe even surpassed, by Simmons's vibrant, both soulful and sexy, unnominated work. (By the way, Shirley Jones's Oscar-winning supporting turn as *Gantry*'s hooker stinks of not-ready-to-leave-acting-class amateurishness.) For anyone who was really paying attention during the 1950s and early 1960s, Jean Simmons was one of a handful of stars who could seriously be considered "the actress" of her time.

Michael Kidd, Dan Dailey, Gene Kelly, and Cyd Charisse

Gene Kelly

IN

It's Always Fair Weather

(1955)

ENE Kelly, the screen's foremost dancing sailor and rain lover, in a really bad mood? That's the case in the ironically titled *It's Always Fair Weather*, but it's not as though there hadn't been hints of Kelly's dark side prior to this. In his remarkably self-assured debut, *For Me and My Gal* (1942), he's an opportunistic heel (until the corny script turns him into an improbable war hero). In the dazzling *Cover Girl* (1944), he broods over his relationship with Rita Hayworth as she climbs from Brooklyn to Broadway. But with *Anchors Aweigh* (1945), clean-cut exuberance became the Kelly specialty, resulting in his sole Best Actor Oscar nomination. (Was it for the way he related to Jerry the Mouse or for teaching Frank Sinatra to dance?) Four years later, trading in their black uniforms for white ones, he and Sinatra (plus Jules Munshin) starred in another sailors-on-leave musical, the much-praised *On the Town*, the first film codirected by Kelly and Stanley Donen. It's an uneven picture, marred by its penchant for excessive silliness; nothing in it tops the surging excitement of its on-location opener, "New York, New York." The second Kelly-Donen film was *Singin' in the Rain* (1952), the high-water mark (pun intended) of the MGM musical and a film that would be hard to overrate; Kelly's title-tune romp is the screen's quintessential expression of uninhibited joy. *It's Always Fair Weather*, the third and final Kelly-Donen musical and a box-office flop, is the anti-*On the Town*, exploring how, a decade after their glory days, the lives of three wide-eyed servicemen panned out. Kelly, more subdued than usual, gives a performance layered with painful self-loathing and stifled potential, expressed in both the scenes and the dances.

Three soldiers, Ted Riley (Kelly), Doug Hallerton (Dan Dailey), and Angie Valentine (Michael Kidd, in the Sinatra slot), celebrating in New York after V-E Day before going their separate ways, pledge to meet again in ten years, believing their bond unbreakable. After being jilted, Ted stays in New York, forsaking law school for gambling. Doug gives up his dream of becoming an artist, finding unfulfilling success in advertising. Angie, now a diner owner and family man, remains the same likeable hick he always was. They all show up for the 1955 reunion, but it's a disaster; they no longer have anything in common, forcing them to confront how the years have changed them. Unbeknownst to them, the story of their reunion is scheduled to be a segment on a live television show, *Midnight with Madeline* (Dolores Gray), an idea hatched by program coordinator Jackie Leighton (Cyd Charisse) for its obvious sentimental appeal.

In the 1945 prologue, Kelly is . . . well, Gene Kelly . . . beaming with postwar possibility until Ted reads the Dear John letter waiting for him. Shattered in an instant, Kelly's Ted is seethingly determined never to be a sucker again. Following an all-night pub crawl, he and his two buddies, now wrecked, take to the streets in a thrilling dance (sort of a drunken "New York, New York") to "March, March," an outlet for their last gasp of battle-charged energy before facing the unknown. (The highlight is the astonishing section in which they dance wearing garbage-can lids on their left feet.) Kelly, who also choreographed with Donen, performs with vigorous abandon, temporarily blotting out his romantic scars. Ten years later, he's a slick, shady character, and yet he doesn't seem really to belong in a world of crooks, mugs, and prizefighters. Oh, he talks the talk and has a nobody's-fool hardness about him, but you know he's too smart for this dead-end lifestyle. Kelly suppresses Ted's real self, shielding his bruised feelings behind a cynical outlook. After the initial delight of the reunion, his defensiveness regarding his worthless life is triggered. He is miserably uncomfortable at their fancy lunch, beginning to see himself as Doug and Angie are seeing him. From different locations, but united by a three-pane split screen, the trio shares a mournful soft-shoe, "Once Upon a Time." Kelly, in the center, uses his poetic grace to convey Ted's disillusionment, paying vivid attention to the tiny flashes of anger in the choreography.

Ted puts the moves on brainy and beautiful Jackie with the smarmy ease of a seasoned lady-killer. They don't truly connect until they recognize each other as similarly *un*connected people. In their costume-shop scene, Kelly drops Ted's cool-dude façade, genuinely depleted by the reunion's reminder of the once-heroic stature he held in his buddies' eyes. Without overindulging the self-pity, Kelly plays this naked admission of failure with mature understatement. Ted spots a chance at redemption when, after learning that his boxer (whom he won in a crap game) is about to take a dive, he punches the pug, deliberately causing the cancellation of the fight. Buoyed by reclaiming a little of his self-respect (even with vengeful racketeers now on his trail), and impelled by the confidence-building romance with Jackie, Ted has taken the first fearless steps to becoming himself (meaning Gene Kelly) again. After hiding in a roller rink, he emerges (still on skates) and launches into the last great dance solo of his career, the traffic-stopping "I Like Myself." Similar in spirit to his puddle-splashing classic, it's a declaration that Ted's decade-long retreat is over. Watch Kelly discover that the title of the song is true, dumbfounded at how far he's come in just one day (after all, it is a musical). At first ignoring gathering onlookers, he soon embraces them as his audience. Through the studio-bound streets of Manhattan, reveling in love and freedom, he, finally, really *smiles*. Let's face it, no one gets as uncontainably happy as Gene Kelly.

The Oscar-nominated screenplay, by Betty Comden and Adolph Green (who also wrote the other two Kelly-Donen films), takes an unusually adult look (for a musical) at life's disappointments and regrets. (Their comic zest shines in their spoofing of sponsor-mad television shows.) The team also penned the lyrics to André Previn's pleasant, if not especially memorable, music. Though the film makes striking and imaginative use of its CinemaScope shape, it's a fairly cheap-looking picture; MGM's cutbacks are apparent. Like Kelly, the underrated Dailey is also very good at burrowing into his less-than-sunny side. Kidd, a brilliant choreographer, doesn't have much screen presence and is, unsurprisingly, given far less to do than his costars. Stunning Charisse is not seen to advantage here: her acting suggests a windup toy, and her only number, the gym-set "Baby, You Knock Me Out," is not one of her best (and has nothing to do with the story). The film's biggest crime is that Kelly and Charisse never dance *together*. But Dolores Gray, with her warm trumpet of a voice, is fabulous in her glittering showstopper, "Thanks a Lot, but No Thanks," complete with "Get Happy" chorus boys.

I can't help feeling that the Kelly-Donen films would have been just as good if Donen had directed them by himself. Keep in mind that Donen made several wonderful, visually exciting movies on his own (*Seven Brides for Seven Brothers* [1954], *Funny Face* [1957], *Two for the Road* [1967]), whereas Kelly didn't direct a single remotely good one (consider the labored lyricism of *Gigot* [1962] or the in-every-way unbearable *Hello, Dolly!* [1969]). But I would never minimize Kelly's impact in front of the camera, where, in this instance, he submerged his patented glee to explore Ted's private anguish. Of course, Gene Kelly's bad mood couldn't last long, but lovers of musicals are all the richer for his letting us get a peek at it.

Robert Mitchum as Harry Powell

Robert Mitchum

IN

The Night of the Hunter
(1955)

JUST because Robert Mitchum never seemed to take himself seriously is no reason for the rest of us to follow his lead. After only two years of bit parts in A pictures and larger parts in B pictures, he made a strong impression as the tough but caring captain in the moving war film *The Story of G.I. Joe* (1945), snagging the only Oscar nomination he would receive. With the broadest shoulders the screen has ever seen and a laid-back intelligence that makes you feel he knows more than you do about how the world *really* works, Mitchum became one of the postwar era's top leading men, a position he held for three solid decades. For an actor who often looked like he had a hangover or had just been roused from deepest sleep (or was about to nod off), the role of the psycho preacher in *The Night of the Hunter* would seem more than a stretch, but as was usual for Mitchum, the effort doesn't show. His personification of pure evil, marked by startling unpredictability, remarkable variety, and perverse humor, is one of the scariest you'll ever see. With his heavy lids fearlessly open, Mitchum's modulated outrageousness results in the performance of his life, in the best American film of 1955.

In a Midwest ravaged by the ongoing Depression, so-called preacher Harry Powell (Mitchum), murderer of twelve widows, is arrested for car theft. He shares a jail cell with Ben Harper (Peter Graves), who's awaiting execution for killing two men in a bank robbery. Only Ben's children, John (Billy Chapin), who's about nine, and Pearl (Sally Jane Bruce), his little sister, know where Ben hid the ten thousand dollars he stole, and they swore never to tell. After Ben is hanged, Harry makes his way to the dead man's family (in search of the loot) and woos Ben's widow, Willa (Shelley Winters), into marriage with his Bible-thumping bravado. Harry murders Willa when she learns his true motive, but the children (and the money) escape his clutches. He chases them down the Ohio River. The children eventually come under the protection of Rachel

Cooper (Lillian Gish), a formidable woman who takes them under her firm wing to join the other strays she's already taken in. Rachel is ready for a fight when Harry tracks them down.

Harry is first seen driving a stolen jalopy, engaging in an oral conversation with the Lord. Mitchum, with a biscuits-and-gravy twang, creates a chummy relationship with Harry's God, speaking of his killings in a guiltless, matter-of-fact way; after all, his ill-gotten gains permit him to continue spreading His word. Harry refers to this as "the religion the Almighty and me worked out betwixt us," and so he lives by his own code. With H-A-T-E tattooed on the back of his left-hand fingers and L-O-V-E on his right, Harry is quite an attention getter. Though he's as physically imposing (and relentless) as Frankenstein's Monster, he has a virile beauty (with a tidal wave of hair above his forehead) and a down-home appeal that country folk can't resist. Harry's amorality allows Mitchum to have a high time verbally seducing anyone in his path. Harry is a born actor, fed by the excitement and risks of a live performance, and Mitchum revels in his audacious fakery (when he passes himself off to Rachel as the children's worried father, he exaggeratedly wipes away a tear with the palm of his hand). In the ice-cream parlor, he assumes his razzle-dazzle, revival-meeting mode, voice booming to dramatize the tale of good and evil; his love and hate hands wrestle each other to surefire effect. Mitchum is even creepier in Harry's more private acts of manipulation and cruelty; when he rebuffs Willa sexually on their wedding night, his intimidating tone is one of holier-than-thou condescension, making her feel small and dirty. On the night he stabs her to death with his trusty switchblade (his "sword"), he enacts a prekilling ritual as if possessed: Mitchum raises his hate-stamped left hand slowly to heaven with chilling grace, rapturously fueling Harry to commit the deed.

The way Mitchum mixes humor with menace is most unsettling. On the day after Willa has been disposed of, Harry, leaning on a tree, calls to John and Pearl, who are hiding in the house. He repeats the word *children* several times with an overdone folksiness, parodying a perfect dad summoning his kiddies. As the money continues to elude Harry, Mitchum reacts to the children with exasperated desperation, fluctuating between bellowing anger and honey-dripping kindness. The bodily harm he incurs in his mad dash to catch them (before they lock him in the basement) plays like slapstick, but when he finds them by the river, Harry is pure animal, untamed and hungry. I have never heard a howl quite like the one Mitchum utters when the kids get away in a rowboat; he starts with a hum that rises steadily in pitch and volume, bursting into wordless, bloodcurdling rage. Perhaps the most disturbing element of Mitchum's work is the soothing beauty and enfolding warmth of his full-voiced hymn singing. When his caressing baritone praises God, which happens often, Harry seems the absolute antithesis of everything he really is. Even a shotgun-holding Rachel is affected by his inspiring rendition of "Leaning on the Everlasting Arms," sung in her front yard. She joins in, and the "divine" music they make together is an ironic, momentary respite from their fierce battle of wills.

A film of astonishing visual imagination and overwhelming emotion, *The Night of the Hunter* is the only film directed by actor Charles Laughton. Ignored in its day, it has come to be recognized as the masterpiece it is. (Had it been a success, Laughton most likely would have directed again.) It certainly was ahead of its time in terms of content, featuring a God-invoking maniac, frank sexuality, and black-comic overtones. Stanley Cortez's cinematography makes it one of the more stunning black-and-white films ever made; no other movie looks quite like it. Some of its images (the dead Willa, entombed underwater; the children's dreamscape journey down the river; the far-off silhouette of Harry's slow but steady pursuit on horseback) take your breath away. Based on a novel by Davis Grubb, James Agee's faithful screenplay, powerful enough to move you to tears, transcends the suspense genre. One flaw: Agee gives Gish too many lines about the endurance of children, overstressing a touching point and making her character too self-consciously wise. But Gish is radiant in the best nonsilent role of her career, imbuing Rachel with plain-scrubbed strength and grandmotherly affection (you start to feel safe the moment she appears). Shelley Winters, continuing her victim phase (following *A Double Life* [1947] and *A Place in the Sun* [1951]), is poignant as misguided Willa. In the difficult role of little John, Billy Chapin is exceptional; his intimately felt transitions quietly enhance the cumulative impact of the story.

Though Mitchum was supremely comfortable trading sly, sexy quips with tough gals like Jane Russell and Susan Hayward, he was even better opposite Deborah Kerr in two of his other versatility-proving highs: his gentle lug of a marine in *Heaven Knows, Mr. Allison* (1957), and his impeccably accented Australian sheep drover in *The Sundowners* (1960). *Cape Fear* (1962) may have given him another crazed stalker role, Max Cady, but revenge-seeking Max is no match for the soulless nightmare named Harry.

Grace Kelly and Alec Guinness

Alec Guinness

IN

The Swan

(1956)

U NLIKE many great stage actors, Alec Guinness had an instinctive
affinity for movie acting that was apparent in his first performance,
a delightfully spirited Herbert Pocket in David Lean's magnificent adaptation of *Great Expectations* (1946). Guinness quickly found international
success as the versatile star of a series of comic miracles produced by Ealing Studios, including *Kind Hearts and Coronets* (1949), in which he triumphed as a master of disguise playing eight members of the D'Ascoyne
family; *The Man in the White Suit* (1951); and *The Lavender Hill Mob* (1951),
which earned him a Best Actor Oscar nomination. He had been a key
player in British films for a decade when he made *The Swan,* his first Hollywood film (he had appeared as Disraeli in a 1950 American film, *The
Mudlark,* but it had been filmed in England). Based on Ferenc Molnár's
play, *The Swan* had already been a 1925 silent and, as *One Romantic Night*
(1930), Lillian Gish's first talkie. A romantic comedy set among royalty,
it was an ideal vehicle for soon-to-be real-life princess Grace Kelly.
Charles Vidor's wide-screen color version is a beauty and boasts an extraordinary cast. Guinness's marvelous performance, as light-haired,
mustache-flicking Prince Albert, makes use of his comic ingenuity, but it
also has a depth that sneaks up on you.

In an unnamed part of central Europe in 1910, Princess Beatrix (Jessie
Royce Landis), matriarch of a Napoleon-dethroned (and exiled) royal
family, receives word that cousin Albert, a crown prince, is coming to her
estate for a four-day visit. Everyone knows he's combing the Continent for
a bride, and Beatrix's daughter, beautiful Princess Alexandra (Kelly), is a
likely candidate. But Albert and Alexandra prove to be uncomfortable
with each other. Sensing the prince's waning interest, Beatrix tries to
arouse his jealousy by creating competition; she decides to invite Nicholas
Agi (Louis Jourdan), her young sons' attractive tutor, to the ball. It turns
out to be an opportunity for Alexandra and Nicholas to acknowledge their

231

long-brewing love for each other, changing the story of a prince in search of his princess into an unexpected love triangle.

Guinness is a stately presence, exhibiting an air of lifelong training in the manners and bearing of a royal personage. Though charming and friendly when greeting Beatrix's family, an awkwardness emerges, and cannot be shaken, upon Albert's meeting Alexandra. Guinness and Kelly share one of my all-time favorite movie introductions. As she bends to curtsey, he reaches to kiss her forehead, and as their timing is off, her rising head crashes into his chin. (In a later scene, notice Guinness as he artfully averts a repeat collision.) Albert is tastefully desperate trying to spark a conversation with the cool, shy princess (Guinness's fidgety body language expertly details his unease), but his attempts at levity fall flat (despite his own laughter), and she flinches at the touch of his hand. Albert is far more jovial playing physical games with her brothers (and their estimable tutor). His boyish enthusiasm is also set free at the ball when he becomes mesmerized by the bass viol in the orchestra. Before he gets up to play it (none too well), watch Guinness absentmindedly mime the fingering, lost in the sensation. Perhaps his slyest comic touch is his foolproof awareness (registered with subtle amusement) of Beatrix's painfully obvious ploys to bring him closer to Alexandra. In one instance, he swiftly sidesteps a dreaded trip to Alexandra's rose garden with a sudden urge to see, of all things, the dairy.

Up until now emotionally guarded, Albert reveals a quietly unsettling anxiety over the disappearance of Alexandra and Nicholas from the ball, following their extended time on the dance floor. Guinness's Albert is no longer childlike or in any way comical; he's a man trying to handle an embarrassing situation as gracefully as possible. When the newly-in-love couple reappears, Albert is slightly inebriated and casually sarcastic. In his increasingly challenging exchanges with his impassioned rival, he struggles valiantly to maintain his good humor, smoothing over his discomfort and lightening the mood with clever comments. Later, when Albert unleashes the firmly controlled anger that has been building inside him all evening, Guinness gives you a glimpse of the future king; he'll not allow an "insolent upstart" to make a fool of him. But when Alexandra plants a tender kiss on Nicholas's lips in his presence, Albert freezes, stunned and deeply wounded that he has lost her. Instead of causing a princely fury, the experience humbles and matures him, diffusing his regal arrogance. Guinness shades the character with a well of feeling that is life changing. Albert discovers what he wants, and though it may be too late, he tries to make amends. The film ends with Guinness's exquisite delivery of a delicately healing speech, in which Albert unfurls a gentle compassion for Alexandra, confronting his own exposed vulnerability in the process. This scene is not a classic, though it deserves to be.

It's hard to believe that this elegant film was directed by the same man who made the tawdry classic *Gilda* (1946), but Charles Vidor directed them both, the two high points of his career. John Dighton's screenplay melds witty comedy, fairy-tale romance, and textured emotion into an irresistible package. *The Swan* was made with the kind of splendor that MGM had all but forsaken by 1956, which must have been a tribute to Kelly's star power (who, by the way, in her virtually all white, swanlike Helen Rose costumes, never looked more ravishing). As for Kelly's acting, this is her warmest, most intimate performance; the same can be said of a never-better Louis Jourdan. Jessie Royce Landis, playing Kelly's mother (as she had in *To Catch a Thief* [1955]), is excellent, and the one-of-a-kind Estelle Winwood, as whimsical Aunt Symphorosa, is peerlessly funny. And, oh, that transporting score by Bronislau Kaper! And yet *The Swan* caused no great stir, either critically or commercially. Atypical of the popular fare of the time, its air of champagne sophistication seems more 1930s than 1950s (you could easily imagine it as an Ernst Lubitsch musical starring Jeanette MacDonald). If its comedy had been more farcical and its love story less bittersweet, it might have found broader appeal (and been far less good). Sadly neglected to this day, it's one of the better films of its year.

The Swan didn't make Guinness the toast of Hollywood, but he didn't have long to wait. He won the 1957 Best Actor Oscar for his fascinating Colonel Nicholson in David Lean's WWII epic *The Bridge on the River Kwai.* (He was nominated the next year for his screenplay of *The Horse's Mouth*, but not for his wonderful work *in* it.) Whether you prefer to remember him as the brilliant center of the Ealing comedies, or as the esteemed Mr. Lean's six-time collaborator, or as Obi-Wan Kenobi of you-know-what (to which he brought a much-needed touch of class), Alec Guinness was one of the screen's all-time great actors. His Prince Albert has been overshadowed by an astounding gallery of characters, but it's time for this ugly duckling to be recognized as a swan.

Robert Bray looks on as Marilyn Monroe
gets into Don Murray's coat

Marilyn Monroe

IN

Bus Stop

(1956)

I'M hardly the first to say it, but it bears repeating: Marilyn Monroe gave her best performance in *Bus Stop*, the screen version of William Inge's hit play. It was her first film after she had interrupted her career, at the peak of her popularity, to study at New York's Actors Studio. It certainly was a new Monroe who returned to Hollywood, and it showed where it counted, on the screen. *Bus Stop*'s Cherie may have been another "dumb blond," but she was markedly different from the dim-bulbed gals Monroe had already played to perfection: Lorelei in *Gentlemen Prefer Blondes* (1953), Pola in *How to Marry a Millionaire* (1953), and the Girl in *The Seven Year Itch* (1955). (Whatever you think of this trio of flicks, Marilyn's comic skills are inarguable.) These light-haired, light-headed characters, happily vacant and confidently poised, were fresh creations, scrumptiously mixing voluptuous sexuality and eternal innocence. Cherie is more complex because, although still funny, she's aware of the lacks in her life, rendering her dissatisfied, even lost. She may be hanging on to pipe dreams, but at least she's got the moxie to try to improve her situation. Monroe gives one of those rare performances that is brilliantly comic *and* a genuine heart-tugger. She abandons her signature breathiness to give Cherie a delicious hillbilly twang, getting a wide range of expressiveness from the uninhibited nature of the thick dialect.

Twenty-one-year-old Bo Decker (Don Murray), a strapping Montana cowboy (and virgin), and Virge (Arthur O'Connell), his sidekick (and surrogate father), head to Phoenix so Bo can compete in the rodeo and, while there, find "a angel" to be his wife. At the dumpy Blue Dragon Cafe, Bo sees scantily clad Cherie performing her solo act and is certain that this Ozark beauty is the bride for him. She's attracted to him, but she has plans to go to Hollywood and wants no part of his persistent stalking. Bo has no idea how to court a woman; after the rodeo, he literally lassos Cherie and before she knows it, she's on a Montana-bound bus with him and Virge. A blizzard strands the bus at a diner, affording Bo and Cherie time to figure out if they do, in fact, belong together.

Self-christened "Sherr-*eee*," and calling herself a "chanteuse," she's doing all she can to rise above the seediness around her. She's used to men pawing her and pushing her around and handles each day's indignities with a fortifying, big-dreamed outlook. In her dressing room, she tells her waitress pal, Vera (Eileen Heckart), about her agenda for film stardom. When she reveals, with her trusty map as a prop, her goal as "Hollywood and Vine!" (where she'll be discovered), Monroe has a bubbling-over naïveté that transcends Cherie's tawdry present and bruised past. And then she sings. In an extraordinary depiction of a rotten performer, Monroe wraps her drawl around "That Old Black Magic" for a roomful of noisy, indifferent drunks (though it's hard to believe that *anyone* could ignore even an untalented Marilyn). Wearing a skimpy blue costume and black gloves, Monroe makes it clear how hard Cherie has worked on this painfully unspontaneous presentation: she emphasizes the lyrics with hilariously literal gestures; she busily swirls her scarf, imagining herself stylish; for her garish lighting effects, she must awkwardly kick switches on the floor. Without condescension or mockery, or a wink to the movie audience, Monroe gives a lesson in how to play a cluelessly terrible performer: with a giving-it-all-you've-got earnestness. Bo interrupts, insists the crowd be quiet, and a pleased Cherie continues. She's still atrocious, but with attentive patrons and this heroic stranger cheering her on, Monroe imbues her with a new confidence. No longer a pathetic puppet, she performs with joy. Briefly, Cherie feels like a star.

Although she is aroused by hunky Bo (Marilyn nearly devours his face on their first kiss) and grateful for his interference on her behalf, she's soon put off by being treated like another of his rodeo events and by his insistence on pronouncing her name "Cherry." His apparent lunacy intensifies, and Cherie futilely plans a getaway; Monroe is touching in her ineptness at lying to him. Once on their bus heading north, she confides in sweet-young-thing Elma (Hope Lange, in her screen debut), telling of her too-many experiences with men and her dream of someone who'll have "some real regard for *me*, aside from all that . . . lovin' stuff," closing her eyes on the last word, evoking all the sexual encounters she wishes she hadn't had. Monroe knew a bit about being treated as an object, and she gives the scene a resonating sadness. Soon after their arrival at the diner, Bo is beaten up by the bus driver (in an outdoor fistfight) for his harassment of Cherie, and his humiliation at the driver's hands humanizes him in her eyes. In a series of apologies and confessions, they at last get to know each other, gingerly exposing delicate truths (his virginity; her promiscuity). Monroe plays these scenes with a sweet openness, never losing track of Cherie's underlying depression about the sorry state of her mixed-up life. Without overindulgence, she allows Cherie sufficient time to absorb and trust Bo's newfound tenderness. Near the end, he offers her his coat, and the emotional climax of the film is watching Monroe get into that coat. So moved at being treated with the gentle care she craves, she slips into it with a look of pure ecstasy, proudly luxuriating in his love. As she savors the moment, Monroe moans softly and, as she leans her head back against his chest, Cherie's longing to be loved has been fulfilled. The act of putting on a coat is a simple one, but I have never seen it accomplished with such shimmering feeling.

Director Joshua Logan, who had brought Inge's *Picnic* to the screen the year before, gives keen attention to his two key players, guiding Monroe to career-topping heights and Don Murray, in his screen debut, to a Best Supporting Actor Oscar nomination for his gawky, immature, sometimes brutish, often tornado-like Bo. Murray and Monroe are naturally funny together, share real intimacy, and are convincingly hot for each other. *Seven Year Itch* playwright George Axelrod sensibly "opened up" Inge's play, dramatizing events that were merely reported on stage, such as the rodeo, Cherie's Blue Dragon gig, Bo's pursuit of her, and her failed escape. (The play begins with the bus's snowy arrival at the diner, which occurs sixty-five minutes into the movie.) Play or movie, *Bus Stop* is likeable but slight, little more than a showcase for two charismatic performers, which it gets in spades in this colorful CinemaScope rendition.

The industry refused to acknowledge the new Marilyn Monroe with a much-deserved Oscar nomination, yet they somehow found room on the ballot for Nancy Kelly's abominably stagy work in *The Bad Seed*. Monroe would again employ her comic sunniness and kicked-around sensitivity when she played Sugar in *Some Like It Hot* (1959). Sugar doesn't have Cherie's depth (and she's secondary to the main plot), but she's still irresistible; who can imagine this mega-classic without Monroe? Both characters want respect and appreciation. Join me in giving those very things to their lustrous portrayer.

Tom Ewell, Henry Jones, Edmond O'Brien, and Jayne Mansfield

Edmond O'Brien

IN

The Girl Can't Help It

(1956)

To describe a performance as cartoonish is usually meant as a criticism. But in the case of Edmond O'Brien's go-for-broke flamboyance as hoodlum Marty "Fats" Murdock in Frank Tashlin's rock-and-roll musical comedy *The Girl Can't Help It*, I can't think of higher praise. Fats is a looney-tunes parody of *every* movie gangster, and more than any live-action film I can think of, *The Girl Can't Help It* feels like an animated movie. Filmed in the brightest colors you'll find in your Crayola box, this toe-tappin' fairy tale sometimes reaches the blissful heights of the best movie musicals of the 1950s. But how in the world did the very black-and-white Edmond O'Brien find himself in this pop-up book of a movie? It certainly was a huge leap from his first important screen role: the unfortunately named Gringoire, Maureen O'Hara's love interest, in the 1939 Charles Laughton version of *The Hunchback of Notre Dame* ("Oh, Gringoire" doesn't exactly roll off the tongue). O'Brien found his proper niche in gritty films of the late 1940s, such as *The Killers* (1946), *White Heat* (1949), and *D.O.A.* (1949). He distinguished himself with his sure-footed portrayal of Casca in Joseph L. Mankiewicz's *Julius Caesar* (1953), a star-studded journey into Shakespeare. Mankiewicz then cast him as the press agent in *The Barefoot Contessa* (1954), and it won him the Best Supporting Actor Oscar. It's a good performance, but I suspect that he won because voters were torn between *On the Waterfront*'s Lee J. Cobb, Karl Malden, and Rod Steiger and that they eventually opted for O'Brien as a way out of their indecision. (Cobb should have won.) *The Girl Can't Help It* is too silly to have won anybody an Oscar, but I think O'Brien's all-out buffoonery makes it his most dauntless performance.

Fats, a has-been crook formerly known as "Slim," wants to marry Jerri Jordan (Jayne Mansfield), an astonishingly endowed platinum blond, but he'd like her to be a "somebody" before they wed (so she'll be worthy of him). Although her manufactured look makes Marilyn Monroe seem like the girl next door, Jerri's an unspoiled sweetie who longs to be a wife and mother, cooking and cleaning her way to happiness. Fats hires washed-up agent Tom Miller (Tom Ewell) to make her a recording star. Tom unwisely starts her publicity buildup before bothering to find out if she has any vocal talent. When Tom and Jerri (are their names a nod to the film's cartoonlike nature?) fall in love, they know that this wasn't what Fats had in mind.

O'Brien burlesques his way through all the clichés of movie gangsters. He must have picked up a few pointers when he costarred with a combustibly over-the-top James Cagney in *White Heat*. But since Fats is never without a cigar to chomp on, he's actually more like Edward G. Robinson (O'Brien's tub scene is the bubble-bath version of Robinson's in *Key Largo* [1948]). When Fats goes wham-bang ballistic (which is often), you half expect smoke to come out of his ears. (At his most agitated, he reminds me of an urbanized Yosemite Sam.) O'Brien yells his lines with gravel-voiced bravado, applying the traditional dis-and-dat accent preferred by thugs, and occasionally detonates his coarse, bellowing laugh. Movie gangsters are usually a spiffy breed, believing that fancy clothes will give them class. Happily for us, Fats has a louder approach to fashion. O'Brien's flashy, neon-lit costumes work like catnip in stimulating his goofy side; he is a tomato-like sight gag storming out of Jerri's apartment in nothing but a bright red nightshirt (red is decidedly *his* color). He also gets to ham it up (the great mobster roles were often sentimental slobs), choking back tears after watching a newsreel about the saddest story he's ever heard: his own untimely downfall from king of the slot machines. Whatever comes Fats Murdock's way, Edmond O'Brien is clearly having the time of his life thrashing through it.

Fats may want to turn Jerri into a canary, but he's the one who's a born entertainer. No one can perform "Rock Around the Rock Pile," one of the many songs he wrote while incarcerated, like Fats himself. In his swell Park Avenue digs, he introduces the song to Tom as a potential career maker for Jerri. O'Brien *acts* the inane prison-life lyrics with all his might; his strenuous commitment to do justice to the terrible song is flat-out hilarious. Later on, before an audience of eager teens, he overcomes his initial nerves and sells the song with furious gestures that could knock you to the ground. Lapping up the spotlight, he throws his whole body into this definitive rendition, hopping around the stage with catchy, up-to-the-minute dance moves. There was a hint of his physical grace in the sidewalk scene in which he readies himself for a bit of tough-guy intimidation aimed at a bar owner: he steps out of his car, adjusts his trench coat and then his hat and, now primed for action, glides his way into the bar with snazzy finesse (Jackie Gleason couldn't have done it any funnier).

Although best known for his string of Jerry Lewis movies, writer-director Frank Tashlin never made anything as original as *The Girl Can't Help It*. (The script was cowritten by Herbert Baker.) The music, the color (a big thank you to cinematographer Leon Shamroy), and the jokes come together in madly enjoyable, bordering-on-surreal scenes: Mansfield's va-va-va-voom walk from her nightclub table to the powder room (accompanied by Little Richard's knockout vocal "She's Got It"); her innocent yet man-demolishing, title-tune stroll to Ewell's apartment; and, best of all, Ewell's Julie London hallucination, in which London taunts him with "Cry Me a River," appearing in a different outfit every few lines (a crash course in 1956 high fashion). Mansfield has a tongue-in-cheek field day with the incongruity of Jerri's colossal shapelessness (Jessica Rabbit's got nothing on her) and her surprising yen for domesticity. Tom Ewell, fresh from the success of *The Seven Year Itch* (1955), once again shows his skill in playing wry, brainy types. *The Girl Can't Help It* pokes affectionate fun at the fad-crazed music industry, but it's also a highly charged celebration of the stars of early rock and roll: Fats Domino, Eddie Cochran, The Platters, and a host of others, each seen to advantage. They make it clear that rock is here to stay.

O'Brien's Oscar-nominated (and hammy) work in the fine Cold War thriller *Seven Days in May* (1964) and his part in the grizzled ensemble of the magnificent western *The Wild Bunch* (1969) were still to come. But nothing he ever did has stayed with me as permanently as his crass, undignified, yet ultimately lovable Fats. As far as I'm concerned, that Oscar he won was presented two years too soon.

*Adam Williams (as the therapist),
Norma Moore, and Anthony Perkins*

Anthony Perkins

IN

Fear Strikes Out

(1957)

[ ]
[ ]
[ ]
[ ]
[ ]
[ ]

IT'S hard to believe there was a time *before* Anthony Perkins was inextricably tied to Norman Bates, and yet, between 1956 and *Psycho*'s release in 1960, he was one of Hollywood's more promising newcomers. Despite being tall, dark, and handsome, he was never going to be a standard-issue leading man because he was better at projecting insecurity than confidence. After James Dean's death in 1955, young Perkins became the screen's foremost portrayer of the angst-filled path to manhood; his performances carry a restless sensitivity, similar to Dean's (though Perkins clearly lacks the swaggering sexuality of the rebel icon). He got a well-earned Best Supporting Actor Oscar nomination for his awkward Indiana Quaker, torn between his pacifist religion and the encroaching Civil War, in William Wyler's *Friendly Persuasion* (1956). The battle scene, in which he cries as he repeatedly fires and reloads his gun, is a great moment in a film with a poky approach to storytelling and an unfortunate fondness for comic relief. His first starring role was as real-life baseball player Jimmy Piersall in *Fear Strikes Out,* the story of Piersall's rise, mental collapse, and road to recovery. This unnerving portrait of a young man being pushed by an impatiently ambitious father plays more like a male version of *Gypsy* than, say, *The Pride of the Yankees*; it's a cautionary tale with a sports father standing in for a stage mother. Perkins's performance, with its clenched intensity and unpredictable mood swings, is a time bomb, and, if he isn't the most convincing actor turned ballplayer, he makes up for his exterior inadequacies with his alertness to Piersall's interior unraveling.

A poor kid from Waterbury, Connecticut, Jimmy Piersall is being groomed for a major-league baseball career by his blue-collar father (Karl Malden). Never satisfied, Dad drives his talented son to be nothing less than perfect through high school, the minor leagues, and at last as one of the Boston Red Sox. Jimmy marries a nurse, Mary (Norma Moore, who has a disconcerting resemblance to Celine Dion), and she stands by him as the nonstop pressure starts to destroy him, culminating in a public breakdown during a game. Sent to an institution, Jimmy begins to come to terms with his father's abuse and wonders if baseball can still be a part of his future.

Jimmy wants more than anything to win the love and approval of his impossible-to-please father; Perkins absorbs every disheartening criticism as fuel to rally Jimmy for his next challenge. There's little joy in this grueling emotional merry-go-round, but Perkins keeps Jimmy's deep-seated unhappiness concealed from everyone, often even from himself. (He will not think negative thoughts about his father.) When the Red Sox send him to their farm team in Scranton, Jimmy says good-bye to Dad at the train station. Perkins beautifully delineates Jimmy's longing for some show of affection from the formidable man; as the elder Piersall rambles on about what his son must do, Jimmy tugs on his upper arm practically pleading for a hug. He settles for an unsatisfying handshake and vacantly stares as the train pulls out but revives himself to shout back how he'll make the major league by next year, knowing it's what his father would like to hear. On his own, it's unsettling the way Jimmy increasingly evokes his father by being as hard on himself, and others, as Dad would be (shades of Norman Bates, taking on the role of an "absent" parent); his flaws *must* be overcome. Alone in his hotel room, he hears a blaring radio program (coming from the next room) that compares him to the "immortals of yesteryear." As it goes on, he gets more and more agitated, soon banging his fists on the adjoining door, demanding the radio be turned down. There's no place to escape the never-ending expectations, and Perkins is pitiable as he conveys that agony.

Each of Jimmy's subsequent outbursts is a little scarier than the preceding one, as his ability to function grows tenuous. In Boston, paranoia sets in when the Red Sox want him to join the team as a shortstop, even though he's trained his whole life for the outfield. He's done everything he's supposed to, so why is everyone turning against him? Arriving at the Waterbury train station, Perkins has childlike irrationality as he unleashes Jimmy's crippling self-doubt to his wife. He runs off at the sound of his father's voice and is speechless when Dad finds him cowering under a nearby stadium's bleachers. He agrees to go on to spring training, making light of his temporary lapse with almost maniacal bursts of laughter (which Perkins utters like cries for help). At a big-league game, Jimmy gets a hit; as he runs the bases, he starts yelling "All the way!," propelling himself to turn a base hit into an in-the-park home run. After crossing home plate, he goes directly to the fans and then to his father, frantically begging to know "How was it?" and "Was it good enough?" and "Did I show them?" It's harrowing to watch Perkins become unhinged, climbing the fence like a caged animal, violently wielding a bat, and screaming his head off as cops tackle him to the ground. In a session with his therapist (after a series of shock treatments), Jimmy defends his father, leading to the movie's big line, "If it hadn't been for him standing behind me and pushing me and driving me, I wouldn't be where I am today." Perkins lets Jimmy hear what he has just said, and it's a revelation he can't face; angry, he knocks a pencil out of his doctor's hands and exits, though he soon returns. In the climactic confrontation between father and son, Perkins's Jimmy works up the courage to confront his dominator, first calmly, then rawly exposing his bottled-up fury and the depth of his pain, aching to be set free.

Fear Strikes Out, produced by Alan Pakula and directed by Robert Mulligan (the team who would bring us *To Kill a Mockingbird* in 1962), is a potent, low-budget black-and-white drama. The screenplay, by Ted Berkman and Raphael Blau, is good at building the tension levels in the father-son relationship, but it's marred by the patness of its fast-curing mental institution (a Hollywood specialty); this last quarter of the film is awfully drab moviemaking. *Fear Strikes Out* is not a one-man show; Karl Malden's portrayal of blinding selfishness and unconscious cruelty (his character always uses "we" and "us" when he speaks of Jimmy's accomplishments) is his best ever.

In between this film and *Psycho*, Perkins's best roles were in a western, *The Tin Star* (1957), a comedy, *The Matchmaker* (1958), and a drama, *On the Beach* (1959). But the success of his phenomenally effective, truly classic performance as Norman Bates put a stranglehold on the remainder of his career, typecasting him as a wacko. Only one post-*Psycho* film fulfilled the promise of his early years: the black comedy *Pretty Poison* (1968), where, as a former arsonist who likes to pretend he's a CIA agent, he falls victim, à la *Double Indemnity,* to Tuesday Weld's amoral majorette. It was a reminder of just how good he had been and could still be. Anthony Perkins was a most valuable player.

Doris Day and company perform "I'm Not at All in Love"

Doris Day

IN

The Pajama Game
(1957)

[ ]
[ ]
[ ]
[ ]
[ ]
[ ]

DORIS Day reigned at the box office for two solid decades, first as the musical sweetheart of the 1950s and then as the light-comic "virgin" of the 1960s. But there's a problem with her screen legacy: few of her movies are any good (and some, like *Julie* [1956] and *Midnight Lace* [1960], are high-camp travesties). She became a star, exuding the kind of fresh-scrubbed warmth and openness that can't be faked, when she sang "It's Magic" in *Romance on the High Seas* (1948), her first film. Warner Brothers immediately put her in a series of weak musicals enlivened by her girl-next-door vivacity, like the 1951 *Meet Me in St. Louis*-wannabe *On Moonlight Bay* (which even hijacked *St. Louis*'s dad, Leon Ames). Day then tackled, with mixed results, some talent-stretching vehicles: *Calamity Jane* (1953), an *Annie Get Your Gun* rip-off, in which she relentlessly overacts; *Love Me or Leave Me* (1955), featuring her impressive dramatic performance as Ruth Etting, though the film belongs to a sensational James Cagney; Hitchcock's mediocre thriller *The Man Who Knew Too Much* (1956), notable for Day's unintentionally hilarious, shake-the-rafters assault on "Que Sera, Sera." Broadway's *Pajama Game* was a 1954 musical-comedy smash and, as rarely happens, nearly the entire original cast re-created their roles in the film version. However, the show's leading lady, Janis Paige (ironically, Day's costar from *Romance on the High Seas*), saw her role go to Day, the film's one concession to the box office. One of the more visually inventive of movie musicals, *Pajama Game* is a coloring book come to life, and it captures Day at her prime moment: no longer the starry-eyed, overeager ingénue, she's a mature and sexy woman, smashingly costumed to accentuate her knockout figure. And since she's not playing a strenuous, I'll-show-you-I-can-act part, she's relaxed, confident, and in peak form.

Sid Sorokin (John Raitt), the new superintendent of the Sleeptite Pajama Factory, is thrust into a dispute between labor and management: the unionized workers want a seven-and-a-half-cent hourly raise. After an altercation with a lazy employee, Sid is confronted by Babe Williams (Day), head of the workers' grievance committee. Sid and Babe fall in love, but just as Babe feared, seven and one-half cents comes between them. Sid is determined to keep his job, get the workers their raise, and win Babe back.

When Babe approaches Sid in her "grievance" capacity, get ready for a no-nonsense Doris Day, unwaveringly committed to her fellow employees and prepared to deal with anyone who mistreats them. Single, she can't conceal her attraction to take-charge Sid. In her first (and best) song, "I'm Not at All in Love," she defends herself to her teasing coworkers with an easygoing toughness, as she casually eats an apple. Though she protests too much (convincing no one), the overriding charm of this wonderful number comes from the fact that Day lets Babe be rather tickled by the attention. (Here and throughout, the star energizes the score with her raspy gusto.) If you maintain an image of Day as the girl who says no-no-no, you'll be surprised when she doesn't fight off, and actually enjoys, Sid's picnic kiss; she then puts her head and her left hand on his chest and closes her eyes. In that one delicate moment, she's a goner, powerless to keep from falling in love with him. When they're alone at her house, she keeps him at a distance during the pleasing duet "Small Talk" — but not to protect her virtue. She tries to resist him because of the pajama factory complications, but by withholding affection, she builds the sexual excitement between them: when he puts his arms around her waist, she nearly passes out. Day has an intimate but ripe sensuality, completely available to her immovable costar, John Raitt. This is the rare case when I wish they had not used the original Broadway star. Oh, his "Hey There" is gorgeously sung, but it may as well be disembodied; he has no presence, sexual or otherwise. It's remarkable how much churning feeling Day works up over him: when he tells her he loves her, she dissolves onto a chair; the second time he says it, she rushes to clasp him. Day's frequent costar, Gordon MacRae (who brought Raitt's other "big" role, Billy Bigelow in *Carousel*, to the screen in 1956), would have made an ideal Sid.

While most of the cast performs at a steady fever pitch, Day grounds the movie in Babe's romantic conflict, working at her own, more spontaneous tempo. Never overpowered by the antics around her, Day balances the film's cartoonish elements with her straightforward acting. The best thing about her performance is that Babe's softness and hardness believably and comfortably reside alongside each other. Babe didn't get involved with the union because there's no man in her life, and love doesn't alter her principles. She'll not be distracted from her cause, and she'll not defer to Sid because he's a man. After their inevitable breakup, she sings a fighting-back-tears reprise of "Hey There," alone in her bedroom. This is the only scene where Day makes a misstep: she indulges in a slow and choppy rendition of the score's biggest hit. I admire her guts here, reaching for greater depths, but her emotions get in the way of the singing, and it's just too much. Aside from that minor complaint, the piercing tenderness that Day locates within her strong-willed portrayal is very affecting.

The Pajama Game isn't one of Broadway's best musicals, but the film surpasses most of the screen versions of better shows. It was codirected by George Abbott and Stanley Donen: Abbott, who also codirected the show in New York, was on board to preserve and protect the material, while Donen's job was to make it cinematic. With fluid camerawork by Harry Stradling, nearly every number soars with pulse-quickening effervescence and kaleidoscopic colors, particularly the get-to-work opener, "Racing with the Clock," and the picnic romp, "Once-a-Year Day." The screenplay by Abbott and Richard Bissell, based on their stage adaptation of Bissell's novel *7½ Cents*, doesn't hold up as well as the snappy, hit-laden score by Richard Adler and Jerry Ross. Hoarse-as-can-be Carol Haney, repeating her Tony Award-winning role as secretary Gladys Hotchkiss, is terrific in the legendary "Steam Heat" (Bob Fosse's choreography is eternally fresh and witty), but, as funny as Haney is in her drunk scene, her outrageous mugging needed to be toned down for the screen. I could also do with much less of charmless Eddie Foy, Jr., as the jealousy-crazed foreman, but more of plump, gray-haired Reta Shaw as a soft-shoeing secretary. Abbott and Donen reteamed to bring *Damn Yankees*, another Abbott stage hit, to the movies in 1958. (Though it's not as vibrant as *Pajama Game*, it's still pretty good.)

The Pajama Game wasn't one of Day's more popular outings, but today it stands as one of her few films with lasting merit. In 1959, her comedy career took off with the whipped-creamy *Pillow Talk*, for which she received her only Oscar nomination. But even in wretched movies (like *That Touch of Mink* [1962]), Day managed to shine; a shine as bright as the one on that long-overdue honorary Oscar the Academy ought to be polishing up for her real soon.

Michael Redgrave and Claude Dauphin (as an inspector)

Michael Redgrave

IN

The Quiet American

(1958)

[ ]
[ ]
[ ]
[ ]
[ ]
[ ]

S IR Michael Redgrave never had the Hollywood success that the other
Shakespearean actors of his generation had: Laurence Olivier hit it
big with his Heathcliff and Maxim de Winter; Ralph Richardson was unforgettable as Olivia de Havilland's tyrannical father in *The Heiress* (1949);
John Gielgud drolly quipped his way to an Oscar in *Arthur* (1981); Maurice Evans, though unrecognizable behind his ape makeup, found a signature screen role in Dr. Zaius of *Planet of the Apes* (1968). Redgrave managed
to have a long, distinguished film career in England, concurrent with his
stage career, but most of his best-remembered films were ensemble pieces
rather than star vehicles: Hitchcock's addictively enjoyable thriller *The
Lady Vanishes* (1938); Carol Reed's moving mining drama *The Stars Look
Down* (1939); Anthony Asquith's dream-cast production of *The Importance of
Being Earnest* (1952). Two roles do stand out from the pack: the ventrilo-
quist driven to madness by a free-thinking (and cruel) dummy in *Dead of
Night* (1945) and the unhappy schoolmaster in *The Browning Version* (1951),
the latter being his best screen work. If just one of his few Hollywood for-
ays had been a hit, he might have been offered roles as good as those as-
signed to Alec Guinness and Rex Harrison. Did anyone *need* to see him in
Mourning Becomes Electra (1947)? Talk about a prestige project: a three-
hour Eugene O'Neill psychodrama (and I do mean *psycho*) costarring Rosalind Russell, Raymond Massey, Katina Paxinou, and Kirk Douglas. It's a
god-awful movie, disastrous for all concerned, but never underestimate the
intimidating powers of a boring classic: Redgrave and Russell got Oscar
nominations (for learning all that ludicrous dialogue?). Writer-director
Joseph L. Mankiewicz's *Quiet American* may have been too grounded in international politics to have been much of a crowd enticer, but it gave Redgrave a great leading role in an American film. He's in nearly every scene,
and the role is complex enough to allow him to work microscopically, deep-
ening his performance with each successive scene.

The film, based on a novel by Graham Greene (but with a markedly different ending), is set in 1952 Saigon. Thomas Fowler (Redgrave) is a middle-aged British news correspondent covering the battle for Indo-Chinese dominance between the Chinese Communists and the French colonialists. With no interest in returning to England or his wife, Fowler has made a life for himself with Phuong (Giorgia Moll), his young and beautiful Vietnamese mistress. Their casual attachment is threatened by the arrival of a goodhearted but mysterious (and curiously nameless) American (Audie Murphy). Is this young, handsome, and optimistic Texan here on a goodwill mission or for some darker purpose? The importance of the question intensifies for Fowler when the American falls in love with Phuong, putting Fowler's convenient arrangement in jeopardy. Suspecting that the American is involved in the sale of explosives, Fowler entangles himself in the local conflict, but his motives remain personal rather than political.

Redgrave's cool detachment and dry cynicism establish Fowler as a man who doesn't seem to believe in anything. His clipped Noël Coward-like delivery does wonders for his snide comments, especially the frequent anti-American ones about rampant consumerism. Claiming no political ideology of his own, Fowler can cover this war without hoping for a particular resolution. But perhaps he's not as cut off as he maintains; there are moments, notably in the watchtower scene with the American, in which he's eloquent about his worldview, eventually shrugging off his words when it appears that he has inadvertently shown concern. Whenever he's ill at ease, he reaches for his two best friends: cigarettes (he often speaks from behind his own cloud of smoke, which acts as a protective buffer) and alcohol (when a comment in a letter from his wife hits too close to the bone, he swills a fortifying gulp and is only then able to continue reading). Redgrave crafts a fallible, self-centered character, fueled by insecurities about his aging appeal and his fear of loneliness. The rivalry between the two men heats up; it's riveting to watch Redgrave's sophisticated façade and guise of certainty start to unravel under Fowler's panic at trying to hold on to what's his.

Fowler never shows any real feeling for Phuong (who seems merely an amusing distraction from his empty life), but without her there's nothing at all. The American tracks down an on-assignment Fowler to reveal his romantic interest in Phuong. Annoyed by this irreproachably aboveboard behavior, Fowler asks him for a cigarette. When the American offers the whole pack, Fowler smacks it to the ground in frustration. Redgrave bristles with disdain for American excess, but what he's really exposing is Fowler's angry realization that this young man is going to upset his whole world. You see a flash of his terror in an intimate moment

with Phuong; he lunges to kiss her, not out of passion but with a fierce-
ness to possess her. Fowler will surprise himself with how far he'll go to
preserve his setup, temporarily numbing his conscience in the process.
Redgrave externalizes the frightened, gullible man who has been hiding
inside the brittle pose; Fowler becomes increasingly agitated and emotionally rattled as the film reaches its climax. For all his theatrical
prowess, Redgrave is a remarkably intuitive film actor, transmitting the
psychological disruptions that shake Fowler to his core and lead to his
undoing, a victim of all-too-human susceptibility.

Mankiewicz took a chance on this dense morality tale in between two
of his biggest hits: *Guys and Dolls* (1955) and *Suddenly, Last Summer*
(1959). Like his *All About Eve* (1950) and *5 Fingers* (1952), it's dialogue
heavy, but its plot isn't as purely entertaining as the plots of those two.
The box-office failure of this smart, pessimistic film couldn't have surprised anyone. (In light of Vietnam's future, it's a fascinating prologue to
the misery yet to come.) Cinematographer Robert Krasker brings nearly
as much black-and-white vitality to the Saigon locations as he did to the
Vienna of *The Third Man* (1949). War-hero-turned-actor Audie Murphy
is an ideal choice to personify America, but he'd seem a less obvious symbol if he'd been given a name (the character is called Alden Pyle in the
novel). It's an unactable role; Murphy must keep us guessing about his
character's intentions, rendering him a story device. (There's much talk
of "plastics" in this movie, and you'll think of *The Graduate* every time
someone mentions them.) A remake, with Michael Caine as Fowler, is
scheduled for release in the fall of 2002.

Fathering (and grandfathering) an acting dynasty is one thing, but you
don't think of Vanessa or Lynn or Natasha when you watch Michael Redgrave on the screen. There's simply too much of interest going on up there
for anything else to occupy your thoughts.

Shirley Booth and Paul Ford

Shirley Booth

IN

The Matchmaker
(1958)

"**H**AZEL won an *Oscar?*" That was my stupefied reaction when, at age ten, I got my first book on the Academy Awards. I assumed that only screen luminaries, not resourceful maids on middling sitcoms, reached such peaks. How was I to know that Shirley Booth was one of Broadway's more esteemed and honored actresses (*three* Tony Awards)? She starred in only four films (all before *Hazel* [1961–66]), so there's not a lot of big-screen footage of hers to sift through. However, there is enough to make you a fan. She made her screen debut, past age fifty, repeating one of her most lauded stage performances, as Lola, the frumpy housewife, in *Come Back, Little Sheba* (1952); while the film cannot be confused with great drama (it is obvious and kitchen-sink mundane), Booth still impresses, suppressing Lola's loneliness and painful past beneath a sunny demeanor and incessant chatter. She won the Best Actress Oscar (in a weak year), beating another stage-to-screen turn, Julie Harris in *The Member of the Wedding* (whereas Booth's work has an utter lack of theatricality, Harris doesn't budge from her proscenium-scaled performance). Did this lead to Booth, a plump matron with a girlish voice (she sounds as if she just took a hit of helium), becoming a film star? No, but she did get one great screen role: her Dolly in *The Matchmaker* is a lesson in comic acting. With a personality as big as Yonkers itself, Booth, with blond hair and fanciful hats, carries this small, winsome film to euphoric heights.

Yonkers, New York, 1884. Dolly Levi, a widow in the matchmaking business, is set on snagging her widowed client, the wealthy merchant (and crusty miser) Horace Vandergelder (Paul Ford), for herself. He, however, has his sights on a young milliner, Irene Molloy (Shirley MacLaine), but so does his innocent, overworked "chief clerk," Cornelius Hackl (Anthony Perkins), who meets her when he runs off to Manhattan for a day of adventure with coworker Barnaby Tucker

(Robert Morse). In twenty-four hours, all their lives will be changed forever, for the better, because Dolly is pulling the strings.

An actress can steamroll her way through a part as indomitable and gregarious as Dolly, but Booth doesn't have to. She gets every one of her built-in laughs, yet you never feel she's "nailing" a punch line; it's one of the most spontaneous comic performances in the movies. She delivers her lines with pauses in surprising places, thinking her way through the words, mining the material for fresh, funny moments you're not expecting. It's a brilliantly put-together performance that looks as if she's making it all up as she sails along. Chattering away, she manipulates nonchalantly, fiddling with her fur piece or gloves, tossing her hands in casual gestures; her "bits" feel like impulses rather than "business." It's a mannered performance in which the manners mask her objectives rather than embellish them. Watch her go into action when Horace tells Dolly that he wants to marry Irene. To tempt him away from the milliner, she creates "Ernestina Simple," outlandishly marketing this fantasy woman as both sex bomb and frugal domestic. Alert to his every response, she breezes through the scene, wheedling him triumphantly. Later, in Irene's shop, she has a ball infuriating him, improvising tales of the madcap "double life" of Cornelius, which Horace, with good reason, refuses to accept. But Booth's energy is so buoyant, and her line readings so off the cuff, that it's futile to argue with Dolly. In their Harmonia Gardens Restaurant scene, Horace barks, "Anybody who lived with you wouldn't have a thought he could call his own," and she jumps at the opportunity to feign displeasure at the notion of their coupling, refusing his nonexistent marriage proposal, discouraging his so-called advances. The lady doth protest too much (wonderfully), ignoring his frustrated attempts to clarify himself. With sustained, velvet-gloved dominance, Booth crowns the moment with "You go your way . . . and I'll . . . go mine," artfully aiming her fork in the same direction for both. Dolly's matrimonial agenda does not, however, distract her from savoring the twelve-course meal set before her. (Booth zestfully eats and drinks almost constantly during this scene.) Horace finally walks out on her, and she consoles herself with both their desserts.

The characters sometimes speak directly to us; Booth establishes a warm, conspiratorial connection with the audience (we're the only ones who know what Dolly is up to). Her into-the-camera reaction shots are always mischievously funny. My favorite scene is her carriage-ride monologue, just after she leaves the restaurant. At first she speaks to her deceased husband, breaking the news that she's going to marry Horace (though her "intended" has no idea). In this private, reflective moment, Booth goes deeper into Dolly, capturing the love she felt for Mr. Levi, but also bringing her genuine affection for Horace to the surface, enlivened by her satisfaction in knowing she can make him happy and that he needs her. Booth then shifts her attention to us, and you'll feel as if Dolly is talking to *you*. She speaks of the benumbing nature of a widow's grief and explains how she snapped herself out of it. Booth's evocation of Dolly's former isolation has an unforced intimacy; nothing is dredged up, it's simply *there*. She elicits our sympathy by not trying to get it; her story is meant to teach *us* a lesson, and so her focus is on her listeners. This scene, like the whole movie, is a call to embrace life, and Booth, with her contagious enthusiasm and bountiful humor, is a multiflavored example of that philosophy in action.

Joseph Anthony's direction is fairly stage bound, but the overall modesty of this black-and-white production allows the story and cast to shine. John Michael Hayes's slimmed-down (and less farcical) adaptation of Thornton Wilder's classic play retains the original's abundant charms. An odd addition is the characters' references to us as moviegoers (when they address us), jolting because of the precinema setting. Paul Ford is a terrific grouch of an actor, tremendously good as the irascible Horace. Anthony Perkins and Shirley MacLaine are ingenuous delights, wide-eyed yet spirited. (Perkins even gets a pre-*Psycho* drag scene.) Robert Morse, repeating his stage role, is a boyish, eccentric performer, and Perry Wilson, as Irene's assistant Minnie Fay, had just played Perkins's mother in *Fear Strikes Out*.

Ruth Gordon played Dolly in the 1955 Broadway production, and Carol Channing took eternal ownership of the part when Jerry Herman musicalized the play as *Hello, Dolly!* in 1964. I prefer the material without songs, and for all of Channing's spectacular brio, I find Booth's, shall we say, subtler approach to be definitive. There isn't a single kind thing to say about the overinflated film version of *Hello, Dolly!* (1969), which bludgeoned the seemingly indestructible appeal of Wilder's play. For all of Dolly's ideal matches, her best one was matching herself to Shirley Booth.

Kay Kendall, Angela Lansbury, and Rex Harrison

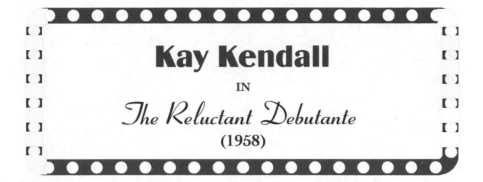

Kay Kendall

IN

The Reluctant Debutante
(1958)

BEFORE there was Maggie Smith, there was Kay Kendall. Like Smith, Kendall was the kind of sophisticated comedienne who had you laughing before she even did anything. You just know that as soon as she speaks or flutters her wrists, she'll send you into spasms of delight. But Kendall was more than just impeccable timing and flamboyant vocal inflections. She also happened to be a glamorous and elegant beauty with a regal ski-slope nose. That she was a beautiful funny lady made her heiress apparent to Carole Lombard and other stunning-looking screwball comediennes of the 1930s. Let's face it: it's funny when a gorgeous woman, dripping with high fashion, falls flat on her face. It certainly brings her down to earth. Kendall's equal adeptness at low physical comedy and witty repartee made her a rare talent indeed.

If you've never heard of Kendall, it's probably because she died of leukemia at the age of thirty-three in 1959. (Lombard also died at thirty-three.) The movies were thus robbed of a lifetime of scintillating comic turns. She made a name for herself in British comedies of the mid 1950s (notably *Genevieve* and *Doctor in the House*). Her first Hollywood picture was the Robert Taylor epic *Quentin Durward* (1955), which did little for her, but was a reliable sedative for audiences. Then came the chic George Cukor-directed MGM musical *Les Girls* (1957), which she promptly stole from its star, Gene Kelly (who seems keenly aware of it and not at all happy). *Les Girls* won her a Golden Globe award and is the American film for which she is best remembered, but I think she's even better in Vincente Minnelli's sparkling comedy *The Reluctant Debutante*.

The film is based on a slight play by William Douglas Home (who also did the screenplay), but it seems to rise to the level of Noël Coward whenever Kendall and Rex Harrison (whom Kendall married in 1957) are on the screen. She plays Sheila Broadbent, wife of banker Jimmy Broadbent (Harrison), and the title role is his American daughter, Jane

(Sandra Dee), from his first marriage. When Jane comes to London for a visit, Sheila decides it'll be irresistible fun to put her new stepdaughter on the assembly line of coming-out balls, culminating in one of her own. This becomes Sheila's life work, despite little enthusiasm from either Jane or Jimmy. Sheila is thrilled to have a contestant in this grueling competition, which turns into a genteel war with her dear rival, Mabel (Angela Lansbury). They turn into the equivalent of stage mothers as each throws a corsaged daughter into the fray. Sheila feels deprived at never having "come out" herself because of annoying interference from something called World War II. And so we're off! The trouble comes when Jane falls hard for David Parkson (John Saxon), an attractive American drummer. Sheila is dead against this match because of David's supposed lurid past but, of course, all works out in the end.

The highlights of the film are the nutty telephone conversations Sheila has throughout the story. Because of wrong numbers or mistaken identities, she's not always talking to the person she thinks she is. Kendall oozes charm while inviting the wrong people to dinner or inadvertently sending her regards to dead people. And while talking, she can always find time to fix a floral arrangement or straighten a picture frame. Kendall gives us detailed, mannered comic acting of the highest order. Another memorable moment is the mad, spontaneous dance she breaks into at one of the balls to avoid a confrontation with Mabel. And has anyone come downstairs with a hangover like Kendall? She positively melts into the floor.

In the sequence where Sheila and Jimmy plot how they'll spy on Jane and David, Kendall turns giddy with mischief as she races through their apartment dressed to the teeth. You can never take your eyes off her . . . which brings us to the subject of her costumes. You can't separate Kendall's performance from her wardrobe, by Pierre Balmain of Paris. She wears one drop-dead knockout after another and not only looks sensational but knows how to use the clothes to enhance her performance. There's never a moment when you think she may be overpowered by her designer's eye-popping creations. And no one can maneuver a feather boa with as much aplomb and for such an extended length of screen time. She uses it as if she suddenly sprouted two extra arms with which to gesture. When she's flitting through the apartment with that gray boa, she looks like a speeding cloud passing by (and is she ever not running?). She's been home from that evening's ball for a good fifteen minutes but simply refuses to remove the boa and eventually falls asleep with it. Her character is defined by her wardrobe and the confidence it gives her in her world. Despite the many mistakes she makes when she opens her mouth, she never makes a *fashion* mistake.

Kay Kendall in *The Reluctant Debutante* (1958)

While the film is clearly a showcase for Kendall's magic, she gets marvelous support in every direction, including direction. Vincente Minnelli gives the picture a supreme sense of style and glamour worthy of her. The material may be stagy, but the movie moves in swirls of color, predominantly red, from Kendall's smashing suit and floppy hat in her first scene to assorted lampshades, drapes, and pillows throughout the picture. (I wish Minnelli had directed the film version of *Auntie Mame* that same year because Rosalind Russell's colossal performance deserved better than the ugly and plodding film that surrounds it.)

After playing Henry Higgins in *My Fair Lady* on Broadway for two years, Rex Harrison seems overjoyed to be doing something so silly and undemanding and doubly pleased to see his wife get such a plum role. Although he lets Kendall walk off with the picture, his work is masterful. Angela Lansbury is an excellent foil for Kendall, and their sparring scenes are delightfully bitchy. (Lansbury's pushiness seems a warm-up for her Mama Rose on Broadway in the mid 1970s.) Sandra Dee and John Saxon are likeable and easygoing and not the boring young lovers you fear they might be. *The Reluctant Debutante* may be a minor gem, but it revels in the major comic talent of the unforgettable Kay Kendall.

Peter Finch and Audrey Hepburn

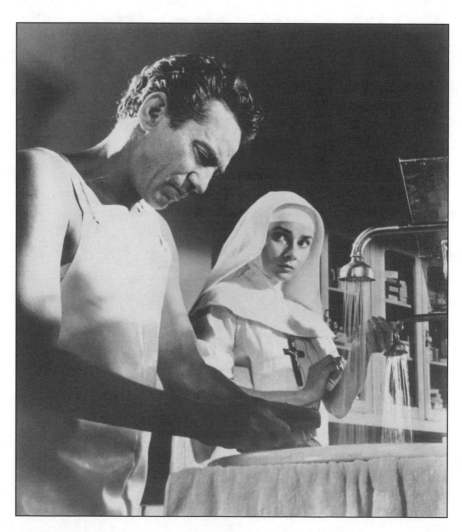

Audrey Hepburn

IN

The Nun's Story

(1959)

I F you think of Audrey Hepburn as an enchanting creature who wasn't much of an actress, then I have three words for you: *The Nun's Story*. As Sister Luke, she's without the elements with which she's most associated: a Givenchy wardrobe, an aging leading man, Henry Mancini on the soundtrack, and posh locales in which to play. It was as if she'd decided to strip away all the glamour and show audiences what she could really do. It worked. Devoid of "Audrey style," she gave what is incontestably the best performance of her career in the best film she ever made. Though highly acclaimed and financially successful in 1959, it seems to have been forgotten: when was the last time you heard anyone mention it? Hepburn's legend is based on the charming and elegant persona she created in *Roman Holiday* (1953) and solidified with *Breakfast at Tiffany's* (1961). *The Nun's Story* doesn't fit in with those dazzling baubles, but it gave Hepburn the chance to go deeper into a character than she ever had before or would again.

The Nun's Story is a far more complex and realistic movie than its title would suggest. If you're expecting *The Bells of St. Mary's* or *The Sound of Music*, you've come to the wrong place. It begins in Belgium in the late 1920s when Gabrielle Van der Mal (Hepburn), an esteemed surgeon's daughter, enters a convent, thrilled to be on a path toward nursing the Congolese natives with her fellow sisters. Her training demands total obedience and a complete lack of pride, and Gabrielle discovers how difficult these things are for her. It's an arduous psychological journey, but after becoming Sister Luke, she makes her way to the Congo, where she assists the brilliant Dr. Fortunati (Peter Finch). The work is rewarding, but Sister Luke struggles with her inability to put her religious life ahead of everything else, including her love of medicine. She returns to Belgium at the start of World War II and tries to find the truest way to serve God, her country, and herself.

Hepburn's great achievement here is her ability to externalize what is essentially an internal drama. *The Nun's Story* takes place in the heart and mind of Sister Luke more than it does in Belgium or the Congo. The central dramatic conflict is whether or not she can subjugate her will to serve God. Her feelings are always transparent to us, even when they're cloaked from the characters around her. She begins the film with a glowing certainty about the future that is increasingly dampened by the difficulties she encounters. Hepburn transmits each small moment of self-discovery as the disappointments, pangs of guilt, and stifled desires accumulate. When asked by a superior to fail a science exam deliberately, as a lesson in humility, her face conveys such disbelief and suppressed indignation that we know her ego is never going to disappear. As Sister Luke matures, Hepburn imbues her with enough strength and courage to figure things out for herself. That she's able to come to definite decisions is a testament to the will that she has always possessed and that has also functioned as the engine of Hepburn's performance.

You don't expect a lot of sexual tension in a movie about a nun. Dr. Fortunati sees Sister Luke as a first-rate (and attractive) nurse and a second-rate (and unhappy) nun. He teases her; he's sarcastic; but it's clear that he feels admiration, deep concern, and probably love for her. His behavior may sometimes seem cruel, but he's convinced that she shouldn't be devoting herself to her religion. Whenever he hits a nerve, Hepburn brings Sister Luke's fragility to the surface. She becomes irritable and emotional in ways she hasn't been before. It's difficult to be around someone who can see right through her, and her careful fortitude becomes painful to maintain. His presence forces her to confront her doubts about her vocation, and the strain makes her ill. Hepburn charts Sister Luke's physical decline not just by looking drab but by driving her to the brink with her brisk efficiency. In her desire to avoid quiet moments of reflection, she winds up in a sickbed where there is time for little else. Hepburn increases Sister Luke's level of discomfort in the intimate scenes in which Dr. Fortunati examines her and tends to her recovery. Without doing anything overt, she conveys Sister Luke's attraction to the doctor. Why else does any spontaneous interaction with him unsettle her so much? Despite her resolve to react otherwise, she cannot conceal that it feels good to receive so much attention and respect from this handsome, accomplished surgeon. Sister Luke tries to ignore this almost-romance, but Hepburn exposes her tender feelings with heartbreaking delicacy.

Fred Zinnemann directed *The Nun's Story* without condescension or judgment, neither sensationalizing nor sentimentalizing the material to make it more commercial. He had the confidence to take his time to re-create the austerity of convent life, then contrasted it with the unbridled lushness of the Congo. Robert Anderson's screenplay, based on Kathryn C. Hulme's novel, has the richness and density so often lacking when books become movies. Cinematographer Franz Planer photographs Hepburn in frequent close-ups not designed to wow us with her beauty but to illuminate Sister Luke as penetratingly as possible. Hepburn takes advantage of this close scrutiny by allowing us to see the core of intelligence from which everything she does stems. Peter Finch is properly sly and hard to resist as the charismatic Fortunati. The other nuns are played by some of the more distinguished stage actresses of the time (Edith Evans, Peggy Ashcroft, Mildred Dunnock, Patricia Collinge, and Beatrice Straight); had the convent folded, they could have started the greatest all-female rep company on the planet. Instead of being cowed by such colleagues, Hepburn meets their challenge and gives as good as she gets.

The Nun's Story reveals Audrey Hepburn as a significant actress who, by the way, just happened to be one of the most illustrious movie stars of the twentieth century. Still to come were noteworthy performances (especially *Two for the Road* [1967]), major opportunities (her underrated Eliza in the overrated *My Fair Lady* [1964]), and occasional missteps (*Paris When It Sizzles* [1964] fizzles) that showcased her unique loveliness and bewitching personality. She could never erase that beauty and charm from any role she played, but when she was Sister Luke, they were simply beside the point.

Edward G. Robinson and Frank Sinatra

Frank Sinatra

IN

A Hole in the Head
(1959)

FRANK Sinatra's recording and film careers famously hit the skids in the early 1950s, but when he was back on top, bigger than ever, it seems he never forgot what it felt like to be down and discarded because those feelings, chasms of insecurity and anguish, informed the best of his subsequent screen work. His comeback role (and first nonsinging part), Maggio, a tough little runt of a soldier in *From Here to Eternity* (1953), resulted in the Best Supporting Actor Oscar for his heated and poignant work. His emotive success was hardly a surprise to anyone who had paid attention to his gift for acting the lyrics of a song (how about "I Fall in Love Too Easily" from *Anchors Aweigh* [1945]?) He outdid himself (and got a Best Actor Oscar nod) as Frankie Machine in the drug-addiction drama *The Man with the Golden Arm* (1955), best remembered for his terrific cold-turkey, kick-the-habit scene, but he's even better at depicting Frankie's against-the-odds struggle to find a viable new life for himself. A third fine Sinatra performance can be found in the comedy-drama *A Hole in the Head*, directed by a past-his-prime Frank Capra and marred by sitcomish writing, a gooey kid, and "High Hopes," the vomitory Oscar-winning song rammed into the middle of the movie. (The main-title theme, "All My Tomorrows," exquisitely sung by Frank, would have made a worthy Best Song.) And yet piercing through these obstacles is a searing, not-to-be-softened Sinatra.

Bronx-born Tony Manetta (Sinatra), a forty-one-year-old widower who owns and runs Miami Beach's Garden of Eden Hotel, is perpetually broke but still dreams (out loud) that he and his eleven-year-old son, Ally (Eddie Hodges), will soon be living on easy street. Facing eviction, he turns, yet again, to his financially secure older brother, Mario (Edward G. Robinson), who disapproves of Tony's irresponsible and highly sexed lifestyle. Mario and his wife, Sophie (Thelma Ritter), fly down from New York, hoping to take Ally home to live with them. To ward this off, Tony agrees to a fix-up with their widowed friend Eloise Rogers (Eleanor Parker), who's living in Miami, but all he's really after is the cash to save the hotel. A call from his old buddy Jerry Marks (Keenan Wynn), now a millionaire promoter, may be his ticket to the big time, but Tony has a way of sabotaging himself, risking everything that means anything to him.

Tony's philosophy is to "put up a big front" (he drives a Cadillac, owns two-hundred-dollar suits), even when his pockets are empty and he can't pay the landlord. Sinatra's bad-boy charm is at its zenith: Tony can talk his way into or out of anything. And yet the older he gets, the harder it is to believe in his pipe dreams; there's real terror stewing beneath Sinatra's ring-a-ding appeal, the fear of being a loser. Averting reality whenever possible, Sinatra plays Tony like a child-man; he may have street smarts, but he naïvely feels safe in his get-rich fantasies. Tony will only be able to like himself when he's a big shot, and since that's unlikely, his dream-weaving holds off the abyss. Little Ally is his audience, and Sinatra's riffs, on subjects as banal as refrigerators and vegetables, are inspiriting time passers (making *anything* sound good), short-term rechargers of Tony's confidence. Sinatra's performance gets fuel from the boy's unconditional love, and it's plain that Tony, despite his undependability as a parent, cherishes Ally.

All his life, Tony has been manipulating Mario, who's more a second father than an older brother. Lying shamelessly to Mario over the phone, Sinatra plays the contradiction in Tony, flaunting his fib-telling expertise but unable to mask his self-disgust at stooping to such money-grubbing tactics. Even in their written-for-laughs, face-to-face arguments, Sinatra is incapable of falseness: his crisp timing, New Yorker inflections, and fast-talking scamming are vastly entertaining and always rooted in character. Tony is the black-sheep relative no one can resist (try as they might), but Mario's tireless cries of "Bum!" rankle him because the insult hits so close to home. Tony needs Mario's money and therefore resents him; Sinatra's pride-rallying anger, in a later dramatic scene between them, has a vindictive bitterness that is aimed outward but clearly meant for Tony himself.

The two women in Tony's life are sexually accommodating Shirl (a prickly good Carolyn Jones) and classy Eloise. Tony's lust for Shirl is palpable, but he subtly moves away from her, realizing that he could never be as "free" as she is; he is happily tied down by his love for Ally. He and Eloise bond in their shared widowhood, and Sinatra brings his lively personality down several notches to confess Tony's lack of interest in their fix-up (which is merely a means to Mario's cash). It's a rare admission of who Tony really is and, for Sinatra, a scene of stripped-bare honesty, tinged with shame but no real remorse.

It's Tony's ambition to open a Disneyland in Florida (no one could call him stupid), but he needs someone to finance it: old pal Jerry. Their pool-party reunion moves to the dog track (in between, Tony sells his car for quick funds). Watch Sinatra, in the film's best scenes, put the "put up a good front" theory in motion as he tries to pass himself off as a player, careful not to appear too impressed by this life he covets. Sinatra is exceptionally vivid at the track, his desperation rising, his "Rat Pack" cool dwindling: Tony is *too* excited when he wins five grand; then, when he heedlessly bets those winnings, *too* involved in the race's outcome (on his feet, rooting for his dog). In the showdown with Jerry that follows, Sinatra is nakedly affecting as Tony fights for a shred of dignity. Each time his chest is poked, Sinatra deflates that much more, facing Tony's festering self-hatred. Darkening the film (for the better), Sinatra plumbs unexpected depths of pain within the confines of a feel-good family film.

Written by Arnold Schulman (expanding his play, which doesn't include the Jerry Marks subplot), *A Hole in the Head* is agreeable, if manufactured-feeling entertainment. Capra never quite congeals its tone-shifting components (drama, sitcom, heart-tugger), relying on Sinatra's verve as the unifying force. Robinson and Ritter provide most of the comic relief, and they are delightful bickerers, but Mario is a character who appears to be waiting for a vacancy in a Neil Simon play, so Robinson, playing it exactly as it was intended, seems stagy (and no one could make work his unfunny recurring bit with a troublesome chair). Ritter comes off better because her role is less of a laugh machine. Eleanor Parker, Sinatra's *Man with the Golden Arm* costar, enters at the halfway mark, looking like she wandered onto the wrong set but playing her underwritten "perfect lady" with her customary grace. And Keenan Wynn gets to show some real ugliness beneath his usual comic bluster.

The Manchurian Candidate (1962), Sinatra's best film (he's the sturdy center of an amazing cast), marked the end of his days as a probing screen actor. However, you'd have to have a hole in your head not to look seriously at his work between 1953 and 1962, which also includes *The Joker Is Wild* (1957) and *Some Came Running* (1958). (I choose to plead amnesia regarding *Johnny Concho, Can-Can,* and a few others.) *A Hole in the Head* is no *Manchurian Candidate* or *From Here to Eternity*, but the dark sting in Sinatra's performance lingers long after the movie's unconvincing happy ending is forgotten.

Ava Gardner and Gregory Peck

Ava Gardner

IN

On the Beach
(1959)

WHILE Hollywood was grooming starlet Ava Gardner into a screen goddess (and, let's face it, they didn't have to do much), something unforeseen happened, something that never happened to Lana Turner or Rita Hayworth: Gardner became an actress. Not much was asked of her at first, though she was the most gorgeous femme fatale in all of film noir when *The Killers* (1946) made her a star. Her screen personality was as natural as her physical perfection; she could be likeably regular and still look like *that*. A goddess, yes, but more comfortable off her pedestal than on it. Her best performances were as boozy broads: flawed, knocked-around goodtime gals with limitless empathy and little vanity. There's no "camp" to be found in Gardner's work (unlike Turner's or Hayworth's); she was too down to earth for that. The 1951 *Show Boat* may not be as good as the 1936 version, but Gardner's downward-spiraling Julie gave the glossy remake a beating heart. (Her rock-bottom confrontation with Howard Keel is its most memorable scene.) As "Honey Bear" Kelly, the flashy comic relief of *Mogambo* (1953), she got her sole Best Actress Oscar nomination (the only recognition in that category ever bestowed on a John Ford film). It was another remake, and nowhere near as fun as the much racier original, *Red Dust* (1932), but Gardner was dazzling and self-assured in the old Jean Harlow role (a durable Clark Gable was the leading man in both versions). By the end of the 1950s, Gardner's face looked lived in, and her worn beauty was the best thing to happen to her acting. Among a big-name cast, it is Gardner, in her peak performance, who provides the pulsating life force in Stanley Kramer's austere *On the Beach*, a cautionary end-of-humanity tale. Gardner is a good argument for the continuation of the species.

It's 1964 (five years in the future), and most of the world's population has been wiped out by radioactive fallout from a nuclear war. Dwight Towers (Gregory Peck) is an American submarine commander whose ship finds harbor at the last safe place, Australia, which has five months before obliteration reaches its shores. Dwight leads a team, including an Australian lieutenant, Peter Holmes (Anthony Perkins), and an English scientist, Julian Osborn (Fred Astaire), on a reconnaissance mission off the California coast. Before they go, Dwight meets playgirl Moira Davidson (Gardner), and at the worst moment in human history, they begin to fall in love.

Facing annihilation, the characters are, unsurprisingly, no barrel of laughs, though Moira knows how to keep up a brave front, still the fun-loving, if increasingly brandy-soaked party girl she's always been. Gardner enters the film with her back to the camera, sent to pick up Dwight at the train station. (No, she doesn't do an Australian accent, but she does have a non-American air about her.) With a mischievous glint in her eye, she's quick with a smile and a laugh. But alone with Dwight following a party, an inebriated Moira unmasks her frightened, crumbling interior. It's an excellent drunk scene; with an unforced sloppiness that rings true, Gardner has the fluidity to tap into every fleeting feeling. Her emotional availability is completely unguarded (she's so *there* at every moment), and it's clear not only that Moira aches to be loved but that she has so much love to give, and she wants to give it to Dwight. They begin a casual but complicated relationship; Dwight embarrassingly confuses her with Sharon, his dead wife. Hurt but not angry, Gardner expands Moira's need to get closer to him and bring him greater comfort as his stoicism disintegrates. As they walk along a crowded street one night, she tells him, with her smoky whisper of a voice, that she doesn't mind being jumbled with Sharon (it's a welcome chance to reinvent herself from a trampy lush into a stable wife). Gardner gives the scene a bare-boned honesty; the softness in her vulnerability is reminiscent of Marilyn Monroe's but is womanly rather than childlike.

Rejected by Dwight, Moira gets loaded and visits Julian, a fellow alcoholic. She confides to him that her great sadness is not that she's going to die but that she has no one to lose, "nothing worth remembering" as time runs out. For all the seeming self-pity in Moira, there's none in Gardner's performance. Without overindulgent clutter, Moira's intimate feelings pour out of her simply and clearly, with the too-late-now residue of life's disappointments. She's a survivor in a world where surviving is no longer possible. When Dwight returns from his mission, it's her, the *real* her, he comes home to. Reborn by a first-time true love, and newly sober, she swells with boundless happiness and satisfaction, come what may, having found her greatest joy through disastrous fate; she now has something to lose. And then Australia is stricken, and Dwight's men want to return to America to die. At the pier, she tells Dwight what he's meant to her, climaxing a performance that has already been uncommonly giving. Gregory Peck is stiffer than he needs to be, but Gardner's liberating spirit, the film's strongest testament to humanity's vitality, more than makes up for him. This was their third and best film together, following *The Great Sinner* (1949) and *The Snows of Kilimanjaro* (1952). Notice that Gardner's last scene is almost identical to her final moments in *Show Boat* (and equally affecting).

One of director Stanley Kramer's best in his series of socially conscious dramas, *On the Beach* is effectively feel-bad without making you want to slit your wrists. The final shot is heavy-handed, but for the most part, the film is straightforward and subdued. The shots of a desolate San Francisco have an eerie stillness and, throughout, Giuseppe Rotunno's black-and-white cinematography has a haunting, elegiac beauty. Despite their in-and-out accents, Anthony Perkins and Fred Astaire perform well, particularly Astaire as the Ferrari-racing scientist, his first nondancing screen role. He and Gardner share a nice rapport (they had played one scene together in *The Band Wagon* in 1953) and, though his hairpiece is dreadful, his work is smartly judged (you never feel he's yearning to burst into song). Kramer had a thing for casting musical stars in dramatic roles; he would later direct Gene Kelly in *Inherit the Wind* (1960) and Judy Garland in *Judgment at Nuremburg* (1961). John Paxton's earnest screenplay, based on Nevil Shute's book, efficiently handles the different storylines, but only Moira comes across as a fully dimensional character, and most of that credit goes to Gardner (who, incidentally, sports a stylish, end-of-the-world wardrobe by the Fontana Sisters of Rome). Finally, after seeing this movie, you'll never need to hear "Waltzing Matilda" again.

In 1964, Gardner had her best post-Moira role: the blowsy, oversexed Maxine in *The Night of the Iguana* (a part originated on stage by Bette Davis). Though many think it's her finest hour, I feel Gardner strains, especially in her forced laughter, and she's ultimately outacted by Richard Burton and Deborah Kerr. But I can't fault a moment of her work as Moira. Oh sure, I can believe our world can end, but I'll never believe the beauty and passions of Ava Gardner can ever really disappear.

Marlon Brando and Anna Magnani

Anna Magnani

IN

The Fugitive Kind
(1960)

[ ]
[ ]
[ ]
[ ]
[ ]

ITALIAN actress Anna Magnani and American playwright Tennessee Williams both hit it big in 1945: she as the star of Roberto Rossellini's neorealist groundbreaker *Open City* (she's such an explosive presence that, after she's gunned down in the street, the film never recovers from her loss), and he as the author of Broadway's *Glass Menagerie*. Who could have foreseen that the Italian cinema's reigning diva and New York's hottest dramatist would join forces so thrillingly a decade later? Williams wrote Serafina in *The Rose Tattoo* for Magnani, but she wasn't confident enough with her English to play it on Broadway in 1951. So, Maureen Stapleton starred, keeping the role warm until Magnani was ready to play it on the screen. By then, she'd had an English-speaking role in Jean Renoir's exquisite film *The Golden Coach* (1952), but *The Rose Tattoo* (1955) would be her first American movie. Atypical Williams, it's a highly enjoyable, primarily comic vehicle in which Magnani, as a volcanically emotional Sicilian-born immigrant seamstress, displays why she is inarguably one of the half dozen greatest screen actresses of all time. Whenever Magnani laughs or cries (which is often), it's as if you've never seen anyone laugh or cry before: has laughter ever been so burstingly joyful or tears so shatteringly sad? Her Serafina is a towering, funny-tragic (and everything in between) tour de force for which she deserved at least two Academy Awards, but a single Best Actress Oscar had to suffice. (Her director, busy Daniel Mann, also guided 1955's other all-out attention getter: Susan Hayward's skid-row descent in *I'll Cry Tomorrow*.) *Orpheus Descending* (1957) was another Magnani-inspired Williams play, and again Maureen Stapleton pinch-hit for her in the disappointing Broadway run. In the film version, retitled *The Fugitive Kind* (but still a critical and box-office flop), Magnani is unforgettable as Lady Torrance, a woman hardened by life's cruelties and a grief that will not fade.

Studly drifter Val Xavier (Marlon Brando), a snakeskin-jacketed guitar player from New Orleans, finds work as a clerk in a small southern town's general store. His boss, Jabe Torrance (Victor Jory), is a dying, bedridden man whose Italian wife, Lady, keeps the business going. Lady entered into her loveless marriage many years ago, just after the local rich boy, David Cutrere (John Baragrey), dumped her. Vigilantes killed her father that same summer, setting fire to his wine garden after he sold liquor to blacks. Val and Lady, each trying to escape a regretful past, begin a passionate affair. He helps her in her attempt to fulfill her dream of opening Lady's Confectionery at the back of the store. Jabe suspects their adulterous liaison, and Val is soon threatened by the sheriff to leave town, but Lady's not an easy person to leave.

When Lady enters, she's completely unconnected to the boisterous commotion attending Jabes's return from the hospital; Magnani exerts not the slightest pretense of being happy to have him home. Lady hates the community that murdered her father, and Magnani wears this bitterness proudly. How else can Lady tell she's alive? She seethes when told that David Cutrere is coming into town to retrieve his recklessly wild sister, Carol (Joanne Woodward). Lady hasn't seen David since their split, and when he arrives in her store, watch Magnani unleash the suppressed fury behind her severe self-possession; it's a showdown that Lady has probably acted out in private hundreds of times. Blaming him for ruining both their lives, she eagerly hurts him with the news that she was pregnant when he left her for a society girl and eventually lost the baby. The haunting sting Magnani puts on repeated phrases like "the summer you quit me" and "the wine garden of my father" is hard to shake. When he moves to kiss her, she screams for him to get out; Magnani makes it clear that, for Lady, resentment won out over lingering love a long time ago. Later, Jabe inadvertently reveals a long-concealed detail about her father's death; Lady grabs at him ferociously to confirm the truth, which he does. Nobody consumes herself with thoughts of revenge better than Magnani; Lady is adamantly unreasonable in her quest never to be defeated again.

Middle-aged Lady quickly recognizes that thirty-year-old Val is another fed-up outsider like herself. Responding to his gentle soulfulness, she hires him, assuring him that she has no "interest" in him. (Magnani states this pointedly enough to suggest otherwise.) Weeks later, she asks Val to move into a tiny room in the store, and he's angered by the implication of "double duty" for him. Lady slaps him (a Magnani specialty) but then exposes herself completely by telling him that she needs him, stripping away any trace of pride. Instead of looking hungrily aroused when he puts his arms around her, Magnani's expression conveys the peace so long denied Lady, the feeling of home. Resurrected by his affection, she makes the confectionery *their* project. As a symbol of her new beginning with Val, a tribute to her beloved father, and an act of rebellion against Jabe, the creation of the confectionery is proof of Lady's rejuvenation. On the evening of the gala opening, she spars verbally with Jabe's snippy nurse (Virgilia Chew); just by looking at her, the white-uniformed icicle accuses Lady of being pregnant by Val. Having her hoped-for suspicion confirmed is a gift that instantly frees Lady from a lifetime of clenched rage; it's a profoundly beautiful transformation by Magnani. No longer feeling contempt, Lady glows with humbling gratitude for the nurse's unintentional generosity in revealing the wondrous truth. Awestruck by this worth-all-consequences blessing, Magnani then delivers the "barren fig tree" monologue; her tender reverence and exalting theatricality make it a heart-stopping, tinsel-covered moment of glory.

Orpheus Descending is not one of Williams's best plays, but its film version is one of the richer cinematic adaptations of his work, free of destructive tampering and commercialization. Sidney Lumet's direction allows the film to breathe in a lazily absorbing fashion; I don't mind its tendency to meander. Williams's screenplay (with Meade Roberts), powerful though it is, could use more of his distinctive humor and less of his self-consciously florid writing. (Magnani is spared the more "poetic" speeches.) Boris Kaufman's moody black-and-white cinematography adds to the texture of shifting emotional undercurrents. Brando, in his second (after Stanley Kowalski) and final Williams role, seems to know that the women have the better parts, resulting in a relatively passive performance of a character who rarely seems believably human (he doesn't even generate as much sexual heat as you'd expect). A raccoon-eyed Joanne Woodward, playing a rich girl bent on "lewd vagrancy" and general debauchery, tears into her boozy slut role with time-of-her-life gusto. She also makes what must be the first attempt to perform oral sex on a man in an American movie. And Maureen Stapleton, good sport of all time, plays the minor role of the sheriff's compassionate wife.

Magnani made two other American films, both costarring Anthony Quinn: George Cukor's *Wild Is the Wind* (1957), for which she received a second Oscar nomination, gets off to a good start, but dissolves into flagrant soap opera; Stanley Kramer's comedy *The Secret of Santa Vittoria* (1969) is just plain bad, wasting her time (and yours). Truth be told, her English isn't always the easiest thing to understand, but that's a small price to pay for the blazing virtuosity of her art.

Marilyn Monroe and Clark Gable

Clark Gable

IN

The Misfits

(1961)

No star epitomized the Hollywood of the 1930s the way Clark Gable, the King himself, did. Unknown when the decade began, he was soon romancing (and sometimes pushing around) MGM's bevy of goddesses onscreen. On loan to Columbia, he became a superstar (and Oscar winner) with the sublime *It Happened One Night* (1934), giving a performance that is light-comic bliss. Back at Metro, his glory days continued with *Mutiny on the Bounty* (1935), in which he's sturdy and commanding (but not a bit English), and *San Francisco* (1936), a crowd pleaser that, with a straight face, informs us that the 1906 earthquake was God's way of punishing an evil city for its sins. There were misfires like *Idiot's Delight*, firm proof that not all of Hollywood's 1939 output was stellar, but he capped that year with his Rhett in *Gone With the Wind*, an ageless performance (though I wish he had used at least a *hint* of a Southern accent). Gable worked steadily in the 1940s and 1950s without making a single distinguished movie. There were decent ones like *The Hucksters* (1947) and *Run Silent, Run Deep* (1958), but more typical were stinkers like *They Met in Bombay* (1941) and *The King and Four Queens* (1956). It wasn't until his final film, *The Misfits*, written by Arthur Miller, that Gable got his first outstanding role since *GWTW*, and his Gay Langland, a past-his-prime cowboy, joins Rhett as his top two dramatic characterizations. *The Misfits* is a far-from-great, sometimes maddening "misfit," but it's Gable's worthiest film since his heyday, and he gives it his all, as if he knows it's his last time in the saddle.

In Reno for her divorce, gorgeous Roslyn Taber (Marilyn Monroe), a onetime "interpretive" nightclub dancer, meets some colorful locals: Isabelle Steers (Thelma Ritter), a seen-it-all divorcée who takes in roomers; Guido (Eli Wallach), a widowed mechanic; Perce Howland (Montgomery Clift), an in-every-way battered rodeo rider; and Gay, a divorced father of two, resolutely committed to his cowboy freedom. Gay convinces Roslyn to remain out west for a while; she moves into Guido's

279

abandoned house, outside the city. She and Gay begin an affair and are quickly living together. With Roslyn (who's hypersensitive to cruelty of any kind) as the catalyst, Gay is forced to confront his outmoded lifestyle: the mustang horses he rounds up and sells used to go to breeders and pet lovers; now they go to the makers of dog food.

Gable, at fifty-nine, still has the roguish charm and secure masculinity to play a longtime womanizer, though the film wisely acknowledges his weather-beaten looks. While Gay enjoys the constant turnover of new divorcées, it's his liberty that he most values. "It's better than wages" is his mantra, a steady job being the worst fate possible. Gable gives Gay a bristling intelligence; he's discomfited by his awareness that the West has changed while he's clung to his rugged romanticism. The first sign that there's more to Gay than meets the eye is in the way Gable responds to Monroe. He's not only bowled over by her beauty but humbled by it. She brings out an unashamed softness in him; he touches her, holds her, and looks at her not just with rapture but with an overwhelming protectiveness. (Gable hadn't connected with an actress so intimately since Vivien Leigh.) After all the women he's had, Gay is reawakened by Roslyn; their bond surpasses sex. However, we don't have an inkling of his private pains until an extended postrodeo drunk scene. Sloppily soused in a bar, he finds Roslyn (who's talking with Perce) and tells her that his two grown children have stopped by, and he wants her to meet them, but, alas, they are gone. (Had they *really* been there?) In the rawest, most exposed scene of his career, Gable, now outside the bar, unleashes Gay's frightening despair, calling for the son and daughter he misses so acutely. It's hard to watch this formidable man become unhinged, as a crowd gathers, because Gable, investing himself completely, makes it feel nakedly personal. He places his loud, crackingly hoarse voice into a higher register, increasing his pitiable vulnerability. His hysteria mounting, he stands on a car, still shouting for them, then kneels and pounds the roof, finally rolling off and passing out. A sweaty Gable, looking like hell, deteriorates in front of us, but he expands our perception of who Gay is.

Roslyn joins Gay, Perce, and Guido on their "mustanging" trip, but she's sickened when she learns the horses' fate; she's a constant challenge to Gay's status quo. Gable, with unerring patience and straight-talking clarity, delivers a long speech, explaining to her how things have been "changed around." Gay's doing what he's always done, but along the way, and through no fault of his, it's become a bad thing. Determined to make her understand, Gable makes such lucid, line-by-line sense of Miller's words that even a scene as quiet as this one becomes riveting and illuminating. The next morning, he tries to remain upbeat, but that becomes difficult once it's clear that they've expended all this effort for only *six* wild horses, which are as scarce as cowboys. After the horses have been caught, Gay has just about decided to set them free when Roslyn offers him money for them. Gable's seething anger speaks volumes about Gay's pride: he'll not be bought, pushed, or tamed. Whatever he opts to do must be *his* choice. Ultimately, Gay is an anachronism brave enough to face not only the pointlessness of his life but the prospect of real change. Gable's lean handling of the final scenes has a mature strength and unsentimental dignity, rendering Gay the most tellingly human element of the film. It's most interesting that it's Gable, the old-time film star, appearing alongside three Method-styled actors (Monroe, Clift, and Wallach) in a "modern" playwright's text, who gives the richest, most revealing performance.

The Misfits is famous not only as Gable's final film but as Monroe's, an unintended elegy to two icons, particularly haunting for its considerable talk of death. Director John Huston, an ideal choice for a potent exploration of men expressing their maleness, gives the film an improvisatory rhythm (it feels like an all-star independent film). Miller's screenplay has a conspicuous "importance," but it also has scenes of startling power and elegiac beauty (hey, at least it's *reaching* for greatness), a forerunner to *The Last Picture Show* (1971), another mournful portrait of America in transition. Monroe has extraordinary moments, but Miller, her then-husband, wrote her an impossible character, exploiting her famous fragility and neediness until her open-wound performance becomes irritating; Roslyn is a glob of compassion for *everything.* Even more breakable is Montgomery Clift's Perce, but the role is never sufficiently woven into the story. Eli Wallach has the worst-written part, becoming a too-easy fall guy for Miller's disgust, but tough old bird Thelma Ritter is terrific company, though she abruptly exits at the halfway mark (similar to the way she regrettably vanishes from *All About Eve*). Russell Metty's stark black-and-white photography has a tactile feel for both the city and country locations.

Gable died twelve days after finishing *The Misfits*. His heart attack was widely believed to have been brought on by the physical strains of the production. So his last film was released posthumously (as was his wife Carole Lombard's last, *To Be or Not to Be*). How satisfying that he "crowned" his long career with an effort worthy of a king.

Maurice Chevalier and Leslie Caron

Maurice Chevalier

IN

Fanny

(1961)

MAURICE Chevalier conquered Hollywood twice: first as a major star of early movie musicals (1929–35), then as the American screen's grand old Frenchman in residence (1957–67). Before the emergence of Fred Astaire, Chevalier was the most important star the movie musical had yet produced, and though he could overestimate his Gallic charm, I think his work holds up surprisingly well (far better than, say, Al Jolson's slobbering desperation, which makes me want to avert my eyes, though neither man is what you'd call fashionable today). Chevalier was esteemed enough to snag Best Actor Oscar nominations for two lighthearted vehicles, *The Love Parade* (1929) and *The Big Pond* (1930). Rouben Mamoulian's breathtakingly innovative *Love Me Tonight* (1932), one of Chevalier's four musicals with Jeanette MacDonald and the first masterwork of the genre, features him at his peak: flaunting champagne effervescence, mischievous wit, gestural flamboyance, and androgynous sex appeal. After two more gems, *The Merry Widow* (1934), the best of his five collaborations with director Ernst Lubitsch, and *Folies Bergère* (1935), he returned to France. His next American film was Billy Wilder's *Love in the Afternoon* (1957), in which he played Audrey Hepburn's father, but it was the next one that put him back on top. Vincente Minnelli's *Gigi* (1958), the last jewel in the MGM musical crown, earned him an honorary Oscar and provided him with two Lerner and Loewe songs that would forever be his: "Thank Heaven for Little Girls" and "I Remember It Well" (yet it's his "I'm Glad I'm Not Young Anymore" that steals the film). Joshua Logan's *Fanny* is his best post-*Gigi* film, and it did something no other Chevalier film had done: it proved that he, now past age seventy, was a marvelous actor. Marcel Pagnol's characters had been the basis for a 1930s French film trilogy, a 1938 MGM film *(Port of Seven Seas)*, a 1954 Broadway musical, and, finally, this adaptation of the musical, which wisely relegated the songs to background music. Honoré Panisse (Chevalier's first name was Honoré in *Gigi* too) is a great role

283

(Walter Slezak won a Tony for his stage portrayal) and Chevalier, exchanging his straw hat for a derby, plays it to the hilt.

Life in the beautiful port of Marseilles is not terribly exciting for Marius (Horst Buchholz), the restless nineteen-year-old son of César (Charles Boyer), a waterfront café owner. Marius is torn between his love for eighteen-year-old Fanny (*Gigi*'s Leslie Caron) and his impulse to lead an adventurous life at sea. Afraid Marius will resent her if she stands in the way of his dream, Fanny painfully rejects him, and he boards a ship set for far-off destinations. She learns she is carrying his child and, to avoid disgrace, she marries sixty-ish widower Panisse, a wealthy local businessman she has refused once before. Her pregnancy is a welcome bonus for the childless Panisse, who is proud to pretend that the child is his. With César playing godfather, the threesome keeps little Césario's true identity a secret. Two years later, Marius returns, still in love with Fanny.

The first half of *Fanny* concentrates on the up-and-down relationship between the young lovers, while the older male characters provide local color and comic relief (by way of juvenile pranks and blustery arguments). Hair parted down the middle, a mustachioed Chevalier certainly looks like he's on hand to get laughs. In César's café, and in plain sight of Marius, Panisse woos Fanny (she flirts back shamelessly to anger the younger man), which leaves an impression of him as a dirty old man, thanking heaven for little girls less elegantly than before. Sometimes gruff, and a joke as a suitor, there's no hint of the character's unsuspected depths until Marius leaves Marseilles. Fanny's acceptance of Panisse's proposal provokes expected delight on his part, but a child to carry his name is more than he could ever have dreamed of. His family has been childless for fifty years, and the satisfaction that his business can finally be called "H. Panisse and Son" is overwhelming; Chevalier lifts the lonely widower to a level of joy that will sustain him for the rest of his life. Thrilled to spend his money on his ready-made family, he's even more thrilled to give them his love and protection. Fanny and Marius's heartbreak has resulted in a new lease on life for Panisse, and his big heart and newfound familial pride cast a warming glow. Chevalier has become the emotional center of the movie.

Panisse arrives home one night to find Fanny and César with Marius, who is hoping to reunite with Fanny (and his newly discovered son); Panisse has been dreading this eventuality for two years. When Marius says that Panisse is not the boy's father, watch Chevalier crumble; being reminded of this devastates the old man, intensifying the younger man's potential to destroy his world. Supported by Fanny and César, Panisse firmly declares that he will never give up the child. Chevalier is deeply poignant when Panisse refers to Césario as "my first child, my last child." He then breaks the tension when he announces that he just heard Césario cough from the next room; since no one else heard the alleged cough, he's wielding his unique, indestructible bond with the boy. No one will ever love that child as dotingly as Panisse does, and he won't take a moment of their time together for granted. Seeing an elderly man have his lifetime longing fulfilled is most satisfying, and Chevalier plays it all with great dignity, never getting mired in the role's sentimentality. In his sickbed scene, the lit-up look on Chevalier's face when the growing Césario visits Panisse reflects the rewarding happiness the last chapter of his life has brought him (and considering the irritating child actor who plays the boy, that's what I call *acting*).

Put *Fanny* on the list of once-popular films that have been forgotten. Tissue-requiring and lushly romantic (bravo to Jack Cardiff's gorgeous color cinematography), *Fanny* received five Oscar nominations, including one for Best Picture. The real shocker was that Charles Boyer got a Best Actor nod and Chevalier didn't. Boyer, who stays on the periphery of the plot, is in no way as memorable or affecting as Chevalier. What were they thinking? Joshua Logan, who also directed the Broadway musical, shaped *Fanny* into one of the better films of his erratic career. (Had he kept the songs, it might have made as sorry a screen musical as his *South Pacific* [1958].) Unfortunately, Logan spends too much time on the strained antics of César and his cronies (including Fanny's mother). Also, there's something odd about watching three great French-born stars, in a quintessentially French story, on French locations, perform in *English*. It lends a whiff of phoniness, or at least Hollywoodization, to the proceedings. Leslie Caron has never looked lovelier, and she's such a fine actress that you forget she began as a dancer. She and Horst Buchholz generate real sparks as a couple (he recently appeared as a Nazi in 1998's *Life Is Beautiful*). Victor Francen's two-minute scene, in which he, as Panisse's older brother, thanks Fanny for the new baby, is unforgettable. *Fanny* lingers as an enticing travelogue, a compelling love story, and, most of all, the paramount achievement of Chevalier's acting career.

Deborah Kerr and Martin Stephens

Deborah Kerr

IN

The Innocents

(1961)

A FTER garnering acclaim in British films of the mid 1940s (notably *Black Narcissus*, the fabulously overheated, Himalayan-set nun drama), ladylike Deborah Kerr was signed by MGM. It seemed logical that the studio would groom her to be the next Greer Garson (whose popularity was waning), but they didn't provide good vehicles to launch her, lazily casting her as redheaded window dressing in costume spectacles like *Quo Vadis* (1951) and *The Prisoner of Zenda* (1952). She had managed to get an Oscar nomination for being the only reason to stay awake through *Edward, My Son* (1949), but as late as 1953, Kerr's talent was still being wasted: she had a supporting role in *Young Bess*, a Jean Simmons vehicle. It was at Columbia, as the blond and adulterous army wife in *From Here to Eternity* (1953), that she broke out of her genteel limbo. Could that really be little Miss Deborah Kerr getting it on with Burt Lancaster in the waves (and trying her best to hit the American *R*s in words like *sergeant*)? After a Broadway triumph in *Tea and Sympathy* (1953), she returned to Hollywood, becoming one of the actresses who would dominate the screen for the remainder of the decade. Although her singing was dubbed by Marni Nixon, no one could touch Kerr as Anna in *The King and I* (1956). (Jodie Foster should be forced to return one of her Oscars for making her Anna a lifeless bore.) Lost in the shuffle of Kerr's most admired films (*Heaven Knows, Mr. Allison* [1957]; *Separate Tables* [1958]; *The Sundowners* [1960]) is perhaps the best one of all: *The Innocents*, an extraordinary adaptation of *The Turn of the Screw*, Henry James's complex horror tale. As Miss Giddens, a ghost-seeing governess, Kerr gives us the unsettling flip side to her nurturing Anna, making it a brilliantly perverse piece of casting.

Miss Giddens (who is nameless in the novel), a country parson's daughter, is hired by a wealthy Londoner (Michael Redgrave) to be governess to his orphaned nephew and niece, ten-year-old Miles (Martin Stephens) and slightly younger Flora (Pamela Franklin), at his lavish country estate. The uncle grants her complete authority, but she must obey one firm rule: *never* contact him about anything. Giddens adores Flora immediately, and Miles arrives soon after, having been expelled from school under unspecified circumstances. All is well until Giddens is plagued by visions of Miss Jessel, her dead predecessor, and Peter Quint, Jessel's dead lover and the master's former valet. She comes to believe that the children are in direct contact with these apparitions, and she's determined to save them from supernatural manipulation. But are these demons actually appearing, or is she imagining them?

Beneath the elegant manners and "Mrs. Anna" hoopskirts, Kerr brims with sexual curiosity. (The character is twenty in the novel; you'll have to forgive Kerr for pushing forty when the role came her way.) At her interview, she's charmed by the roguish bachelor uncle into accepting the position. She beams when he takes her hand, asking for her help. He's never seen again, but Kerr's reactions to subsequent mentions of him hint at Giddens's fantasies of someday being one of his romantic conquests. Arriving at the estate, this inexperienced woman is overwhelmed by both the beauty and the violence of the natural world: lush gardens, predatory insects, flapping pigeons, fierce wind and rain. While cutting roses, she's unnerved to find an unidentified man looking at her from the watch-tower. (Watch Kerr eerily *feel* his presence before she sees him.) He next appears (peering at her from outside a window) moments after she has stumbled upon a photograph of Peter Quint in the attic; she then realizes that her menacing stranger is the man in the photograph. She acknowledges his handsomeness when she relates her terror to housekeeper Mrs. Grose (Megs Jenkins), who reveals that Quint is *dead*; now, as a bad spirit, he becomes Giddens's obsession. She later concludes that Miles is possessed by Quint, and there's a shocking good-night kiss encounter: Miles plants a prolonged mouth-to-mouth kiss on her, and she doesn't pull away. Kerr's stunned expression exposes Giddens's guilt in allowing herself to make contact with Quint through the boy. In the supposed interest of discovering what these devils want, she presses Mrs. Grose to tell her all of the indecent details of the abusive relationship between Quint and Jessel; Giddens is transfixed by the lurid tales. In the final showdown, she insists on being alone in the house with Miles (meaning Quint?), feverishly setting the stage for inevitable disaster.

If hallucinations of Quint come from Giddens's sexual repression, Jessel's appearances denote the governess's enormous insecurity about her ability to do her job and win the affection of the children. Told of Flora's love for Jessel, Giddens has a nagging interest in her deceased rival. Miles's past worship of Quint adds to her feelings of exclusion; she can't handle the competition, even if it's from beyond the grave. Although she *thinks* she loves the children, she has no conception of how to relate to them, misinterpreting their actions and blind to their fragility. She's even jealous of their closeness to each other, which intensifies her suspicion that they're in collusion with the ghosts. Kerr's Giddens is distressingly schizophrenic around the children: she's either smothering them with maternal warmth or perceiving sinister motives behind their every move. She even turns angrily on ever-supportive Mrs. Grose. As Giddens comes apart at her elaborate seams, Kerr sustains the character's furious conviction to fight evil, leaving no room for the possibility that she may be acting rashly or wrongheadedly. Kerr's convincing semblance of lucidity prevents us from ever dismissing Giddens as merely crazy, but her crusade is frighteningly marked by increasing paranoia and unending susceptibility. The clarity of Kerr's acting brings psychological logic to a character in whom logic has little place.

Jack Clayton, fresh from directing the searing *Room at the Top* (1959), turned James's classic into a breathtaking movie; he never loses sight of the fact that *all* of the characters are innocents. Every frame of Freddie Francis's cinematography provides sensory overload, and the ghost scenes are among the most nightmarish black-and-white images I've ever seen. The penetrating screenplay, by William Archibald and Truman Capote, embellishes the story with small, deft touches not in the novel (a hide-and-seek game, a music-box tune, Quint's photo, an outdoor climax among statuary). Since Martin Stephens had been so chilling the year before as an emotionless alien child in *Village of the Damned*, you really can't blame Kerr for suspecting the worst; his Miles is preternaturally precocious. *The Innocents* is far superior to the other adult fright flick of the time: *The Haunting* (1963), Robert Wise's talky, pretentious, and unsatisfying effort.

Kerr holds the record for the most (six) Best Actress Oscar nominations without a win. And she wasn't nominated for her Miss Giddens, or for her final important screen role, Tennessee Williams's Hannah Jelkes in John Huston's *Night of the Iguana* (1964). She was presented with an honorary award in 1994. Nice try, Academy, but I'd call it a too-little-too-late gesture.

Yvette Mimieux and Olivia de Havilland

Olivia de Havilland

IN

Light in the Piazza
(1962)

U NINTERESTED in developing the beautiful and gifted Olivia de Havilland into a prestigious actress, Warner Brothers utilized her in unchallenging, love-interest parts in a series of Errol Flynn adventures, the
best being the altogether perfect *Adventures of Robin Hood* (1938). She got
to prove her acting mettle on loan to other studios, notably in *Gone With
the Wind* (1939), featuring her immortal Melanie, and *Hold Back the Dawn*
(1941), for which she famously lost an Oscar to her younger sister, Joan
Fontaine *(Suspicion)*. When she broke free from Warners, winning a lawsuit that thereafter prevented studios from adding an actor's suspension
weeks to the ends of their seven-year contracts, she quickly became the
foremost screen actress of the late 1940s. Under Mitchell Leisen's guidance (he had also directed *Hold Back the Dawn*), she won the Oscar for *To
Each His Own* (1946), one of the last (and best) of the unwed-mother sagas.
Then came her two biggies: *The Snake Pit* (1948), *the* mental-institution
picture of its time, hasn't aged well, but her startling, vivid work gives it
a depth not found in the script; *The Heiress* (1949), which contains her
greatest performance (and won her a second Oscar), is a lesson from
William Wyler in how to bring a play to the screen. Unfortunately, she
couldn't sustain the momentum; she isn't even the central character of her
two best films of the 1950s, *My Cousin Rachel* (1952) and *The Proud Rebel*
(1958), which focus, respectively, on Richard Burton and Alan Ladd. But
one more plum role came her way. She's in nearly every scene of the unusual *Light in the Piazza,* gracing it with her emotional transparency and
mature intelligence. It's a film topped only by *Summertime* (1955) in the
Italy-does-strange-and-wonderful-things-to-Americans genre.

Wealthy, middle-aged Meg Johnson (de Havilland) is on a leisurely vacation in Florence with her blond, lovely, twenty-something daughter,
Clara (Yvette Mimieux). When Clara was a child, a pony's kick to her
head resulted in her never progressing mentally past age ten. When well-

off shop owner Fabrizio Naccarelli (George Hamilton) pursues Clara, Meg tries her best to discourage him (without revealing why). But Clara and Fabrizio fall in love and, primarily because of the language barrier, her condition isn't obvious to him or to his family. Though aching to see Clara find happiness, Meg is flummoxed as to what she ought to do. She takes Clara to Rome, where they're met by Meg's pragmatic husband, Noel (Barry Sullivan), who thinks it's time to put Clara in a "school." Revulsed by that option, Meg takes Clara back to Florence (and Fabrizio), determined to see them wed. (This all plays infinitely better than it sounds.)

Meg appears to be a typical guidebook-clutching tourist (albeit one with a smart Christian Dior wardrobe), but you'll soon spot the unceasing strain beneath her Winston-Salem manners and glamorous façade (flattered by caramel-colored hair). De Havilland's Meg carries the sadness of clinging to an impossible dream: to see her beloved Clara lead a normal life. But every time Fabrizio appears, Meg tightens, behaving politely but not friendlily, as she does her best to dissuade him, until she realizes that he and Clara share an unmistakably special connection. De Havilland is keenly attuned to Meg's fluctuating impulses, torn between fleeing (to shield Clara) before disaster strikes and weakening to the possibility of an answer to her prayers. As she becomes further embroiled in the Fabrizio situation, her cool reserve gives way to flat-out bewilderment. De Havilland has the immediacy of playing each scene as if she has no idea where it's headed: watch her carefully checking the Naccarellis' reactions to Clara's more pronounced childlike responses; her uncharacteristic snapping at the American consul for his lack of sympathy regarding her circumstances; her increasing mystification at her own inaction in allowing the courtship to continue. There's a telling, metaphoric scene in which Meg takes a ride in a horse-drawn carriage. As the driver's quickening speed unsettles her, Meg's fragile composure is punctured; *all* of her mounting fears rise disruptively (and unconsciously) to the surface as she, too, drives cautionless into an unknown she may not be able to control.

De Havilland makes Meg's snowballing dilemma that much more complex by enlightening her with an awareness of the irrationality of her hopes for Clara. In Rome, she defends the scenario of Clara's uncomplicated, pampered future (with Fabrizio) to her skeptical husband, Noel, but is really trying to convince herself. When he mentions an expensive "home" for Clara as the inevitable answer, it's all Meg has to hear. The moment he leaves for the States, she takes Clara back to Florence, resolved to see her daughter marry her Italian. With her mission clear, de Havilland sheds years of Meg's inhibiting pain and doubt, smiling easily and openly as she gets closer to securing a happy ending. When she tells

Fabrizio's father (Rossano Brazzi) that she won't leave Florence until their children are married, de Havilland says it simply but firmly. Then a crisis erupts, and she consoles Clara, preparing her for the real possibility of a return to their pre-Fabrizio existence. In no mood for Noel at this moment of pending defeat, his phone call prompts Meg to reach desperately (and most amusingly) for a stress-reducing cigarette. Answering his questions with casually stinging sarcasm, she has a spontaneously funny, transatlantic minibreakdown. It's de Havilland's choicest moment, a loosely controlled comic display of frayed nerve endings. But the story isn't over yet, and de Havilland has a memorable final line that she delivers with the full weight of everything that has come before it. (If you've seen the movie, I suspect you remember what she says.)

Director Guy Green never permits the Italian scenery to overpower the dramatic content, and he tastefully avoids the plot's potential for maudlin excess. Based on a story by Elizabeth Spencer, Julius J. Epstein's screenplay goes deeper than you'd expect from an on-location romance; it's a far more adult and intimate film than, say, *Three Coins in the Fountain* (1954). A believably Italian George Hamilton and a beguiling, unself-conscious Yvette Mimieux, both alumni of *Where the Boys Are* (1960), so surpass everything else they've ever done that you can hardly believe it's them. And no Italian-set movie of the time would be complete without the official presence of Rossano Brazzi; from *Three Coins* to *Summertime* to *Rome Adventure,* it was practically a Hollywood commandment to employ him in such films. In a subplot, which is a nice complement to the main action, de Havilland is hardly immune to Brazzi's allure, taking subtle pleasure in his smoldering attentions, hinting at Meg's desire for an Italian escapade of her own.

After giving this richly shaded performance, de Havilland met the same fate as her contemporaries: cheesy horror films in the 1960s *(Lady in a Cage)* and all-star disaster films in the 1970s *(The Swarm).* (At least 1964's *Hush . . . Hush, Sweet Charlotte* gave her the satisfaction of stealing a film from Bette Davis.) The light in the piazza was de Havilland herself, and the movie gave her a final opportunity to bring her illuminating warmth to a role that was worthy of her.

Katharine Hepburn and Dean Stockwell

Katharine Hepburn

IN

Long Day's Journey Into Night
(1962)

KATHARINE Hepburn made history when she won an unprecedented *four* competitive acting Oscars, and no one was more deserving of so lofty an achievement. However, as impressive as she is in her award-winning roles, does anyone feel she was honored for her best work? How could she win for *Morning Glory* (1933) when that same year she gave one of her more enduring performances in *Little Women*? After losses for classic turns in *The Philadelphia Story* (1940) and *The African Queen* (1951), both among her twelve nominations (which don't include *Stage Door* [1937], *Bringing Up Baby* [1938], or *Adam's Rib* [1949]), her remaining Oscars came for late-career mother roles in domestic comedy-dramas: *Guess Who's Coming to Dinner* (1967), *The Lion in Winter* (1968), and *On Golden Pond* (1981). Oscar was going out of his way to correct an oversight: her greatest "mother" performance, as Mary Tyrone in *Long Day's Journey Into Night*, a superlative screen version of Eugene O'Neill's autobiographical drama, was an Oscar also-ran. (Anne Bancroft won for *The Miracle Worker*.) In one of the theatre's most colossal parts, in a play that is a candidate for America's finest (featuring the all-time dysfunctional family), Hepburn is magnificent: her uncompromisingly ugly portrait of despair may be the most complexly detailed breakdown you'll ever see on film. It's daunting to analyze her work as Mary: there's simply so much going on at all times. Ironically, this mercurial, brilliant performance by our most revered movie actress happens to be one of her lesser-seen.

On the New England coast, in the summer of 1912, retired touring actor James Tyrone (Ralph Richardson), his drug-addicted wife, Mary, and their two grown sons, self-destructive alcoholic Jamie (Jason Robards) and sensitive drifter Edmund (Dean Stockwell) spend a harrowing day of blistering confrontations as two things become agonizingly clear: a thought-to-be-cured Mary (who became an addict when a doctor prescribed morphine during her illness following Edmund's birth) has returned to dope two months after her release from a sanatorium; and Edmund's lingering ailment is, in fact, consumption and can no longer be dismissed as a "summer cold."

Hepburn greets the morning with a forced gaiety and nervous chatter that make it apparent that Mary is concealing something. Straining to distract the family from realizing she's back on morphine, she is paranoid (and rightly so), believing that their every comment harbors suspicion. When anyone makes delicate reference to her problem, she defiantly feigns ignorance, becoming coldly defensive as her carefree façade erodes. If her delusions are challenged directly, Hepburn's Mary can be ferocious, incensed at being forced to confront what she can't face (such as the severity of Edmund's illness). Hepburn also insidiously conveys that Mary wants to hurt her family, spitefully assigning blame for their individual contributions to her misery. No saintly victim, Hepburn's Mary is a woman whose selfishness cannot be discounted. But the ravages of her addiction, her loneliness, and her own guilt are sometimes expressed with devastating lucidity. To Edmund she confesses her unending torment with, "One day, long ago, I found I could no longer call my soul my own," and the depth of her self-awareness is startling. Much later, when Edmund calls her a dope fiend, she grows very still, too pierced by his comment and its accuracy to do anything but feel how much it hurts.

It's a performance that soars on pure emotion, tears and laughter constantly fleeting by, calibrated by one of our faster-*thinking* actresses; Hepburn makes transitions through Mary's dark psyche at lightning speed, yet you don't miss a beat of the logic behind her mood swings. Though she speaks her lines rapidly, her instincts for when to stop for a knife-twisting pause, or to highlight a moment with a splash of self-pleasing humor, are ingenious, as are her haunting choices for when to whisper her words. Sometimes she deepens her voice to venomous gravel, railing against her husband's miserliness or venting her hatred of doctors. At lunch, she steamrolls over talk of Edmund's diagnosis with a plate-crashing tirade against quacks, clinging to the belief that her son will soon be well. And throughout the film, Hepburn remains attuned to just how narcotically fueled Mary is at any given moment, modulating the levels of her fidgety body language and erratic personality with astounding facility.

Mary's only peace comes in her extended respites into the memories of her happy youth. With her Irish servant, Cathleen (Jeanne Barr), as her audience, her idyllic version of her past (and her "rheumatism") can go unquestioned. When Cathleen asks why she never went on the stage, Mary, at first caught off guard, touches her hair glamorously (she can't help but be flattered) before appearing slightly insulted that someone as well brought up as she might be mistaken for an actress. When she casually mentions that she got on pleasantly with the actors in James's company, Hepburn's line reading suggests otherwise: Mary felt superior to them and maintained a cool distance (you just know that they didn't care for her either). As she recounts her schoolgirl days (in which she dreamed of being either a nun or a concert pianist) and her love-at-first-sight, dressing-room meeting with James, her voice becomes lighter, girlish, and her excitement is of a teenage variety. The years visibly melt away as Hepburn luxuriates in Mary's lyrical evocation of that wondrous time. (She daringly acts much of this scene with her eyes closed.) Later, for James and Edmund, she gets lost in a reverie of her wedding-gown fitting, playacting the scene with fanciful gestures as she revels in her joy and her beauty. Before life collided with her innocence, Mary felt protected by her beloved Blessed Virgin, and she now believes that her only chance for salvation is in recapturing the faith she lost; Hepburn's yearning for that spiritual rescue is quietly shattering.

Director Sidney Lumet trusts and nurtures his cast, knowing that the effectiveness of this black-and-white, nearly three-hour film (indeed a *long* journey) would be derived from the actors rather than from "opening up" the play. Ralph Richardson's work peaks in the scene where James recalls, with deep regret but no self-pity, his misguided career. (I just wish he had the worn, matinee idol looks the role requires.) Dean Stockwell is, by turns, fragile and fierce, but always intelligent. And Jason Robards, repeating his 1956 stage role, is superb; his lengthy drunk scene is electrifying, funny, and moving. If you didn't feel the enormous love the Tyrones feel for each other, despite their bitter resentments and accusations, the piece would be unbearable unpleasantness. As they are doing the best they can, it tears your heart out.

Amazingly, Hepburn was equally believable playing stunning beauties (as in *The Philadelphia Story, Woman of the Year, The Lion in Winter*, and, yes, *Long Day's Journey*) *and* wallflowering spinsters (as in *The African Queen, Summertime*, and *The Rainmaker*) without significantly altering her famously high-cheekboned appearance. (Only the rarified nature of her Bryn Mawr speech put limits on what she could play.) But however exquisite or plain she convinced you she was, Hepburn acted with such unique verve that she could make four Oscars seem insufficient praise.

James Garner and Julie Andrews

Julie Andrews

IN

The Americanization of Emily

(1964)

I fell in love with Julie Andrews in 1964: she was sparkling onscreen in *Mary Poppins,* I was an entranced three-year-old in the audience. Seeing her in it again thirty-eight years later, she can still do no wrong, but the movie, despite an exceptional cast and terrific tunes, is overlong and lumpy (and has too many poorly paced scenes without her). She performs with elegant precision and a firm lack of saccharine, but there's not much else for her to do with the role. She'd just lost out to Audrey Hepburn in her bid to preserve her legendary stage performance as Eliza Doolittle in the film version of *My Fair Lady. Mary Poppins* was her consolation prize, culminating with that year's Best Actress Oscar (Hepburn's fair lady wasn't even nominated). But next, it was her turn to take someone else's stage role, and though Hepburn couldn't erase memories of Andrews, Andrews obliterated Mary Martin's association with Maria von Trapp. Often accused of being goody-goody, Andrews is actually the antidote to the sentimental "trapp"-ings of *The Sound of Music* (1965). Her beguiling humor (for which she has never been given enough credit) and her galvanizing energy drive the three-hour film and, with the help of scenic Salzburg, make it invigorating. You may not believe this, but Andrews made a film in between her two blockbusters; not only was it not a musical, it wasn't even filmed in color. *The Americanization of Emily,* a biting anti-war comedy, was her first and best nonmusical film. Her Oscar might better have gone to her for her softly sensual Emily, since the part extended the boundaries of what could be expected from the versatile star. You never feel you're watching a musical star "attempt" a straight role; she doesn't have to work hard to prove she can act. Her role may be secondary to James Garner's, but she gives a mature, crisply intelligent performance.

Set in 1944 London, the film follows U.S. Lieutenant Commander Charlie Madison (Garner); he's a confirmed coward, a likeable rascal, and the personal attendant to Admiral Jessup (Melvyn Douglas). As a "dog-robber," it's Charlie's job to ensure that his admiral gets the best food and liquor (and anything else in demand) available during wartime. Emily Barham, an English girl working in the military motor pool, drives Charlie around the city as he makes his procurements. Although initially put off by his Yankee excesses, Emily initiates a sexual encounter that leads to their falling in love. Jessup, on the verge of a mental breakdown, declares, "The first dead man on Omaha Beach must be a sailor." It's his wish to bring attention to the navy's overlooked contribution to the upcoming Normandy invasion, and so he orders Charlie and his buddy, "Bus" (James Coburn), to make an on-location movie about it. But Charlie, now engaged to Emily, has absolutely no intention of crossing the English Channel on D-day.

At first, Emily quietly fumes with anti-Americanism, refusing Charlie's invitation to one of his much-touted soirees without a moment's hesitation (she seems to be the only English girl around too staunchly proud to indulge). When he calls her a prig for turning him down, she states that she doesn't mean to be, but his put-down rankles. Back in her quarters, she confesses to a coworker that, though she may appear priggish, she's actually anything but, labeling herself "grotesquely sentimental." Emily has lost a husband, a father, and a brother in this war, and she's found intermittent solace bringing sexual comfort to the beds of soldiers who will soon be shipped off. Andrews delivers this expository monologue with touching matter-of-factness, free of self-pity or embarrassment. She externalizes Emily's grief in her anger at the Yanks, whose seeming enjoyment of the war offends her. But needing to get out of her unhappy rut, she goes to Charlie's party and thoroughly enjoys it, capping the evening with her uninvited (but welcome) appearance in his bedroom. Through with "doomed men," she finds a cynical survivor an attractive alternative. Their love scenes are unquestionably the hottest of Andrews's career (admittedly, there's not much competition). As she kisses him hungrily, he tries to slow her down ("Easy, tiger") to no avail. The chemistry between Andrews and Garner is so palpable (cozy yet prickly) that I'd call him her best leading man. (The sparks were still there eighteen years later in *Victor/Victoria*, the best of her too many films for her husband, writer-director Blake Edwards.)

Andrews's sexuality will surprise you, but her performance is unpredictable all the way through; sometimes she's calmly bemused when you expect her to lash out (at his anti-British insults), and other times she's perturbed by a casual gesture (like his gift of Hershey bars). Emily is more complicated than her "girlfriend role" status suggests, and Andrews is alert to the character's inner workings. She's particularly good at conveying the clash between her tenderly passionate need for Charlie and her intellectual discomfort with his self-preservation-at-all-costs morality (even though this is what first drew her to him). This love-hate friction explodes when they say good-bye on an airport runway during a torrential downpour; he's off to D-day but very pleased with himself because he knows he'll arrive too late to be part of it. Appalled by his smugness, she rips into him, liberating her amassed frustrations and breaking off their engagement. Andrews's fierce conviction packs enough righteous indignation and disgust to compete handily with the raging storm around her. He won't let her get away with this, confronting her with her inability to commit to anyone and accusing her of hiding behind her fantasy of superior British ideals. (Isn't she also protecting herself from the possibility of having to mourn someone else?) Andrews gives him a look that could kill, followed by two walloping slaps to his face. James Garner has the effrontery to call Julie Andrews a bitch!

Paddy Chayefsky's still relevant screenplay, based on William Bradford Huie's novel, makes for an unusually thought-provoking comedy (the romantic half of the story is decidedly less comic than the war half). However, Chayefsky has a tendency to overwrite; the memorable tea scene at the home of Emily's mother (the brilliant and eccentric Joyce Grenfell) is nearly undone by his putting too many too-articulate sentences about Charlie's philosophy of war into Garner's mouth. It sounds more like rehearsed speechmaking than talking. Chayefsky also botches the final scene, in which Andrews utters so much semantic mumbo jumbo that I defy anyone to make sense of the ending. Despite these lapses, Arthur Hiller's direction balances the film's varied tones into a cohesive entertainment. Handsome, smart, and funny, Garner is excellent in a role you could easily picture Jack Lemmon playing (except for the love scenes). Melvyn Douglas is super as Jessup, fighting to stay strong as he falls apart. And fans of television's *Laugh-In* should watch for Judy Carne and Alan Sues in small roles.

Andrews's reign as box-office queen was fleeting; her last success was the delightful but bloated Roaring Twenties musical *Thoroughly Modern Millie* (1967). I must be one of the few who actually went to see her in her back-to-back career-shattering flops, *Star!* (1968) and *Darling Lili* (1970). I'm just grateful she got to Hollywood in time for the last gasp of movie musicals. She remains beloved for Mary, Maria, and Millie, but Emily gives you an idea of the impressive alternate route her career might have taken if she hadn't been blessed with those glorious vocal cords.

Richard Burton as Alec Leamas

Richard Burton

IN

The Spy Who Came in from the Cold

(1965)

I
T'S somewhat miraculous that, after all the tabloid hysteria about his adulterous affair with Elizabeth Taylor during the making of their 1963 debacle *Cleopatra*, Richard Burton more than recovered with four superb performances that made him one of the premier film actors of the 1960s. He had come to short-lived Hollywood prominence a decade before with his Heathcliff-like turn in *My Cousin Rachel* (1952) and his rather stiff Marcellus in *The Robe* (1953). He won Oscar nominations for those two and stood poised for a major career that didn't happen. A few disasters (remember *The Rains of Ranchipur*?) ruined his momentum, and he left Hollywood. His career was revitalized by the British film *Look Back in Anger* (1959) and by a Tony Award for the Broadway musical *Camelot* (1960). It was then that he set off for Rome, Liz, and scandal. After his listless Marc Antony, he and Taylor starred in the junky, all-star film *The VIPs* (1963). The title role in *Becket* (1964) put his movie career on track, and his onscreen sparring with Peter O'Toole made for one of the more exciting matchups of the decade. Burton was outrageously funny and sexy as the defrocked minister in *The Night of the Iguana* (1964), playing opposite Deborah Kerr and Ava Gardner. And just before *Who's Afraid of Virginia Woolf?* (1966) proved that he and Taylor could actually make an excellent movie together, he gave an extraordinary performance in Martin Ritt's film *The Spy Who Came in from the Cold*.

Based on John Le Carré's Cold War novel, the film follows the latest assignment of longtime British agent Alec Leamas (Burton). He must establish himself in London as an embittered, broken-down *ex*-spy in order to entice the enemy into approaching him about defecting. He'll then attempt to topple Mundt (Peter van Eyck), an important East German agent, by implicating him as a British double agent. In the meantime, he takes a job as a library assistant, where he meets an attractive and idealistic communist named Nan Perry (Claire Bloom), who becomes his lover. The other side eventually makes contact, and the plan is set in motion. Fiedler (Oskar Werner), Mundt's second in command, despises his superior and is unwittingly used by Leamas in the plot to paint Mundt as a traitor. Twists, double twists, and betrayals lead to a nail-biter climax at the Berlin Wall.

Being a spy means being an actor twenty-four hours a day. At the start of his mission to portray himself as an unemployed and bitter drunk, there's a brief, wordless scene of Leamas walking down the street. His vacant eyes, aimless gait, and unkempt appearance represent his total immersion in his role whether or not he's actually being watched at that moment. This man, whom no one seems to notice, looks as if he hasn't spoken to anyone in days. Burton's incisive attention to detail convinces us that Leamas can make people believe anything about him. But Burton is also subtle enough to suggest that Leamas's assumed personality isn't that far from his real one. Does the pretense become an outlet for his own feelings of despair? His violent outburst with a grocer may be a calculated move, but the anger that rises to the surface seems to come from genuine frustration. The truth is that his own life is as lonely and empty as that of his "character." He speaks of spies as people who want to brighten their small existences, but there doesn't seem to be much fun involved and not a shred of glory. He can never tell anyone what he's up to, so there's no one to comfort or applaud him. In a later interrogation, he savors a shot of whiskey as if it were a magic potion. Is he still playing his part? Or does the gesture express Leamas's own desperate thirst for alcohol? Burton delicately blurs the separation between Leamas and his creation, and it's fascinating to try to figure out where one leaves off and the other begins.

Burton loosens up the character on his first date with Nan, behaving spontaneously and with humor. Leamas speaks easily of his cynicism regarding the world situation while keeping his actual work a secret. He resists his attraction to Nan because he doesn't want to place her in danger. Although he balks at their first kiss, Nan's persistence allows him to accept the fact that he cares for her. Loving someone gives him a vulnerability on the job that he has never had before. Once he "defects," Leamas is nearly always seen in the presence of Fiedler or his associates. There are a few private moments when Burton has a chance to reveal what's going on inside of Leamas. Nan's safety has become the only thing of personal importance to him. When he learns that a London paper has reported him missing, a kind of quiet terror invades his face. Did Nan notify the police? Is she now being watched? Did the communists leak information of his disappearance? Was Nan alarmed when she read about it? Fiedler later mentions Nan, and Leamas, hiding how startled he is, casually dismisses his relationship with her. As Fiedler leaves the room, we can see from Burton's pale, faraway expression that Leamas's distress over Nan's fate supersedes the perils of his mission. Even in public scenes like the tribunal, Burton's razor-sharp concentration permits us to read the thoughts simmering behind his eyes. His ability to bring a fire-breathing intensity to a cerebral role provides visceral power to the film's final moments.

The Spy Who Came in from the Cold is sure to cure any James Bond fantasies you're still harboring about the spy racket. Martin Ritt's meticulous direction builds the story incrementally as each piece of the puzzle is sorted out. This film both demands and deserves your undivided attention. The grim but beautiful black-and-white cinematography of Oswald Morris is ominously expressive. The great Austrian actor Oskar Werner gives a cunningly persuasive performance as Fiedler. This character, who looks like a Beatnik poet, appears to have more energy than all his comrades put together. Werner and Burton's characters develop an uneasy friendship, which is all the treacherous circumstances will allow. Cyril Cusack, as Leamas's "Control," has an air of cool detachment that's both amusing and disturbing. And Michael Hordern has a brief, but memorable, role as a gay agent.

Burton received an Oscar nomination for his Alec Leamas; Werner was in the same Best Actor race but for his outstanding work in the rather dreary *Ship of Fools* (which lasts longer than your average cruise). It couldn't have felt very good to lose that Oscar to Lee Marvin's appealingly goofy work in the western spoof *Cat Ballou,* but then Burton would make a career of being overlooked by Oscar (seven times). Despite his staggering talent and sonorous voice, the Motion Picture Academy preferred to keep him out in the cold.

Kate Reid and Natalie Wood

Natalie Wood

IN

This Property Is Condemned
(1966)

NATALIE Wood is not exactly a "must" for inclusion in a book about great performances. She was every inch a star, but her acting might best be described as hit or miss. Often extraordinarily effective, she could also be embarrassing (remember her big scene at the end of *Gypsy* or *all* of *Sex and the Single Girl*?). Her precocious Susan of *Miracle on 34th Street* (1947) remains one of the best-loved child performances in movie history (surprisingly, she was not given a juvenile Oscar for it), but no comparable roles followed. Just as she was about to disappear into ex-child star oblivion, she was cast as wild (but tender) Judy in *Rebel Without a Cause* (1955), becoming the poster girl for the new youth and receiving an Oscar nomination for supporting actress. This reactivated a sagging career, but good parts didn't materialize (she's hardly a high point of *The Searchers*). Her banner year was 1961 with the back-to-back releases of *Splendor in the Grass* and *West Side Story*. In *Splendor*, she showed previously untapped emotional resources under Elia Kazan's careful guidance (too bad he wasn't as mindful of the cast's more overwrought members and the varying quality of William Inge's Oscar-winning screenplay). It was the first film in Wood's trilogy of sensitive, sexually explicit (for the time) love stories, followed by *Love with the Proper Stranger* (1963), a real winner, and *This Property Is Condemned*. This threesome constitutes her best work, and although the first two were very popular (and won her Oscar nominations), the last was undeservedly lost in the shuffle. Wood delved deeply into *This Property*'s Alva Starr, savoring her Southern accent, uninhibitedly at ease with her considerable erotic nature, and illuminating the character with an open-wound rawness that *West Side Story* fans might not expect of her.

Writers Francis Coppola, Fred Coe, and Edith Sommer expanded Tennessee Williams's brief one-act play into a full-length screenplay. In Depression-era Mississippi, Hazel Starr (Kate Reid) runs a boarding-house near the railroad tracks with her two daughters: beautiful Alva and gangly, teenage Willie (*To Kill a Mockingbird*'s Mary Badham). Times are hard, and Hazel is not above using Alva to keep her male clientele happy, promising them her daughter's "niceness" (and hoping to benefit financially). Owen Legate (Robert Redford) is a railroad official who's come to town to lay off employees, ensuring his unpopularity and placing the boardinghouse's future in jeopardy. Owen and Alva fall in love, but Hazel won't let go of her meal ticket, and she causes the couple's breakup. The lovers reconcile in New Orleans, but Alva now has a secret that could destroy their happiness.

Wood's Alva has mastered the role of fun-loving party girl, but the sadness beneath her dazzling act soon emerges. She finds solace in her fantasy life; she's reminiscent of Blanche DuBois, trying to blot out the ugliness and see only the magic in the world. Watch her process any unpleasant life-as-it-really-is moment and struggle not to let it break her fanciful façade. After Alva falls for Owen, Hazel plans a move to Memphis, contingent upon Alva's "availability" to a Mr. Johnson (John Harding). Bolstered by love, Alva refuses, but her mother uses guilt (regarding Willie's future) and lies (about Alva's father) to get her way. Wood's life-preserving strength crumbles as Hazel tears at Alva's memory of her beloved dream-ridden father (who abandoned them). When told that he thought her selfish and vicious, Alva repeats, "Papa never said that," over and over, desperately trying to hold on to her cherished image of the man. Wood's fighting tigress regresses into a helpless, sobbing child, crystallizing the fact that Alva has been suffering Hazel's abuse since she was a little girl (it's like watching a flashback superimposed on the scene). Alva's eventual collapse at the bathroom sink is the final proof that she is not yet a match for her ice-cold mother. Once Owen leaves, Alva is emboldened by having nothing left to lose. At a nightclub with Mr. Johnson, Hazel, and Hazel's beau, J. J. (Charles Bronson), Alva fortifies herself with liquor ("loaded like a pistol"), drowning her sorrows with a vengeance. She wields her desirability as the potent weapon it is, rendering Mr. Johnson *and* J. J. powerless to refuse her every request. Revenge is hers when she seduces J. J. in front of Hazel, brandishing the cruelty her mother has taught her so well. Wood's excessive laughter and reckless gestures give Alva a mercurial electricity that makes her barely concealed hopelessness all the more pitiful.

Her relationship with Owen has an instant sexual spark, but it takes a while for them to connect. In a manner that would make even Scarlett O'Hara wince, Alva is an outrageous flirt. Men like her obviousness, but Owen sees through it; his rebuffs baffle and infuriate her (and must be overcome). She doesn't know any subtler way to attract a man and has certainly never tried being herself. Owen thinks she's deluded and aimless, and he challenges her to be something more. She can't see the harm in elaborate dreams and, when he tells her that he has none, Wood looks at Redford like he's the saddest creature on earth. Falling in love with Owen opens up a world of real-life possibility, unfettered by fantasy. When he lies beaten by some angry locals, she offers her aid, which he initially resists. When he then reaches for her, Wood overflows with the joy of being needed (rather than used) by someone, and Alva is, for the first time, the happy young woman she was meant to be. She'll cling to that happiness as long as she can.

Wood's spangling flamboyance and Redford's intelligent reserve complement each other beautifully. Owen may be an undercooked character, but Redford's leading-man perfection makes this hardly noticeable. This film was a marked improvement over the pair's first teaming, *Inside Daisy Clover* (1965), which was yet another mindlessly overblown tale of big, bad Hollywood. Kate Reid is frighteningly good as Hazel, the *most* loathsome of Wood's dysfunctional movie moms. (Roz Russell may have led her to stripping, but at least had the good taste to stop short of prostitution.) Sydney Pollack's direction too often settles for glossy when it should be striving for gritty. He should have demanded that the almost-ruinous, ever-intrusive musical score and revolting theme song be excised, never to be heard again. Also irritating is that no attempt was made to give Wood's hairstyles and costumes the slightest period flavor. Despite these flaws, *This Property Is Condemned* is better than some of the more acclaimed film versions of Williams's plays (I'm thinking of *Cat on a Hot Tin Roof* and *Summer and Smoke*). Unfortunately, it came too late in the series of Williams adaptations; audiences had grown wearily familiar with his steamy (and much-imitated) plots by 1966. Wood had been the 1960s' key portrayer of the trials and tribulations of young love, and then she capped the decade with the groundbreaking "free love" comedy *Bob & Carol & Ted & Alice* (a film that screams "1969" as quintessentially as *Easy Rider*). Did any other actress go through as many cinematic sexual upheavals in the 1960s as Natalie Wood?

Vanessa Redgrave as Isadora Duncan

Vanessa Redgrave

IN

Isadora

(1968)

THE 1968 Best Actress Oscar race featured two nominees honored for playing celebrated performers from the early part of the twentieth century: Barbra Streisand as Fanny Brice in *Funny Girl* and Vanessa Redgrave as Isadora Duncan in *Isadora*. As artists, Brice, a Ziegfeld entertainer, and Duncan, mother of American modern dance, could not have been more dissimilar, and the same is true of the films made about them. *Funny Girl*, despite its Broadway pedigree and superlative score, is pretty conventional fare, hardly tampering with the showbiz clichés that had kept musical biographies churning for decades, from Alice Faye as Lillian Russell to Betty Hutton as Texas Guinan. What it has going for it is Streisand, and her spectacular performance is its only reason to exist. The same is true in Redgrave's case, though *Isadora* is anything but standard: it is a bold, freewheeling biopic that's overlong, chaotic, excessive, and maddening, but it does breathe life into a stale movie genre. Yeah, it's a mess, but that's part of its rebellious appeal; it's completely in the spirit of its untamable subject, transcendently realized by Redgrave in a tour de force performance. Her unfailing commitment to the character, at all ages, with each lover, and, primarily, in the dance sequences, has you convinced: no one else could have played this part as fully as she. Now, back to Oscar night: when Streisand tied for the award, it was justified, but it was with Redgrave, rather than Katharine Hepburn (*The Lion in Winter*), that she should have shared her moment.

On the French Riviera in 1927, Isadora Duncan, middle-aged and needing money, is writing her memoirs, flashing back to her beginnings in San Francisco and the relentless drive that led to her becoming a revolutionary dancer and the toast of Europe. The film covers three major love affairs, two children (from whose drowning deaths she never recovers), her time in Communist Russia, and her resulting disastrous return to the United States. As she recalls her past in these final days of her life, she's obsessed

311

with finding the dark, handsome stranger (Vladimir Leskovar) she's recently glimpsed from her hotel balcony (and nicknamed "Bugatti," after his car), and who may, in fact, be Death himself.

Redgrave's virtuosity as a dancer is the revelation here (outdoing her singing skills in *Camelot* [1967]). Beyond having the physical capabilities to enact a dancing legend, the key to Redgrave's success is that she is believable as someone who is most alive when dancing; her need to dance seems primal. Every time she begins to raise her arms, it's as if she were invoking Terpsichore herself. She moves not merely with grace and poetry but with power (she's a tall woman, a magnificent specimen), fulfilling the demands of Litz Pisk's choreography with the sensitivity, passion, and stature of a great artist, turning each dance into a one-act play. She's a beautiful, barefoot nymph in flowing Grecian frocks, sometimes using a swirling panel of fabric as a partner. The newness of Isadora comes through in Redgrave's surging sense of discovery. Her rapture expresses, with heart-racing energy, humanity's wondrous exaltation of life. She personifies boundless possibility. Vital to Redgrave's effectiveness is her ability to communicate through the music; she responds to the distinct emotional tones of each piece. Her concentration takes her to another realm, and her eyes often have a glint of madness. Yet in her electrifying self-absorption, she never loses her performer's savvy, her instinct for wowing spectators. Could the real Duncan have been as extraordinary as Redgrave? As with Streisand and Brice, has the interpreter surpassed her subject? In Redgrave's all-out fervor and tingling sensuality, and as her inner and outer beauties converge, she turns bare stages into "theatre."

Redgrave brings an innocent's faith and a renegade's fire to Isadora's blind ambition to fulfill her destiny. Guilelessly, and with indestructible enthusiasm, she simply has no choice. But when she meets set designer Gordon Craig (James Fox), she discovers something else: all-consuming love. Her sexual awakening is dramatized in a daring scene: without an audience, an intimately candid Redgrave, beginning flat on her back and looking up into the camera, dances the life-altering, humbling power of carnal ecstasy, in what I'd describe as a choreographed interior monologue (it plays like a dream sequence). There's less youthful ardor in her relationship with millionaire Paris Singer (Jason Robards). Redgrave, though aroused by his confidence and his financial ability to make anything possible, exhibits more affection than raw desire for him. After their split and the deaths of her children (a daughter from Craig, a son from Singer), Isadora flings herself, on her 1921 visit to Russia, into a destructive, reality-escaping affair with a moody Russian poet, Sergei Essenin

(Ivan Tchenko). The scene in which he smashes the photos of her children becomes, in Redgrave's ravaged face, a reliving of their deaths.

The Isadora of 1927 is an eccentric, fading star who behaves like a madwoman with her coterie of friends and staff, abusing them as they try in vain to help her. Redgrave's capricious behavior, darting from bitchiness and batty humor to desperate neediness and paranoia, creates a portrait of a woman in ruin. At her most pathetic, she's a garish joke, but the more we see of her, the more Redgrave reveals that Isadora is steeped in forgetting, haunted by the endless horror of her beloved children's tragedy, depending on mind-numbing diversions to get her through each day. Finally, there's Bugatti, a figure of romantic fantasy. She persists in finding him, rushing heedlessly to her dance of death.

Karel Reisz's direction is imaginative and impassioned, but it lacks tautness; the film feels as if it were assembled in a haphazard fashion. Seriously flabby (it really bogs down in Russia), it has good scenes undone by their length and others that never go anywhere. Reisz's filmmaking is at its most assured when Isadora is dancing. The screenplay, by Melvyn Bragg and Clive Exton, has an unshackled spirit, but only the title character has dimension; the three leading males are types, with two or three bald characteristics on which to hang (barely) a character. (James Fox is another British star who played a dancing American, in *Thoroughly Modern Millie* [1967].) That's Bessie Love, star of the Oscar-winning musical *The Broadway Melody* (1929), as Isadora's mother. *Isadora,* as immodest as the lady herself, is a lavish production, and though the film has many flaws, a lack of integrity isn't one of them. I'm surprised that Old Hollywood didn't devise a sanitized, eye-popping "Isadora" musical for dancing goddess Rita Hayworth. It would have made an intriguing companion piece to Redgrave's definitive interpretation.

My favorite later Redgrave performance is her cast-against-type turn in *Howards End* (1992), the zenith of Merchant-Ivory. As a sickly, submissive matron, she has an ethereal warmth, especially in the loving friendship she develops with Emma Thompson's character. It's like watching Redgrave pass the torch of "preeminent British screen actress" to the worthy Thompson.

Gene Hackman confronts Melvyn Douglas

Gene Hackman

IN

I Never Sang for My Father
(1970)

I think of 1967, with *Bonnie and Clyde* and *The Graduate,* as the official kickoff of the American cinema's modern era, in which filmmakers would have the unparalleled freedoms of the movies' new permissiveness. Stage actor Gene Hackman, playing Clyde's brother, joke-telling Buck Barrow, was among the screen actors to click at this exciting moment; his Oscar-nominated performance as a good ol' boy (and ex-con) remains one of the key ingredients of this thrilling, tone-shifting classic. In 1971, Hackman became a star and won the Best Actor Oscar as "Popeye" Doyle, the racist, volatile cop of *The French Connection.* He gave it his all, but it's not much of an acting role, and despite the film taking the Best Picture Oscar, two great suspense set pieces do not a great movie make. William Friedkin's direction is a muddle, and Hackman's Oscar should have gone to Peter Finch *(Sunday, Bloody Sunday).* If you want to experience the breadth of Hackman's talent, skip Popeye and go right to *I Never Sang for My Father.* Overall, the film isn't much (at best a good family drama), but Hackman's contemplative performance, carrying the baggage of an uneasy relationship with a difficult parent, peels away layers of scarred sensitivity in his yearning for closure.

Gene Garrison (Hackman), a middle-aged teacher and author, is a recent widower who lives in New York City, near his aged, suburban parents, Tom (Melvyn Douglas) and Margaret (Dorothy Stickney). Gene adores his mother but has always had trouble communicating with his intimidating, never-satisfied father, a self-made business success who rose from poverty (and abandonment by *his* father). After Margaret dies from a heart attack, Gene and his older sister, Alice (Estelle Parsons), who was banished by Tom when she married a Jew, try to figure out how to take care of the stubborn, increasingly frail, and memory-losing old man. Gene jeopardizes his plans to leave New York and marry a California doctor, Peggy (Elizabeth Hubbard), knowing that his father will give him grief if he tries to go. Hoping for a last chance at having the father-son bond that's eluded them, Gene remains, temporarily, seeking a resolution that may never come.

Hackman's plaintive narration starts with the haunting "Death ends a life, but it does not end a relationship." The story then begins in the recent past: Hackman makes plain Gene's draining routine of absorbing his father's criticisms (and guilt-inducing comments), responding with short laughs and tight smiles, biting his tongue when he'd like to scream. Tom does most of the talking, Gene *all* of the listening. Having never been able to stand up to his indomitable elder, Gene's been swallowing his true thoughts and feelings his whole life, faithfully waiting for his father's love and appreciation. Gene has always tried to please him, but being Tom Garrison's dutiful son is a thankless, time-consuming job. Hackman's rueful eyes bear the toll of ceaselessly accumulating familial strain (there's also defeat in his walk). Contrast this overriding discomfort with Hackman's open and tender demeanor in the bedroom scene between Gene and his ailing mother; with her, he breathes freely, without a trace of the tension his father's presence precipitates. In his scenes with Melvyn Douglas, Hackman steels himself: Gene dreads these futile, one-sided talks. He must tell Tom about his California plans, but he cannot bring himself to force the issue. Needing to let off steam, he visits his friend Norma (Lovelady Powell) for some stress-reducing sex. In a postcoital chat, Hackman, holding her like a security blanket, releases Gene's stewing exasperation, words he'd like to tell his father. The central conflict in Gene, wrenchingly felt by Hackman, is that he hates hating his father, resenting the old man for not *letting* him love him. Hackman makes emotional inertia interesting: counterpoint to his bristling anger is Gene's sinking depression at witnessing the pitiable effects of old age on a once-vital man.

Gene has always gotten the support he needs from the women in his life: his mother, his deceased wife, bosom buddy Norma, fiancée Peggy, and sister Alice (here from Chicago for their mother's funeral). With the female cast members, Hackman brims with an abundance of love to give; Gene clings to Alice and then Peggy as his dealings with Tom grow unavoidably unpleasant. Hackman and Parsons develop a strong sibling dynamic (it helps that they worked together in *Bonnie and Clyde*), believably sharing both history and affection. In their one-on-ones, Hackman vigorously elucidates Gene's mounting frustrations with his father's selfishness, but underneath are the shadows of how belittled and sickened he is by his own passivity. It's Alice, still smarting from Tom's cruelty to her, who sparks a confrontation, insisting that he hire a live-in housekeeper. Reacting to Tom's outrage at being labeled helpless, Gene decides to stay with him, endangering his future with Peggy but powerless to do anything else. The film climaxes with the big showdown you've been waiting for, and Hackman, giving articulate voice to Gene's predicament, plays it as if every moment up until then has been building toward this point. The beauty of Hackman's work here is the agony behind his barrage of words. There's no vindictive triumph; it costs Gene dearly to be pushed to the breaking point. He still wants nothing more than to love his father, and what Hackman unleashes is pain rather than rage.

Robert Anderson's adaptation of his 1968 play, more personal feeling than the countless movies of the week it seems to have spawned, derives its strength from its two- and three-person scenes rather than from attempts to open it up. The same is true of Gilbert Cates's direction, which is rightly invisible when it simply trusts the story and the cast. Anytime Cates goes "cinematic," as in Gene's horror-movie tour of nursing homes, the movie is terrible. Another mistake is the music, primarily a pointless, touchy-feely song accompanying Gene as he walks through his parents' house. Melvyn Douglas is outstanding, both fragile and formidable (and never a villain), navigating Tom's moods and diminishing capabilities with consummate control. Despite a bad hairdo, Estelle Parsons, refreshingly cast as a normal person, does a solid job with her dense scenes. Hackman and Douglas were both deservedly Oscar nominated, but Hackman for Best Supporting Actor and Douglas for Best Actor. (Hackman, second billed, was not yet a star.) In hindsight, they should have switched categories since Hackman's role is considerably larger, and it's Gene's story being told.

Hackman's gifts for economy, simplicity, and truthfulness (not to mention his unglamorous looks) made him, more than any of his peers, the Spencer Tracy of the last third of twentieth-century film, even "emerging" in 1967, the year of Tracy's death. Whereas most male stars of the period seemed highly influenced by Brando's bravura realism, Hackman emulated Tracy's meat-and-potatoes approach.

Richard McConnell and Robert Duvall

Robert Duvall

IN

Tomorrow

(1972)

[ ]
[ ]
[ ]
[ ]
[ ]
[ ]

WHEN Robert Duvall appeared as Boo Radley at the end of *To Kill a Mockingbird* (1962), he not only made a haunting feature-film debut (in an instant classic, no less), but he forged a significant cinematic association with the film's screenwriter, Horton Foote. Two decades later, *Tender Mercies* (1983), an original work by Foote, resulted in Duvall taking home the Best Actor Oscar for his beautifully fleshed-out portrait of a broken-down country singer (complete with his *own* singing). Just about exactly between these two peak achievements (in both men's careers) was the instantly forgotten, Mississippi-set heart-tugger *Tomorrow*, a Foote screenplay (based on his own play version of a William Faulkner story) starring Duvall and released the same year that *The Godfather* secured him as one of the movies' first-class actors thereafter. Extremely low budget, *Tomorrow* was an obvious labor of love for its makers, and that dedication shows in each of its individual contributions, none more so than Duvall's. His aptitude for playing unsophisticated rural types without condescension or showiness makes Jackson Fentry one of the more convincing backwoods characters you're likely to see. Duvall's faultless technique, devoid of studied tics and mannerisms, conceals unsuspected depths that reveal themselves slowly, then wipe you out.

Leaving his daddy's cotton farm, Fentry travels thirty miles (on foot) to live in isolation as the winter caretaker of a sawmill. On Christmas Eve morning, he hears the moans of Sarah Eubanks (Olga Bellin), a pregnant woman who, sometime earlier, had fainted outside the mill. Fentry takes her in and cares for her (she had recently been abandoned by her husband), and she accepts his offer to stay with him until the baby arrives. He comes to love her, but after the baby is born Sarah's frail health worsens, jeopardizing their chance of being a happy family and also any subsequent claim by Fentry as the little boy's rightful father.

With his hard-sounding, flat-toned, and mighty thick country accent (in no way charmingly hillbilly), Duvall may initially strike you as an actor in need of subtitles, but you'll adjust your ear soon enough. Trudging along comfortably in Fentry's worn shoes, Duvall plays the role with a distinct rhythm (efficient without hurriedness) and energy (sturdy without overexertion). Watch him toil at his chores, be it picking cotton or doing laundry or chopping wood; no fuss, just another day's work. This plain man appears untouched by life, but here, in the middle of nowhere, life finds him, and he's more than up to meeting the ensuing challenges and embracing the rewards. Fentry is a man of few words, but that's not to be confused with limited intelligence; Duvall is unobtrusively, yet acutely, aware of everything around him, and this becomes particularly evident in his sensitive handling of Fentry's burgeoning relationship with Sarah. Though she does most of the talking, chattering on about any number of topics, Duvall, a great listener, takes in every word; Fentry is always thinking, processing things quietly but fully. His early shyness gives way to his growing contentment in having her companionship, and their newfound pseudo-marriage develops at an unforced tempo. It turns out that gentlemanly, faithfully dependable Fentry is a born "caretaker," and in making life easier for Sarah, true happiness seeps into him. The austere dignity and unwavering devotion that Duvall brings to Fentry is thankfully free of any patronizing whiff of simple-folk-are-beautiful quaintness.

When he and Sarah sit outside, on opposite sides of the boiling laundry kettle, he suddenly blurts, "Marry me, Sarah," even though he knows she's still married. Duvall says these words without making eye contact, continuing to stir the pot, unsure how she'll react. (She's caught off guard but clearly not unsympathetic.) When he mentions marriage a second time, on a different day, with the same three pointedly uttered words, he's nearer to her and looking directly at her. He's become freer with her, more confident in the rightness of their union, and unconcerned with the husband who deserted her. Infused with love and his vision of an idyllic future in a new house promised him by his boss (on a piece of land Fentry proudly picked out himself), he holds tight his dream, determinedly believing that he has the force of will to keep Sarah alive, even vowing to do so. When he welcomes her infant boy into the world, it's love at first sight; he's as committed to the child as he is to Sarah, beginning an openly affectionate bond with his "son." Fentry has the fortitude to take whatever comes his way, however painful, and deal with it without self-pity. In the harrowing climax, he resorts to physical force in order to protect a promise he made but, true to Fentry's reserved nature, Duvall never gets explicitly emotional. The scene is that much harder to shake for his lack of the cathartic tears you might be waiting for, though Fentry's eyes are branded, ever after, with the wounds he will not speak of. Would he have been better off if Sarah had never appeared on his doorstep? Wouldn't that have deprived him of the most enriching chapter of his life? The astonishing capacity for love and goodness with which Duvall imbues Fentry is especially fascinating in a character so unreadable at first glance.

Tomorrow, photographed in black-and-white by Alan Green, has the unvarnished look of Walker Evans photographs, giving it an authentic sense of place, which seems to have been accidentally stumbled upon by the camera. Joseph Anthony's understated direction sets the tone for the cast as they make their delicate, leisurely journey to the scalding conclusion. With her weathered prettiness, Olga Bellin, in her only screen appearance, captures Sarah's wistful, sad-hearted warmth. Among the supporting players, two stand out: Sudie Bond as Sarah's midwife and Richard McConnell as the son of Fentry's unseen boss. Foote's graceful, poetic script has a density that permits Duvall to keep things subtle, knowing that his painstaking performance will be enhanced by the carefully rendered storytelling.

Another major, nearly-as-ignored Duvall performance, featuring yet another Southern setting for the San Diego-born actor, is his charismatic and often very funny turn as the father in *Rambling Rose* (1991), a far more extroverted character than Fentry but another who is more than meets the eye, which is a key component of Duvall's artistry; he takes us places we thought we'd been before but, alas, had not. It wasn't for nothing that Duvall graced the cover of a 1981 issue of *American Film* magazine with the tag line, "America's Hard-Boiled Olivier." No one objected.

Robert Redford as Bill McKay

Robert Redford

IN

The Candidate

(1972)

[ ]
[ ]
[ ]
[ ]
[ ]

GOLDEN boy Robert Redford was *the* movie star of the 1970s, but as this was the heyday of the anti-movie star, he was something of an anomaly. Nicholson, Pacino, Hoffman, and De Niro reigned, and Redford's prodigious lower-key abilities weren't much lauded. (Hey, just try picturing any of those heavyweights in *The Way We Were*.) He and Warren Beatty carried the torch of "classic" film star into the '70s, but they also made significant, challenging films that helped define that decade as a second Golden Age of Hollywood. Redford had come out of television (remember his chilling *Twilight Zone* episode?) and the theatre. He re-created his 1963 Broadway success in *Barefoot in the Park* in its 1967 film version, demonstrating what a terrific light comedian he was. (He reminds me of Joel McCrea in his proficiency at getting laughs without discernible effort.) But it was as Sundance to Paul Newman's Butch in *Butch Cassidy and the Sundance Kid* (1969) that Redford found his inevitable stardom. His playful rapport with Newman was reminiscent of the teasing camaraderie once shared by Clark Gable and Spencer Tracy. They reteamed for the multi-Oscar winning hit *The Sting* (1973), for which Redford received his sole Best Actor Oscar nomination. If you have fond memories of these two films, I wouldn't advise revisiting them: neither is as good as you remember, proving just how far the stars' charisma carried them. Far better, and the film that contains Redford's best screen performance, is *The Candidate*, still the most trenchant film about the American political process.

Bill McKay (Redford), son of an ex-governor of California (Melvyn Douglas), is approached by political insider Marvin Lucas (Peter Boyle) about becoming the Democratic challenger to the unbeatable Republican incumbent, Crocker Jarmon (Don Porter), in the Senate race. McKay, a lawyer for liberal (mostly ecological) causes, feels nothing but cynicism about politics, a world he saw firsthand as a child. Since his victory is impossible, Lucas assures him that he may say what he wants on the issues;

with the best intentions, McKay accepts. He slowly starts making headway: he has looks, brains, and ideas. The more popular he gets, the clearer it becomes that he's going to have to modify his opinions to gain broader appeal. He reluctantly succumbs to the strategies of his advisors because of the campaign's obvious success, and as Election Day nears, McKay bears little resemblance to the change-seeking man he was at the outset.

There isn't a moment when you can detect Redford acting; his performance feels captured unaware by a hidden camera. No one listens to his fellow actors with more concentration than he does, and there's much to listen to in this movie; Redford visibly absorbs everything coming at him, quickly and fully. The most interesting thing about the character is that, instead of becoming more vivid as the movie progresses, he gets vaguer and vaguer as his campaign team repackages him. Despite his resistance at every turn, you can witness the "blanding" of McKay in his key public appearances. At his first press conference, in his law office, he is refreshingly blunt in his responses, even stunning reporters with an actual "I don't know" answer. He's out of his element at his first banquet (he hasn't yet learned to smile automatically when making a speech), but he's still honest and he's *real.* By the time of his debate with Jarmon, McKay is a far more confident performer, but in his closing remarks, he breaks with rehearsed banalities, speaking out about race and poverty with the conviction he once did. It's the last we'll see of the old McKay because, as the compromises mount, there's no turning back. In his last major speech, to an audience of union members, Redford exhibits McKay's complete mastery of applause-inducing political rhetoric. There's a moment when you can see him on the verge of saying something unplanned and rebellious, but he opts not to; he's been seduced by the hoopla surrounding him. Registering McKay's pleasure in being able to manipulate a crowd, Redford gleams. McKay's transition (external and internal) from lost-cause crusader to "dream candidate" is assiduously thought out by Redford; he makes each incremental step of McKay's rise (or fall?) feel resoundingly true.

In addition to the stress of being refashioned for public consumption, McKay is also tested in his personal life. Bristling at every mention of his spotlight-loving father, and determined not to include the old man in the campaign, Redford shoulders a lifetime of resentment, maintaining an unforgiving distance from the man whose selfishness and neglect have had a lasting impact on him. The father-son conflict is more sharply defined than the scenes depicting McKay's relationship with his cool, ambitious wife (Karen Carlson). If the campaign forces him to deal with familial discomfort, it also provides its share of absurdity. Redford incorporates his refined comic skills when the relentless schedule makes him punchy. He "snaps" in

the backseat of a car, verbally fiddling around with the speech he's delivered countless times, chewing on phrases and improvising silly sounds and
voices with a stream-of-consciousness looseness that makes sense under
the trying circumstances. At a television studio, as tape rolls, he bursts into
laughter, unable to regain his composure (a model "bloopers" moment).
Because he seems so perfect, Redford is irresistibly enjoyable cracking
under pressure. He understands that these unpredictable losses of control
are McKay's only outlets in which to feel free and spontaneous in a situation where neither is appropriate (or conducive to victory).

Jeremy Larner's Oscar-winning screenplay captures the runaway-
train madness of modern politics with amazing prescience; everything in
it has only intensified in the last thirty years. Director Michael Ritchie
utilizes a documentary style that heightens the you-are-there frenzy of
the campaign. (Ritchie's other outstanding film about American culture
is the 1975 beauty-pageant satire *Smile*.) There's dead-on support from
Peter Boyle, Don Porter, and the ever-great Melvyn Douglas (who'd
won an Oscar as Paul Newman's dad in *Hud* [1963]). Redford's two-
time costar Natalie Wood makes a cameo as herself, congratulating
McKay on winning the primary.

After starring in another benchmark political movie, *All the President's
Men* (1976), Redford won the Best Director Oscar for his first directing
venture, *Ordinary People* (1980), a beautifully acted family drama that bore
his signature integrity. The most disappointing thing about Redford's career is that, since he began directing, his acting has been lackluster; he gave
surprisingly lazy, low-energy performances in *The Natural* (1984) and *Out
of Africa* (1985). The only way to excuse his work in *Indecent Proposal* (1993)
is to conclude that he must have been preoccupied with his next directing
assignment, the excellent *Quiz Show* (1994), featuring Ralph Fiennes in a
Redford-like role. Although he's done great work helping new filmmakers
at his Sundance Institute and proven himself no flash-in-the-pan director,
I still really miss Robert Redford, the actor.

Jon Voight as Conrack

Jon Voight

IN

Conrack
(1974)

[ ]

[ ]

[ ]

[ ]

[ ]

[ ]

MOST people had never heard of Jon Voight when *Midnight Cowboy* was released in 1969. Some must have thought that director John Schlesinger had found an unknown Texan to play the title character, but Voight was actually from Yonkers, New York. His terrific performance established him as a major new talent for the screen. In 1972, he had a smash hit with *Deliverance,* and in 1978 came his touching, Oscar-winning work in *Coming Home.* You may find yourself hard-pressed to think of another Voight film from his first decade in the movies. There were others, but none that really connected with audiences or got across-the-board critical approval—unfortunate because *Conrack* contains one of his best performances. As good as Voight has always been, I don't think "charming" is a word that springs to mind when describing his acting. Yet as Pat Conroy in the autobiographical *Conrack,* he's warm, funny, and appealing in ways I don't think he ever was before or has been since.

The film is based on Conroy's book *The Water Is Wide* and begins with his arrival as the new grade school teacher on a small island off the coast of South Carolina in 1969. It's unusual for a white man to be teaching at this all-black school in this isolated place, but Conroy is clearly an unusual guy. None of his students has ever left the island, and he soon realizes that he must go far beyond the curriculum to educate them. The world has already given up on them, and they're being raised without hope for anything better. They nickname him "Conrack" because they can't (or won't) pronounce *Conroy.* The basic story is how Conrack's impassioned interest in teaching leads them to a kind of self-respect and thirst for knowledge that's completely new to them. This may sound like a variation on the old one about a teacher who's resented and resisted but ultimately adored by forever-changed pupils (think of *The King and I; To Sir, with Love,* and so on), and that's exactly what it is. But its unique setting and Voight's striking unpredictability make it seem new again.

We get very little background to the character, but that's fine because Conrack is fully dimensional from the moment he appears. Voight inhabits the role so completely that he's incapable of making an unconvincing move or expression, and his Southern accent flows effortlessly. We sense that he's a lost soul trying to find his place in the world. One of the few personal details he reveals is that he was once a rabid racist who has been atoning for his past in assorted ways. Guilt may be the springboard that lands him on the island, but finding a use for his talents is what makes him belong. Voight's Conrack shows us that changing young lives perceptibly every day is a natural high of which he can't get enough. It's the kind of role that could easily be overplayed by an actor who overestimates his own likeability and then shamelessly courts the audience's adoration (dare I say Robin Williams?). The key to Voight's performance is that he seems genuinely turned on by his interaction with the children; he gets everything he needs from their faces. Voight's lack of self-consciousness and mix of thoughtful intelligence and razzle-dazzle make it impossible to imagine the movie without him. Jon Voight, to quote innumerable movie posters, *is* Conrack.

It is very satisfying to watch Conrack get results as he teaches the children how to swim, play football, appreciate Beethoven, even experience their first movie (Tyrone Power in *The Black Swan*). Through each of their adventures (including Halloween on the mainland), the vigor of Voight's performance is a nice contrast to the languor of the setting. It was only a matter of time before Conrack's boss (Hume Cronyn) questioned his unconventional methods of taking school out of the classroom. The outstanding results of his teaching technique led a foolish Conrack to believe that he was irreplaceable and highly regarded by all concerned. When Conrack's situation on the island is jeopardized, we feel it all the more for the restraint with which Voight handles it. By keeping his emotions in check, but still conveying all that he's feeling, he is deeply moving. Conrack has finally connected with the world in a richly satisfying way, but he may not be allowed to continue his new life's work. Though an unapologetic heart-warmer, the film earns its effects honestly.

Perhaps what'll stay with you more than anything is the joy that Voight radiates. He makes it very entertaining to be in Conrack's company. He's particularly delightful in a scene with an older woman of the island who can't help noticing his attractiveness. He's both confident and uncomfortable in her presence, with endearing results. The role suggests Voight's potential as a light comedian. After showing such spontaneity and an obvious flair for getting laughs, I wish someone had written him a smart romantic comedy, pairing him with Diane Keaton or

Goldie Hawn. He could once again have used the sparkling brashness and ingratiating vulnerability that are so irresistible here. In recent years, Voight has found renewed career activity as a character actor in hits like *Heat* (1995) and *Mission: Impossible* (1996), not to mention his Oscar-nominated, Halloween-mask performance as Howard Cosell in *Ali* (2001). (He has also received plenty of attention as the father of Oscar winner Angelina Jolie.) However, it's still not too late for someone to offer him a role that would give him the opportunity to revitalize the charm and comic invention that he brought to *Conrack* a quarter century ago.

Conrack was directed by Martin Ritt, who had a particular affinity for stories of the South *(The Long, Hot Summer; Norma Rae; Cross Creek)* and for making audiences feel the heat of the locations. The Carolina sun permeates *Conrack*, but not as much as the warmth and passion in Jon Voight's fiercely committed performance.

Cliff Robertson and Geneviève Bujold (as Sandra)

Cliff Robertson

IN

Obsession

(1976)

CLIFF Robertson may be an Academy Award-winning actor but, perennially situated on the brink of real stardom, he never quite made it in Hollywood. After a supporting role in *Picnic* (1955), a popular and critical hit, he nabbed his first leading role, playing an unbalanced May to Joan Crawford's nobly suffering December, in the camp classic *Autumn Leaves* (1956). I'm almost certain he's the only actor to have thrown a typewriter at Joan (onscreen anyway). He looks justifiably embarrassed (or merely bored stiff) as the aging surf bum in *Gidget* (1959), and there's not a whiff of Cape Cod in his flavorless John F. Kennedy in *PT 109* (1963). I much prefer him as the revenge-seeking antihero of Samuel Fuller's kinetic film noir, the wonderfully wacko *Underworld U.S.A.* (1961), and as Henry Fonda's opponent in the fine political drama *The Best Man* (1964). Then came camp classic number two, *Love Has Many Faces* (1965), which would have been more appropriately titled *Lana Has Many Costumes*. The title role in *Charly* (1968), a retarded man who becomes a genius after experimental surgery (only to regress), had the smell of Oscar all over it. Yet it's such a poor film that, amid amateurish direction, atrocious dialogue, and annoying visual tricks, it's hard to assess Robertson's work in it. The Oscar he won for it did little for his career; it was as if *Charly* never happened (we should be so lucky). I can't be objective about Brian De Palma's *Obsession* because I fell in love with it when I was fifteen, and no matter how many times I see it, it never fails to cast a spell over me, and Robertson's performance invariably moves me. Dismissed as a rip-off of Hitchcock's *Vertigo*, which it is to a point (having seen *Obsession* first, the similarities were meaningless to me), the film and its star deserve recognition, unfettered by comparisons to a masterwork.

In 1959, wealthy New Orleans real-estate developer Michael Courtland (Robertson) is stunned when his wife, Elizabeth (Geneviève Bujold), and their nine-year-old daughter, Amy, are kidnapped and held for ransom. In a police rescue attempt condoned by Michael, both are killed. Sixteen years later, Michael, still emotionally numb, goes on a business trip to Florence with his partner, Bob Lasalle (John Lithgow). Visiting the church where he first met his wife, he sees twenty-ish Sandra Portinari (also Bujold) restoring a wall painting, and she looks *exactly* like Elizabeth. Mesmerized, Michael pursues her, eventually taking her to his New Orleans mansion with the intention of marrying her, a bigamous melding of past and present. Michael's obsession with Sandra is soon matched by her consuming interest in Elizabeth.

Before the kidnapping, Michael is a serenely happy man. He gazes at his wife and daughter like a man who doesn't take his good fortune for granted; that indestructible love is the foundation upon which Robertson's performance is built. The 1975 Michael continues to mourn their deaths, going through the motions of business deals, functioning rather than living. He doesn't come out of this coma until he encounters Sandra. Pulled as if by an invisible string, and oblivious to the beauty of Florence all around him, Robertson, in his long black coat with the collar turned up, stalks her like a private detective. When she speaks to him for the first time, from her scaffolded work station in the church, he cannot get the smile off his face. She who restores art is about to restore a man's life. She asks him what he does, and he looks as though he's forgotten; when he does answer and she tells him how important it sounds, Robertson instantly says that it isn't, candidly emphasizing the emptiness of Michael's success and his overpowering feeling that nothing can ever be as meaningful to him as the love he lost *or* the chance to reclaim it. Incapable of rational thought and operating in some half reality, he courts Sandra with gentle persistence, swept away by the illusion of Elizabeth's return, thereby assuaging his lifelong guilt regarding her death. He can't explain what's happening, and he's simply too happy to try. Whenever she speaks, Robertson's moist eyes stare at her so intensely that it's clear Michael isn't always listening to what she's saying: his absorption is total, and he never gets used to the sight of her.

Robertson's joy becomes more expansive as Michael, wanting to ritualize his rebirth in a public way, envisions a cathedral wedding. Resolved to secure and protect his "new life," Robertson reveals Michael's tightly controlled anger at his partner and his psychiatrist as they try to dissuade him from rash behavior. Hurt and betrayed but undeterred, Michael wants to wed Sandra before anything can prevent it; Robertson remains hypnotized by his character's belief in a redemptive second chance. In a dream, he puts his arms around Sandra/Elizabeth and says, "I've waited so long," and it carries the weight of sixteen years of misery being lifted. When a repeat of the 1959 tragedy is inexplicably set in motion, Robertson drives the rest of the film with a pulsating, sanity-shaking fever; at first, Michael's intent on making things right this time around, but then he's possessed with punishing his tormenters. In an overwhelming airport-set finale, where slow motion, swirling cinematography, and the rapturous strains of the score come together, Robertson is the restrained center of it all. As you watch him absorb the incredible events of Michael's life in the film's final minutes, Robertson makes a multilayered, connect-the-dots journey through the character's jumbled emotions in a performance worthy of the virtuosic filmmaking supporting him.

Dazzlingly directed by Brian De Palma, who never allows the technical bravado to overpower the story, *Obsession* can be a transcendent experience. Paul Schrader's cunning script pays homage to *Vertigo* not only in the seeming reappearance of a dead female but also in the way it mixes obsessive love with guilt. Neither as complex nor as provocative as Hitchcock's 1958 classic, *Obsession* is its worthwhile kid brother. There are other Hitchcock references: a young woman's fascination with her predecessor *(Rebecca)* and the use of scissors in a killing *(Dial M for Murder)*. Vilmos Zsigmond's probing camera gives the film a dream-state fluidity, bordering on hallucinatory. And Bernard Herrmann's extravagant score, a major component of the film's moody grandeur, is nearly as great as the one he composed for *Vertigo* itself. Bujold impresses in her showy dual role, but an overly flamboyant John Lithgow plays his Southern businessman like he's auditioning for Big Daddy. And did the inspector have to sound like Clouseau? And why name him Brie?

De Palma's and Schrader's careers were on the rise (1976 also brought us the former's *Carrie* and the latter's screenplay for *Taxi Driver*), as Robertson, past fifty, saw his continue to decline. Though he has never been the kind of actor to generate a fan's obsession, watching him undergo one on the screen is a haunting experience.

Art Carney as Ira Wells

Art Carney

IN

The Late Show
(1977)

I can still remember my fourteen-year-old mouth dropping open when Glenda Jackson announced that Art Carney had won the 1974 Best Actor Oscar for *Harry and Tonto*. Hold on. Did Ralph Kramden's best friend, Ed Norton (everyone's favorite sewer worker), really just win the Academy Award? Not only that, but he beat Al Pacino *(The Godfather Part II)*, Jack Nicholson *(Chinatown)*, Dustin Hoffman *(Lenny)*, and Albert Finney *(Murder on the Orient Express)*. None of these fellows had won an Oscar at this point (only Finney has yet to win), and I'd say it should rightly have been Michael Corleone's night. Director Paul Mazursky's casting of Carney in the low-key role of Harry was a major surprise; the part would require none of the inspired idiocy that had made him one of America's best-loved clowns. As an old man who takes an adventurous cross-country journey with Tonto, his orange cat, Carney gives a smart, unsentimental performance. The film itself is too long, and not all of its episodes are satisfying, but Carney's restraint is always affecting as Harry tries to find dignity and independence in his remaining years. As good as he undoubtedly is in this minor comedy-drama, the Oscar still seems an excessive tribute for an effective change of pace. Three years later, Carney would justify his Oscar-winning status with a bristling performance in *The Late Show*, writer-director Robert Benton's deft blend of film noir and offbeat comedy, that would leave memory of *The Honeymooners* even farther behind—and do its part to prove that Art Carney is an actor without detectable limitations.

What would a 1940s private eye (such as Philip Marlowe) be doing thirty years after his glory days had passed? That's the intriguing question posed by *The Late Show*. Living in a rented room in 1977 Los Angeles, Ira Wells (Carney) is a forgotten man, an anachronism who belongs to a world of dames and chiselers that no longer seems to exist. Actually, only the styles have changed, and Ira soon finds himself in a plot convoluted and labyrinthine enough to suit him (and please fans of *The Big Sleep* and *Out of the Past*, who like their mystery stories impenetrable). The ensuing accumulation of shootings, blackmails, infidelities, and murders is merely a backdrop for the developing relationship between two wildly disparate characters: out-of-step Ira and up-to-the-minute Margo Sperling (Lily Tomlin), a purely 1970s kind of kook. The death of Ira's buddy Harry Regan (Howard Duff) and the disappearance of Margo's cat (another important role for a feline in a Carney movie) are somehow connected, and the duo becomes the unlikeliest of unofficial partners. Can a liberated, marijuana-selling, sometime actress bond with an obsolete mug who's been living inside a Mickey Spillane novel?

Ira still expects women to behave according to the rules of yesteryear; the broads of his time specialized in glamour, mystery, and a need to be protected. He may call Margo a "doll," but even he notices that she doesn't quite fit the bill. Carney's demeanor in their earliest scenes together is so uncomfortable that he can barely look her in the eye. Her unladylike manner irritates him, but it's her incessant chatter on all manner of subjects that he finds unbearable. (Ira is a guy who speaks only when it's absolutely necessary.) One night in her apartment, following an adrenaline-filled car chase that has left them feeling invincible, Ira seems to be exhibiting a grudging fondness for Margo as she gives her spirited recap of the night's events. (Is that a smile finding its way onto Carney's determined-to-stay-gruff face?) When Margo makes her impulsive suggestion that they become real partners (Nick and Nora Charles for the '70s), watch the way Carney activates Ira's emotional retreat. Margo's always-in-the-moment approach to living is too fast and unpredictable for Ira, who resorts to an "I'm a loner" defense to sidestep her attempt at bringing them closer together. When Carney raises that protective curtain, it's clear that Ira Wells can't even imagine himself as anything but a solo act.

At first, Ira seems fueled by his desire to avenge Harry's grisly murder, but his objective soon goes deeper than that. Harry's death becomes the opportunity for Ira to make a stab at rejoining the human race. Although Carney retains his brusque, surly manner, he allows us to see that this case is slowly bringing Ira back to life. Thinking of himself as someone in the present, rather than the past, is just what he's needed. Ira's investigation leads him to the estate of Ron Birdwell (Eugene Roche), a suspiciously friendly crook who specializes in hot merchandise. Birdwell's henchman Lamar (John Considine) brutally beats and humiliates Ira, but the pummeled old-timer vows revenge, spewing enough tough-guy jargon to save face. I love the fact that Carney keeps dabbing his bloody nose throughout his subsequent conversation with Roche instead of instantly recovering from his bruises in the great tradition of movie he-men. When Ira later gives Lamar that promised beating, it's a major victory for his pride. He recounts his triumph to Margo with a level of enthusiasm we haven't seen in Ira. No longer is he someone who used to be Ira Wells, but the man himself. Although he maintains his gumshoe cool, everything about Carney's work in this scene quietly screams, "I'm back!"

Unfortunately, Ira's body is immune to the restorative powers of crime solving. Let's face it: he's a coughing, Alka-Seltzer guzzler with a perforated ulcer and a bum leg. These ailments give Carney an outlet to humanize a remote, self-reliant character. Ira doesn't want anyone's help or pity, but sometimes there's no disguising the fact that he's in intolerable pain. Margo is with him when he collapses in a restaurant, and his fragile state causes him to speak openly about his deteriorating health in a way that is uncharacteristic for this emotionally-in-check man. He confides in her about his previous operations and his determination to avoid a return to the hospital. This is as close as Ira comes to reaching out to someone, and Carney gives us a brief, but penetrating, glimpse into the private hell beneath Ira's crumbling tower of strength.

Lily Tomlin is a uniquely gifted comic talent (is there *anyone* like her?), and the lovably self-dramatizing Margo is a role rich enough to deserve her. Carney may have become a household name playing one of the loopier characters in pop culture, but this film permitted him to play straight man, leaving Tomlin to take care of most of the laughs. Supported by Robert Benton's consistently fresh take on the detective genre and its denizens, Carney conveys Ira's considerable (if unspectacular) growth, from a man who carries his disappointments and hard luck on his face and body to someone clearly on his way to connecting with the contemporary world. To watch Carney undergo this believably paced rejuvenation is to observe how an actor can seem to be doing very little and yet achieve so much.

Tommy Rall, Steve Martin, and Robert Fitch perform "It's the Girl"

Steve Martin

IN

Pennies from Heaven
(1981)

STEVE Martin was already one of America's best-loved funnymen when *The Jerk* (1979) made him a big-time movie star. It was just the kind of vehicle that fans expected from their "wild and crazy guy," a man who interrupted his stand-up with sudden attacks of "happy feet." He could have spent the 1980s in an unbroken stream of dumb-and-dumber comedies, potentially wearing out his comic persona. I can't conceive of a bigger risk than the film he selected for his follow-up to the pleasurably infantile *Jerk.* It would have been self-destructive enough to do a musical at a time when the genre was inarguably dead, but to choose one that wasn't even a musical *comedy* seemed like career suicide. The Depression-set *Pennies from Heaven* is the bleakest of MGM musicals, but it's also one of the few fascinating pictures in the genre over the last thirty years (please, never mention 2001's execrable *Moulin Rouge!* in my presence). Its no-show at the box office and mixed critical reaction couldn't have surprised anyone; its fans should be grateful it got made at all. Bernadette Peters, Martin's *Jerk* leading lady, was logically cast beside him again; she was not only an accomplished musical performer but had made her name in another 1930s-set piece, the stage musical parody *Dames at Sea.* So it's Martin who's the surprise here *and* the revelation. His role required enough tap-dancing skill to warrant a young Astaire or Kelly; Danny Daniels's intricate period choreography would test just how "happy" Martin's feet could really get.

Arthur Parker (Martin) is a traveling sheet-music salesman in 1934 Chicago. His marriage to prudish Joan (Jessica Harper) is sexually frustrating, but Arthur has a much more severe problem: he keeps expecting life to be like the optimistic songs he peddles and aches to find a place where the songs are *true.* In musicalized daydreams, Arthur experiences the sunny alternatives to the actual events in his hard-luck life. (Martin and the rest of the cast lip-synch to 1930s pop recordings rather than burst into song with their own voices.) Striving to escape *his* Depression,

Arthur may have found storybook love (and sexual gratification) in virgin schoolmarm Eileen Everson (Peters).

Arthur is a selfish, lying, undependable womanizer, and though he's hardly likeable, it's easy to empathize with his yearning for a life of joy and beauty. Depression songs were meant to lighten people's spirits in tough times, not provide a textbook for living; Arthur is sadly deluded by his distorted perceptions and expectations. He falls in love with Eileen in an instant, as in a song, but it's he who mucks up their affair. (Even he can't prevent the intrusions of real life.) Martin provides piercing access to Arthur's misguided longings, moving restlessly from one shortsighted moment to another and trying to escape his accumulating responsibilities. At a movie theatre, as Arthur and Eileen watch *Follow the Fleet*, Martin makes a haunting transition into one of his dreamscapes (he usually clicks right into them). His face is glued to the screen—he's hypnotized, really—and he begins unconsciously to mouth the lyrics to "Let's Face the Music and Dance" as Fred sings it to Ginger. He's out of synch at first, but his confidence builds, and when he turns to Eileen, he's utterly possessed (and in synch); the effect is both soothing and unsettling. A later scene provides Arthur's unavoidable collision with reality, the moment it catches up to him. As he hears a newsboy shout a headline about *him*, Martin's look of frozen shock turns to one of resigned inevitability; no accompanying fantasy follows.

This isn't a case of a nondancer barely getting through the combinations, unable to disguise his fright. (Remember the cast of the 1975 sinking ship called *At Long Last Love*?) Martin utilizes the grace that makes him an inimitable physical comedian, putting over his numbers with astonishing self-assurance and gleeful panache. The bank-loan number, "Yes, Yes!," is the film's Busby Berkeley-like extravaganza, and Martin leads it commandingly, even with eye-catching competition from leggy chorines and gigantic coins. "It's the Girl" is a stage-set vaudeville routine, reminiscent of "Fit as a Fiddle" from *Singin' in the Rain* (1952). Clad in plaid suits and bowler hats, Martin and two other salesmen perform the fanciest footwork in the picture in an athletic celebration of lusty urges. In his and Peters's Fred-and-Ginger fantasy, Martin surges with romantic elegance, taking carefree refuge in the black-and-white illusion. (He's no Astaire double, but his wholehearted embrace of ballroom dancing nonetheless dazzles.) Martin also responds in intimate ways to his lip-synched lyrics; the words bring Arthur's suppressed feelings to the surface. When he mouths Bing Crosby's "Did You Ever See a Dream Walking?" at his first sight of angel-faced Eileen, it doesn't feel like a spoof. He locates the cores of these transporting (literally, in his case) tunes, surrendering to their uninhibited emotion. In a climactic rendition of the title tune, using his *own* voice, he gives a softly plaintive interpretation; he's still trying to see the bright side and still able to find comfort where he always has: in a great song.

Pennies from Heaven's first incarnation was as a six-part British miniseries in 1978, written by Dennis Potter and starring Bob Hoskins. I may be the only person who prefers the lavish film to the modestly produced series (which tries my patience). The big budget allowed for a natural expansion of Arthur's fantasy life, and Potter wrote the Oscar-nominated screenplay. It's the best movie musical of the post-*Cabaret* era, and like Bob Fosse's brilliant 1972 feel-bad classic, you might call it an antimusical. Herbert Ross surpassed himself when he took a break from commercial fare (like *The Goodbye Girl*) to direct this colorful, stylized piece, a film that looks better and better with each passing year. Gordon Willis's strikingly lit cinematography and the witty production design (featuring two breathtaking re-creations of Edward Hopper paintings) make wondrous contributions. Peters got her best movie role (she won a Golden Globe), and is not only as poignant as you'd expect but has a surprising inner strength: Eileen is able to face the darkness in her life head-on. Christopher Walken, whom I usually loathe, shows up as a pimp in a seedy bar and hijacks the movie. His sensational tap-dancing striptease to "Let's Misbehave" is the finest five minutes of his career; he's jubilantly sleazy. And lovers of *old* MGM musicals will spot the still amazing Tommy Rall *(Kiss Me Kate, Seven Brides for Seven Brothers)* as one of the "It's the Girl" trio.

Martin has continued to sprinkle his film career with surprising choices (like *The Spanish Prisoner* [1997]) though, admittedly, nothing as startling as *Pennies from Heaven*. He was even an unlikely winner of the New York Film Critics' Best Actor prize for his spastically bravura work in *All of Me* (1984). But his best work has to be *Roxanne* (1987), which he also wrote, a glorious update of *Cyrano de Bergerac*. And, to think, he can tap too.

Woody Allen and Mia Farrow

Mia Farrow

IN

Broadway Danny Rose
(1984)

A s daughter of director John Farrow *(Wake Island)* and actress Maureen O'Sullivan (Tarzan's favorite Jane), Mia Farrow is Hollywood royalty. Television's *Peyton Place* and her brief marriage to Frank Sinatra made her a celebrity in the mid 1960s, but it was the big screen's *Rosemary's Baby* (1968) that proved she need never again be referred to as anybody's daughter or wife. Her electrifying performance in that still shocking thriller should have led to major stardom in the 1970s. It didn't. Farrow would have to wait until her partnership with Woody Allen in the 1980s to have the movie career she deserved. Allen's longtime costar Diane Keaton was off testing her dramatic potential in films like *Reds* (1981) and *Shoot the Moon* (1982), and Farrow became his new leading lady on (and off) the screen. *A Midsummer Night's Sex Comedy* (1982) cast Farrow in a role that seemed tailor-made for Keaton, and her performance was little more than an awkward Keaton imitation. It was an inauspicious beginning. Next came the clever *Zelig* (1983), but her secondary role offered no opportunity to shine. Allen didn't seem to know how to use her. *Broadway Danny Rose* was the breakthrough: it became clear that her real strength was as a character actress. Just write great parts and she'll surprise you with her ability to bring them to life. Perhaps the biggest shock of all was how funny she could be.

Danny Rose (Allen) is a small-time theatrical agent whose most promising client is has-been singer Lou Canova (Nick Apollo Forte), who's on the verge of a comeback. Danny is seen in public with Lou's mistress, Tina (Farrow), when he tries to convince her to show up at Lou's concert that evening. Misunderstandings follow, and Danny and Tina soon have mobsters on their trail and are running for their lives. Danny doesn't know that Tina has been encouraging Lou to dump him as his agent. (All of Danny's clients leave him when they get their first taste of success.) Of course, Tina hadn't been through a life-threatening adventure with Danny when she was scheming against him. Now she likes the schnook.

343

Wait a minute. Wispy Mia Farrow as tough-talking, chain-smoking Mafia widow Tina Vitale with bleached hair piled high on her head? It sounds like disastrous casting but proves inspired. The first time she appears she's screaming at her boyfriend over the phone, and it doesn't quite register that it's Farrow behind those sunglasses. She slips on this no-nonsense character so effortlessly that, from the first moment, we never doubt her veracity. Although her bimbo looks and New Yawk accent are impeccable, it's Farrow's believability as a woman with street smarts and a more than colorful past that grabs our attention. Tina is no caricature. She's a lot smarter than this type of character usually is and too shrewd to let anyone know what she's thinking. (Is that the reason for the often-present sunglasses?) When Tina reveals her philosophy of life, she rattles off several variations of "looking out for number one," and you know she's not kidding. Farrow transforms herself completely into this bruised but resilient broad who's nobody's fool.

Farrow plays straight man to Allen's constant barrage of one-liners. She never blinks at any of his punch lines. Tina doesn't find Danny funny, and she's hardly hanging on his every word. Farrow has plenty of funny lines herself and delivers them with deadpan marksmanship, getting every laugh that Allen sets up for her without the slightest bit of exertion. The story of Tina's wiseguy husband's career and gruesome demise is very funny because Farrow tells it so matter-of-factly. Tina's ideas for decorating Danny's apartment in gold, pink, zebra skin, and bamboo are ghastly, and Farrow delivers this kitschy brainstorm in utter earnestness. You can never catch her "acting," and her timing is flawless.

At the start, we learn that Tina thinks guilt is a waste of time. Her relationship with Danny teaches her something about it, though, and she becomes a more complicated character. Farrow lets us see Tina slowly become less sure of herself and more irritable in the process. She can't seem to find her way back to the old, in-control Tina, which turns out to be not such a bad thing. And yet there were chinks in her armor from the beginning. She's almost childlike in the self-doubt she expresses to Danny regarding her decorating career (even realist Tina Vitale has big dreams). He may be a loser, but he does have a way of cutting through her steel veneer as no one has before. She also devoutly believes in a local fortuneteller's advice in times of crisis. Tina doesn't have all the answers; she just looks as if she does. Farrow starts with a potentially stereotypical character, makes her fresh and surprising, and then reveals the uncertainty beneath her arsenal of strength.

Broadway Danny Rose is short, fast, and fun, a valentine to those people on the fringes of show business. Woody Allen received Oscar nominations for his direction and screenplay. He includes a little in-joke when Danny shows Tina his photo with Frank Sinatra (who by this time had long been Farrow's ex-husband). I also need to mention Gordon Willis's inventive black-and-white photography. There's a scene at the Macy's Thanksgiving Day Parade warehouse with the giant inflated balloons that is startling, eerie, and magical.

Allen and Farrow were never quite the great comic team that Allen and Keaton were. Farrow proved to be an ensemble player in his stock company of actors and didn't even always have the leading female role in their thirteen films together. Tina wasn't the best part he wrote for her (that would be the movie-obsessed waitress in *The Purple Rose of Cairo* [1985]) or the most popular (the title role in *Hannah and Her Sisters* [1986]), but it was the turning point in their collaboration. There would never again be any doubt that she was a gifted and intuitive comedienne. She and Allen parted company after *Husbands and Wives* (1992), and neither of their careers has recovered. (His entrancing *Bullets over Broadway* [1994] is a notable exception in an otherwise disappointing decade for him.) She hasn't had a choice film role since then, and Allen has yet to find a muse to replace her. That she did not receive a single Oscar nomination for any of the movies she made with Allen (nor for *Rosemary's Baby*) is unfathomable to me. How many other actresses of her generation have shown such versatility?

Robin Williams as Vlad

Robin Williams

IN

Moscow on the Hudson

(1984)

BEFORE Robin Williams's movie career went into the stratosphere with the box-office and critical success of *Good Morning, Vietnam* (1987), which netted him his first Oscar nomination, there had been doubt about whether his manic comic brilliance (which many had first encountered on television's *Mork & Mindy* in the late 1970s) could click on the big screen. His pre-*Vietnam* features, such as *Popeye* (1980) and *The World According to Garp* (1982), are a quirkier group of films than the commercial-minded goo that would dominate his work in the 1990s. His exceeding popularity turned some of the decade's worst movies, notably *Hook* (1991) and *Mrs. Doubtfire* (1993), into hits. If you want to see what an extraordinary *actor* Williams once was (and could still be), you have to go back to his pre-glory, meager ticket-selling days: *Moscow on the Hudson*, a multishaded, funny but rocky tale of a Russian musician's defection to New York, contains his finest screen work. Without trying to make us love him (he's ingratiating without effort) or snapping into out-of-character comic riffs, Williams, with a bushy beard and an unruly mop of hair, gives a meticulously disciplined performance.

Vladimir Ivanoff (Williams), a saxophone player in a Russian circus, is passive in his dealings with the indignities of Soviet life (the incessant lines, the cramped housing), yet when the circus comes to New York, it is he, in an unplanned burst of defiance, who defects (in the middle of Bloomingdale's). He forms two lasting attachments right there in the store, with Lionel (Cleavant Derricks), the African-American security guard who takes him in until he can find his own place, and with Lucia (Maria Conchita Alonso), an Italian-born salesclerk who becomes his girlfriend. Vlad struggles to make a go of his daunting new life, sometimes wondering if it's all been worth it.

The first thing to mention is Williams's phenomenally convincing Russianness. The language rolls off his tongue second-naturedly, and as the first twenty minutes are almost entirely subtitled, he has quite a lot to spit out. He's even more impressive with the Russian-accented English, speaking with the frustrating uncertainty and intense concentration of an overwhelmed novice, but noticeably improving with each successive scene. (It's an achievement comparable to Meryl Streep's in *Sophie's Choice*.) Though you may forget that Williams *is* American, his accomplishment would be no more than a technical feat without his accompanying emotional investment. Vlad lives with his caring family (parents, sister, grandfather) and has a steady girlfriend, but it's still a debilitatingly cautious, ever-monitored existence. When he performs "Take the 'A' Train" (for himself and the circus animals), it's an isolated moment of self-expression, foreshadowing the yearning that's about to make itself known.

The teeming, unbridled humanity of New York, wonderful and terrible, is a real eye-opener for him. Though Vlad has been trying to convince his miserable friend Anatoly (Elya Baskin), a clown, *not* to defect, it is Vlad, on the troupe's final stop before the airport, who snaps at Bloomie's. Intending only to buy "bloo jins," he's overtaken by something bigger, his previously unadmitted desperation to be free. After splashing his face at a water fountain, he meekly says, "I defect," to security guard Lionel, gaining confidence each subsequent time he says these two words. Fleeing the KGB by hiding under Lucia's skirt, then crawling around the store on all fours, Williams has some low-comic fun without undercutting the enormity of the situation. The Feds arrive and, in a fitting-room interview (as Williams clutches Vlad's designer-jeans purchase like a security blanket), he quickly realizes how frighteningly alone he is and runs out of the store to wave good-bye to the "Liberty" bus of departing Russians (and his sax). Williams's rapturous, broad smile of freedom can't quite fend off his uncontrollably encroaching tears. He manages to choke out a "nice to be here" to the press, but looks as if he's about to disintegrate from exhaustion.

Ironically, domestic life at Lionel's family's apartment is a duplication of the overcrowded home he left behind. There's a great scene at a supermarket (he has offered to do the grocery shopping) where the endless coffee brand choices result in such a sensory overload for Vlad that he essentially malfunctions, collapsing to the floor. He's determined to make good, working tirelessly at every job that comes his way (busboy, hot dog vendor, McDonald's employee, cab driver, limo driver). But without Lionel's friendship and the burgeoning romance with Lucia, the path to a more authentic life would be unbearable. An unabashedly loving Williams connects with them, not merely affectionately but in a way that gives meaning

to Vlad's life; they and Orlando (Alejandro Rey), his Cuban-American immigration lawyer, *are* his American world. At a party celebrating Lucia's
new citizenship, he asks her to move in with him, which sparks their
breakup. She has other plans for her future. Without her, and with Lionel
off to Alabama, Vlad grieves the loss of his second family. On his own in
the East Village, he confronts assimilation in anonymity, questioning the
wisdom of his defection. Vlad is unraveling, anesthetizing the pain with a
vodka-drenched nightlife, and a seething Williams eventually voices the
anger and bitterness stewing inside him.

Director Paul Mazursky, who cowrote the observant script with
Leon Capetanos, seamlessly weaves comedy and drama. *Moscow's* humor
rises naturally from the events, while its exploration of "America" is rich
in optimism without being rose-colored. I could do without the occasional flashes of homophobia, such as the sinister, Bernard Herrmann-
like music that accompanies a gay character as he follows Vlad down the
street. Maria Conchita Alonso and Cleavant Derricks provide bright,
energized support to Williams as he transforms Vlad's Soviet innocence
into New York endurance.

Williams received Oscar nominations for the yucky and pretentious
Dead Poets Society (1989) and the infinitely superior *Fisher King* (1991),
though the latter is Jeff Bridges's film more than his. Actually, his best
work of the 1990s is his hilarious voice-only turn as the Genie in Disney's
Aladdin (1992). He did win an Oscar, a supporting one, for his sensitive
shrink in *Good Will Hunting* (1997), a well-done feel-good drama in which
he admirably restrains himself from getting too warm and fuzzy. It's the
last Williams film I've seen, unable as I am to bring myself to the ennobling
(and presumably sickening) likes of *What Dreams May Come* (1998), *Patch
Adams* (1998), *Jakob the Liar* (1999), and *Bicentennial Man* (1999). (Let's
hope this phase of his career is over.) But before he "defected" to synthet-
ically manipulative fare, he turned Vlad's potholed ride to freedom into an
unqualified seriocomic triumph.

Diane Keaton as Kate Soffel

Diane Keaton

IN

Mrs. Soffel

(1984)

NO screen comedienne of the last thirty years has brought me as much undiluted pleasure as Diane Keaton, the woman who refined stammering insecurity into an ingratiating art. Her 1970s partnership with Woody Allen created a male-female comedy team as immortal as that of William Powell and Myrna Loy. In the 1980s, Keaton confirmed her dramatic mettle with a series of uncompromising, unlikeable characters (no scrappy farm heroines, no corporate-fighting crusaders for her). Yes, she had already been in the first two *Godfather* movies, playing Kay, a mostly thankless role, though she's the last face you see in the first film and, in the second, has a blowout confrontation with Al Pacino. Then there was the cautionary *Looking for Mr. Goodbar* (1977), a hateful, empty movie that brought her raves, even though it's one of her less distinctive efforts. Things improved with *Reds* (1981), in which she gives an insightful portrayal of Louise Bryant, playing her as both burdened and fueled by an awareness that her drive and ambition far outclass her writing talent. *Shoot the Moon* (1982), *The Little Drummer Girl* (1984), *Mrs. Soffel,* and *The Good Mother* (1988) followed. None of these knotty, demanding characters cuddled up to audiences (interesting, since Keaton's comic persona is so appealing). My favorite of these is her Mrs. Soffel. I usually want to groan when a performance is described as "brave," but Keaton's work, unpredictable and free of star vanity, is just that: a gripping portrait of a woman who, without apology, devours her chance to feel alive. It's both an awakening and a breakdown, and therein lies my fascination with Keaton's work.

Based on a true story, *Mrs. Soffel* is set in 1901 Pittsburgh. In the Allegheny County Prison, the Biddle brothers, Ed (Mel Gibson) and Jack (Matthew Modine), outlaws in their mid twenties, await hanging for murder (though they maintain their innocence). Kate Soffel, the warden's wife and mother of four, is emotionally and physically fragile, a response to her suffocating, immobile life. First meeting the boys on one of her Bible-dispensing rounds, she comes to believe in their innocence, but more important, she falls in love with the charismatic, poetry-writing Ed. She not only helps them plan their escape but, at Ed's amorous invitation, runs out on her family, recklessly joining the brothers in their hazardous attempt to flee to Canada and freedom.

Like an Ibsen heroine, Kate is a woman for whom life's expected joys (marriage, children, household) bring stifling frustration. Her depression manifests itself in an undiagnosable illness, but when she emerges from her three-month sickbed, her air of healthiness seems forced and questionable; Keaton quickly establishes Kate's precarious hold on her life. Living within the prison, she is as much an inmate as those behind bars, and she seeks solace in her faith. She listens for God's guidance, but it's clear that, despite her prayers, religion has never given Kate peace. Bible in hand, she's uneasy in her initial encounters with the smart, beautiful Ed, but she's not scared off. Keaton begins the process of incrementally shedding Kate's propriety, tapping into her rush of stimulation after years of numbness; before long, there's no going back. In the obvious vulnerability beneath her warden's wife "role," Kate is susceptible to losing control, aroused by Ed's audacious flirtations, and though flustered by them, comes back for more. Their theological discussions, supposedly meant to comfort him, weaken her resolve to make the best of her unhappy life, and her reliance on an unanswering God dwindles. (It's Ed who's converting her.) Keaton's alert presence conveys that Kate, sitting outside the bars of Ed's cell, knows she's being manipulated by him, but it doesn't matter. As the embarrassment and discomfort he instills in her show signs of disappearing, so too does "Mrs. Soffel." From here on, in his proximity, Keaton sprinkles her performance with involuntary smiles, spasms of joy that can't be contained, glimpses into a reborn soul. Though always aware of what she ought to do, she instead does what she wants; Kate is in love. A headiness takes over: a message from Ed, slipped to her via a third party, gives her a clandestine thrill; she's naughtily tickled by Ed's touch as he removes, from her boots, the two saws she's smuggled for him. There's a brief scene in which she makes a last-ditch attempt to reach out to her husband (Edward Herrmann), asking him to take her away for a month. Keaton plays the scene with a rising desperation, which deflates into hopelessness when Kate's earnest plea is denied.

When the boys break out, Ed comes for her, but she resists. (His genuine feelings for her are a leap you may have trouble accepting.) His kisses render her helpless, and—boom—she goes with them, in only her nightgown and coat, laughing and running out into the snow. It's her escape as much as theirs. Sexual fantasy, imminent danger, and an upturned reality

Diane Keaton in *Mrs. Soffel* (1984)

commingle, and it's liberating. Keaton carries the sensation of being turned on by these exciting, romantic risks. When she jumps off a train, she's jumping into a new world: the unknown. Deliriously in love, a no-regrets Kate has never been more "herself." When they finally consummate the relationship (after finding shelter in an old couple's house), it's Kate who instigates it. Keaton is no bombshell, but she embraces her eroticism with an uninhibited need that makes you feel you shouldn't be looking. Rather than bare her body, she bares Kate's thirst to love and be loved, to be touched, to *feel* her life. Her abandon makes it one of the more honest, thematically relevant (and therefore ungratuitous) of sex scenes. Time is their enemy, but she's savoring every crazy, precious moment. Later, with her long hair unpinned and blowing free, she shoots a gun, warning onlookers to keep their distance, and then she laughs. For Kate, it's this life of passion and impulse or nothing. As they're being chased (in their horse-drawn sleigh) and about to be overtaken, she begs Ed to shoot her. Keaton cries, "Yes! Yes!" in a fierce, startlingly orgasmic way that's brilliantly appropriate for the new Kate. Come what may, the smile Ed can elicit in her will never be far away, nor will the feelings that transformed and defined her.

Gillian Armstrong's direction, both disciplined and free-spirited, probes the central character's provocative complexities with immaculate care, making *Mrs. Soffel* an unusually sweeping, anything-may-happen love story. Gorgeously designed, the movie transports you in that magical way achieved only by the best period films. Russell Boyd's cinematography adds to the stirring evocation of the era, surpassing itself in capturing the imposing, ominous beauty of ice-blue snowscapes. Ron Nyswaner's well-built screenplay handles the exposition skillfully and succintly, layering what will become a riveting exploration of an atypical character. (The film might have been a commercial hit if it were easier to categorize Mrs. Soffel and her story.) A pre-*Lethal Weapon* Mel Gibson, an arresting up-and-comer with bedroom eyes, is neatly cast and gives his all, matching Keaton's searching, voracious commitment to the piece.

Jeff Daniels (as Tom) and Mia Farrow

Jeff Daniels

IN

The Purple Rose of Cairo
(1985)

T HE first time I saw *The Purple Rose of Cairo,* I was sure of two things: Woody Allen had made his masterpiece and Jeff Daniels was going to be a major star. Well, one out of two ain't bad; I still contend that *Purple Rose* is Allen's best film. Daniels's big break had come with Flap, Debra Winger's unreliable husband, in *Terms of Endearment* (1983), in which he managed to hold his own among a cast of colorful veterans. The plum dual role in *Purple Rose* is an actor's dream, and Daniels's performance is a sustained high; he gives *two* comic tours de force, an exhilarating achievement that leaves me light-headed. Whenever a leading man shows such polished comic skills, it activates my impulse to proclaim that we've found the next Cary Grant (as hopeless a mission as seeking the new Audrey Hepburn). Daniels's quicksilver wit, freewheeling energy, and appealing self-mockery should have been parlayed into a Grant-like career, but since *Purple Rose* was no box-office smash, he got neither the attention nor the Oscar nomination he deserved.

In Depression-era New Jersey, Cecilia (Mia Farrow) spends all her spare time at the movies, escaping her unhappy marriage to brutish Monk (Danny Aiello). After she loses her waitressing job, she eases her sorrow with repeated showings of *The Purple Rose of Cairo* at the Jewel Theatre. The movie (mixing *Dinner at Eight*'s sophistication with *The Mummy*'s exotica) is about Tom Baxter (Daniels), a wide-eyed explorer-poet-adventurer who befriends a coterie of ritzy New Yorkers. During Cecilia's fifth viewing, Tom speaks directly to her and walks off the black-and-white screen into a world of color to meet her, leaving his fellow characters unable to move their plot forward without him. Whereas Cecilia has been craving Hollywood fantasy, Tom yearns for a real life. When swollen-headed actor Gil Shepherd (Daniels), who plays Tom in the movie, hears that his creation has run amok, he comes east to coax him back onto the screen before a scandal erupts. Both Tom and Gil become smitten with a stunned Cecilia; she is suddenly juggling the attentions of a fictional hero and a red-blooded movie star.

A delightful contrast to the jaded martini swillers he meets inside an Egyptian tomb, Tom is clad in a safari suit, knee-high boots, and a pith helmet (and enough eye makeup to rival Valentino). He's impossibly enthusiastic about everything, gleefully accepting their impromptu invitation to Manhattan. It's pleasurably unnerving when, later, he looks into the audience at Cecilia, hesitates with his lines (in a scene we've already seen twice before), and then speaks to her. Stepping out of the movie is his impulsive bid for freedom; he's a celluloid alien, eager to take in the sensations of reality. Tom knows only what's been written into his character; he's a sweet, polite dreamboat (and a great kisser) who's unaware of life's unfairness. His "movie talk" convinces Cecilia of his love and loyalty; Daniels's romantic abandon and childlike purity are hard to resist. When Tom explains to a group of hookers (led by Dianne Wiest) that he must respectfully decline their friendly offer because of his devotion to Cecilia, the girls are dumbstruck by his disarming sincerity. Tom and Cecilia's whirlwind escapade climaxes when he takes her on a nightclub-hopping date *inside* the movie he came from. (He insists the other characters accept his new fiancée.) Daniels's golly-gee-whiz sprightliness never wears thin because his pangs of excitement vibrate from every pore; his giddy inflections on words like *madcap* and *fetching* twinklingly display the "cheerful bravado" Gil says he used to play Tom.

A sleek product of the Hollywood machine, Gil Shepherd is an on-the-brink-of-stardom careerist whose favorite topic, whose *only* topic, is himself. Casually quoting his good reviews, which are never far from Gil's thoughts, Daniels gives an unceasingly hilarious, dead-on portrait of actorly ego. Gil is panic-stricken that Tom's actions will give him a reputation for being difficult, and the only things that can distract him from Tom's threat to his future are conversations about how talented he is. His self-absorbed antennae home in on Cecilia when she begins to speak of his "magical glow." Her compliments are an addictive tonic, and Gil, who agrees with her perceptive insights, becomes open, warm, and captivated. (Daniels's fleeting flashes of false modesty are quite funny.) Finally, someone who understands him and his struggle! In a clever touch by Daniels, Gil remains oblivious to the Depression squalor of Cecilia and her miserable town. Their reenactment of a tender love scene from *Dancing Doughboys* leads to a tender love scene of their own (in which Gil exhibits some of the gentle ardor he brought to the role of Tom). When Gil confronts Tom, Daniels has a ball contrasting the star's highly stressed, down-to-business attitude with the hero's uncluttered innocence. Compare the subtle but marked difference in the characters' speaking voices: Daniels keeps Tom's boyishly light, employing a lower-pitched hard edge for Gil's.

Reminiscent of *Sherlock Jr.* (where a man walks *into* a movie) and *Pennies from Heaven* (which mixes the Depression with fantasy), *Purple Rose* is a great film, a fabulous-looking swirl of comic inspiration, aching pathos, and technical wizardry; it's my absolute favorite film of the 1980s. Allen's miraculous script pays tribute to the escapist and healing power of movies; whatever befalls Cecilia, a darkened theatre will never let her down, even *after* the boundaries between movie life and real life have been blurred. Mia Farrow, who had just scored in Allen's other "Rose" film, *Broadway Danny Rose*, is heartbreakingly sympathetic; she is as worn out by the Depression as Sylvia Sidney is in films like *Dead End* (1937), but she's also understatedly funny, taking everything in stride as Daniels's two characters turn her life upside down. The final close-up of her is as fascinating to probe as Garbo's fadeout in *Queen Christina* (1933).

Daniels later starred in Jonathan Demme's tingly black comedy *Something Wild* (1986), which toyed with audience expectations with its jolting mix of laughs and terror. There's little else worth mentioning on his film résumé. He's appeared in more than his share of family films, such as *101 Dalmatians* (1996) and *Fly Away Home* (1996), and he had a big hit opposite Jim Carrey in *Dumb and Dumber* (1994), which effectively killed my Cary Grant fantasy for his career. He had a cameo in Allen's *Radio Days* (1987), but I'm surprised the tireless writer-director hasn't snagged him for another leading role. When *Sweet and Lowdown* (1999) was released, some hailed Sean Penn's Oscar-nominated work as the finest male performance in any of Allen's films in which the filmmaker himself did not star. Penn was awfully good, but Daniels's classic double whammy in *The Purple Rose of Cairo* still holds that distinction for me and probably always will.

Rosanna Arquette and Nick Nolte

Nick Nolte

IN

New York Stories
(1989)

MANY of us saw Nick Nolte for the first time in the television minis-eries (and classy soap opera) *Rich Man, Poor Man* (1976), giving a sensational, I-have-arrived performance; a big-screen career seemed a foregone conclusion. *The Deep* (1977), a *Jaws* wannabe, is a terrible movie (noteworthy for making the wet T-shirt part of our cultural heritage), but it did put him on the box-office map. His best roles over the following decade were as the physically wracked football pro in *North Dallas Forty* (1979), a smart, fresh sports movie, and as the homeless man who changes the lives of a wealthy, mixed-up family in the grand comedy *Down and Out in Beverly Hills* (1986). *New York Stories* is comprised of three short films: Martin Scorsese's bravura *Life Lessons*, Francis Ford Coppola's underdone *Life Without Zoe* (a deadly attempt at whimsy), and Woody Allen's adorable *Oedipus Wrecks*, a clever fantasy. Nolte stars in Scorsese's entry, the opener (and the best of the trio), a forty-five-minute drama about a famous (fictional) painter. Whether confronting the physical canvas or exploring the emotional one, Nolte gives an intense and intricate portrait of an artist, less romanticized than what the movies have historically given us.

Lionel "The Lion" Dobie (Nolte), a celebrated artist for the past twenty years, is holed up in his cavernous downtown loft-studio, under enormous pressure to finish new works for an upcoming show. Meanwhile, he's having trouble holding on to Paulette (Rosanna Arquette), his blond twenty-two-year-old assistant and lover, an art student of negligible talent. She's determined to break away from him, despite his insistence that he's provided her with an ideal setup to pursue her art. She agrees to stay, no longer sleeping with him. (Withholding sex is her only power.) The differences in their ages, finances, talents, and commitments (to painting) make for a combustible combination.

Standing in front of a mostly white canvas (a massive rectangle), Nolte has a disheveled look (his longish brown hair and graying beard make him look like Kris Kristofferson) and the penetrating concentration of a predatory animal. Peering through his glasses, his nothing-else-exists expression is focused on the unformed work, looking to see what isn't yet there. Nolte's tunnel vision eloquently transmits Lionel's isolation. *Life Lessons* shows an artist *making* art, and it's certainly more exciting than watching Charlton Heston paint the Sistine Chapel. When inspiration strikes, Lionel is a man possessed: energized, swooping his body with passionate strokes, spattered in oily hues. Nolte is as voluptuously alive as the bold colors and slushy sensuality of Lionel's explosive, nonrepresentational pieces. To the accompaniment of stimulating audiocassettes (Procol Harum's great rock single "A Whiter Shade of Pale" serves as Lionel's theme), a rapt Nolte soars in a zone of creativity. Scorsese's visual delirium in these productive outbursts—enhanced by the carpet-ride flow of Néstor Almendros's cinematography and the heart-racing precision of Thelma Schoonmaker's editing—puts you inside the process, somewhere between Nolte, his brush, and the canvas itself.

The only other light in Lionel's life is Paulette, his muse of the moment, and Nolte looks at her in much the same way he does a canvas; her ankle-braceleted foot, her lacy panties stop him dead. Their relationship has passed its peak, another episode in Lionel's cycle of doomed, though art-fueling, affairs. Lionel uses women, fed by their beauty, escaping into their beds. Without malice, he simply cannot see Paulette as anything more than a character in *his* life. With his husky whisper, Nolte makes Lionel a soothing manipulator, easing her back into his life by playing on her doubts and insecurities: under a guise of sincere unselfishness, he's intent on making her feel guilty about her impulse to ditch her artistic aspirations; he vaguely compliments her work but is careful to avoid direct criticism (though it's clear he's unimpressed); he tries to steer her away from other men, sometimes with smirking condescension regarding his rivals, other times in a state of feverish desperation, flaring a raging jealousy. Nolte plays these beats as a rush of instinctive strategies in self-preservation. Lionel may have agreed (at least temporarily) to Paulette's spitefully empowering no-sex stipulation, but he's rattled when she brings another guy into her bed. In a rapturous scene, emotionally choreographed to the aptly chosen, surging strains of Puccini's "Nessun dorma," Nolte's riveting stillness gives way to a longing that lifts Lionel out of his chair, pulled by the music, staring up at her room through paint-flecked glasses, lost in his fixation. Later, on a rainy street, after he's craftily helped to botch her attempt to reconnect with an ex-lover (Steve Buscemi), she's irate, but he puts his arms around her as she fights him. When Nolte looks into her eyes and says he loves her, it's tremendously stirring (and convincing), and for the moment it appears to be true. (The other times he spouts "I love you" and "I'll do anything," he's dipping into Lionel's arsenal of handy time-tested salves, short-term fixes.) In a scene near the end, furiously finger painting and railing (to himself) against women, Nolte, in a sudden, devastating transition, puts his green-stained hand over his mouth and holds it there, unexpectedly *feeling* all that has happened.

Written by Richard Price (Scorsese's collaborator on *The Color of Money* [1986]), *Life Lessons* packs an incendiary palette of emotional tones into its limited running time. Scorsese approaches the screen the way Lionel stalks his canvas: his direction is as kinetic and kaleidoscopic as one of Lionel's epic paintings. Scorsese appears to have connected personally with his main character's discord, trying to connect life and art, have them feed each other in the desired doses, all too aware of the complications involved. A well-cast Rosanna Arquette has a clear understanding of Paulette, though the shrillness of her voice can, at times, be grating.

Nolte received two Best Actor Oscar nominations, for *The Prince of Tides* (1991), in which he was everything readers of Pat Conroy's book could have hoped for in their page-to-screen Tom Wingo; and for *Affliction* (1998), where, struggling with a legacy of violence, he effected a disturbing meltdown. He reteamed with Scorsese on *Cape Fear* (1991), a repellent remake of a decent 1962 thriller, rendering the original a classic by comparison.

Michelle Pfeiffer

IN

Frankie and Johnny

(1991)

STUNNING Michelle Pfeiffer made a remarkable big-screen climb in the 1980s, from her inauspicious 1980 debut as Suzie in *The Hollywood Knights* to her 1989 prize-winning Susie in *The Fabulous Baker Boys*, which features her atop-a-piano rendition of "Makin' Whoopee" (rivaling Rita Hayworth's "Put the Blame on Mame" from *Gilda* [1946] in the sexiest-musical-number-ever sweepstakes). Her breakout year was 1988 when a trio of performances declared that she had emerged decisively from the sidelines of stardom: in *Married to the Mob*, she disappeared delightfully into her tough-talking Mafia wife; in *Dangerous Liaisons*, her translucent vulnerability won her a supporting Oscar nomination; in *Tequila Sunrise*, she flashed undeniable old-time Hollywood glamour. *Frankie and Johnny*, not to be confused with the Elvis Presley movie, gave her one of her better (and least likely) roles; how could anyone have cast the movies' latest goddess in a role played on stage by—brace yourself—Kathy Bates? Major irony: though Bates was a screen unknown when *Frankie and Johnny* was being cast, she was the reigning Best Actress Oscar winner *(Misery)* when the film was released. Those who dismissed Pfeiffer's casting as Tinseltown wrongheadedness underestimated her ability to make the part her own. Her Frankie is a fresh creation, a beautiful woman whose unhappy romantic history has caused her to de-emphasize her looks, shutting down from the possibility of a recharged personal life. Whether short fused or slow burning, tartly funny or starkly exposed, Pfeiffer is luminous, elevating a sometimes sentimental, sometimes synthetic comedy-drama with an unflinching portrait of emotional paralysis that stays with you well after the feel-good elements around her have faded from memory.

Frankie, officially "retired from dating," is a waitress at a Greek diner in New York's pre-hip Chelsea section. Enter Johnny (Al Pacino), an ex-con (who served eighteen months for forgery) hired as the new short-order cook. Gregarious and unpredictable, he pursues Frankie, much to her annoyance. But he starts to wear her down, and they begin a rocky relationship. Frankie, still suffering the grief from previous attachments and unwilling to risk being hurt again, isn't ready to believe in anyone. However, Johnny remains committed to his theory that they're made for each other.

Pfeiffer slings sarcasm with the weary ease of a longtime urbanite; she can do hardboiled without suggesting a slumming movie star. There's a good running gag in which all her coworkers come to her to open tightly sealed jars, none as airtight as Frankie herself. A counterpoint to Pfeiffer's don't-get-too-close deportment is her sensitivity to those worse off than she; Frankie nurtures the diner's aging regulars and her lost-soul colleagues, seeing herself (and possible future) in them. Sleepwalking through a rudderless life, she's mired in a sadness that she fiercely protects as being preferable to the hazards of getting involved with someone new. She does all she can to go unnoticed (nondescript clothing, little makeup), thereby less likely to attract trouble. Pfeiffer wears Frankie's disappointment like a winter coat, stymied as to how to turn her life around. Wary of Johnny, but curious too, Frankie begins a stop-start, baby-stepped rejuvenation process, astutely detailed by Pfeiffer. Steely and suspicious at first, she's increasingly flustered by his attentions. When he unexpectedly arrives at her walk-up to escort her to a work-related party, she's having a bad hair day *and* wearing a sorry-looking dress. Pfeiffer's discomposure is most disarming, achieved with her second-nature gift for unforced comedy, which is also on view in a later scene in which Frankie rambles on about her dead parakeet while grudgingly granting Johnny's request to gaze at her open-robed nakedness. Though drawn to his uninhibited approach to living (she is charmed by his mad, improvisatory Greek dancing at the party), Frankie will do all she can to bust up their blossoming romance before it can explode in her face.

Unnerved by Johnny's fast-tempoed upheaval of her predictable, if lonely, routine, Frankie keeps finding opportunities to retreat, even though she feels good around him. Soon after they have consummated their relationship, Johnny shows up unannounced on her bowling night and tells her that he loves her, wants to marry her and have kids with her, forcing her closer to acknowledging and confronting her painful past. Provoked by his smothering intensity and relentless brashness, she is harsh toward him, though Pfeiffer makes it apparent that Frankie is disintegrating inside. Her panicking, fight-picking flare-ups dare him to continue wanting her; besides, she's just waiting for him to prove himself another untrustworthy heel. Still unable to believe it's her he wants (he barely knows her), she moves tentatively nearer to baring all of her private anguish, splintering her hard-shelled exterior. When Johnny shares his own anxieties, about his first postprison reunion with his two kids (his wife remarried), she's there for him. With the focus off herself, she utilizes her strength in helping others; Pfeiffer's Frankie sees and responds to a new, not-so-certain Johnny. When she finally tells him about the ex-boyfriend she's avoided talking about (the last of her barriers to come down), Pfeiffer unguardedly peels away the layers of Frankie's lingering sorrows and ongoing fears. She aches to feel the safety of his love but is still unsure if she's capable of doing so.

Warm, likeable *Frankie and Johnny* is one of the few good adult romantic comedies of its decade. Anytime Garry Marshall's direction threatens to make things too self-consciously neat (the convenient, abusive "rear window" drama playing out in the building across from Frankie's apartment; the ambulance-racing NYC-is-hell ambiance), Pfeiffer reanchors the movie in Frankie's messy, honest struggle. Terrence McNally seems to have had a good time restructuring and expanding his two-character play, *Frankie and Johnny in the Clair de Lune,* for the screen, conceiving a colorful crew of supporting characters, including Frankie's gay buddy (Nathan Lane) and a randy waitress (Kate Nelligan), who though frequently entertaining are clichéd and even anachronistic. (The diner's atmosphere and its occupants feel hijacked from an old movie.) Pacino, with whom an on-the-rise Pfeiffer appeared in *Scarface* (1983), gives a soulful and loopy performance; he puts on Shakespeare-quoting Johnny like an oversized sweater. Though the character may seem too good to be true, the actor is totally engaging, and he and Pfeiffer truly connect. The film's box-office failure was blamed on its unlucky opening weekend: the nation stayed home to watch the unfolding Clarence Thomas–Anita Hill real-life drama on television.

Although Pfeiffer was poised to dominate the 1990s as Meryl Streep had done the 1980s, she wasn't able to maintain the momentum. She did net a third Oscar nod, for *Love Field* (1992), and sizzled as Catwoman in that same year's *Batman Returns* (though television's Julie Newmar still *owns* the role), but there was also junk like *Wolf* (1994) and *Up Close and Personal* (1995) and admirable disappointments like *The Age of Innocence* (1993). Pfeiffer's Frankie was passed over for an Oscar nomination (though Bette Midler's hideous work in *For the Boys* somehow made the cut), but she should be as affectionately recalled as the tune that inspired the film's title.

Robert Downey, Jr., as Charlie Chaplin

Robert Downey, Jr.,

IN

Chaplin

(1992)

A film about Charlie Chaplin would seem to have everything going for it (rags-to-riches protagonist, family insanity, sex scandal, political turmoil, *and* the glamorous overkill of Hollywood), but there was one element I thought insurmountable: they could *never* find an actor who could encompass everything audiences would demand from someone playing the legend. In addition to the staggering technical skills involved, he would have to be credible as one of the funniest men on earth, the most identifiable icon the movies have ever produced. Well, irony of ironies, Richard Attenborough's *Chaplin* has almost nothing to recommend *except* the stupendous title-role performance at its center. Despite colossal odds against him, Robert Downey, Jr., is so convincing, at every age, on stage and off, *and* hilarious, that it's a felony the film surrounding him is so pedestrian. Nevertheless, Downey, who got a much-deserved Best Actor Oscar nomination, is undaunted in his pursuit to give us a more complete Chaplin than we had any reason to expect, and his work never feels like a facile stunt or bloodless mimicry.

Following the two actors (a child and a teen) who play Chaplin through poverty, the workhouse, and his entry into vaudeville, Downey officially assumes the role on a London stage, as a sloppy drunk in a theatre box who wordlessly, yet continually, disrupts an emcee's spiel. Downey's whole performance rides on this sequence: if he's not funny, Chaplin-sized funny, then we can all go home. Well, he proves to be a consummate physical comic, falling out of and into the box with the grace, timing, and wit that make you believe this young man is gifted enough to take on the world. Each gag and pratfall, each emerging smile from his straight-faced drunkenness, is executed so flawlessly that you know you can relax for the rest of the movie. His next routine is an impromptu audition for Mack Sennett (Dan Aykroyd), in which he demonstrates to the blustery, skeptical director that, despite his boyish looks, he's the drunk who impressed Sennett on stage. (Chaplin had arrived in America touring with a British vaudeville show.) Improvising some mayhem with his luggage, followed by a nose-burning cigarette bit, Downey, once again, scores. Not only can you see the essence of Chaplin in this shtick but there's something else: Downey's work has the excitement of capturing, before our eyes, the formulation of Chaplin's art. He's both the celluloid Chaplin we know and a hungry new-comer finding his way to immortality . . . which brings us to the Tramp. After haphazardly piecing together the costume, he heads to the set; with his back to us, Downey spontaneously "discovers" the Tramp's brisk wad-dle as he walks off. With Sennett's camera rolling, the Tramp interrupts the taking of a wedding-day family photo. Inspiration has struck Chaplin, but also Downey, who nails the Tramp's giddy, childlike quality (flirting with the bride), his balletic dexterity (as he's chased by the riled family), plus the judiciously used smiles and feminine flourishes key to the character. (Attenborough has such confidence in Downey that he freely uses clips from Chaplin's actual films without fear of breaking the illusion.)

Downey has the additional task of aging through the role. His young Chaplin is a Cockney-accented, ambitious kid. As his success balloons, Downey, in subtle stages, transforms him into a classy figure, adopting a casually refined air and a cultured English accent, accurately re-creating the mellifluousness of the Chaplin voice. The movie repeatedly cuts to 1963 Switzerland, where the star, now seventy-four and in exile from the United States (because of the "Communist" tag that dogged him), is going over the manuscript of his autobiography with his editor (Anthony Hopkins, in a fictional role), who's encouraging him to get past his natu-ral reticence and be more personal in his writing. Unrecognizable behind extensive age makeup and a head of white hair, Downey, using a meas-ured pace, is remarkably "old" without resorting to artificial doddering, and his gentle, even dainty, reserve is touching. In a scene near the end, he tells the editor how he didn't have the talent to achieve his artistic as-pirations. Stating this candidly, Downey unearths Chaplin's abiding, deep-seated disappointment rather than false modesty.

Downey shades the character with a persistent undercurrent of sadness, a by-product of his battered childhood. The teenage Chaplin regretfully committed his unbalanced mother, Hannah (Geraldine Chaplin, playing her own grandmother), to an asylum. His father, who abandoned him, died from drink, and his first love, Hetty (Moira Kelly), the prototype for the *many* teenage girls that followed, married another. When Downey reads her Dear John letter (Chaplin is by now a star), he submerges the blow; his pain is a guarded aspect of the man. No matter how celebrated Chap-lin becomes, Downey retains a remoteness, allowing him to find peace in only two relationships: his relaxing friendship with easygoing Douglas Fairbanks (Kevin Kline) and his happy marriage to Eugene O'Neill's daughter, Oona (again Moira Kelly, pointing up the fact that, in her *exact* resemblance to Hetty, Chaplin has recaptured true love). All else is the driving perfectionism of his work and its "humanist" messages (which will make him a target of ongoing FBI scrutiny), funneling his social conscience and political outrage into comedy. Chaplin instinctually challenges authority, and Downey endows him with the courage of his convictions (yet he rarely needs to raise his voice). Downey's triumph is both inward (Chaplin's perennial outsider status rings true) and outward (in one flashy scene, he even gets to do Chaplin imitating Nijinsky!).

Attenborough's mundane direction can't elevate the film beyond a schematic film-star biopic. One touch, the staging of certain scenes from Chaplin's life in the style of slapstick comedy, is a cheap, lame idea. The conventional screenplay, written by William Boyd, Bryan Forbes, and William Goldman (based on Chaplin's autobiography and David Robinson's biography) clumsily rams as many facts as it can into each line of dialogue (and the clunky narration), blandly dramatizing material that is anything but bland. And the case for Chaplin's romantic obsession with Hetty (and her return as Oona) is not especially plausible. With a big-name cast that flits by, *Chaplin* reduces most of its characters to stick figures. Anthony Hopkins behaves as if he's completing some dreaded, judge-imposed community service, while Diane Lane, who brings just the right regular-gal likeability to her Paulette Goddard, is wasted in the film's fashion-parade conception of her part. Only Geraldine Chaplin, clearly moved by playing her deteriorating grandmother, gives a haunting, detailed performance (witness her tea-and-crackers scene). The production values are sumptuous, but without nimble direction or a probing script, the effect of all the expense is one of newly painted artifice rather than transport to bygone eras. Downey, carrying the entire epic on his modest build, is unfazed, bringing unrivaled meaning to the term *Chaplinesque.*

Jeff Bridges as Max Klein

Jeff Bridges

IN

Fearless

(1993)

I N fifty years, when the final two decades of twentieth-century American film are talked about, that faraway era's most highly esteemed actor will be none other than Jeff Bridges. Though he's received consistent critical praise (and four Oscar nominations), he still hasn't gotten the widespread attention commensurate with his limitless versatility, go-for-broke instincts, and reverberating intelligence. He has paid a price for the eclecticism of his résumé: Bridges has hardly been big box office, leading to his being overlooked in favor of Mel Gibson, Kevin Costner, Harrison Ford, and Michael Douglas. None has shown Bridges's range, but as I've said, time will eventually settle the score. He made his mark (no longer *just* Lloyd's son or Beau's baby brother) as part of the amazing ensemble of *The Last Picture Show* (1971), the wholly absorbing, elegiac tale of early-1950s Texas. He received a supporting Oscar nomination for it and another one for *Thunderbolt and Lightfoot* (1974), but it wasn't until *Starman* (1984) that he joined the A list. As an alien who takes human form, Bridges is funny and inventive, far better than the film itself, and he was justly nominated for a Best Actor Oscar. After *Jagged Edge* (1985), one of his rare popular movies, he hit his stride with a string of outstanding performances, in *Tucker* (1988), *The Fabulous Baker Boys* (1989), *The Fisher King* (1991), and *Fearless*, an unusually disquieting drama in which he plays a man whose sense of reality is severely altered after he survives a plane crash. Bridges gives an impassioned, mercurial performance, charting his character's complex, unwieldy breakdown with all the courage of the title.

When a San Francisco-to-Houston plane crash-lands in Bakersfield, Max Klein (Bridges), an afraid-to-fly architect traveling with his business partner, not only survives but saves many lives. Feeling suddenly immortal, Max begins a strange, dangerous odyssey in which he's addicted to testing his loss of fear and apparent invulnerability to death and is no longer able to connect with his old life, including his wife, Laura (Isabella

Rossellini). His only fulfilling human contact now comes in his friendship with fellow crash victim Carla (Rosie Perez), who is suffering guilt over her baby's death in the accident. Max is instrumental in helping her face life again, but he isn't any closer to confronting his own trauma. For him, simply being alive may be the scariest thing of all.

The film begins eerily: Bridges, in suit and tie, wends his way through a cornfield, carrying a baby and holding a boy by the hand, followed by other survivors, moments after the crash. With smoke from the explosion, it looks like a scene from a jungle war movie, with Bridges an oddly calm, dazed but purposeful leader. Without overt emotion, he seems removed from the event, not sure if he's alive or dead. Either way, Max is a changed man. In a diner, he tests his mortality (and God) by ordering a bowl of strawberries, something he's deathly allergic to, but he has no negative reaction. None of the old rules apply anymore, and Bridges begins Max's believable, ever-worsening inability to reconnect with his life. (Max is not unlike Starman; each has a hard time assimilating after crashing to earth.) He's distant, moving through his world as if invisible, and impatient, flashing raging cynicism and sarcasm. At his postcrash homecoming, surrounded by loved ones, he abruptly slaps a well-meaning therapist (John Turturro) with a casualness that chills the room. In a car, as a lawyer (a too-comic Tom Hulce) rambles on about cash settlements, he shuts the man up with an extended primal scream. Max can find momentary euphoria in speeding on an empty road (with his head hanging out the window and his eyes closed) or in crossing a busy street without looking, but his illusory invincibility takes its toll; the more recklessly Max defies death, the more fragile Bridges appears. Clinging to his seemingly empowering, fear-conquering agenda, and still incapable of resuming his former life, Max goes to the edge: the ledge of an office building's roof. Atop it, he overtakes his fear with a king-of-the-mountain roar, then savors his victory, breathing deeply, laughing, floating in the wind with his arms outstretched, his coat flapping in the breeze. Spinning in circles, he has beaten fear once again, but at what cost? Bridges's abandon is thrilling and scary as he drives Max to leave behind the fear-filled tendencies of his old self.

In the first plane flashback, we meet the ordinary, though nervous, Max. As the terror of the impending crash mounts, he sees a flash of white light and accepts his fate. (His subsequent "fearless" actions are also preceded by these blinding bursts: call them death-wish nudges.) His fear dissipates, and he's transformed into a placid hero. "We're safe because we died already," he later tells Carla. Bridges incisively conveys Max's deep-seated refusal to reengage, opting for his supposedly indestructible existence rather than returning to the normal fears and compromises that come with being human. At a Thanksgiving blowup with his wife, he says about his son, "I don't want him to grow up to be a frightened child in a man's body," and it's clear that he's speaking about himself. While Bridges maintains Max's resistance to the past, he allows him genuine pleasure and tender feeling as Carla's new friend. There's a wonderful mall scene where he impulsively decides they should buy Christmas presents for the dead: her baby and his beloved father (whom he lost at age thirteen). It's a bittersweet, cathartic scene, spurred by Bridges's touchingly boyish energy. The difference between them is that Carla is willing to be helped; Max prefers to remain a "ghost." He won't be well until he *wants* to be saved. In the film's final moments, Bridges, repeating two words, wrenchingly mixes laughter, tears, and a walloping surge of emotion into a profoundly moving, unforgettable climax.

Peter Weir directs with elegant control, but he's also unafraid to tackle the searing emotionality of the story head-on, crafting a film satisfying to both mind and heart. His staging of the flight and crash scenes is astonishing in its realism and therefore deeply upsetting. Rafael Yglesias's screenplay, based on his novel, is fascinating in its exploration of disturbing psychological terrain. (This *ain't* entertainment, folks.) Despite the to-hell-and-back situation, *Fearless*, superbly shot by Allen Daviau, is nevertheless rewarding, carried by the fullness of Bridges's churning, committed acting, though it does lose its tautness whenever he's not onscreen. Rosie Perez, known for her brassy "attitude," received a supporting Oscar nomination for her softly affecting, change-of-pace Carla.

After *Fearless*, Bridges continued to challenge himself, dramatically in *Wild Bill* (1995), comedically in *The Big Lebowski* (1998), and, somewhere in between, with his cagey U.S. president in the embarrassingly self-important film *The Contender* (2000), which earned him a third supporting Oscar nomination. (He also emerged unscathed from *The Mirror Has Two Faces*, Streisand's 1996 everyone-tell-me-I'm-pretty fiasco.) Put Bridges with Joel McCrea, Joseph Cotten, and Robert Mitchum, other taken-for-granted actors who unassumingly created tremendous bodies of work.

Leonardo DiCaprio, Johnny Depp, and Juliette Lewis

Johnny Depp

IN

What's Eating Gilbert Grape
(1993)

I F Jeff Bridges is the premier screen actor of the baby-boomer generation, then Johnny Depp is *the* actor of the younger-than-Tom-Cruise set. Depp, of the dark-chocolate eyes and Garbo-like cheekbones, made the leap (elusive for so many) from television to the big screen after three years on *21 Jump Street,* quickly categorizing himself as someone who wouldn't be categorized. Two "Eddie" roles for director Tim Burton, *Edward Scissorhands* (1990) and *Ed Wood* (1994), showed that he was more interested in challenges than in stardom: in the former, his latter-day Frankenstein's Monster has sweet humor and unforced pathos; in the latter, as the cross-dressing schlockmeister, his all-out zaniness is affectionate and free of snickering condescension. In between these theatrical parts came another title role, Gilbert Grape, a young man stymied by his dead-end life in a nowhere town, bound by family duties progressively taking their toll on him. Depp clearly enjoys altering his looks from role to role, and here he has reddish brown, shoulder-length hair, parted down the middle. In a story peopled with colorful characters, Gilbert is the quiet center, and Depp, who's in nearly every frame, grounds the movie, sorting through Gilbert's cluttered psyche with poignant introspection. The film's pulse is his conflicting love 'em or leave 'em inclinations toward his family (and the town). A role as potentially inert as this one could lead to drab acting, but don't worry: even when Gilbert is just going through the motions, Depp is *there.* With sadness in his eyes, shame in his comportment, and reserves of love waiting to be expressed, Depp moves Gilbert closer to activating his stalled life.

In Endora, a small midwestern town, Gilbert lives in an isolated, crumbling old house with his family: his mother (Darlene Cates), who began on the road to obesity when her husband hanged himself in the basement and is now so large she hasn't left the house in seven years; his older sister, Amy (Laura Harrington), who's become the surrogate mother; his mentally retarded brother, Arnie (Leonardo DiCaprio), a handful who's about to turn eighteen; and his fifteen-year-old sister, Ellen (Mary Kate Schellhardt), with whom he doesn't get along. In addition to the huge responsibility of being Arnie's primary caregiver, Gilbert works in a grocery store, which allows for "deliveries" to Betty Carver (Mary Steenburgen), the married woman with whom he's having void-filling sex. Becky (Juliette Lewis), a free-spirited young woman touring around (in a camper) with her grandmother, arrives in Endora and turns out to be the catalyst for getting Gilbert out of his funk.

In the opening narration, Depp has just enough defeat in his voice to set the tone for Gilbert's suffocating situation; he's as pinned down by routine and obligation as Momma is by her weight. The most memorable aspect of the movie is the affecting relationship between Gilbert and Arnie. Depp and DiCaprio are amazing together, sharing a physical ease with each other that connotes familial closeness and long-standing trust; you believe that their rituals (hide and seek; Arnie's baths) have been repeated countless times. An unself-conscious DiCaprio, who received a supporting Oscar nomination, is technically and emotionally extraordinary in this showy role, but Depp, whose aching simplicity was (unsurprisingly) underappreciated, is equally fine. Acting opposite a character of limited capabilities only makes Depp intensify his focus on DiCaprio, as he tries to reach the part of Arnie that will understand him; he balances overwhelming protectiveness with accumulating impatience (a *Rain Man*-ish dynamic). Gilbert's love for Momma is less explicit; ashamed of her freak status, he makes unkind remarks about her (outside the home), which Depp delivers with a casual, impersonal sting. (He'll call her a whale before anyone else can.) It seems that everyone relies on him (boss, lover, buddies), and he is there for each of them without meeting, or even expressing, his own needs. Inside, he's retreating from all of them. (Depp looks as though he were fading away.) But where exactly is he headed? Is Gilbert on the same trajectory as his beaten father? Avoiding overt anger or bitterness, Depp burrows inward, into the privacy of Gilbert's paralyzing limbo. But in his keen gaze is the subtle comic glint that registers the absurdities of those around him. He doesn't give the character *too* much awareness though; Gilbert doesn't readily see the depth of pain in Momma or in sexmate Betty.

Then Becky comes to town. After Gilbert drives her from the grocery to her camper, he's drawn to her relaxed openness. He is amusingly clueless at first, unsure how to respond to her musings on nature, unable to hold up his end of the conversation, but attracted to her positive energy. Gilbert is an uncomfortable blank when she asks him what he wants from life; if he's honest, he'll have to confront the impulse to escape, and so he

Johnny Depp in *What's Eating Gilbert Grape* (1993)

withdraws. After his sweet numbness in his scenes with Mary Steenburgen's Betty, Depp comes slowly, perceptibly alive through this new relationship. He and a for-once-not-weird Juliette Lewis chart a first love that is refreshing because it is not driven by hormones; they unite in a disarming, unaffected way. New frustrations arise: splitting his time between Becky and his family; the embarrassment that keeps him from bringing her home to meet Momma; Becky's imminent departure. And Depp, in a startling scene, snaps. Finally expressing anger, Gilbert unfortunately directs it at his brother, smacking him around the bathroom when he wildly refuses to take his bath. Following this troubling episode, Gilbert is able to speak to Becky frankly about his family history, which deepens their intimacy. Depp persuasively brings Gilbert out of his detachment, coming to terms with the love and loyalty that were always beneath his drudgery, even, in a tender, restrained scene, helping to give Momma the gift of self-respect. Depp has scrupulously, though with invisible technique, made Gilbert's story a true coming of age.

Unhurriedly paced and quirky without artificiality, *Gilbert Grape* is a lovely family drama. Director Lasse Hallström cast it beautifully, right down the line; the family members may not resemble each other, but you believe they share that house and its past. Hallström also does wonders with two actresses I don't usually respond to: a funny, touchingly desperate Mary Steenburgen and a warm, radiant Juliette Lewis have never been better. As for DiCaprio, why watch him in that "boat" movie when you can see him in this? Peter Hedges's compassionate screenplay, based on his novel, alternates between, and sometimes mixes, pain and humor. Sven Nykvist's bright-colored cinematography gives the film a fable-like beauty, saturated in rural America's striking skies and vast landscapes, not to mention the kitschiness of small-town Endora.

Depp and Hallström reteamed on *Chocolat* (2000), a pleasant, overrated trifle to which Depp, in a love-interest supporting role, lent his star power. (Did he owe Hallström a favor?) But, you know, as good as Depp is as Gilbert or as Ed Wood or as Donnie Brasco, I imagine that his best work is yet to come.

Shirley MacLaine as Tess Carlisle

Shirley MacLaine

IN

Guarding Tess

(1994)

I N Alfred Hitchcock's black-comic misfire *The Trouble with Harry* (1955),
moppet Shirley MacLaine, in her screen debut, looks like she's doing
whatever Hitch told her to do without really understanding what it's all
about. (Can you blame her?) Not long after, she made her mark with two
Oscar-nominated performances, in *Some Came Running* (1958) and *The
Apartment* (1960), that still stand as her most enduring achievements. In the
former, her funny-sad portrait of Ginny, a perennially innocent, helplessly
dim heart-of-gold tramp, has a startling openness; the result is a certifiable
heart-shredder. In the latter, a film that modulates between comedy and
drama as naturally as any ever has, she and Jack Lemmon give two of the
screen's more perceptive portrayals of the diminutizing effects of big-city
loneliness. None of the rest of her 1960s work can compare with it. In the
endless *Sweet Charity* (1969), she overworks her vulnerability, while Bob
Fosse's too-many-ideas direction wears you out. After a semicomeback
with *The Turning Point*, a 1977 take on a 1940s-style woman's picture (in
which she outacted Anne Bancroft), her full-scale resurgence came with
her prickling, unpredictable Aurora in *Terms of Endearment* (1983), an in-
consistent, sometimes shameless film, one that doesn't meld laughter and
heartache as ably as *The Apartment* (her scenes with a prime Jack Nicholson hold up best). She won an it's-about-time Best Actress Oscar for this
showy role, which set the tone for most of the parts that followed: formidable, intimidating women barricading their weaknesses. The best of these
was Tess Carlisle in *Guarding Tess*, an odd-couple comedy given considerable heft by MacLaine. One of her stronger performances, it exemplifies
her no-stone-unturned approach to making a character live onscreen.

Secret Service agent Doug Chesnic (Nicolas Cage) is fed up with his
ongoing assignment: protecting former First Lady (and major handful)
Tess Carlisle at her Ohio residence. Doug, who had been an agent in
Tess's late husband's White House, yearns for more active duty, but

whenever he tries to leave, Tess uses her power with the current president (who never appears) to ensure that Doug remains on her team. Taking out their unhappiness on each other, Doug and Tess eventually come together, forging the kind of parent-child relationship that has eluded Tess with her own two grown children. It's a bond that will be tested (and fortified) when Tess's life is endangered.

Withdrawn from public life, Tess feels discarded and useless, expressing her bitterness and diminished self-respect by being difficult with those who must deal with her. When Doug delivers a breakfast tray to her bedroom, she ignores his entrance and continues to cut clippings from a newspaper. Tess artfully knife-twists her displeasure at his recent attempt to leave her. With controlled, mocking condescension, MacLaine gives her lines real bite. Her alertness to everything around her displays the character's incisive intellect, even though Tess, like some faded film star, seems past her peak. Delineating Tess's severe depression, rooted in loneliness, isolation, and fallen pride, MacLaine gutsily darkens the film into something richer than the light fare it would first appear to be. Her run-ins with by-the-book Doug aren't pleasant, but they are the liveliest events in her cast-aside life. MacLaine and Cage are well matched in these battles of wills, giving as good as they get. After Doug inadvertently (and publicly) humiliates Tess when she falls asleep at the opera, she fumes, but watch MacLaine in the scene that follows. Exiting, Tess is met by a crowd of adoring fans, and nothing could be more healing. Shedding twenty years, she lights up. For the first time, we see an in-her-element Tess, temporarily nourished and restored. She brightens again when her son, Barry (Edward Albert), makes a rare visit. If you want proof of just how good MacLaine can be, watch her in what is, for her, an almost wordless scene. Barry has come to get Tess's endorsement for a questionable real-estate venture. As he tries to convince her of his deal's merits, she first absorbs the crushing fact that this treasured visit is more like a meeting. Listening intently, she then realizes that her integrity will not permit her to give her son what he's come for, followed by the resulting pain of knowing that this will widen the divide between them. She's plainly brokenhearted as she refuses him simply and unalterably. Her eyes are inconsolably sad, flecked with anger at being used, but also guilty and regretful over how her son turned out.

Tess and Doug's exhausting, challenging collisions wear them down, and they finally make peace over a highball. (Tess is quite the drinker.) She's no fool and sees in Doug a genuine caring and loyalty she'll never find in her own son. Needing a real friend, she carefully opens up about her time as First Lady and her less-than-perfect husband (for whom she gave her all). MacLaine, with a cocktail cooling her weary forehead, has

a one-on-one directness, allowing Tess to share details of a personal nature with an acuity that broadens our perception of who this woman is
(and was). She loosens up, and this unlikely duo, ending up at a local bar,
even laugh together. Tess is also revived (try as she might to appear blasé)
by the news that the president will attend the dedication of the final wing
of her husband's library. In a brief tour de force, MacLaine graciously
steamrolls over the man in charge of the ceremony. Supposedly willing to
defer to his plans, she briskly voices her specific vision of the event and
makes it more than clear (though never disrupting her warm smile) that
her suggestions had better be carried out. She's sparked by the high of
feeling like her old self. When the president cancels his visit, thereby less-
ening the occasion's importance, she admirably saves face. In her speech
at the dedication, MacLaine rallies Tess's winning charm and dignified
grace, masterfully concealing her extreme disappointment. After a somewhat farfetched climax, the president returns a phone call she made to
him. In no mood for chitchat, she gets right to her point, gets him to agree
to what she's asked, and then bye-bye. Her blunt, efficient manner contrasts with the resonant private feelings behind her request; MacLaine's
insinuating way around the film's sentiment heightens its impact.

Despite the formulaic setup, *Guarding Tess* delivers the goods, an-
chored not just by MacLaine's layered work but by Cage's funny hy-
perintensity and hangdog sweetness. He's particularly good at conveying just how humorous humorlessness can be. Director Hugh Wilson
gives us a handsome, well-paced picture, and his screenplay, which he
cowrote with Peter Torokvei, keeps the silliness to a minimum and
spares us unnecessary love-interest subplots. Among a crack supporting
cast, the ever-offbeat Austin Pendleton, as Tess's high-strung chauffeur,
and a terror-stricken Susan Blommaert, as Tess's jittery secretary, stand
out. Ultimately, MacLaine's Tess is a worthy companion to her Fran
Kubelik in *The Apartment*; both are disheartened women at dead-end moments in their lives who, despite what they may think, haven't quite extinguished their capacities to connect with another human being.

Don Cheadle and Denzel Washington

Denzel Washington

IN

Devil in a Blue Dress

(1995)

ENZEL Washington made his name in films with a social conscience, modern-day message pictures, such as *A Soldier's Story* (1984), *Cry Freedom* (1987), *Glory* (1989), *Malcolm X* (1992), and *Philadelphia* (1993), winning a supporting Oscar for *Glory*. Then he starred in *Devil in a Blue Dress*, a 1940s-set mystery. A superior entertainment, it was a nice break from Washington's "important" films, more an outright star vehicle than Oscar bait. Even without the patina of prestige, *Devil in a Blue Dress* is a movie in which race plays a potent, encompassing role. Washington, showing more of the power, presence, and versatility he brought to the aforementioned films, emotionally grounds this one, making it a film noir with genuine weight (and he becomes a full-blown movie star). The labyrinthine plot is incidental; it's Washington's character, Ezekiel "Easy" Rawlins, and his connection to his community that constitute the film's real content.

Los Angeles, 1948. Houston-born Easy, a single WWII veteran, has been out of work three weeks, a particularly troubling situation for a man with a mortgage. At a local hangout, he meets Dewitt Albright (Tom Sizemore), a white gangster who offers him good money to track down Daphne Monet (Jennifer Beals), a white woman who frequents black clubs. Dewitt says he's acting on behalf of Todd Carter (Terry Kinney), a mayoral candidate and Daphne's fiancé. Before long, the police suspect Easy of two connected murders, and so he enlists the aid of Mouse (Don Cheadle), his trigger-happy pal from back home. The intrigue surrounding Daphne, involving dirty politics, interracial love, blackmail, and sex crimes, keeps on twisting, but in the process it looks as though Easy has found his new profession: private investigator.

Washington quickly establishes Easy as a man who derives considerable strength from his pride in owning a house. The dignity-reducing outside world, one of racism and unemployment, doesn't impinge on his carefully tended domain, as long as he can keep up the payments. Well-muscled Washington, in sleeveless white T-shirts, emits peace and contentment from this corner house, a haven that fortifies and sustains Easy. In his early dealings with Mr. Albright, Easy is cautious; he doesn't want to get mixed up in anything crooked. However, he needs cash, and the job (keeping his ears open about Daphne) seems harmless enough. Money in his pocket puts a spring in Washington's walk, and as Easy interacts with old friends at a jazz club, it's clear that he is a well-liked guy. On the trail of information, a reluctant Easy is seduced by Coretta (Lisa Nicole Carson), a buddy's gal, and he pumps her (if you will) for facts. While servicing her, Washington has a funny moment after she halts their near-to-climax business, and he, with a voice growing high and scratchy, blurts out anything he can think of to get her to continue. There's less enjoyment ahead, and Washington delves deep, allowing Easy to feel the toll of the losses that accumulate around him, ever fearful of causing harm. Violence, whether inflicted on him or on others, sickens him (witness his reactions to the sadistic Albright). In his run-ins with brutal cops, Washington's Easy stews with anger, confusion, and fear, but he's careful to cooperate with them and to control his temper as best he can; one wrong move could cost Easy his life. For all his sensitivity, he's still an ex-soldier, a powerful man who can take care of himself, with the brains to use that force wisely. Yes, he's out of his element, but he adapts. When Daphne at last appears, Washington and Jennifer Beals, with innuendo and possibility dangling between them, keep the sexual sparks flying.

Easy plays the patient, responsible big brother to an immature, impulsive delinquent in his relationship with Mouse. But even when they're arguing, there's an enduring bond of love and history between them. His contrast with Mouse's amorality heightens Easy's sense of accountability. (Just look into Washington's pensive eyes at any given moment.) Easy is not an altogether blameless bystander, and Washington registers the character's everlasting guilt in the presence of Dupree (Jernard Burks), the friend he betrayed by fooling around with Coretta. But as the case gets closer to solution, and as Easy becomes more personally affected (and threatened), Washington turns into an action hero the honest way: through purposeful conviction. He has a point-of-no-return fury, but that doesn't mean he's having a vindictive good time or that he isn't afraid. Nothing rolls off of Easy; his actions, and those of Mouse and the others, stay with him in a kind of collective human consciousness carried inside. After the mystery is unraveled, the film ends with a beautiful scene on Easy's street (not to be confused with easy street). Watering his lawn, interacting with neighbors, and taking in the bustling life around him, Washington swells with Easy's sense of fulfillment, stepping out of this moment in time in order to savor it. Most importantly, he suffuses Easy with optimism: for himself, his community, the world. Right here, on this block, is what all the struggling is about, and he absorbs that with a doesn't-get-much-better-than-this smile (even though, as represented by the intrusive appearance of a police car, the struggle is by no means over). As the camera pulls back and the rays of the California sun bathe the street, Washington narrates Easy's final thoughts. He has a great last line, and he says it with such profound satisfaction that its effect is both moving and exhilarating.

Carl Franklin's direction has the smoky glamour associated with the genre, but by placing character over plot in his attention to Easy, a most *un*easy hero, he gives the film its originality. Franklin's script, based on Walter Mosley's book, embellishes sexy, gun-toting nostalgia with a refreshing, socially aware outlook, saying, in effect, that while Bogart and Mitchum were out cracking their cases, here's what was going on in a lower-profile part of town. Yet in the classic noir tradition, the mystery in *Devil in a Blue Dress* is appropriately convoluted. With a mid-century period look as detailed and colorful as that of *L.A. Confidential* (1997), *Devil* has a time machine's authenticity. Jennifer Beals is no Mary Astor or Barbara Stanwyck in the femme fatale department, but she fulfills her shady-lady requirements rather well. It's a sensational, startlingly funny Don Cheadle who emerges from the supporting cast, declaring himself a young actor with a big-time future.

The film finishes with everything in place for a sequel, and I can think of few recent screen characters I would welcome in a series as much as I would Easy. To see him develop his investigative skills and nestle further into his beloved neighborhood would have put me in line for opening-weekend tickets. Unfortunately, *Devil in a Blue Dress* wasn't successful enough to warrant a second, never mind third or fourth, installment. Though Washington has kept busy, even winning a second Oscar, this time for Best Actor, for *Training Day* (2001), contemporary movies could still use the shot in the arm that his Easy would so bracingly provide.

Laura Dern as Ruth Stoops

Laura Dern

IN

Citizen Ruth

(1996)

[ ]
[ ]
[ ]
[ ]
[ ]

TWO gifted actors, Bruce Dern and Diane Ladd, are the parents of Laura Dern. So it's no shock that she inherited sufficient talent to excel in the family business. It was clear to anyone who saw her in *Mask* (1985), *Smooth Talk* (1985), and *Blue Velvet* (1986) that young Dern, still a teenager, was no nepotism-riding starlet, soon netting herself a well-earned Best Actress Oscar nomination for *Rambling Rose* (1991). In that title role, she was a heady combination of vulnerability, humor, and sexuality, the likes of which hadn't been seen since Marilyn Monroe in *Bus Stop* (1956). Though Dern then starred in *Jurassic Park* (1993), its box-office muscle did little for its human cast members. (Who even remembers them?) In the decade after *Rambling Rose*, Dern had only one role of Rose's caliber: the aptly named Ruth Stoops in *Citizen Ruth*, an outrageous, satirically funny "abortion" comedy. Rose and Ruth share certain things: both are lost, impulsive, not-real-smart misfits taken into the homes and under the wings of strong older women; but, whereas Rose is irresistibly warm and sympathetic, Ruth is a druggie nightmare. With ferocious comic gusto (and all vanity out the window), Dern attacks the role, reveling in Ruth's stridence and crudity.

Ruth, who is unfit for motherhood (having given up four children for adoption) and usually high, lives a mooching, hand-to-mouth (make that drug-to-nose) existence. Arrested for "hazardous vapor inhalation" (for the sixteenth time in eighteen months), she learns that she's pregnant, and an exasperated judge tells her that if she gets an abortion he'll see about reducing the charges against her. In jail, she meets Gail (Mary Kay Place), a "Baby Saver," whose mission it becomes to prevent Ruth from aborting her baby. After paying Ruth's bail, Gail and her husband, Norm (Kurtwood Smith), take Ruth home with them. But Ruth proves to be unmanageable, and she's quickly "adopted" by the pro-choice camp, who are determined to see that she gets her abortion. Suddenly, Ruth is at the center of a media circus, with both sides doing all they can to win her to their cause. An apolitical Ruth is only concerned with which group will pay her the bigger cash prize.

Dern is ravenously committed to Ruth's unredemptive behavior and never tries to endear herself to the audience or soften the character in any way. With a mane of dirty-blond hair, a trailer-park wardrobe, and a long-legged, mannish walk, she's a sight: a white-trash Barbie. Dern doesn't play down to Ruth. She grants this unique, innately unmaternal protagonist her take-me-as-I-am due. Loud and in your face when pissed off, Dern gives Ruth a short fuse, even though, as (essentially) a homeless person she has to depend on the kindness of others. Dern fire-breathes her foul-language dialogue; expletives are Ruth's prime self-defense and make her feel powerful. She's coarsely, untamably funny as she spews obscenities in moments like her stoplight chance encounter with an old boyfriend, or her public reunion with her mother (a cameo by Diane Ladd). Ruth, free of self-awareness, wants what she wants without seeing farther than five minutes in front of her. Dern wittily plays her like a spoiled child; she turns the waterworks on and off with the facility of someone who's had a lot of practice, always ready to play the victim if it'll help. Her gangly, convulsive movements, sometimes bordering on slapstick, evoke an adolescent boy, which is appropriate for someone with as little self-control as Ruth. Believable as an addict, Dern's first drug scene is unforgettably bizarre: she sprays patio sealant into a paper bag, then breathes it in, leaving her face looking like it fell into a blueberry pie. (Her quest for new things to sniff is freaky fun, whereas watching her, say, stick a needle in her arm would not be.) In a later, high-seeking tour de force, Dern, alone in a bedroom, gulps from a liquor bottle, pounds her instantly burning chest, takes another swig, shudders involuntarily, and then tries to kill the taste by inhaling bathroom-cleaning fluid, which causes her to cough, curse, and then opt for another snort of booze. In this surprisingly funny sequence, Dern, with more revulsion than pleasure, immerses herself in Ruth's collision-course compulsions.

You can try to help Ruth, just don't expect anything in return, not even gratitude. Though she becomes the "project" of both factions, she's impervious to change; they all want to use her, but she does most of the using. She can't commit to anything (except drugs), and as Ruth is out only for Ruth, her loyalties swing like pendulums. Dern gives her a basic shrewdness (she is, after all, trying to get all she can out of every situation), but you wouldn't call Ruth bright; the rest of the world is one big haze to her. She's completely oblivious to abortion as an issue. When she switches to the pro-choice team, she is unconvincing in her defense of her decision as she spouts her new "beliefs" to the Baby Savers; Dern makes it clear that Ruth is more concerned with trying to remember what those beliefs *are* than with their meaning. The only way to hold Ruth is to buy her. Ensconced in the pro-choice headquarters, she watches, on television, as the Baby Savers offer her fifteen thousand dollars if she'll have her baby. (Dern reacts like a game-show winner.) As her appalled pro-choice "sisters" try to talk her out of accepting the money, Dern goes into one of Ruth's bratty tantrums, screaming, stamping, sobbing; Ruth is more a baby than the one living inside her. No one can stand Ruth after a while, and you end up sympathizing with *everyone* who has to deal with her. Her impending "choice" provokes a bidding war and, after the pro-choice security man, Harlan (M. C. Gainey), a Vietnam veteran, offers to match the other side's bid, Ruth tells him her lavish plans for the money, proving that she has no idea what things cost. Dern plays Ruth here like a girl fantasizing about what she'll be when she grows up. (Only money sparks her attention the way, say, sniffing glue can.) Despite the story, there's a perennial innocence in Dern's work; Ruth, exposed to a great number of ideas and a great deal of passion, absorbs nothing.

Directed by Alexander Payne, who cowrote the screenplay with Jim Taylor, *Citizen Ruth* is a sharp, tasty comedy that lampoons both sides of a hot-button issue and brilliantly places a strung-out blank in the eye of the storm. Payne dexterously builds the encroaching hysteria while he maintains a light touch (a nice contrast to his title character, who is anything but light). The always-great Mary Kay Place leads a terrific supporting ensemble; it's hard to resist a film that casts Burt Reynolds and Tippi Hedren as opposing leaders in the abortion war (he's the Baby Saver; she's pro-choice). Payne and Taylor followed *Citizen Ruth* with *Election* (1999), another scathing, crackerjack comedy. (Keep 'em coming, guys!) And, whether you're pro-choice or anti-choice, how can you not be pro-Laura Dern after *Citizen Ruth*?

Debbie Reynolds and Albert Brooks

Debbie Reynolds

IN

Mother

(1996)

DEBBIE Reynolds hadn't starred in a movie since *What's the Matter with Helen?* (1971) when director Albert Brooks asked her to play his *Mother.* Not even Brooks could have anticipated what blessed casting this would prove to be. *Singin' in the Rain* (1952) may have launched Reynolds as the epitome of the perky girl next door, but it hardly scratched the surface of her capabilities. She became one of few musical stars who survived the end of that era and grew in popularity as a star of romantic comedies until the end of the 1960s. Some of these disposable movies, such as the spunky *Second Time Around* (1961), are rather pleasing, but others, including the laugh-free *My Six Loves* (1963), are nothing less than moronic. Reynolds's persona of later years has been brassy Vegas entertainer and Zsa Zsa-imitating talk-show guest (and, of course, Princess Leia's real-life mother). Her knock-'em-dead style led me to expect that she would really "sell" her performance in *Mother,* but nothing could have been further from the truth. It turned out to be a reminder of the acting talent she displayed when roles challenged her to be more than adorable. In *The Catered Affair* (1956) and *The Rat Race* (1960), Reynolds turned off her musical comedy energy and showed that she could develop a character with real conviction and poignancy. It's funny that my least favorite Reynolds performance is the one that brought her the most acclaim: *The Unsinkable Molly Brown* (1964) may have garnered her an Oscar nomination, but her work in it has a tiring, desperate-to-please quality that you won't find anywhere in *Mother.*

Written by Albert Brooks and Monica Johnson, *Mother* is a small film with a big subject. Almost a two-character piece, it explores the inner workings of a mother-son relationship. John Henderson (Brooks) is a recently divorced novelist suffering from writer's block who wonders why he always attaches himself to women who don't believe in him. He decides to move back home to see if his relationship with his mother,

Beatrice (Reynolds), is at the root of all his troubles with women (and everything else). He tries hard to break through her reluctance to deal with the past and ultimately comes to see her as a complicated person whom he's never really known.

When Beatrice first appears, she's giving a television installer a hard time about picture quality, and it looks as though she's going to be a stock character, another sitcom mom with zany, maddening qualities designed to make us roll our eyes in recognition. Beatrice can't master Call-Waiting or a picture phone and has a penchant for keeping cheese and salad in her freezer. Though Reynolds is delightful in these scenes, Beatrice becomes less and less silly as we get to know her better. There's a pivotal scene with her son, in a restaurant, where a martini loosens her up a bit. She lets down her guard and reveals a more spontaneous Beatrice than we've seen so far; no longer just John's mother, she's a bright woman with definite opinions about his books. Reynolds reveals her character in small increments, and the more vivid she becomes, the younger she seems. John gets closer and closer to the girl she used to be, and it's as if he is meeting a complete stranger. Reynolds uses the dotty qualities shown at the beginning of the film as Beatrice's protective armor, as though she's playing the "mother" character that everyone expects her to be, whether or not that's who she actually is.

Reynolds is not afraid to show us the character's coldness. Beatrice is in no mood for a let's-blame-Mommy-for-everything scenario and is uncomfortable with her son's intrusion on her life. When she catches John innocently going through a box of her belongings that he finds in his closet, her quiet anger is tempered by her vulnerability at being confronted with reminders of her past. Beatrice is controlled, and even her outrage is balanced. Reynolds's work is a lesson in economy. It really is thrilling to watch someone who's been around so long who's better now than she's ever been. When John gives Beatrice his analysis of their relationship in the film's climactic confrontation, watch the way Reynolds listens to what he says, absorbs it, and responds to it. It has to be the richest moment of her career, and Lillian Gish couldn't have played it more fully. Although Beatrice and John move closer to mutual understanding, Reynolds doesn't become all warm and cuddly, nor does she try to make us love her (as if Beatrice were merely the senior-citizen version of Tammy). She stays true to the character in a remarkably unsentimental performance.

Mother spells everything out for us, but Reynolds retains a complexity that makes Beatrice (and all mothers of her generation) linger in the mind after the movie ends. As with *Guarding Tess* (1994), it's refreshing simply to see a contemporary American movie in which the female lead

Debbie Reynolds in *Mother* (1996)

is a woman of a certain age. And as Beatrice is attractive and sexually active, this is certainly no *Driving Miss Daisy* (1989). Brooks and Reynolds play off each other with a kind of easy rhythm that makes their unlikely teaming a perfect match. The scene in which they haggle over prices and brand names at a grocery store is a model of give-and-take partnering. Unfortunately, the movie fares less well whenever any other character enters the scene. But as long as the focus stays on the mother-son conflict, it's funny, touching, and absorbing.

Despite *Mother*'s failure at the box office, Reynolds seemed a shoo-in for an Oscar nomination. I didn't see how Academy members could resist the combination of her superb performance and the sentimental value of her comeback but, alas, they did. Perhaps if she had milked the early scenes for broader laughs or if she'd been more blatantly emotional toward the end, she would have been recognized. Her truthfulness and restraint proved too subtle for her peers. This movie asks you to look at your mother as you've never seen her before—and to look at Debbie Reynolds in that same way.

Al Pacino as Lefty

Al Pacino

IN

Donnie Brasco

(1997)

I N a bit of ingenious casting, Al Pacino, three-time portrayer of Michael Corleone (the screen's premier Mafia don), signed on as *Donnie Brasco's* Lefty, an insignificant goodfella who couldn't get within hand-kissing distance of Corleone. Pacino is so convincing as a low-level mug (and hit man) that it's hard to believe it's the same guy who brought such poker-faced remoteness and icy glamour to his godfather. Stringing together one classic scene after another, *The Godfather* (1972) is one of the movies' supreme dramatic entertainments, whereas *The Godfather Part II* (1974), with its parallel storylines in two different periods (charting the family's rise and decline), is a complex and ambitious sequel, a great elegiac epic, and a masterpiece. As Corleone hollows out emotionally and spiritually, Pacino, whose stillness has an unyielding intensity, gives a most human portrait of dehumanization. (The problem with 1990's *Godfather Part III* is not merely that they waited too long to make it but that the story is *over* at the end of the second part.) *Donnie Brasco,* based on a true story, put Pacino in what might be labeled Joe Pesci territory. Although Lefty can be a funny guy, Pacino gives him the ongoing pain of being a nobody aching to be a somebody, even as time is running out.

In 1978, FBI agent Joseph Pistone (Johnny Depp), alias Donnie Brasco, goes undercover to infiltrate a New York mob family at its lower rungs. Benjamin "Lefty" Ruggiero, a thirty-year wiseguy (with twenty-six hits to his credit), takes Donnie under his wing. Though Lefty hasn't been able to rise within the ranks, he knows all there is to know about the Mafia; Donnie is an eager student. Whenever he can, Donnie sneaks home to visit his wife (Anne Heche) and three daughters, but as he becomes more entrenched in his new role, and as his closeness to Lefty deepens, which is his *real* life?

Pacino's New York dialect is gruff, hard, and usually loud, but his line readings have a "neighborhood" rhythm that's musical and inflections that

mine the dialogue for its considerable comic value. In his most broadly entertaining moments, such as his embellishing of points with "fuhgedabou-
dits," he reminds me of Sid Caesar, though he never crosses the line into
caricature. Pacino's self-conscious enjoyment of acting and his flair for
grand gestures only enhance his effectiveness. With a bad-taste fashion
sense in which he takes pride, Lefty is a sight, but Pacino's alert eyes constantly remind you that, despite the bravura comic streak, Lefty isn't stupid. Hey, he's survived thirty years in the mob. His wisdom, though limited to his area of expertise, is for real, and when he opens his mouth, it's
obvious that he's not as dopey as he looks. In Donnie, with whom Lefty
hits it off pretty quickly, he sees someone to whom he can impart decades
worth of brutal, scheming know-how, which couldn't come at a better
time in his used-up life. Pacino fleshes out the man behind the thuggish
exterior. Lefty is the "connected" guy who needs to connect. He's revived
by this chance to be of use to a protégé and feels like a big guy with important knowledge, molding his subject and becoming personally involved. (Call Lefty a Henry Higgins with bad speech.) He's found a
much-needed friend and a surrogate son. Lefty's real son, who's about
Donnie's age, is a junkie. Donnie shows real potential as an up-and-comer,
whereas Lefty is going nowhere. Pacino's face is marked with the strain of
watching younger guys pass him by while he stays in place. Though he
has the self-awareness to refer to himself as a "spoke on a wheel," Lefty
retains hope that it's not too late to be "upped," firmly believing in the system. If he lets go of that faith, his life is meaningless. But whenever the
bosses are around, Lefty fades into the background. Even though he's, by
far, the oldest guy in his crew, Pacino stares at the big shots the way an
awed teenager, dreaming of money and power, might. It's fascinating to
see how Pacino, such a colossal presence, can, at will, blend colorlessly
into groups; two-bit Lefty is surprisingly easy to ignore.

Through bad moods and blistering cracks, Pacino expresses Lefty's
festering rage at the way his life turned out, while he remains devoted to
the organization that has so often forgotten him. In a world where your
best friend may literally stab you in the back, the trust that develops between Lefty and Donnie is special. When Pacino utters, "I love you, Donnie," it's deeply felt but simply said; he doesn't even look him in the eye.
The moment passes, but you know he'd do anything for Donnie. Their
unity is tested after Lefty whacks an innocent "snitch" (the film doesn't
shy away from showing Lefty at murderous work), and Donnie confronts
him on the subject as they ride in a car. (Many of the movie's best scenes
are the car-ride conversations between them.) Though defending his actions, Pacino bares Lefty's uneasiness in knowing his steadfast belief in

the always-right, no-questions-asked code has been shaken. Remorse unsettles him. But, far worse, Lefty soon has reason to doubt Donnie. In a parked car (a scene whose intimacy evokes the classic Brando-Steiger one in *On the Waterfront*), Lefty tells Donnie what it would mean to him to find out that Donnie is a rat. A near-the-edge Lefty *knows* it must be true, but allows himself to believe Donnie's assurances. How else can he go on? Pacino's final scene is played with reserves of dignity; no self-pity, no temper, no regrets, just a guy who knows the score.

Englishman Mike Newell, director of *Enchanted April* (1992) and *Four Weddings and a Funeral* (1994), would seem a bizarre choice to helm an in-your-face New York movie (with a disco beat), but he's incisively good at maximizing the material's humor, thereby shocking us with the disturbing blasts of violence. Paul Attanasio's pungent screenplay, based on Joseph Pistone's own book, explores the lower echelons of Mafia life in vivid detail, an authentic backdrop for the central relationship. The infiltration plot is nothing new, but the bond between Lefty and Donnie makes it feel fresh. In a high-wire act for both character and actor, Depp impressively modulates the intricacies of what's going on inside Donnie at any given moment.

Pacino has been criticized lately for being a major ham in movies like *Heat* (1995) and *The Devil's Advocate* (1997). Well, at least he hasn't lost his passion for acting or his gumption to take risks. I'd rather watch a scenery-chewing Pacino than latter-day Robert De Niro, who has been giving monotonous, predictable performances for twenty years, coasting on his long-ago aura of greatness. I'll take Al any day.

Fiona Loewi, Jason Priestley, and John Hurt

John Hurt

IN

Love and Death on Long Island
(1998)

TWO distinguished English actors had 1998 screen triumphs as lonely, aging, esteemed men of the arts, each of whom becomes infatuated with a comely young man. Sir Ian McKellen received much praise, including two major critics' prizes and an Oscar nomination, for his role as film director James Whale in *Gods and Monsters*, an admirable but unexciting movie. John Hurt, in his best movie role in nearly two decades, was even more impressive in *Love and Death on Long Island*, a quirky update of *Death in Venice*, but he was ignored at award season. (Neither film caused a ripple at the box office.) Hurt had gotten his cinematic break in the unflashy role of Richard Rich in *A Man for All Seasons* (1966), a multi-Oscar winning historical drama, just dripping with prestige. In the 1970s, he gave two of the greatest performances I've ever seen, both for television: his flamboyant Quentin Crisp in the biopic *The Naked Civil Servant* (1975) and a frighteningly erratic Caligula in *I, Claudius* (1976). His big-screen career took off with a Best Supporting Actor Oscar nomination for his prison inmate in the maddeningly unrestrained *Midnight Express* (1978), followed by a Best Actor nod for the title role in David Lynch's haunting and beautiful film *The Elephant Man* (1980), in which he gave a performance worthy of Lon Chaney. In between, he appeared in the sci-fi smash *Alien* (1979), giving birth to the title character with a memorable stomach-exploding delivery. More character actor than star (he's still confused with *William* Hurt and John *Heard*), he's a scrawny version of Charles Laughton, another outrageously inventive craftsman. *Love and Death on Long Island* finds him in a gentle key, bringing refined comedy and engaging eccentricity to Giles De'Ath (get it?), a character who breaks out of his staid existence when an unlikely romantic obsession strikes.

A renowned but publicity-shy British writer, widower Giles De'Ath leads a reclusive London life, untouched by modern technologies (even television). His world goes topsy-turvy when, expecting to see the latest E.

M. Forster film adaptation, he enters a theatre showing *Hotpants College 2*. Just as he's about to walk out, teen idol Ronnie Bostock (Jason Priestley) appears onscreen, and Giles is hypnotized. Unable to shake his thoughts about the twenty-something actor, Giles learns everything he can about him via teenybopper magazines and video rentals. He impulsively travels to Ronnie's Long Island town and sets himself up in a motel. Eventually, he befriends Ronnie's girlfriend, Audrey (Fiona Loewi), who will be the one to introduce him to his golden boy. Ronnie is thrilled by the mentor-like attention he receives from such a classy gentleman, but he's unaware of the depth of Giles's feelings for him.

Giles prefers the secluded comfort of his large house to the outside world, which baffles him. That is until Ronnie's "pizza boy" entrance pierces him like Cupid's arrow. From that first pang, Hurt treats Giles's compulsion as fact; he doesn't question it, struggle with it, or try to suppress it. Though it's implied that his marriage was no love match (she was "rather older than myself"), the film never labels Giles as gay; he seems asexual rather than a closet case. Not a sensitive coming-out tale, Giles's pursuit of Ronnie defies neat explanation, and the movie wisely avoids an unnecessary examination of his dawning sexuality; it plays like a caution-less ride into uncharted territory. Hurt is acutely aware of the amusing incongruity of an eminent man's craggy-faced propriety and his insatiable yearning for a sitcom-trained heartthrob. It's embarrassing, but unavoidable, when those who sell him movie tickets or video memberships enjoy making him feel like a dirty old man. Hurt maintains a valiant, fragile hold on Giles's dignity in these grown-man variations of those familiar scenes in which a teenage boy works up the courage to buy a condom or ask for a nudie pictorial by name. One night, with the surreptitious finesse of a secret agent, he discards his stash of boy-crazy magazines in a public trash bin. There's a character-defining moment when Hurt crystallizes the fact that Giles is aware of his absurdity but powerless to behave otherwise: while watching a video of Ronnie in *Skid Marks*, he's openly appalled by the inane dialogue, but he's still helpless with the irrational glee that only Ronnie can induce. In a game-show dream sequence, Giles chooses Ronnie as his area of expertise; Hurt answers the trivia questions with drolly humorless precision. At a lecture, he turns his dull existential topic (the death of the future) into an impromptu appreciation of film acting (as inspired by Ronnie). It's a treat to watch a great actor dissect his own profession (Hurt passes Giles's criteria for excellence without any trouble).

Giles's self-inflicted degradation intensifies with his arrival on Long Island as he roams the streets of Ronnie's neighborhood (in hat and raincoat) in search of him. After deliberately crashing his supermarket shopping cart into Audrey's, he begins the single-minded process of charming his way into Ronnie's world. When he hears Ronnie's voice (calling from L.A.) on the young couple's answering machine, Hurt tingles with the sensation of just how close he's getting to his object of desire. Just before their at-long-last meeting, Giles watches Ronnie walk along the beach with his dog. Hurt puts his hands to his mouth in an involuntary gesture that illuminates Giles's reverent gratitude for, and nervous anticipation of, coming face to face with his prince. As he praises the fledgling star's talent during dinner, Hurt delicately balances Giles's genuine belief in Ronnie's specialness with the calculating flattery of someone who'll say whatever he must to get what he wants (witness his sympathy for the failure of *Tex Mex*, Ronnie's "message" picture). Ronnie is profoundly affected by Giles's confidence in him, but Audrey begins to see through their new best friend. This offbeat triangle climaxes at a roadside diner when Giles circuitously confesses his love to Ronnie. There's a definite moment when you can watch Hurt shift gears in midsentence; Giles makes the risky decision to turn the subject from male friendship to male lovers, paving the way for what's to come. However it ends, Giles's mad escapade has made him feel more alive than ever before.

This graceful comedy, based on a novel by Gilbert Adair, was written and directed by Richard Kwietniowski, who has a knack for highlighting the laughs in a potentially uncomfortable situation. Jason Priestley, who knows a little something about being a teen idol, is an ideal Ronnie, and Fiona Loewi's Audrey, looking like a dark-haired Melanie Griffith, has a warm, open presence. Less convincing is the vague Long Island setting (that's Nova Scotia standing in). I may not believe the location, but I can't fault Hurt's microscopically observant portrayal of Giles's life-altering odyssey.

Martin Donovan and Lisa Kudrow

Lisa Kudrow

IN

The Opposite of Sex
(1998)

LISA Kudrow first came to national attention as Ursula, the impossibly stupid waitress on television's *Mad About You*. The series' stars, Helen Hunt and Paul Reiser, got a lot of mileage out of reacting to Ursula's confident incompetence and roundabout logic, and it was only a matter of time before Kudrow got a series of her own. As Phoebe Buffay on the ensemble sitcom *Friends*, she became an overnight sensation (as did her five attractive costars). The ensuing media blitz surrounding *Friends* often sidelined the fact that the show was extremely funny and the six performers remarkably gifted. None more so than Kudrow. She's the latest link in the chain of blond comediennes with a talent for playing the not very bright. And like the best of them, she is not an imitation of *any* of the ones who have preceded her. When writer-director Don Roos cast her as Lucia Dalury in his big-hearted black comedy *The Opposite of Sex*, it was anything but typecasting. Since Lucia is an uptight, mid-thirties, intensely smart, brown-haired high school teacher, no one could have read the character description and said, "Get Lisa Kudrow!" To go from Phoebe, a famously flaky twenty-something, to Lucia, a repressed character with a quick tongue, is all a chance-taking actress could ask for. Kudrow is a marvel: without altering her appearance in any significant way, her tightly wound Lucia seems old enough to be Phoebe's mother. Not only that, but Kudrow's blazing wit makes it temporarily impossible to imagine her playing anything but the most intelligent characters.

Dedee Truitt (the astonishingly self-possessed Christina Ricci), a sixteen-year-old blond vixen, runs away from her mother in Louisiana (after creating an unpleasant scene at her stepfather's funeral) and decides to visit her half brother, Bill (Martin Donovan), a thirty-five-year-old high school English teacher in Indiana. Bill lives in a fabulous house with his decade-younger lover, Matt (Ivan Sergei), who's gorgeous and sweet but no intellectual giant. Bill's money was inherited from his former lover, Tom, a successful stockbroker who died of AIDS. Tom's sister, Lucia, has remained close to Bill, but not as close as she'd like. The plot kicks into high gear when Dedee lures Matt from Bill, reveals that she's pregnant, steals ten thousand dollars from Bill, and sets off for Los Angeles with Matt in tow. Soon on their trail are Bill, Lucia, and a local cop, Carl Tippett (Lyle Lovett).

Kudrow gets to deliver a steady stream of caustic comments and, in addition to being acidly funny, she fuels Lucia with an ever-present, deep-seated anger. Her pain doesn't make her any less funny; she's actually *funnier* because the humor is rooted in character, rather than merely coming out as clever one-liners arriving at marked intervals. Lucia has little faith in humanity, and her stinging barbs are a way of dealing with the world (keeping it at a distance but also getting some revenge on it). She can't understand Bill's incessantly good nature and prefers to be at the ready with no-punches-pulled remarks. If Bill won't protect himself from outside forces, she will. Only Dedee is a real match for her; it's almost—but not quite—fun to have this verbally-equipped terror for a sparring partner. Lucia makes an attempt to connect with Dedee when they first meet; she tells her the story of why her name is pronounced "*Loo*-sha" rather than the more Italian-sounding "Loo-*chee*-a." Hardly charmed by Lucia's Wasn't-I-an-adorable-child? anecdote, Dedee immediately brandishes her ignorance about AIDS and proceeds to rub Lucia's romantic feelings for Bill in her face. Kudrow's startlingly unamused reactions make it clear that Lucia has come to detest this demon child in one brief conversation.

It was Lucia who introduced her brother to Bill, and we can assume that it was not so the two men would become a couple. Kudrow gives a knowing portrait of a straight woman unhappily in love with a gay man; she knows she can never expect anything more from Bill, yet she can't help resenting him because of *her* inability to get over him. (It's his fault she's single and bitter, right?) When Matt runs off with Dedee, Lucia becomes a fixture at Bill's house, assuming her imagined rightful place. Their trip to Los Angeles punctures her domestic fantasy and puts an increasing strain on their relationship. Kudrow's best scene comes in a motel when Lucia exposes some of her bottled-up feelings to Bill. The scene starts in a comic vein: she tries to get a heterosexual rise out of him by holding up her just-washed bra and by flinging the word *vagina* at him. The futility of this tack leads to an admission of her fed-up frustrations with sex; she claims to prefer the simpler, safer pleasures of back-rubs and shampoos. Now she's really rolling, moving on to her thinly concealed fury at Bill for risking his career and reputation by chasing Matt, whom she cannot accept as anything more than a boy toy. When the subject turns to Tom and AIDS, issues of blame and disapproval arise, and Bill lashes back by implying that Lucia has homophobic impulses she'd rather not confront. By the time he's had enough of her analysis of his life and storms out, she's truly shaken; snappish Lucia is left speechless for the first time. Kudrow hits many notes in this one life-changing scene, faultlessly shifting from Lucia's comfort zone of sarcasm to the riskier area of her true feelings. She digs deeper and deeper into Lucia's jealousy and self-pity, her wounding rejections and aching loneliness. Lucia is now far too complex to be dismissed as comic relief.

Kudos to Don Roos for this wicked, full-of-surprises treatise on the common struggle to make and maintain meaningful human connections. Christina Ricci's Dedee is one scary teen (sort of a granddaughter to the smart-mouthed tarts Ida Lupino used to play), but it's hard to dislike a character who's this funny. Her shocking, *un*politically correct narration is a consistent source of evil amusement. Martin Donovan makes a gentle, sympathetic Bill (and is also excellent in another gay portrayal in the British film *Hollow Reed* [1997]), and Ivan Sergei is engaging as confused Matt. Lyle Lovett's appealingly amateurish performance contrasts nicely with Kudrow's consummate control in their shared scenes. It was a wonderful surprise when the New York Film Critics Circle cited Kudrow as the Best Supporting Actress of 1998; Lucia would have liked being singled out as someone special.

Diane Lane as Pearl Kantrowitz

Diane Lane

IN

A Walk on the Moon
(1999)

S a brainy seventh-grader, an American in Paris who falls in first love, Diane Lane made her screen debut in the beguiling film *A Little Romance* (1979). Obviously a *real* actress (for all her prettiness, there was nothing "cute" about her), she grounded the film's considerable whimsy with a smart, natural, and mature performance, stealing the film from a location-chewing, French-accented Laurence Olivier, past seventy and shameless. Cut to twenty years later (in the interim, Lane was Francis Ford Coppola's favorite actress of the 1980s, featured in his films *The Outsiders* [1983], *Rumble Fish* [1983], and *The Cotton Club* [1984]): Lane, now in her mid thirties, gave *another* smart, natural, and mature performance, in *A Walk on the Moon,* playing a Jewish housewife whose early midlife crisis manifests itself in an affair that rocks her family's stability. Attuned to every murmur of feeling in her character's jangled impulses, Lane should have been in that year's Oscar race and thereby elevated to Hollywood's A list. However, the film's box-office failure meant that most people missed a well-acted domestic drama, as well as Lane's liberating performance.

In 1969, Pearl Kantrowitz (Lane) and her two children, fourteen-year-old (and sexually burgeoning) Alison (Anna Paquin) and much-younger Danny (Bobby Boriello), plus mother-in-law Lillian (Tovah Feldshuh), leave New York City, as always, to spend the summer upstate, renting a lakeside bungalow at an all-Jewish vacation spot; Pearl's husband, Marty (Liev Schreiber), a television repairman, will join them on weekends. Feeling trapped and unfulfilled, thirty-ish Pearl, who *had* to get married at seventeen, recklessly begins a steamy affair with Walker Jerome (Viggo Mortensen), known as "The Blouse Man," a hunky, flirty traveling salesman who makes stops at the camp. Marty eventually learns the truth, and he and Pearl (who's had an offer to run away with Walker) face imperfect reality: they either end or salvage their relationship.

Pearl is a good wife and mother; Lane, whose New York Jewish inflections and accent are unforced, builds the performance from a foundation of love for the family. There's nothing *wrong* with her life, but there's no vitality; she feels anonymous, worn out by the rut she's in. Seeing Alison on the brink of womanhood, Pearl is especially sensitive to the passage of time. (The film parallels the plights of mother and daughter; both step into uncharted sexual waters, both are on the road to self-discovery.) Visible beneath Pearl's pleasantness are the rumblings of dissatisfaction, stemming from her long-ago loss of options (brought on by her teen pregnancy). Lane plays Pearl with a surging ache to *feel* something new and *be* someone new. It's not too late, and as she's a beautiful woman, adventure can come her way pretty easily. When she meets Walker, selling his wares from his bus, she's flustered by his attractiveness (and longish blond hair). Lane's Pearl, trying not to be obvious about his having caught her eye, is charmingly self-conscious and uncomfortable making small talk with him. Another day, he gives her a gift of a tie-dyed shirt, and there's a line-crossing moment when he bites the tag off it, right at her shoulder. Caught off guard, this intimacy takes her breath away. And with nice-guy Marty away so much of the time, she's vulnerable to Walker's magnetism. Lane conveys that, for all her conscience, tentativeness, and lack of confidence, Pearl is swept away by overpowering, unapologetic need. (Ironically, as she's trying to control her frisky daughter, she's "letting go" herself.) In his bus, at night, Lane has no coyness about why she's there, and as they make love, a never-before ecstasy shimmers over her, and her nervous chatter subsides. The sexual revolution reaches Pearl as the moon landing is being televised; she's being penetrated on "one giant leap for mankind." (Okay, the symbolism is a tad bludgeoning.) It's an erotic awakening, and Lane glows thereafter. (In other scenes, she literally goes weak in the knees at the sight of him, or appears to be memorizing every pore on his face.) She even wakes with one of those naughty Scarlett O'Hara morning-after smiles.

There's a fierce honesty in Lane's acting: truth radiates from her eyes; intelligence energizes her expressions. After her mother-in-law questions her about the affair, Pearl breaks it off with Walker; when he says he understands, watch Lane's face flash Pearl's hurt and disappointment that he doesn't put up a fight. But as Lane makes passionately clear, Walker is more than a fling and can't easily be forgotten. The movie sets up the conflict with refreshing complexity: Pearl isn't a victim; Marty isn't a villain; and Walker isn't a cad. At Woodstock with Walker (she couldn't stay away from him), she expresses her unbridled freedom, including her insatiable hunger for him, in public. When Marty later confronts her, Lane's dominant emotion in the scene is Pearl's sadness at having hurt him rather than regrets for her actions or self-pitying defensiveness or crawling-back cowardice. (Her searching performance refuses to make the final outcome a foregone conclusion.) She's more volatile in her showdown with her daughter, fearing that Alison, who's furious at her mother for her adulterous behavior, will make the same all-the-way mistake Pearl made at seventeen. Mothering her confused child takes precedence over defending her transgressions. Lane's consuming tenderness, physical as well as emotional, overrides any anger; Pearl's prime objective is to make Alison feel just how loved she is. Lane and Anna Paquin, listening to each other intently, play together beautifully (one child actress to another). Here and in a climactic scene with Marty, softly trying to make him understand what's been going on inside her, Lane proves herself an actress of moment-to-moment availability and under-the-skin investment.

Pamela Gray's lovingly detailed, nonjudgmental screenplay tells a small story, but one whose universality comes through in the fully developed main characters. *A Walk on the Moon* also has a transporting period flavor, affectionately evoking a sense of Jewish community. (An unseen Julie Kavner's public-address announcements, which keep the bungalow residents informed, are very funny.) Since it was directed by actor Tony Goldwyn, it's not surprising that the acting is the film's strongest suit. Liev Schreiber modulates Marty's pain, outrage, and insecurities with remarkable variety and well-placed humor. (It's a role that could have been played by Dustin Hoffman, one of the film's producers, in younger days.) Anna Paquin ably delineates Alison's rebellious streak without losing sight of the little girl she hasn't quite grown out of. Tovah Feldshuh is terrific in the "Jewish mother" role, funny and canny and no cliché. Only Viggo Mortensen is stranded with an implausible character; dreamboat Walker is a figure of fantasy, not only a sexual god but a sensitive guy too!

If even half as many people who saw Lane (in an ensemble role) in the box-office smash *The Perfect Storm* (2000) had seen her as Pearl, she might have joined the bankable ranks of Julia Roberts, Sandra Bullock, and Meg Ryan. If she ever does, they better watch out.

Renée Zellweger as Betty Sizemore

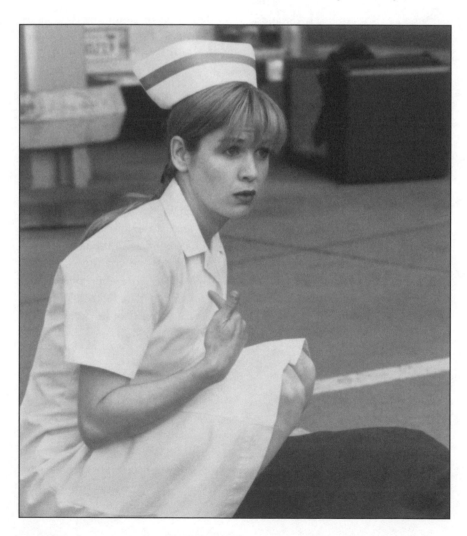

Renée Zellweger

IN

Nurse Betty

(2000)

FOR those of us who had just about given up on seeing a smart, adult, romantic comedy ever again, Cameron Crowe's *Jerry Maguire* (1996) was a godsend, featuring a career-best Tom Cruise, a rocket-firing, Oscar-bound Cuba Gooding, Jr., and, in Renée Zellweger, an unequivocal case of a star being born. (Speaking of *A Star Is Born*, "Renée Zellweger" is a name that, in Old Hollywood, would have lasted about as long as "Esther Blodgett.") With palpable warmth, on-the-button comic instincts, and an unexpected maturity, she went from unknown to major find in a little over two hours (1940s and '50s film buffs may catch the fact that marriage makes her character "Dorothy Maguire"). Since then, *Nurse Betty*, one of the more ambitious commercial comedies of recent years, is the film that has best employed her immensely likeable screen presence and sizable talent. With an irresistible blend of pluck and poignancy, Zellweger is reminiscent of Margaret Sullavan in *The Good Fairy* (1935) and Jean Arthur in *The More the Merrier* (1943); it's easy to imagine her in remakes of both films. Zellweger's effervescent spirit carries Betty out of her doldrums and into a loopy, if dangerous, coming of age.

Betty Sizemore is an unhappy Kansas waitress who finds much-needed escape in *A Reason to Love*, a television soap opera. When Del (Aaron Eckhart), her loutish car-salesman husband, is murdered by two hit men, Charlie (Morgan Freeman) and Wesley (Chris Rock), because of stolen drugs, an unseen Betty witnesses the grisly episode. It sends her into posttraumatic shock: she blocks out Del's death and suddenly believes that her favorite soap character, Dr. David Ravell (Greg Kinnear), is not only real but her ex-fiancé. She drives to Los Angeles to locate him. Charlie and Wesley, deducing that she's run off with the missing drugs, pursue her. When Betty finds "David," actor George McCord, he interprets her odd behavior (talking to him as if he were his character) as that of an enterprising actress with amazing improv skills;

411

he's charmed and intrigued. Betty is transported by his interest in her, but sooner or later, he's going to find out that she isn't pretending, at about the same time that Charlie and Wesley arrive in town.

There's something anachronistic about Betty (even her name suggests another era): she's living in a house with a white picket fence with a husband who's more boss than mate. (He won't let her fulfill her aspiration of becoming a nurse, a natural vocation for someone as innately compassionate as Betty.) With her puffy-cheeked, squinty-eyed vulnerability and the about-to-give-out scratchiness of her sandpaper voice, Zellweger doesn't have to push to gain our sympathy. She plays the early scenes like a windup doll; if Betty stops being perky and capable for a second, she'll have to confront reality and might not be able to go on. Highlighting the fact that Betty is essentially playing a role, Zellweger exaggerates her chipper facial expressions, effortfully compensating for how dejected Betty is (more than she can admit). She's an efficient waitress, but she seems distracted and unconnected. The wear and tear and the heartbreak seep through Zellweger's clear blue eyes, which are most alive when Betty is lost in her soap opera. She knows Del is an all-around creep, but she keeps her contempt in check. (Zellweger evokes a Stepford wife who's about to malfunction.) When her loving coworkers remember her birthday and give her a life-size cutout of Dr. Ravell, her emotions gently spill out; the depth of her appreciation makes it clear how seldom Betty gets to feel special. The horror of seeing Del tortured and killed causes her to snap (something Zellweger accomplishes with the ease of flipping a switch), and she's cheerfully blank and unperturbed when questioned about what she saw. Locked in Betty's quest to find true love with "David" (she thinks she's walked out on Del), Zellweger has a buoyant purposefulness; Betty is a life force in search of a life.

Zellweger is sunnier than all of southern California, and her openness is what makes Betty so ingratiating. Her trauma is a release, and Zellweger manages to be both funny and touching all the way through. She hits her laugh lines so nimbly that you don't anticipate them or their beguiling effect: watch her levelheadedly perform an emergency medical procedure in an ambulance ("It's okay, I've seen it done once"), or tell Rosa (Tia Texada), her new roommate, about David's history, matter-of-factly recounting the soap's outlandish storylines. And then, there he is, at a gala benefit. She walks over to him and his entourage and knocks their socks off with her "in character" speech about her past with David, in what appears to them to be a bold audition for the show. Zellweger is so sweetly assured, speaking the insipid lines with such sincerity, that Betty believably bowls him over and glides, like Cinderella at the ball, into his life. It isn't hard to be entranced by her luminous smile and her astounding belief in what she's doing ("Your dedication scares me," he tells her). In the few happy scenes with him, Zellweger achieves a sustained high of pure elation that is most infectious. Betty is "inside" her soap, but her meltdown isn't far off. David brings her to the set, and it's an accidental slap of paralyzing reality, which Zellweger's Betty, drawing into herself, movingly faces.

Neil LaBute's well-paced direction shows sensitivity for the soul-stirring yearning in the script. He goes too heavy on the violence, though it's clear he's trying to jolt us as much as Betty. The screenplay, by John C. Richards and James Flamberg (story by Richards), is a galvanizing mix of genres with bright, funny dialogue spoken by assorted dreamers and realists. The formidable Morgan Freeman makes Charlie's surprising obsession with Betty a hauntingly affecting transition out of his cynicism. Giving Freeman lots of lip, Chris Rock is a consistent laugh getter. Greg Kinnear is just smashing as the glossy actor, twinklingly amusing when it's required, then startling in the virulence of his mean streak. If 1985's *Purple Rose of Cairo* (whose plot also features a miserable waitress, her bully of a husband, and a heartthrob actor) were made today, Kinnear would be the guy for Jeff Daniels's role. Standing out from *Nurse Betty*'s ace supporting cast is Harriet Sansom Harris, who, as a down-to-earth Arizona bartender, is so truthful and unsentimental that you're sorry she doesn't follow Betty to Los Angeles.

Zellweger won a Golden Globe for *Nurse Betty*, but was slighted at Oscar time, though there was space on the ballot for Joan Allen *(The Contender)* and Juliette Binoche *(Chocolat)*, two fine actresses who gave dull performances in underwritten roles. Oh well, no one was going to beat Julia Roberts *(Erin Brockovich)* anyway.

VIDEO AVAILABILITY GUIDE

MOST of the one hundred movies featured in this book are currently available on VHS and/or DVD. Here's some help in catching up with the rest.

With their extensive library of MGM and Warner Brothers oldies, cable television's Turner Classic Movies (TCM) is the place to find the following: *He Who Gets Slapped, Five Star Final, Jimmy the Gent, Deep Valley, The Pirate, The Actress,* and *Light in the Piazza. The Quiet American,* a United Artists release, has also played on TCM.

In recent years, I have seen *The Affairs of Cellini, The Good Fairy, Hold Back the Dawn, Desert Fury, Nightmare Alley,* and *Ace in the Hole* on cable television's American Movie Classics (AMC). *Dance, Girl, Dance,* an RKO film, has aired on both TCM and AMC.

While writing this book, I saw *A Royal Scandal, The Breaking Point,* and *The Model and the Marriage Broker* on Cinemax, which shows a good number of older films, mostly from Twentieth Century-Fox, that aren't on home video.

Some of the films not on video at present *were* available in the past. So if you have a rental store with a large stock, you might be able to locate these once-issued selections: *He Who Gets Slapped; Dance, Girl, Dance;* and *The Pirate.*

My two cents: *It's Always Fair Weather, The Swan, The Reluctant Debutante, Fanny,* and *The Americanization of Emily* (each a wide-screen film) are on video, but I suggest you wait to see them, in all their rectangular glory, in the letter-box editions shown on TCM. Trust me.